DIAN HANSON

AF185794

THE LITTLE BIG BOOK OF Breasts

The Compact Age of Natural Curves

TASCHEN

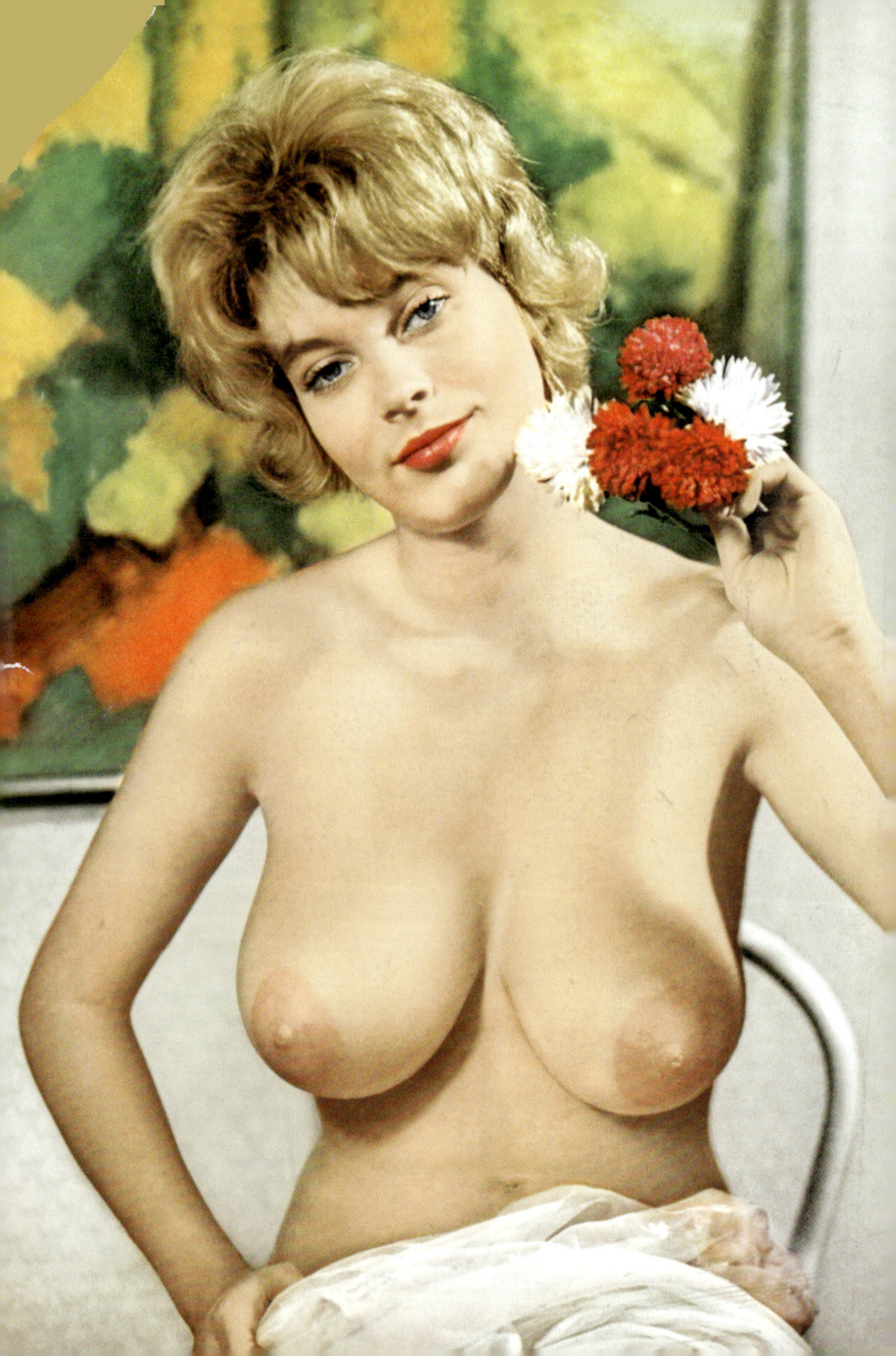

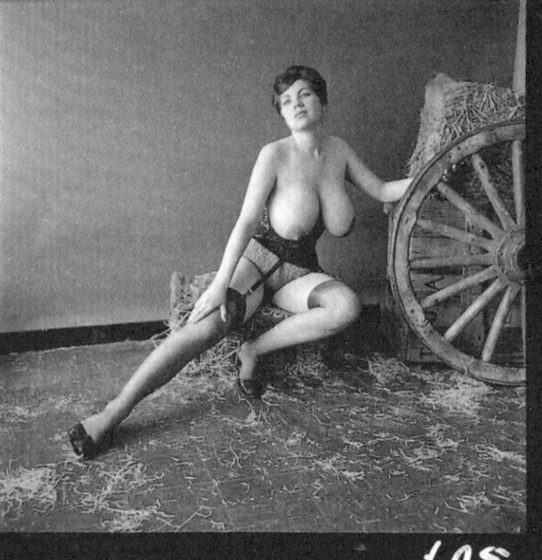
105

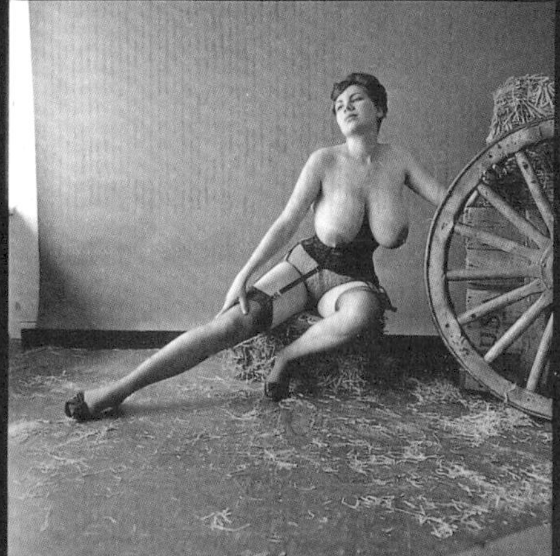
104

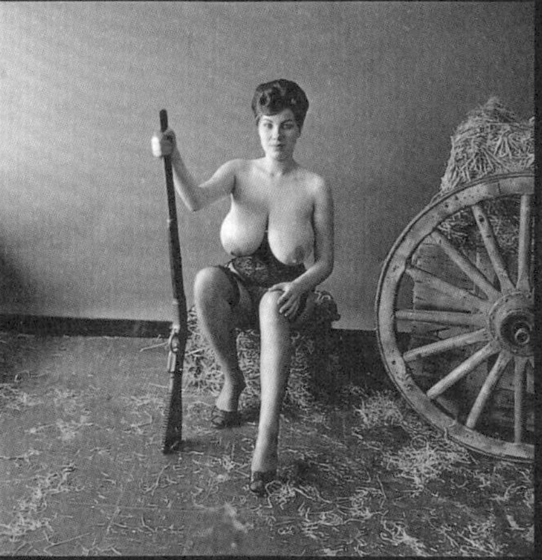
106

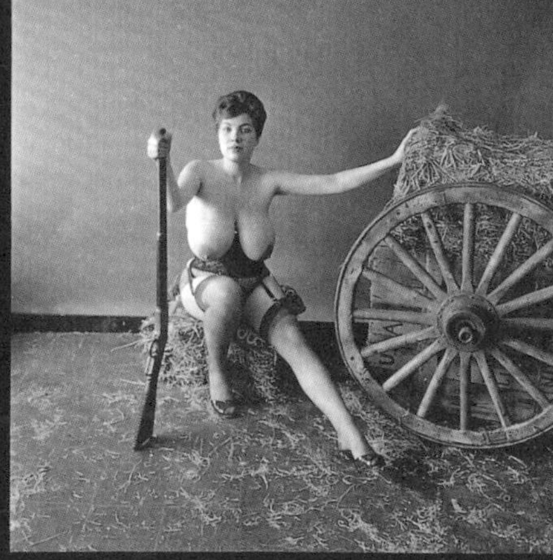
108

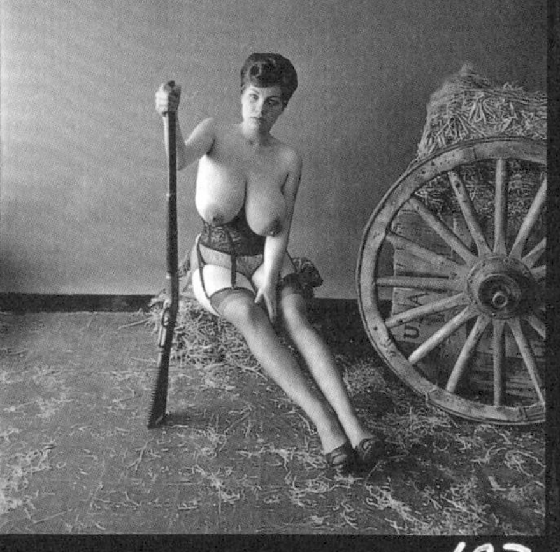
107

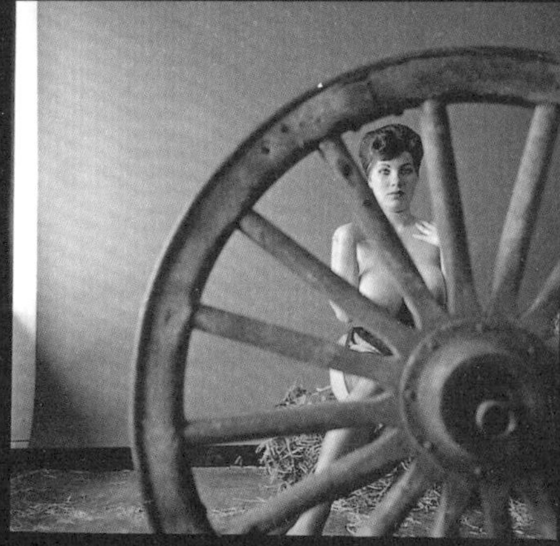

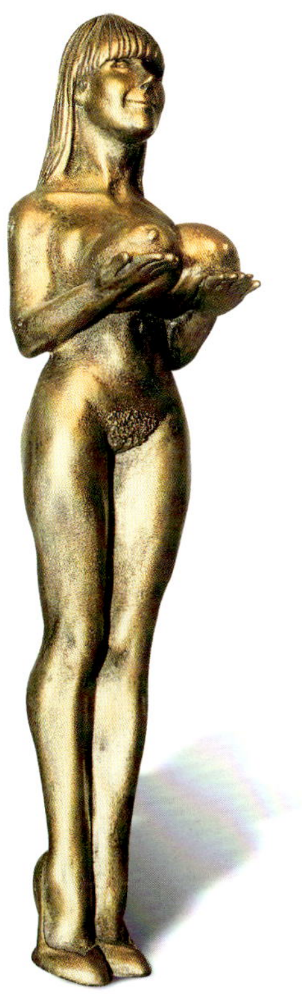

"It's a refreshingly silicon–free display of natural beauty."

—*Loaded*, London

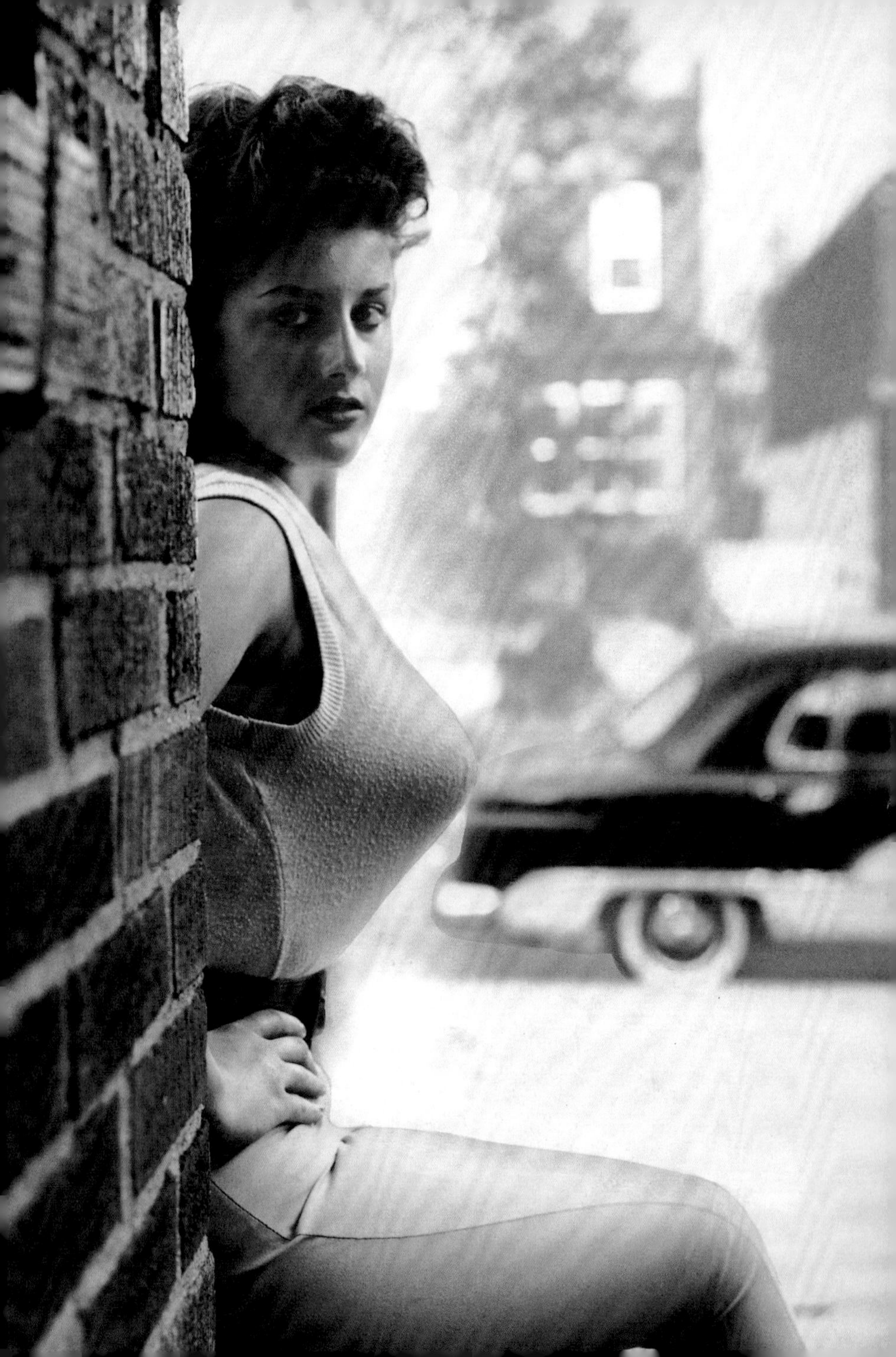

> "I am a breast, a mammary gland disconnected from any human form, a mammary gland such as could only appear, one would have thought, in a dream."
>
> — Philip Roth, *The Breast*, 1972

The Bigger The Better

By Dian Hanson

In *The Breast* a man is transformed into a giant disembodied boob with a hypersensitive nipple in place of his penis; most would say a uniquely American fantasy. By 1972 America's breast fanaticism was so well known and well entrenched that for Roth's contemporaries, men who came of age in the 1940s and '50s, a 155-pound breast would indeed have been a dream come true. We accept America's singular fascination, but how did a country come to fixate so completely on one secondary sexual characteristic — on this soft, simple mass of fat and glandular tissue?

The first American magazines to show bare breasts appeared around 1925, including *Art Group Quarterly*, *Artists & Models*, *Dawn*, *Hotdog*, *Jazza Ka Jazza*, *Paris Studio*, *Shadowland* and a magazine bluntly titled *Sex*. The so-called "girlies" prospered until alcohol Prohibition ended in 1933 and citizens' decency leagues were

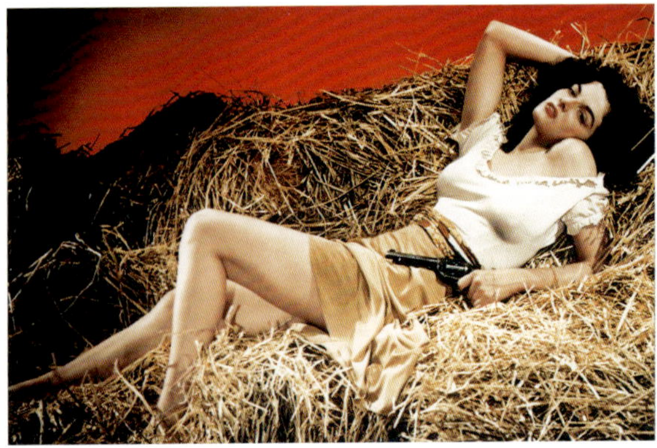

left with no sin to suppress. All those bare breasts on the newsstand offered a natural new target and by 1935, under pressure to censor or cease publishing, editors had replaced the photos with line drawings and spicy fiction. The government made much of keeping the newsstands photo-free right up until World War II, when suddenly girlies became a patriotic necessity.

America's WWII pin-up effort is unique in history. It was anecdotally a response to the thousands of men who were infected with venereal disease during World War I. When a second war loomed it was decided the only way to keep troops safe from Europe's carnal temptations was to distract them with pin-ups. You couldn't just hand a boy a nudie magazine and tell him to jerk off, though. Moral standards had to be maintained. So while the photos returned to the magazines, bathing suits and tight sweaters chastely covered every breast. And they had a time doing it, as these '40s breasts were noticeably bigger than the bare breasts of the '20s and early '30s. I've heard conjecture that the voluptuous pin-up queens were selected as fertility symbols, to inspire soldiers to survive and propagate. That sounds plausible — unless you've met any men's magazine publishers. Since I have, I imagine the thinking was more, "If you can't give 'em bare boobs, at least give 'em big ones!" Sweaters proved the ideal environment for creative padding.

The new, bigger breasts quickly spread from the magazines to the Hollywood screen. Lana Turner became the first official "sweater girl" in 1941. Rita Hayworth made her screen debut that same year, but was best known for a negligee pin-up so popular it was later painted on the atomic bomb dropped on Bikini Atoll in 1946. When French fashion designer Louis Reard named his brief bathing suit the "bikini" later that year there was more of Rita than the island in his choice.

Admittedly, Lana and Rita weren't busty by today's standards, but their breasts were emphasized in a way not seen before the war, and 1941 also produced a star needing no special emphasis. Jane Russell's

PAGE 4 Annette Casir, circa 1965.

OPPOSITE A promotional photo of Jane Russell, shot by George Hurrell in 1943 for Howard Hughes' *The Outlaw*.

RIGHT Busty covergirl Jane Dolinger (*Modern Man*, 1959) was a world adventurer and author of seven travel books.

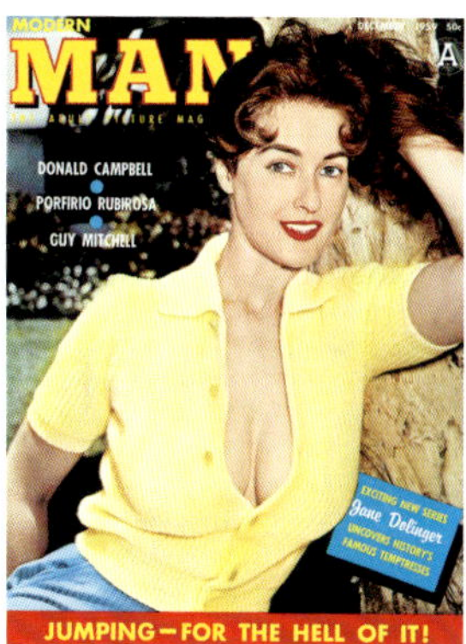

talents were so obvious in Howard Hughes' *The Outlaw* that the film was banned for nearly 10 years.

Hughes discovered 18-year-old Russell working in his dentist's office. *The Outlaw's* script wasn't much, and not even Howard believed Jane could act, but the eccentric billionaire's breast fetish overwhelmed all obstacles. Hughes' subsequent promotion of *The Outlaw* as a showcase for Jane's breasts, including the boast that he'd personally designed her bra based on aerodynamic principles, created so much controversy that the film was banned until 1943. Following a brief release it was banned again, and again, and again, before it finally passed inspection in the breast-friendly atmosphere of 1950. A wealth of Russell pin-ups and publicity stills did make it out in 1941, though. They showed Jane reclining on a bed of hay, her breasts straining a white peasant blouse beside the tagline "What Are the Two Great Reasons for Jane Russell's Rise to Stardom?" It was a question any American man could answer.

And so it went from 1941 to 1945.

Hoarded in footlockers and tacked to barracks walls, tucked into wallets and blazoned on fighter planes, big American breasts were the fighting man's constant companions. Then the war ended and the guys had to forsake their paper girlfriends and come home to real women, leaving the men's magazines struggling for survival. Clearly there was no place for *War Laffs* or *Who's Your Pin-Up Girl?* in peacetime America, so publishers launched a host of new "bad girl" magazines between 1948 and 1951. *Night and Day*, *Modern Man*, *Gala*, *Frolic*, *Swagger*, *Follies* and *Cavalcade of Burlesque* all gambled that the newly domesticated vets still yearned for a little wild life. It was a good guess; the burlesque-themed magazines prospered with models that were flashy, brash, and above all else, busty.

The first stripper to build a career on breast size was Busty Brown, debuting around 1941. Jennie Lee, The Bazoom Girl, followed in 1945 while a senior in high school. Tempest Storm arrived in 1950, and two of the greatest legends, Virginia

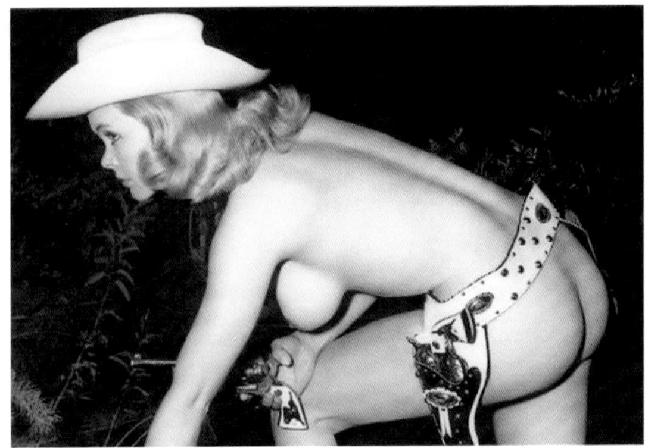

LEFT AND OPPOSITE Curvaceous stripper Candy Barr shot one husband, dated mobster Mickey Cohen, served time for marijuana possession in 1950s Texas, and was a "person of interest" in the Kennedy assassination. Here by unknown photographer, circa 1958.

"Ding Dong" Bell and Candy Barr, debuted in 1954. Candy's 34Ds may have been the most perfect breasts ever released to the public, but Virginia's were bigger, and in the mid-'50s size definitely mattered. Soon even Miss Bell was upstaged by the monumental Gee Whiz, her name inspired by fans' reactions to her watermelon-sized breasts.

Along with the strippers, postwar men's magazines introduced the concept of the professional topless model. Caren Castro, Maria Stinger, Linda West, and Jane Dolinger all fit this description. Jane was unique in being a bona fide journalist who accompanied her topless photos with tales of her adventures in Africa and the Amazon jungle. Buffering the topless models were glamour girls like Irish McCalla, Betty Brosmer, Meg Miles, and Jayne Mansfield who were so breathtakingly busty they could get away with keeping their clothes on. Only Jayne went on to pose topless, yet on a magazine cover all could outsell more daring, but less endowed, models.

By the 1960s big breast mania was so entrenched that it could support its own magazine genre, titles including *Gem*, *Gent*, and *The Swinger*, soon changed to *BUF*, short for Big Up Front. Among the notable models appearing in these magazines were Michelle Angelo, Joan Brinkman, Diane Curtis, Shawn Devereaux, Candy Earle, Lisa Matthews, Linda McClung, Starr Murphy, Janice Orames, Suzanne Pritchard, Janie Reynolds, and Julie Wills.

In addition to the big names, the late '60s brought the first wave of transient magazine models, girls who did a few shoots for quick cash and then disappeared, often leaving no record of their real names. In the '70s this trend intensified when the Sexual Revolution stripped the moral baggage from nude modeling. Young hippies drifted in, made a few bucks, and drifted on. By the time magazine readers were aware of a potential new star she was often long gone, to the great frustration of all. Still, the decade produced its share of stars, including Karen Brown, Linda Corrigan, Darlene English (aka Yum Yum), Linda Gordon, Lois Harmon, Theresa Jackman, Bonnie Locke, Joyce Mandell, Sylvia McFarland, Roberta Pedon,

"Hoarded in footlockers and tacked to barracks walls, tucked into wallets and blazoned on fighter planes, big American breasts were the fighting man's constant companions."

Candy Samples, Joyce Spaeth, Keli Stewart, and Mary Waters.

Busty magazines continued to prosper through the 1980s, but increasingly showcased breasts more silicone than Mother Nature. Like student loans, big breasts had become a career investment, a springboard to success in adult films or on the strip circuit. In the early '90s some dancers "upsized" with new and larger implants every year, while women with naturally large breasts had to go bigger too, just to stay competitive. By 1995 "big as your head" was considered a reasonable guideline for breast enhancement. Then the nasty side effects of stretching skin beyond its limits kicked in, the government cracked down, and the super-sized fad faded.

The super-sized implants may be gone, but we'll never return to that golden age of the '50s, '60s, and '70s when big breasts were safely assumed to be real. This book is for all who have looked upon a spectacular rack and wondered, "Are they, or aren't they?" Here you can cast doubt aside and cuddle up to some of the most celebrated natural breasts ever molded by Mother Nature. And if you still yearn for Roth's 155-pounder, just check out Annie Hawkins-Turner, aka Norma Stitz, on page 189. According to the *Guinness Book of World Records* her endowment comes pretty darn close.

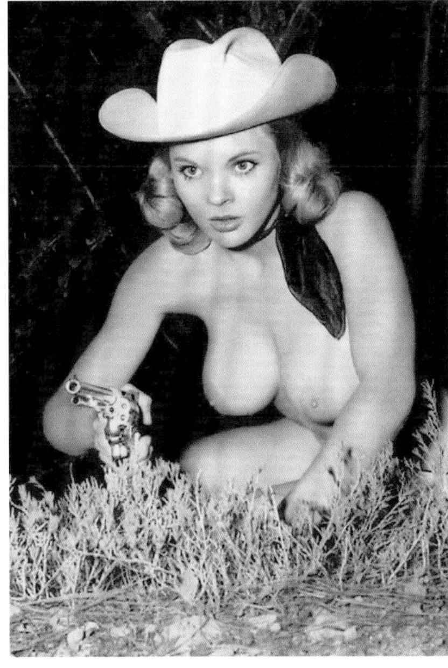

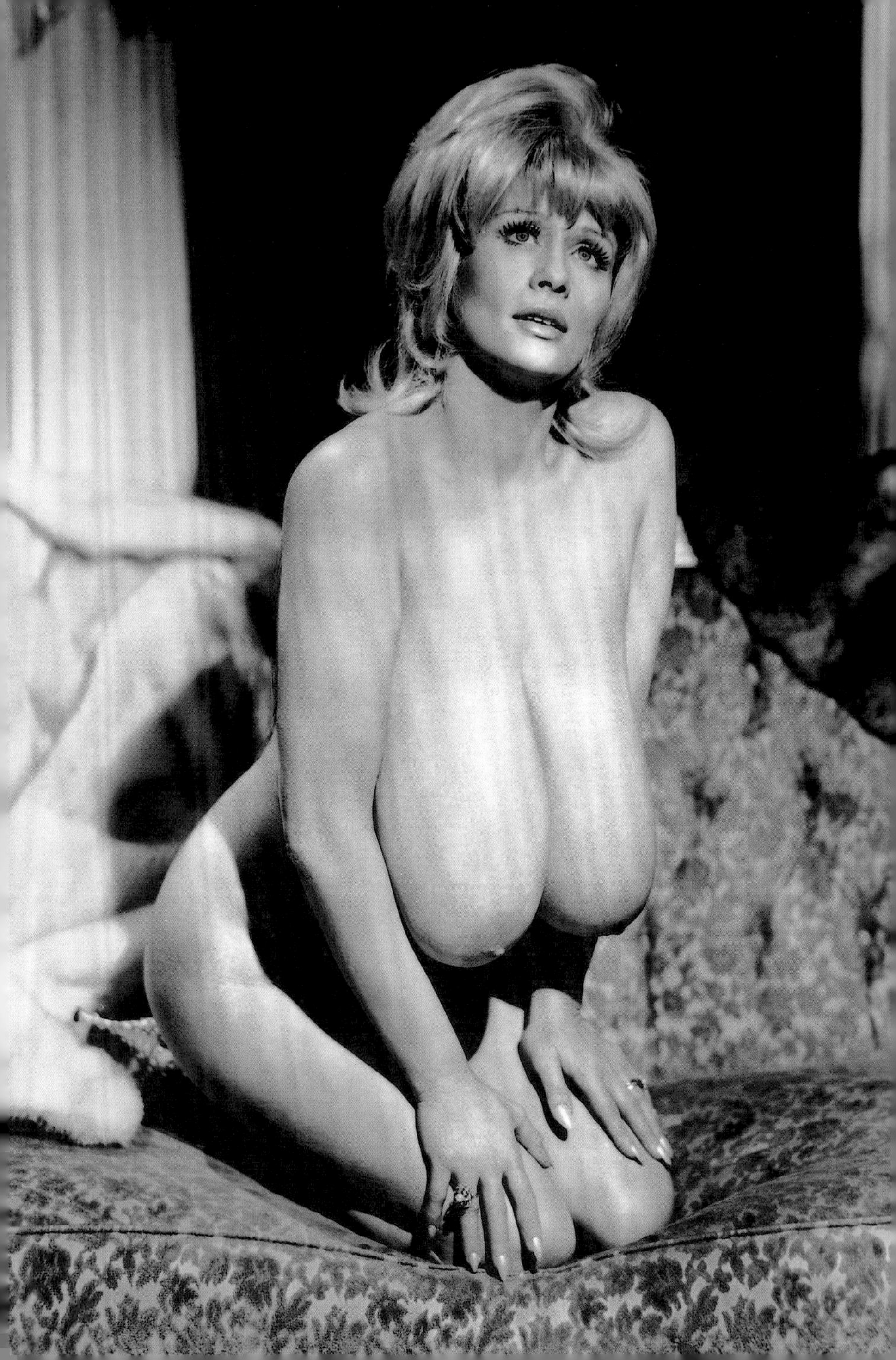

> „Ich bin eine Brust ... in eine jeglicher menschlichen Form entbehrende Milchdrüse verwandelt, in eine Brust, wie sie eigentlich nur im Traum ... denkbar ist."
>
> — Philip Roth, *Die Brust*, 1972

Je voller, desto doller

Von Dian Hanson

In Philip Roths Roman *Die Brust* wird ein Mann in eine einzige gigantische Titte verwandelt, mit einer überempfindlichen Brustwarze anstelle des Penis. Die meisten würden sagen, das sei eine typisch amerikanische Fantasie. 1972 war der Busenfanatismus unter Amerikanern so weit verbreitet, dass eine Brust von 70 Kilogramm für Roths Zeitgenossen, Männer, die in den 1940er- und 1950er-Jahren herangewachsen waren, tatsächlich die Erfüllung aller Träume gewesen wäre. Doch wie konnte es geschehen, dass ein ganzes Land auf ein sekundäres Geschlechtsmerkmal, auf jene weiche Masse aus Fett und Drüsengewebe, so versessen war?

Die ersten amerikanischen Magazine, die blanke Busen zeigten, darunter *Art Group Quarterly*, *Artists & Models*, *Dawn*, *Hotdog*, *Jazza Ka Jazza*, *Paris Studio*, *Shadowland* und ein Magazin, das unverblümt *Sex* genannt wurde, kamen um 1925 auf den Markt. Diese „Girlies" genannten Blätter prosperierten, bis das Alkoholverbot der Prohibitionszeit 1933 aufgehoben wurde und die Moralwächter nun keine offizielle

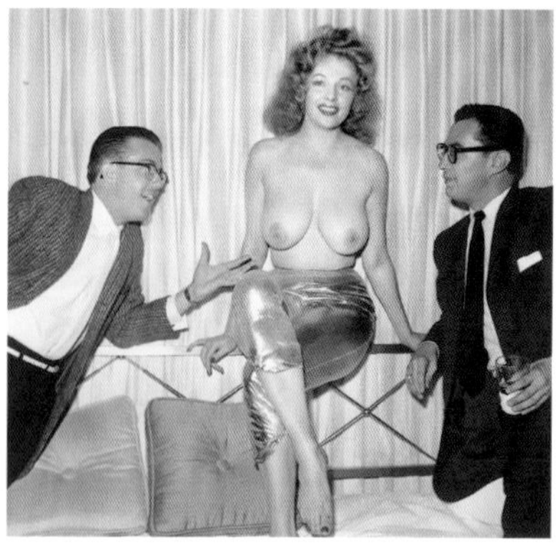

PAGE 10 Chesty Morgan left Poland for America to turn flesh into fortune. Hers were the biggest natural breasts on the strip circuit.

LEFT AND OPPOSITE Tempest Storm insured her breasts for $1,000,000 in the 1950s, dated Elvis and John F. Kennedy, and at age 86 was still stripping occasionally. Photos by Earl Leaf.

Sünde mehr hatten, die sie anklagen konnten. Da boten sich all die nackten Brüste an den Zeitungsständen als neues Ziel an, und so mussten die Verleger unter dem Druck der Zensur ab 1935 die Fotos von Nackedeis durch Strichzeichnungen oder pikante Texte ersetzen. Bis zum Zweiten Weltkrieg waren die Behörden sehr bemüht, die Zeitungsstände busenfrei zu halten, doch plötzlich mauserten sich die Girlie-Magazine zu einer patriotischen Notwendigkeit.

Amerikas Bemühungen, die Pin-ups während des Zweiten Weltkriegs zu fördern, sind einzigartig. Es heißt, diese Anstrengungen seien eine Folge der Geschlechtskrankheiten, die sich Tausende von Männern während des Ersten Weltkriegs zugezogen hatten. Als sich der zweite große Waffengang abzeichnete, entschieden die Verantwortlichen, die Truppen von Europas fleischlichen Verlockungen fernzuhalten, indem sie ihnen zur Zerstreuung Pin-ups boten. Nun tauchten in den Magazinen zwar wieder Fotos auf, doch blieben die Busen züchtig von Badeanzügen oder eng anliegenden Pullovern bedeckt. Diese saßen allerdings gehörig straff, denn jene Brüste der 1940er-Jahre waren deutlich draller als die nackten Busen, die es in den 1920er- oder den frühen 1930er-Jahren zu sehen gab. Ich habe Mutmaßungen gehört, die üppigen Pin-up-Queens seien als Fruchtbarkeitssymbole auserkoren worden, die den Überlebensdrang und den Fortpflanzungswunsch der Soldaten steigern sollten. Das klingt plausibel – doch nur, wenn man nie mit Herausgebern von Männermagazinen zu tun hatte. Da ich über diese Erfahrung verfüge, meine ich, dass der Hintergedanke eher ein anderer war: „Wenn man ihnen schon keine nackten Titten bieten kann, dann sollen sie wenigstens dralle Titten haben!“ Pullover erwiesen sich als ideale Umhüllung für fantasievolle Polsterungen.

Sehr bald schon hatte es der neue, drallere Busen von den Seiten der Magazine auf die Hollywood-Leinwände geschafft. Lana Turner war 1941 das erste offizielle „Sweater-Girl“. Im selben Jahr gab Rita Hayworth ihr Filmdebüt, viel berühmter aber war sie durch ein Pin-up, auf dem sie im Negligé zu sehen war. Dieses Bild war

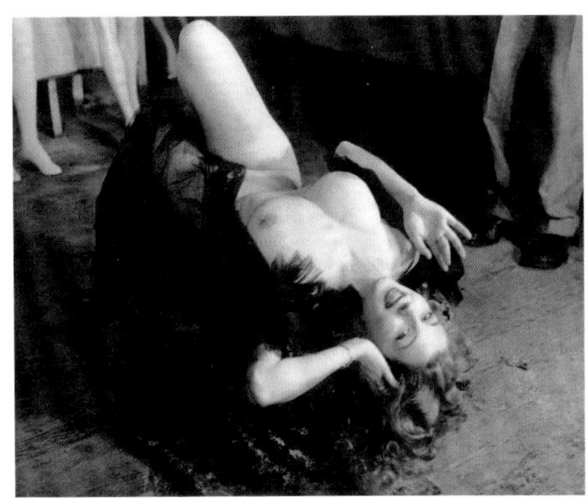

so populär, dass es später sogar auf die Atombombe gemalt wurde, die 1946 über dem Bikini-Atoll niederging. Als der französische Modeschöpfer Louis Réard noch im selben Jahr einen knappen zweiteiligen Badeanzug entwarf und ihn Bikini taufte, hat er wohl eher an Rita gedacht als an das Korallenriff in der Südsee.

Zugegeben, nach heutigen Maßstäben waren Lana und Rita gar nicht so vollbusig, doch ihre Brüste wurden in einer bis zum Zweiten Weltkrieg unbekannten Weise betont. 1941 trat dann ein neuer Star ins Rampenlicht, bei dem nichts hervorgehoben werden musste. Jane Russells Vorzüge waren in Howard Hughes' *The Outlaw* (*Geächtet*) so augenfällig, dass der Film fast zehn Jahre lang verboten blieb.

Hughes hatte die 18-jährige Russell in einer Zahnarztpraxis entdeckt, wo sie arbeitete. Das Drehbuch gab nicht viel her, und nicht einmal Howard glaubte, dass Jane schauspielern könne, doch der exzentrische Millionär schob mit seinem Busenfetischismus sämtliche Hindernisse beiseite. Der Umstand, dass Hughes den Film anschließend wie einen Werbefilm für Janes Brüste vermarktete und sogar prahlte, er persönlich habe ihren Büstenhalter nach aerodynamischen Prinzipien entworfen, sorgte für so viel Zündstoff, dass der Film bis 1943 verboten blieb. Dann durfte er für kurze Zeit gezeigt werden, wurde aber anschließend immer wieder auf den Index gesetzt, bis er im busenfreundlichen Jahr 1950 endlich freigegeben wurde. Zahlreiche Pin-ups und Werbefotos mit Jane Russell gelangten allerdings ab 1941 an die Öffentlichkeit. Sie zeigten, wie Jane sich auf einem Heulager räkelt und ihr Busen eine weiße Bluse ordentlich strafft. Daneben stand geschrieben: „Was sind die beiden schwergewichtigen Gründe für Jane Russells Aufstieg zum Star?" Jeder amerikanische Mann konnte diese Frage beantworten.

Und so wurden zwischen 1941 und 1945 diese Bilder in Spinden gehortet, an Kasernenwände geheftet, in Brieftaschen verstaut und als Zierde auf Jagdflugzeugen angebracht. Große amerikanische Brüste waren ständige Begleiter der kämpfenden Soldaten. Dann war der Krieg vorbei, die Jungs mussten ihre Freundinnen aus Papier

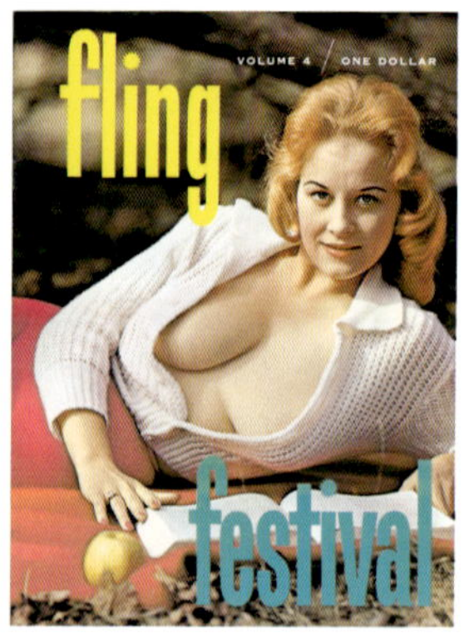

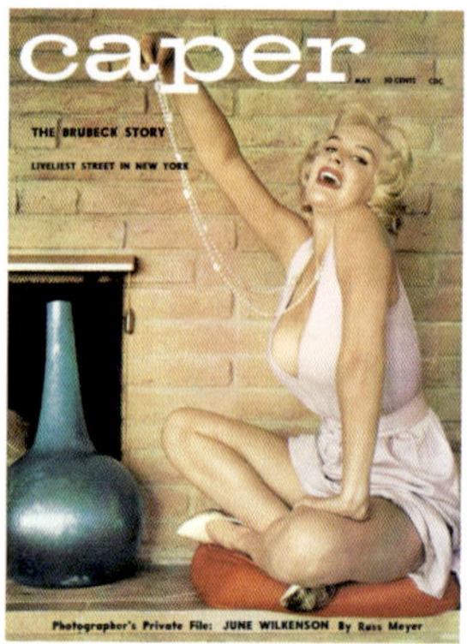

verlassen, zu richtigen Frauen nach Hause zurückkehren, und die Männermagazine durften sehen, wie sie überlebten. Im Amerika der Nachkriegszeit war eindeutig kein Platz für Zeitschriften wie *War Laffs* oder *Who's Your Pin-Up Girl?*, also lancierten die Verleger zwischen 1948 und 1951 eine Reihe neuer „Böse Mädchen"-Magazine. *Night and Day*, *Modern Man*, *Gala*, *Frolic*, *Swagger*, *Follies* und *Cavalcade of Burlesque* spekulierten allesamt darauf, dass sich die Heimkehrer noch immer nach einem Leben sehnten, das wenigstens ein bisschen wild war. Diese Vermutung traf den Nerv. Die Magazine boomten mit Modellen, die halbseiden, keck und vor allem vollbusig waren.

Die erste Stripperin, die dank eines ungewöhnlich großen Busens Karriere machte, war Busty Brown, die um 1941 debütierte. Jennie Lee, das „Bazoom Girl", folgte ihr 1945 noch als Collegeschülerin. Tempest Storm betrat 1950 die Bildfläche, und Virginia „Ding Dong" Bell sowie Candy Barr, zwei Legenden, traten 1954 zum ersten Mal ins Rampenlicht. Candys Brüste, die 75 D beanspruchten, zählten zu den perfektesten, die die Öffentlichkeit je erblickt hatte, Virginias Busen war allerdings mächtiger, und in der zweiten Hälfte der 1950er-Jahre kam es eben besonders auf die Größe an. Doch bald schon wurde selbst Virginia Bell von der großzügig ausgestatteten Gee Whiz (*Gee whiz! – Menschenskind!*), die ihren Namen den melonengroßen Möpsen zu verdanken hatte, in den Schatten gestellt.

Die Männermagazine der Nachkriegszeit publizierten neben Bildern von Stripperinnen nun auch regelmäßig Aufnahmen von professionellen Topless-Modellen. Caren Castro, Maria Stinger, Linda West und Jane Dollinger übten allesamt diese neue Tätigkeit aus. Jane war etwas Besonderes, denn sie war zugleich eine seriöse Journalistin, die zu ihren Oben-ohne-Fotos auch Geschichten von ihren Abenteuern in Afrika und im Amazonasdschungel lieferte. Diese Topless-Modelle wurden allerdings von professionellen Covergirls wie Irish McCalla, Betty Brosmer, Meg Miles und Jayne Mansfield in den Schatten gestellt, die so atemberaubende Brüste hatten, dass sie sogar angezogen ziemlich

OPPOSITE LEFT *Fling* (1960) was America's first magazine devoted to large breasts.

OPPOSITE RIGHT 1959 *Caper* cover of June Wilkinson by breast-obsessed filmmaker Russ Meyer.

RIGHT British beauty June Wilkinson posed for *Playboy* at 17, while still a virgin.

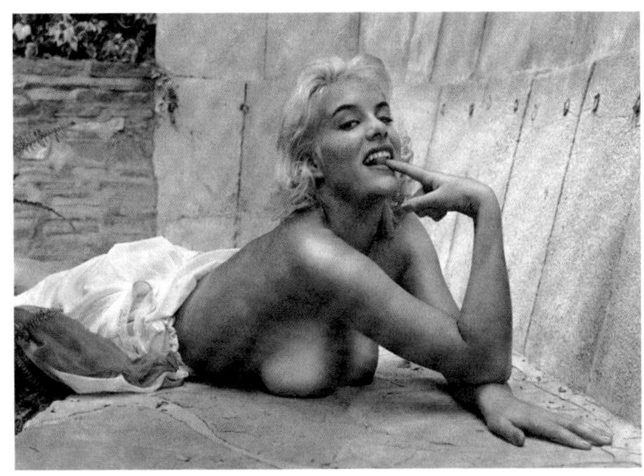

aufregend wirkten. Nur Jayne wagte später den Schritt, auch oben ohne zu posieren.

In den 1960er-Jahren war der Dicke-Titten-Wahn dann so etabliert, dass er ein eigenes Genre von Magazinen tragen konnte, zu denen Titel wie *Gem*, *Gent* und *The Swinger* gehörten, ein Blatt, das seinen Namen kurz darauf in *BUF* änderte (ein Kürzel für „Big Up Front"). Zu den herausragenden Modellen, die in diesen Magazinen zu sehen waren, gehörten Michelle Angelo, Joan Brinkman, Diane Curtis, Shawn Devereaux, Candy Earle, Joyce Mandell, Lisa Matthews, Linda McClung, Starr Murphy, Janice Orames, Suzanne Pritchard, Janie Reynolds und Julie Wills.

Abgesehen von diesen großen Namen trat Ende der 1960er-Jahre eine erste Riege von Gelegenheitsmodellen auf die Bühne, namenlose junge Frauen, die für schnelles Geld ein paar Aufnahmen machten und dann aber wieder von der Bildfläche verschwanden. In den 1970er-Jahren, nachdem die sexuelle Revolution moralische Bedenken gegen Nacktaufnahmen hinweggefegt hatte, verstärkte sich dieser Trend sogar. Junge Hippiemädchen schneiten herein, machten ein paar Dollar und wurden nie wieder gesehen. Gleichwohl brachte auch dieses Jahrzehnt seine Stars hervor, zu denen Karen Brown, Linda Corrigan, Darlene English (aka Yum Yum), Linda Gordon, Lois Harmon, Theresa Jackman, Bonnie Locke, Sylvia McFarland, Roberta Pedon, Candy Samples, Joyce Spaeth, Keli Stewart und Mary Waters gehörten.

Busenmagazine florierten auch noch in den 1980er-Jahren, doch stellten diese Hefte zunehmend Brüste zur Schau, die mit Silikon geformt worden waren. Brust-OPs waren nun eine wichtige Investition für die Karriere. In den frühen 1990er-Jahren möbelte manche der Tänzerinnen ihre Titten Jahr für Jahr mit neuen, immer größeren Implantaten auf, und so mussten auch Frauen mit natürlichen großen Brüsten ihre Möpse aufmotzen, nur um konkurrenzfähig zu bleiben. Um 1995 galt „so umfangreich wie der Kopf" als angemessene Vorgabe für Brustvergrößerungen. Dann jedoch traten die Nebenwirkungen auf, die Behörden griffen ein, und der Megatitten-Fimmel flaute ab.

„Und so wurden zwischen 1941 und 1945 diese Bilder in Spinden gehortet, an Kasernenwände geheftet, in Brieftaschen verstaut und als Zierde auf Jagdflugzeugen angebracht.“

Mit den übergroßen Implantaten mag Schluss sein, doch jenes Goldene Zeitalter der 1950er-, 1960er- und 1970er-Jahre, in dem man sicher sein konnte, dass alle großen Brüste echt waren, wird nie wiederkehren. So widme ich dieses Buch all jenen, die schon einmal mit spektakulären Titten konfrontiert wurden und sich fragten: „Sind die nun echt oder nicht?“ Hier, liebe Leser, können Sie Ihre Zweifel beiseiteschieben und sich an so manche berühmten naturbelassenen Titten schmiegen. Wer jedoch immer noch nach Roths 70 Kilogramm schwerer Titte lechzt, mag einen Blick auf Annie Hawkins-Turner alias Norma Stitz (Seite 189) werfen. Dem *Guinness Buch der Rekorde* zufolge kommen ihre Möpse dieser Vorstellung ziemlich nahe.

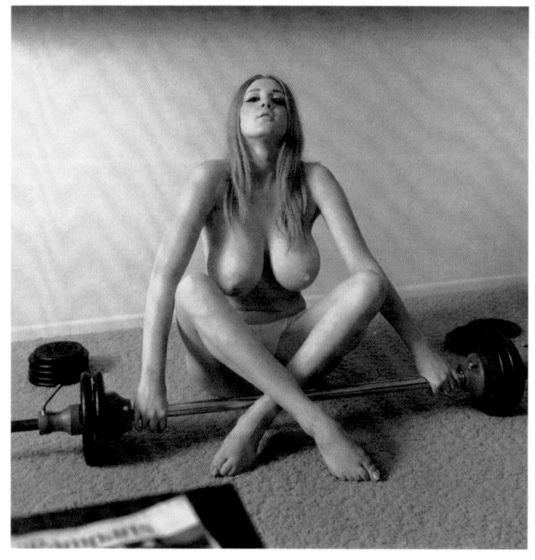

LEFT Unknown model by Lance Kincaid, circa 1968.

OPPOSITE 1960s favorite Suzanne Pritchard in a Los Angeles backyard.

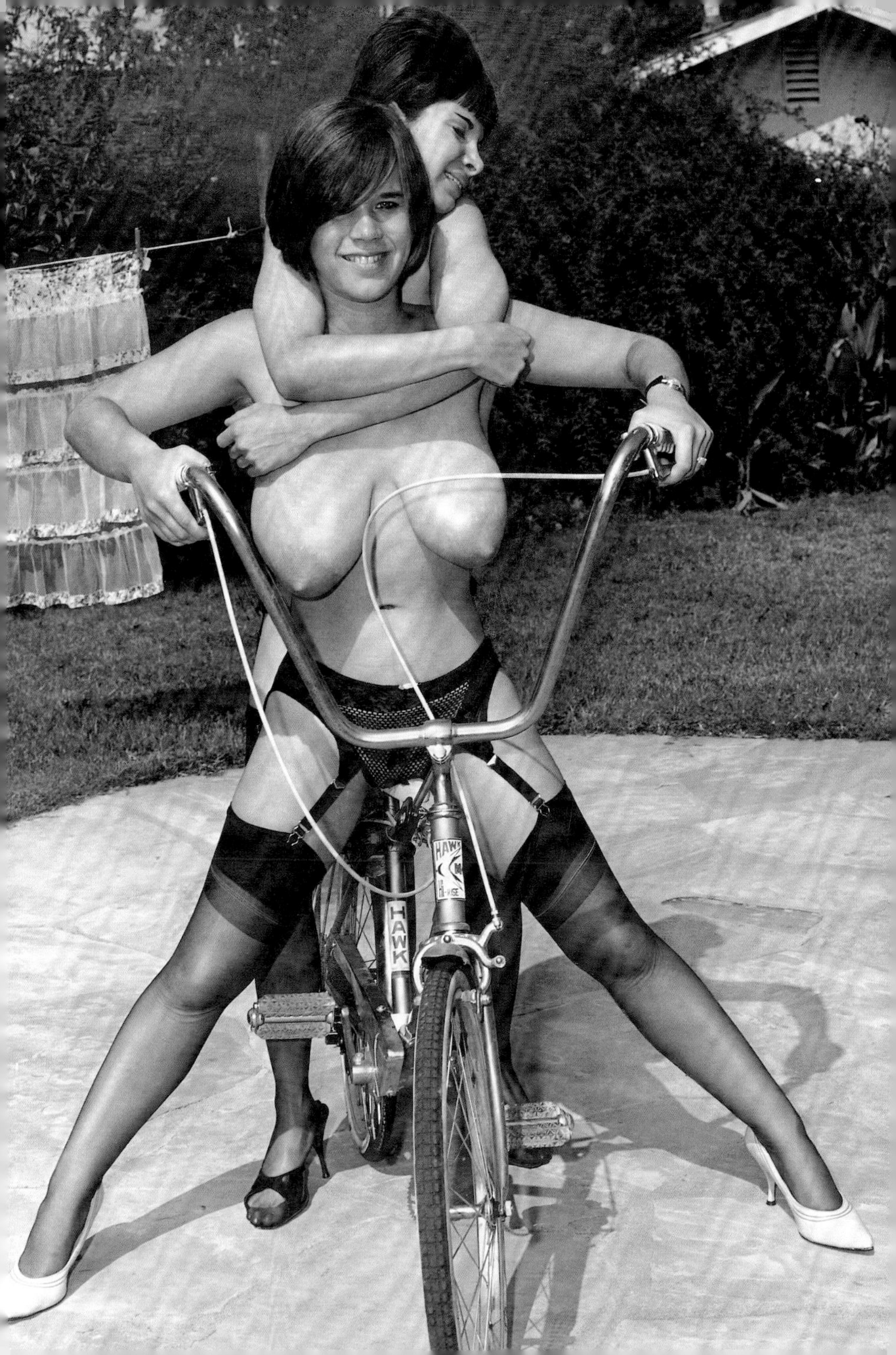
HAWK
HAWK

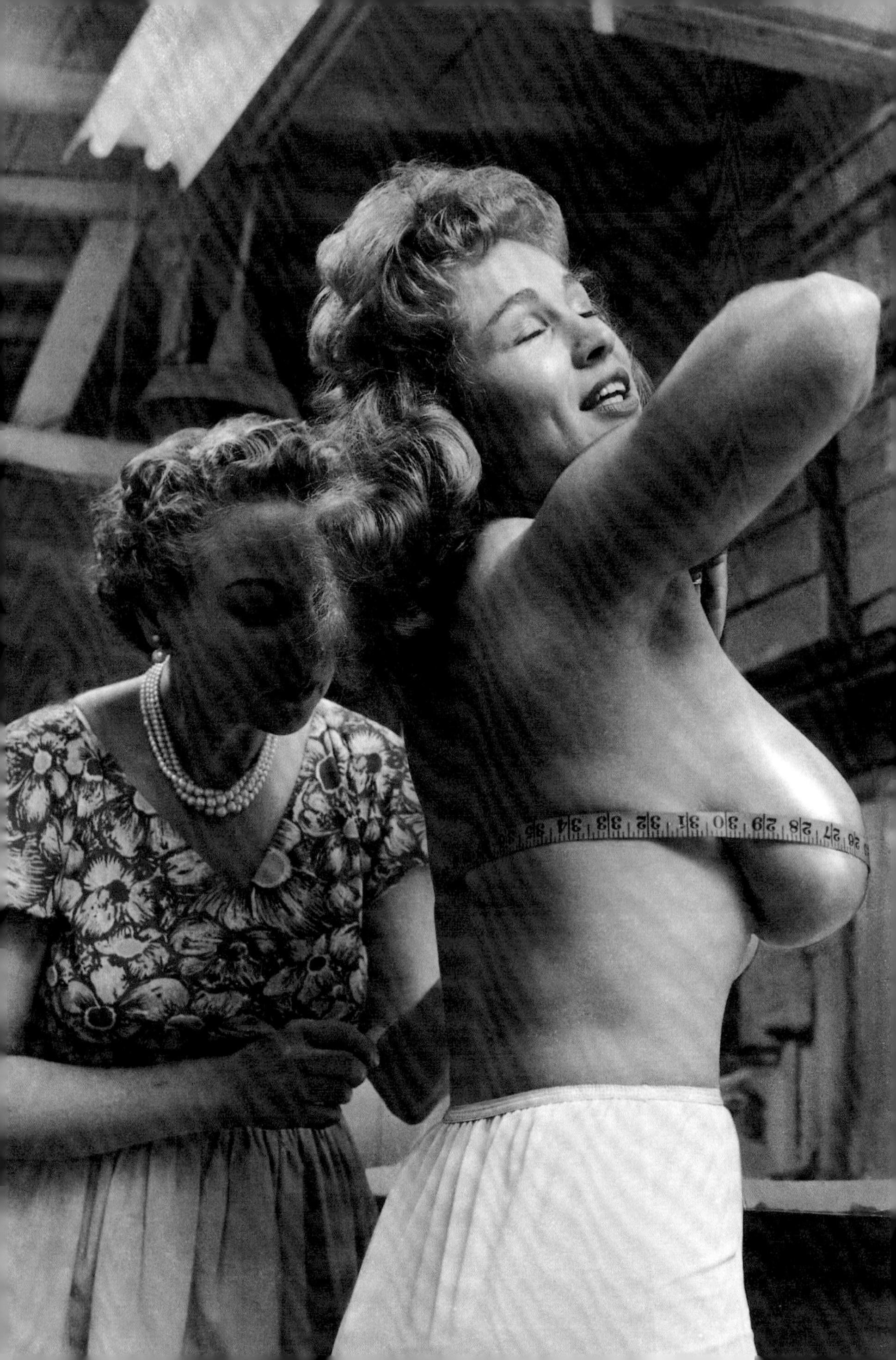

« Je suis un sein [...] une glande mammaire qui n'est reliée à aucun corps humain, une glande mammaire telle, aurait-on pu croire, qu'on n'en pouvait voir qu'en rêve ... »

— Philip Roth, *Le Sein*, 1972

Plus c'est gros, plus c'est bon

Par Dian Hanson

Dans *Le Sein*, un homme se retrouve transformé en nichon géant avec un téton hypersensible à la place du pénis ; fantasme typiquement américain, diront certains. Il est vrai qu'en 1972, la passion de l'Amérique pour la poitrine était si intense et enracinée qu'aux yeux des contemporains de Roth, devenus majeurs dans les années 1940 et 1950, le roploplo de 70 kilos représentait bel et bien un rêve devenu réalité. Nous admettons de bon cœur cette singulière fascination américaine, mais comment un pays entier est-il devenu si obsédé par cet attribut sexuel secondaire – cette masse douce et simple de graisse et de tissus glandulaires ?

Les premiers magazines américains à montrer des seins nus parurent aux alentours de 1925 : *Art Group Quarterly*, *Artists & Models*, *Dawn*, *Hotdog*, *Jazza Ka Jazza*, *Paris Studio*, *Shadowland* ainsi qu'un magazine crûment intitulé *Sex*. Les modèles, les fameuses *girlies*, prospérèrent jusqu'à la fin de la Prohibition, en 1933, lorsque les ligues citoyennes pour la vertu cherchèrent un autre vice à éradiquer. Toutes

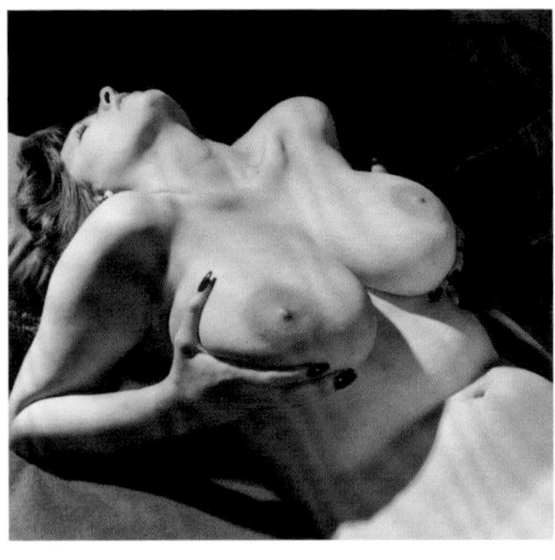

PAGE 18 Virginia “Ding Dong” Bell had some of the biggest breasts on the 1950s strip circuit.

LEFT Nanette Shetler, popular 1960s magazine model.

OPPOSITE Unknown model from the 1960s.

ces poitrines exposées en devanture de kiosque étaient une proie idéale, et en 1935, menacés de fermeture administrative sous la pression constante des censeurs, les éditeurs avaient remplacé les photos jugées licencieuses par des dessins et des feuilletons olé olé. Le gouvernement veilla à ce que les kiosques restent vierges de seins qu’on n’eût su voir jusqu’à la Seconde Guerre mondiale, quand soudain les *girlies* devinrent une nécessité patriotique.

La vague de *pin-up* déversée par l’Amérique à cette époque est d’une ampleur unique dans l’histoire. Au départ, cette campagne sensuelle avait pour objectif d’éviter que des milliers de soldats soient victimes de maladies vénériennes, comme cela avait été le cas pendant la Première Guerre mondiale. Lorsque la seconde se profila à l’horizon, il fut décidé que le seul moyen d’empêcher les *boys* de céder aux tentations européennes était de les distraire avec des *pin-up*. Pour autant, le gouvernement ne pouvait pas donner un magazine de femmes à poil à un gamin et lui ordonner de se branler… les valeurs morales conservatrices prévalaient malgré tout. C’est ainsi que les photos de *girlies* reparurent dans les magazines, mais on veilla à couvrir de maillots de bain ou de pulls moulants les parties les plus intimes de leurs corps, ce qui faisait tout sauf les camoufler. Car les poitrines des années 1940 étaient notablement plus grosses que les seins nus exhibés dans les années 1920 et au début des années 1930. J’ai entendu dire que ces petites reines voluptueuses étaient choisies pour évoquer la fertilité, de façon à ce que les soldats aient envie de rentrer au pays et de se reproduire, une noble intention qui n’est crédible que si l’on n’a jamais rencontré un patron de magazine masculin. Comme je connais bien cette espèce, j’imagine que l’idée était plutôt : « Si on ne peut pas leur donner des nichons nus, au moins qu’ils soient gros ! » Les pull-overs moulants s’avérèrent les alliés parfaits d’une gorge bien rembourrée.

Ces nouveaux seins, plus gros, passèrent rapidement des magazines aux écrans de cinéma. Lana Turner devint la première *sweater girl* en 1941. Rita Hayworth fit ses débuts à Hollywood la même année, mais

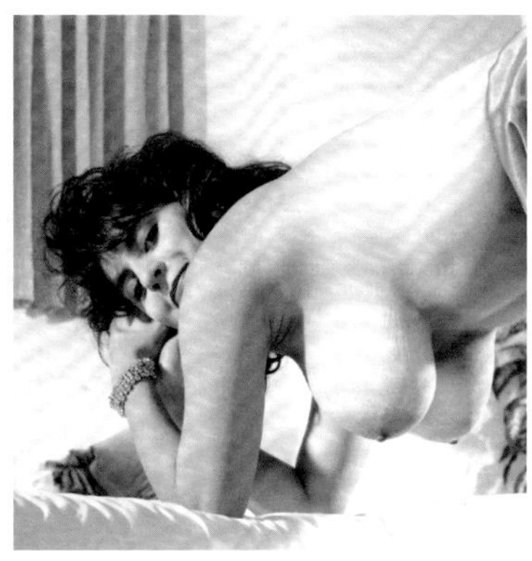

c'est en pin-up « dévêtue » d'une nuisette qu'elle est devenue célèbre : une image si populaire qu'elle décora la bombe atomique lâchée sur l'atoll de Bikini en 1946. Et quand le créateur de mode français Louis Réard baptisa son maillot de bain rikiki « bikini » quelques mois plus tard, ce fut davantage en hommage à Rita qu'à cette île micronésienne.

Il semblerait que Lana et Rita n'aient pas été si girondes que cela par rapport à la norme actuelle, mais leur poitrine était mise en valeur comme jamais jusqu'alors. Une autre vedette naquit en 1941 qui n'avait nul besoin d'artifices : les talents de Jane Russell sautaient tellement aux yeux dans *Le Banni*, de Howard Hughes, que le film fut interdit pendant près de dix ans.

Hughes découvrit Jane Russell lorsqu'elle n'avait que 18 ans, chez son dentiste. Le scénario du *Banni* n'était pas un chef-d'œuvre, et même Hughes ne la pensait pas capable de jouer la comédie, mais la passion du millionnaire excentrique pour les belles poitrines abattit tous les obstacles. Pour faire sa promotion, Hughes n'hésita pas à clamer qu'il s'agissait d'une ode à la poitrine de Jane Russel, et se vanta d'avoir lui-même conçu son soutien-gorge à partir de principes aérodynamiques ; le scandale fut tel que *Le Banni* se vit interdit jusqu'en 1943. Brièvement présenté en salles, il fut ensuite interdit à nouveau, et encore, et encore, avant d'enfin passer avec succès l'épreuve de l'inspection en 1950, alors que les seins étaient en pleine gloire. Des centaines de photos de Jane Russel en pin-up circulèrent cependant dès 1941. Jane y est allongée dans le foin, ses seins gonflant à en faire exploser un corsage blanc de paysanne, et l'image est accompagnée d'une question à laquelle n'importe quel mâle américain sait répondre : « Quels sont les deux gros alliés de Jane Russell dans son ascension vers la gloire ? »

Cette tendance perdura jusqu'en 1945. Entassées dans des cantines, punaisées aux murs des baraquements, glissées dans les portefeuilles ou peintes sur le nez des bombardiers, les poitrines américaines accompagnèrent les soldats dans tous leurs combats. Ensuite la guerre prit fin, et les *boys* abandonnèrent leurs compagnes de papier pour retourner auprès de femmes

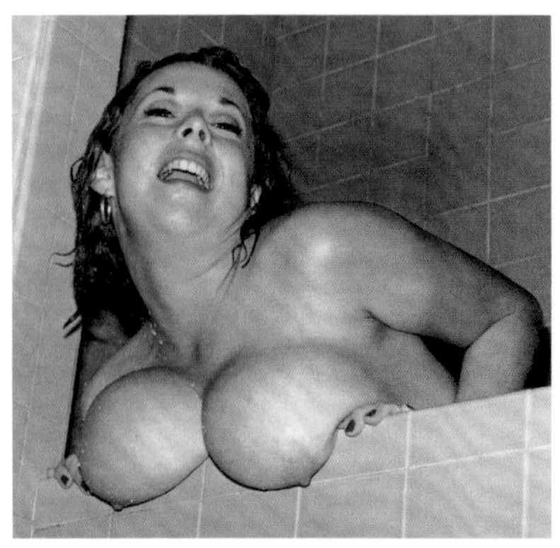

bien réelles, au grand désespoir des éditeurs de magazines masculins. Il devint évident que des publications comme *War Laffs* ou *Who's Your Pin-Up Girl?* n'avaient pas leur place en temps de paix, si bien qu'entre 1948 et 1951, ils lancèrent une série de magazines dédiés aux bad girls, les « vilaines filles » : *Night and Day*, *Modern Man*, *Gala*, *Frolic*, *Swagger*, *Follies* et *Cavalcade of Burlesque* faisaient le même pari, à savoir que les vétérans fraîchement démobilisés étaient en manque de sensations fortes. Pari gagnant. Les magazines dits « burlesques » firent un tabac grâce à des modèles hautes en couleur, effrontées, et surtout, pourvues de fortes poitrines.

La première effeuilleuse à se faire un nom avec son tour de poitrine fut Busty Brown, qui fit ses débuts vers 1941. Jennie Lee, « The Bazoom Girl », prit sa suite en 1945 alors qu'elle n'était encore qu'en terminale. Tempest Storm arriva en 1950, et deux légendes parmi les opulentes, Virginia « Ding Dong » Bell et Candy Barr, démarrèrent leur carrière en 1954. Les 90C de Candy sont alors les seins les plus parfaits jamais dévoilés au grand public, mais ceux de Virginia étaient plus gros, et dans les années 1950, la taille était vraiment ce qui comptait le plus. À la fin de cette décennie, même Miss Bell fut supplantée par la sculpturale Gee Whiz, dont le nom d'artiste s'inspire des réactions que ses seins gros comme des pastèques provoquaient chez ses admirateurs.

Outre les stripteaseuses, les magazines masculins de l'après-guerre poussèrent sur le devant de la scène les modèles professionnels spécialisés dans le sein : Caren Castro, Maria Stinger, Linda West et Jane Dolinger entrent dans cette catégorie. Jane était cependant unique en son genre, puisqu'elle était journaliste indépendante et accompagnait ses photos seins nus du récit de ses aventures en Afrique et dans la jungle amazonienne. La plupart de ses consœurs étaient des starlettes comme Irish McCalla, Betty Brosmer, Meg Miles et Jayne Mansfield dont les seins étaient d'un volume si époustouflant qu'elles n'avaient pas besoin d'enlever leurs vêtements. Seule Jayne posa poitrine nue, mais même vêtue, elle éclipsait les modèles plus audacieux et moins généreusement pourvus.

OPPOSITE Bonnie Locke, circa 1975.

RIGHT Jennie Lee, known as "The Bazoom Girl," started stripping as a 17-year-old high school student in 1945.

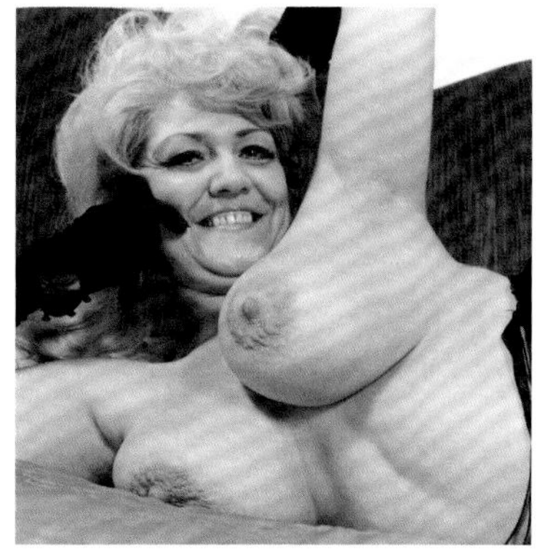

Dans les années 1960, la fixation sur les gros seins était si enracinée dans l'imaginaire et l'iconographie américains qu'elle alimentait un nouveau genre de magazines spécialisés, parmi lesquels *Gem*, *Gent* et *The Swinger*, bientôt rebaptisé *BUF*, pour Big Up Front (Dodue Devant...). Leurs modèles fétiches étaient Michelle Angelo, Joan Brinkman, Diane Curtis, Shawn Devereaux, Candy Earle, Joyce Mandel, Lisa Matthews, Linda McClung, Starr Murphy, Janice Orames, Suzanne Pritchard, Janie Reynolds et Julie Wills.

À la fin des années 1960, une première vague de modèles opportunistes éphémères se joignit aux grands noms, des filles qui faisaient quelques photos pour se renflouer et disparaissaient, souvent sans laisser leur vrai nom. Cette tendance s'intensifia dans les années 1970, lorsque la révolution sexuelle libéra le nu du joug moral. De jeunes et jolies hippies empochaient quelques dollars en montrant leurs seins et continuaient leur route. Quand les lecteurs découvraient une nouvelle déesse potentielle, elle avait souvent disparu de la circulation depuis longtemps... Vous parlez d'une frustration ! Cette décennie n'en produisit pas moins son lot de stars, notamment Karen Brown, Linda Corrigan, Darlene English alias « Yum Yum » (Miam miam...), Linda Gordon, Lois Harmon, Teresa Jackman, Bonnie Locke, Sylvia McFarland, Roberta Pedon, Candy Samples, Joyce Spaeth, Keli Stewart et Mary Waters.

Les magazines « de nichons » prospérèrent au fil des années 1980, mais les seins gonflés à la silicone y prirent une place croissante. Les gros seins devinrent un investissement, comme un prêt étudiant, l'accessoire de choix pour lancer une carrière dans le film porno ou le strip-tease, jusqu'à la surenchère. Au début des années 1990, certaines « danseuses exotiques » augmentaient leur tour de poitrines chaque année, poussant les femmes naturellement dotées de grosses poitrines à se faire opérer aussi, pour résister à la concurrence. En 1995, dans ce milieu, le mot d'ordre était « aussi gros que la tête ». Ensuite on parla des complications, la plus bénigne et courante étant l'étirement

« Entassées dans des cantines, punaisées aux murs des baraquements, glissées dans les porte-feuilles ou peintes sur le nez des bombardiers, les poitrines américaines accompagnèrent les soldats dans tous leurs combats. »

excessif de la peau, et le gouvernement mit fin au délire mammaire artificiel.

Les implants surdimensionnés ont peut-être disparu, mais nous ne reviendrons jamais à l'âge d'or des années 1950, 1960 et 1970, quand on pouvait être sûr que les gros seins étaient naturels. Ce livre s'adresse à tous ceux qui ont reluqué un décolleté spectaculaire en se demandant : « Ce sont des vrais, ou pas ? » Dans ces pages, vous pourrez laisser vos doutes de côté et savourer les poitrines les plus célèbres jamais modelées par Mère Nature. Et si vous rêvez encore des 70 kilos de Roth, jetez donc un œil à Annie Hawkins-Turner, alias Norma Stitz, page 189. D'après le *Livre Guinness des Records*, son « talent » s'en approche sacrément.

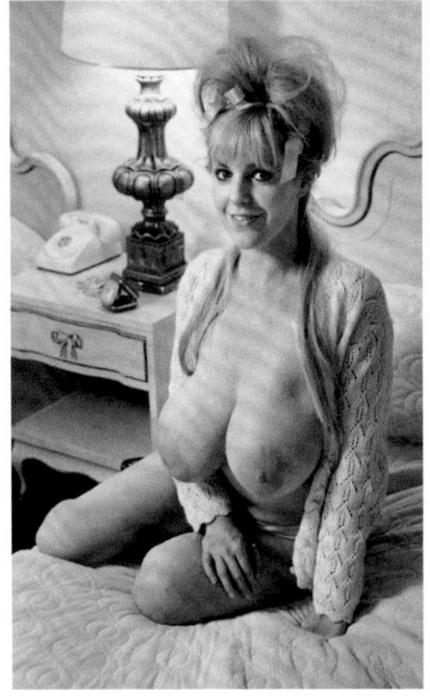

LEFT Ann Marie, real name Kathy Ayers, played an evangelical radio preacher in Russ Meyers' final film, *Beneath the Valley of the Ultravixens.*

OPPOSITE Janie Reynolds in one of the most treasured photos from my personal collection.

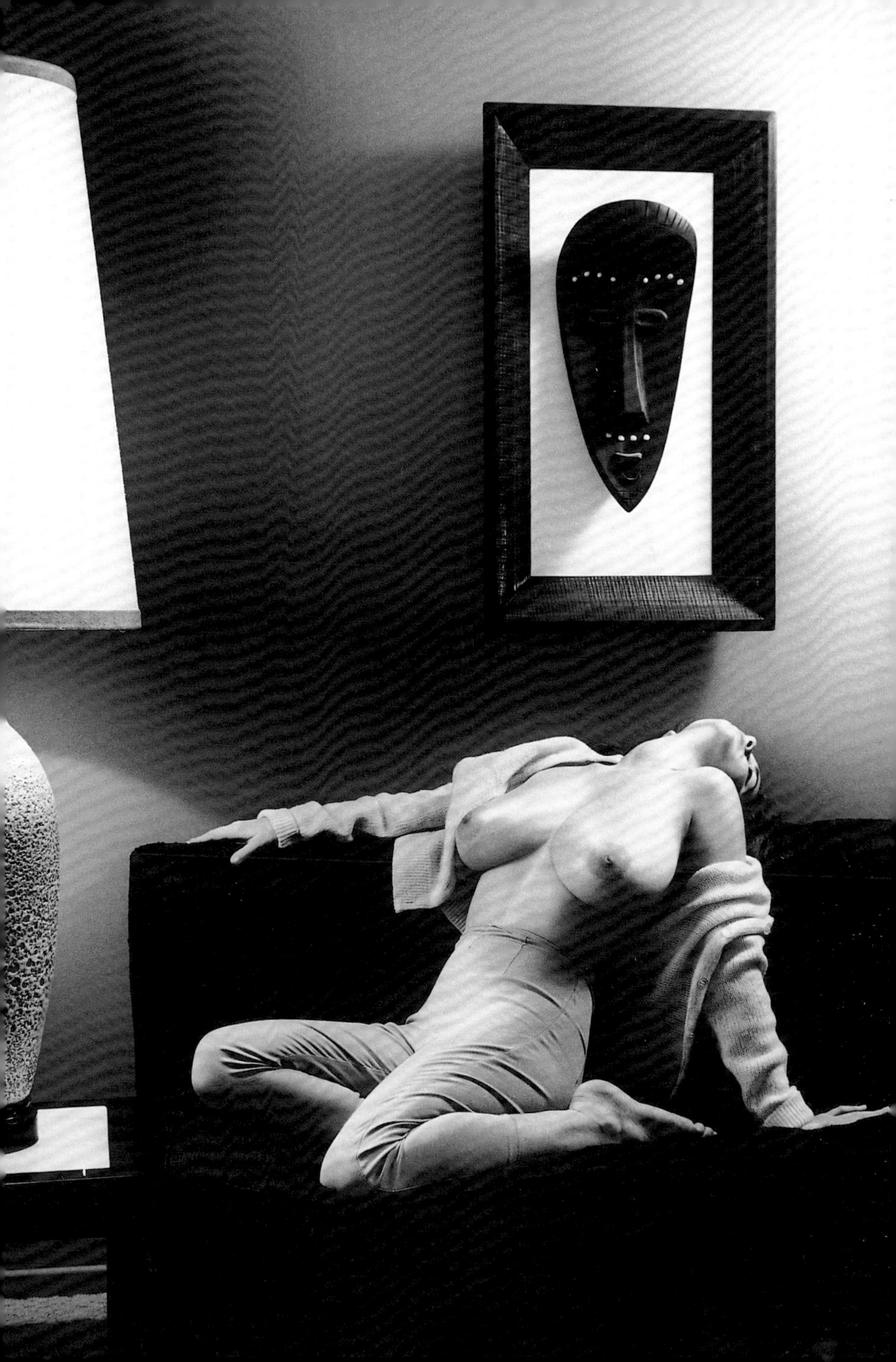

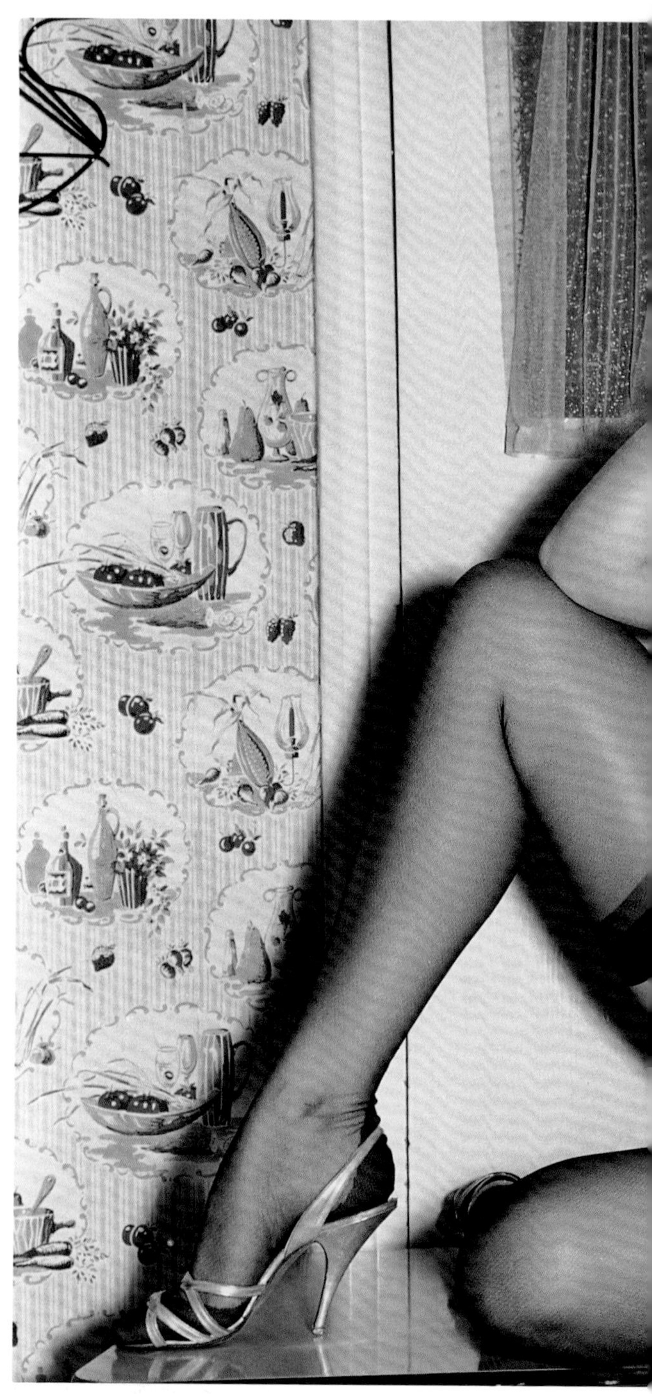

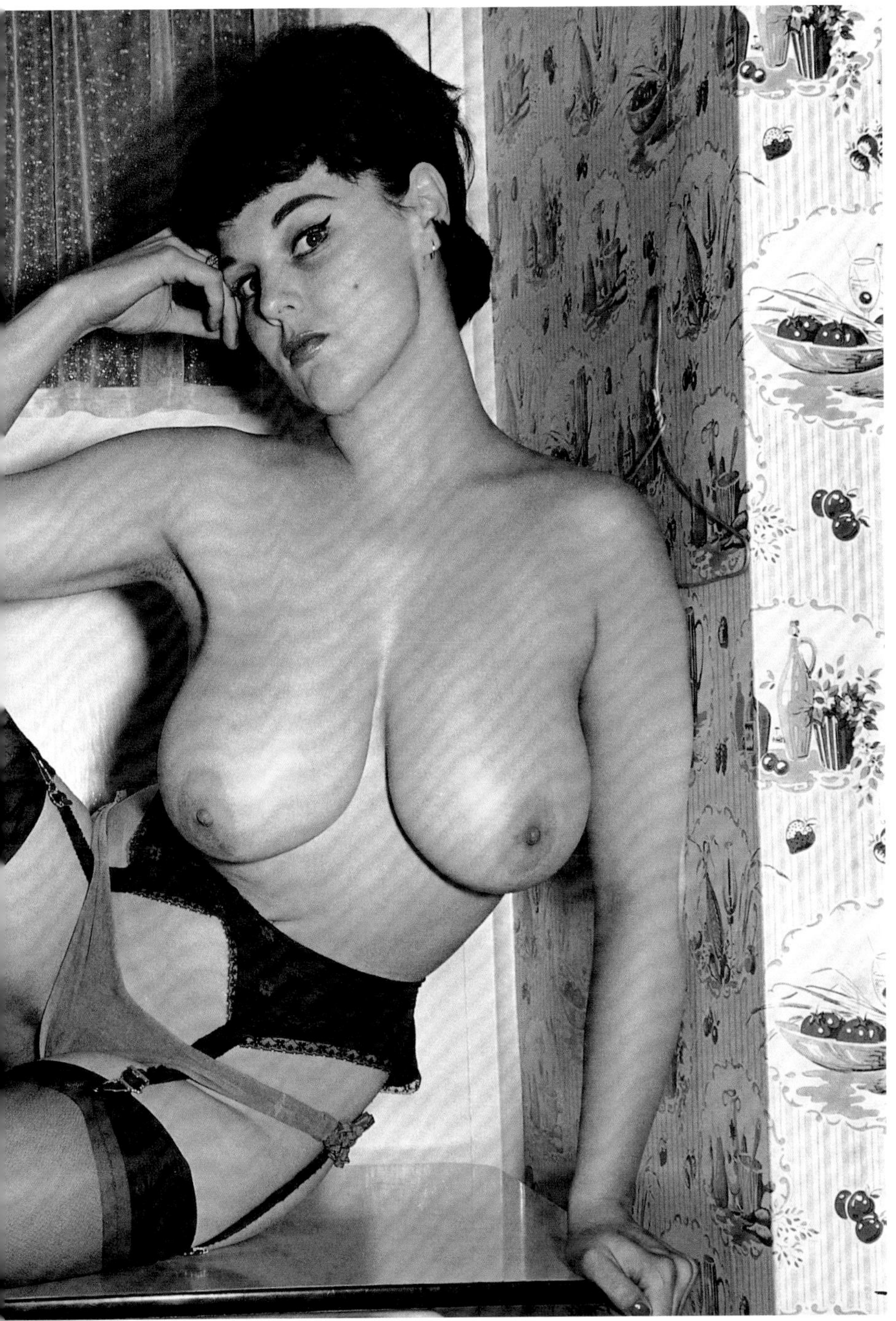

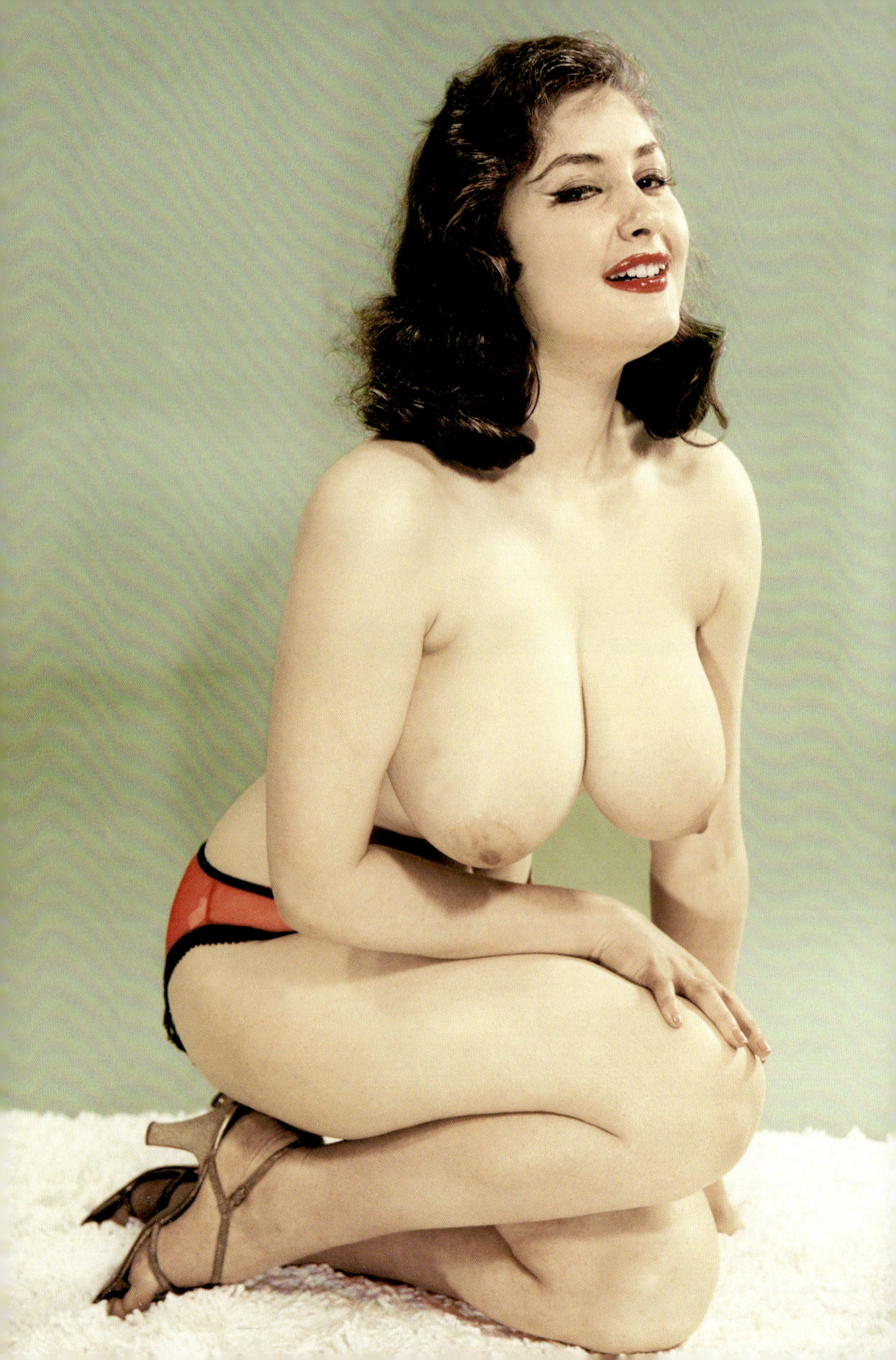

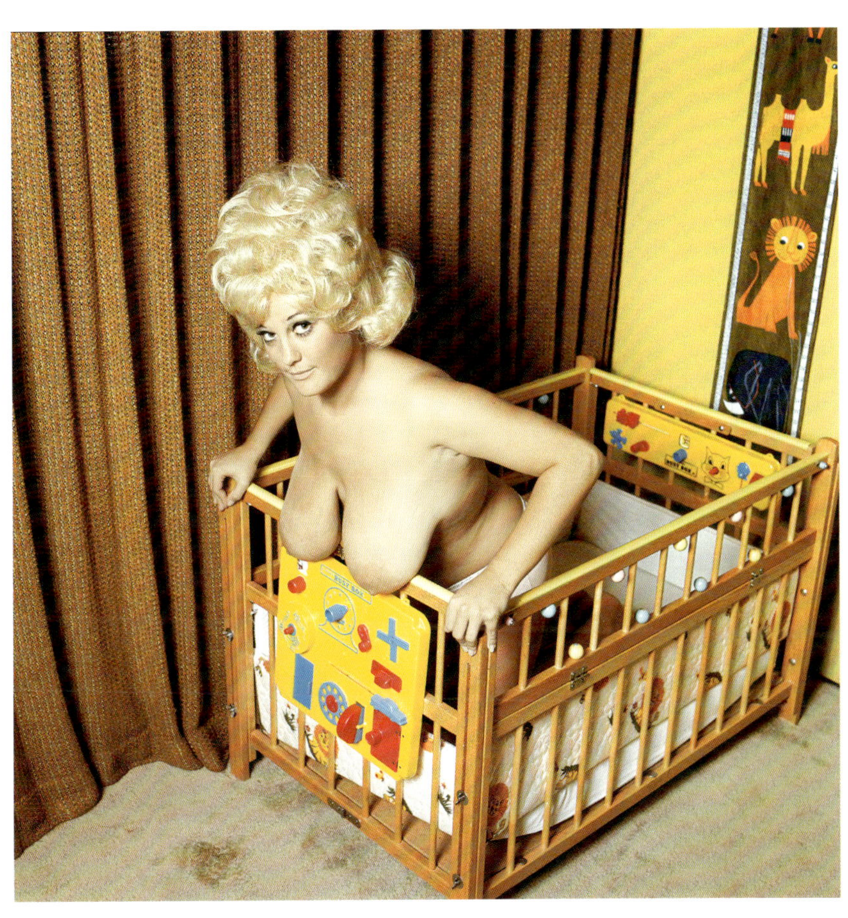

PAGES 26-27 Lorraine Burnett OPPOSITE Ann Austin ABOVE Unknown

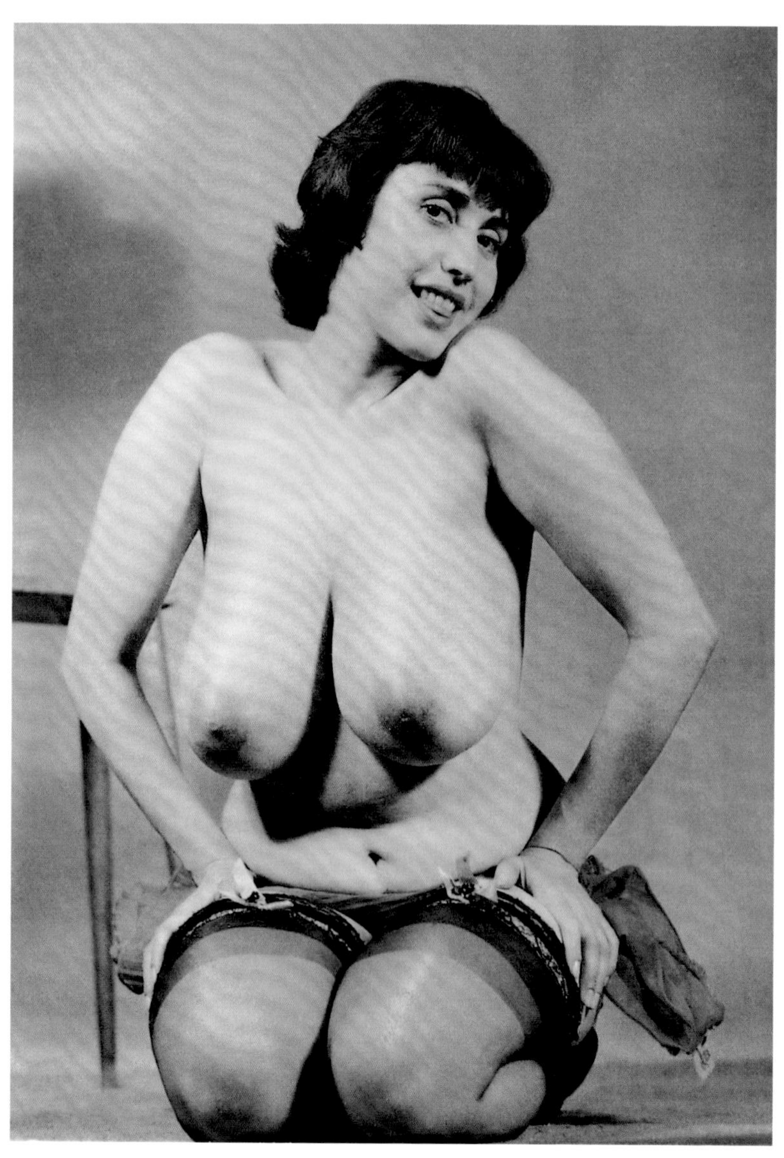

Linda West

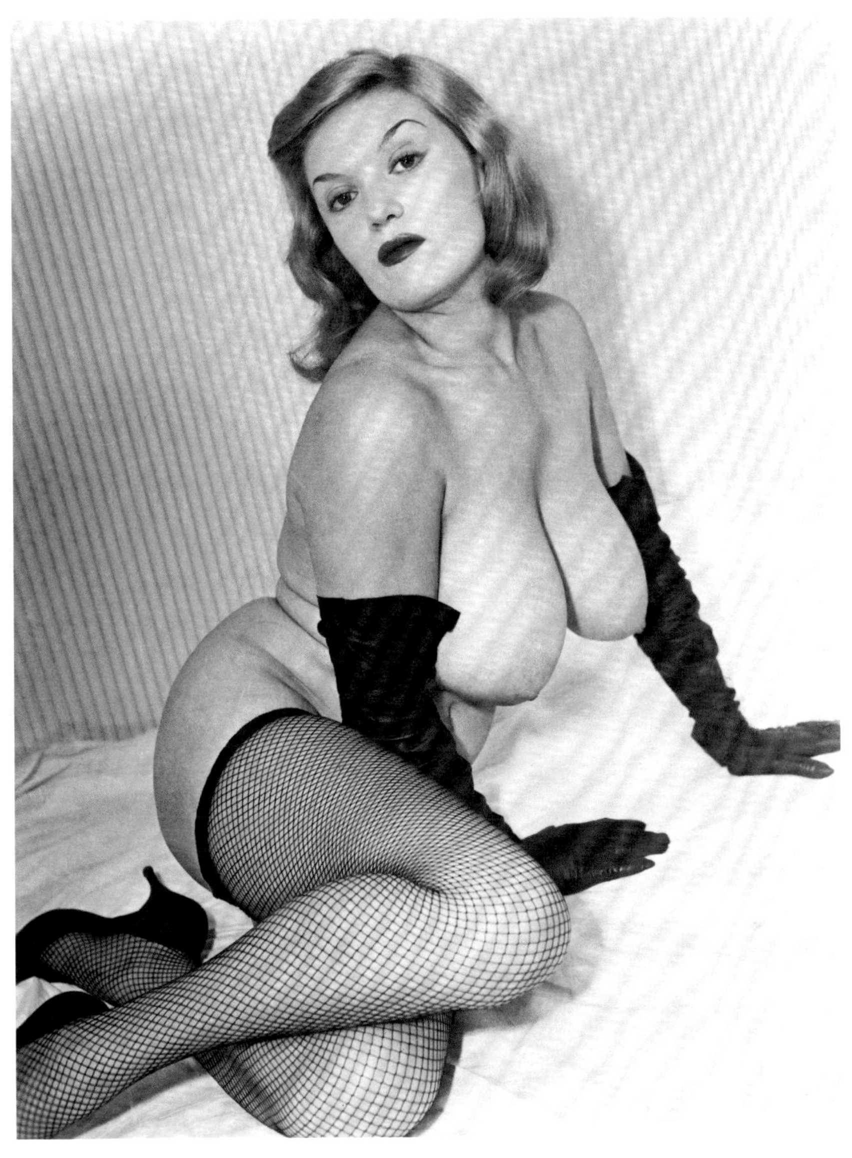

ABOVE Paula Page PAGES 32-33 Caren Castro

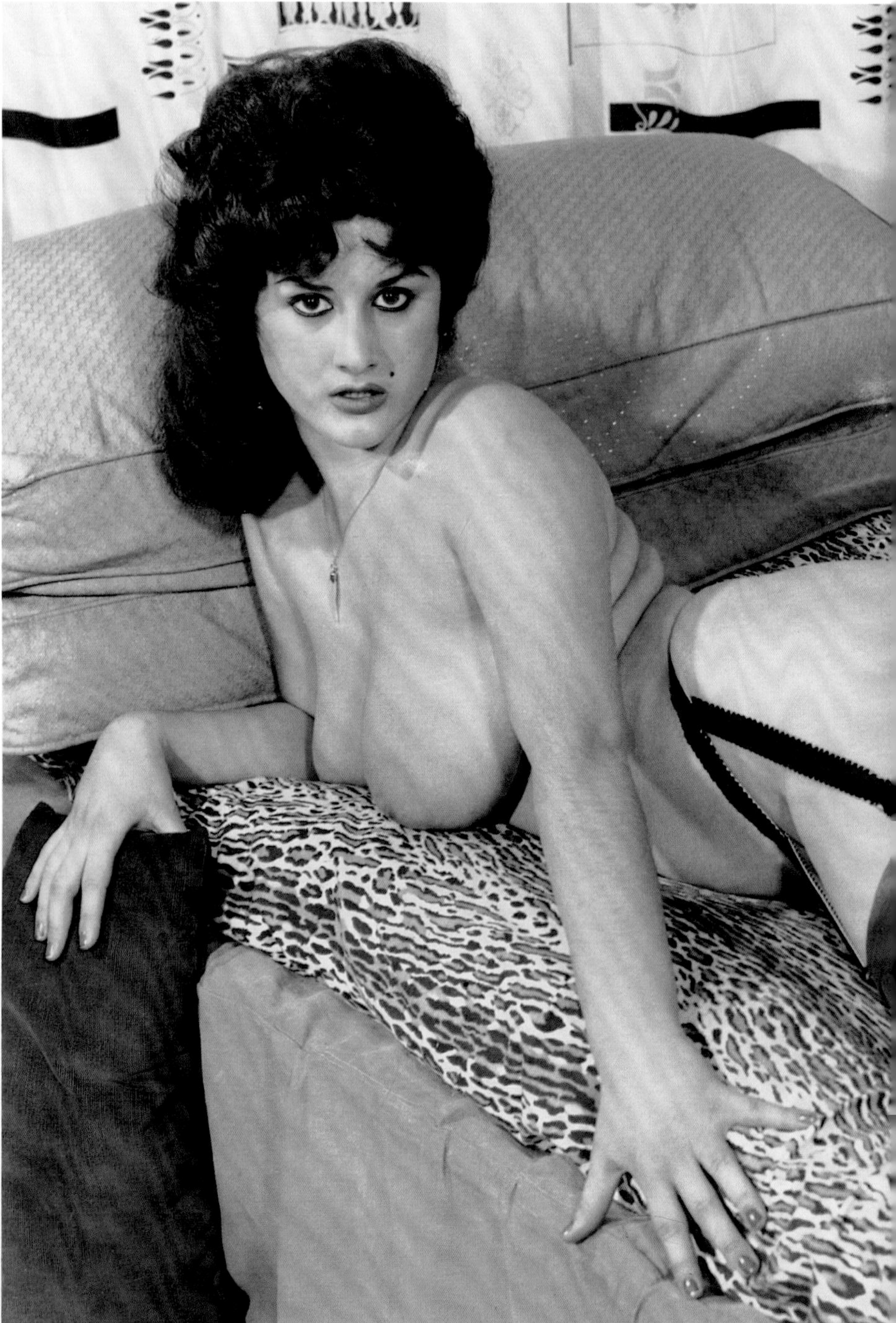

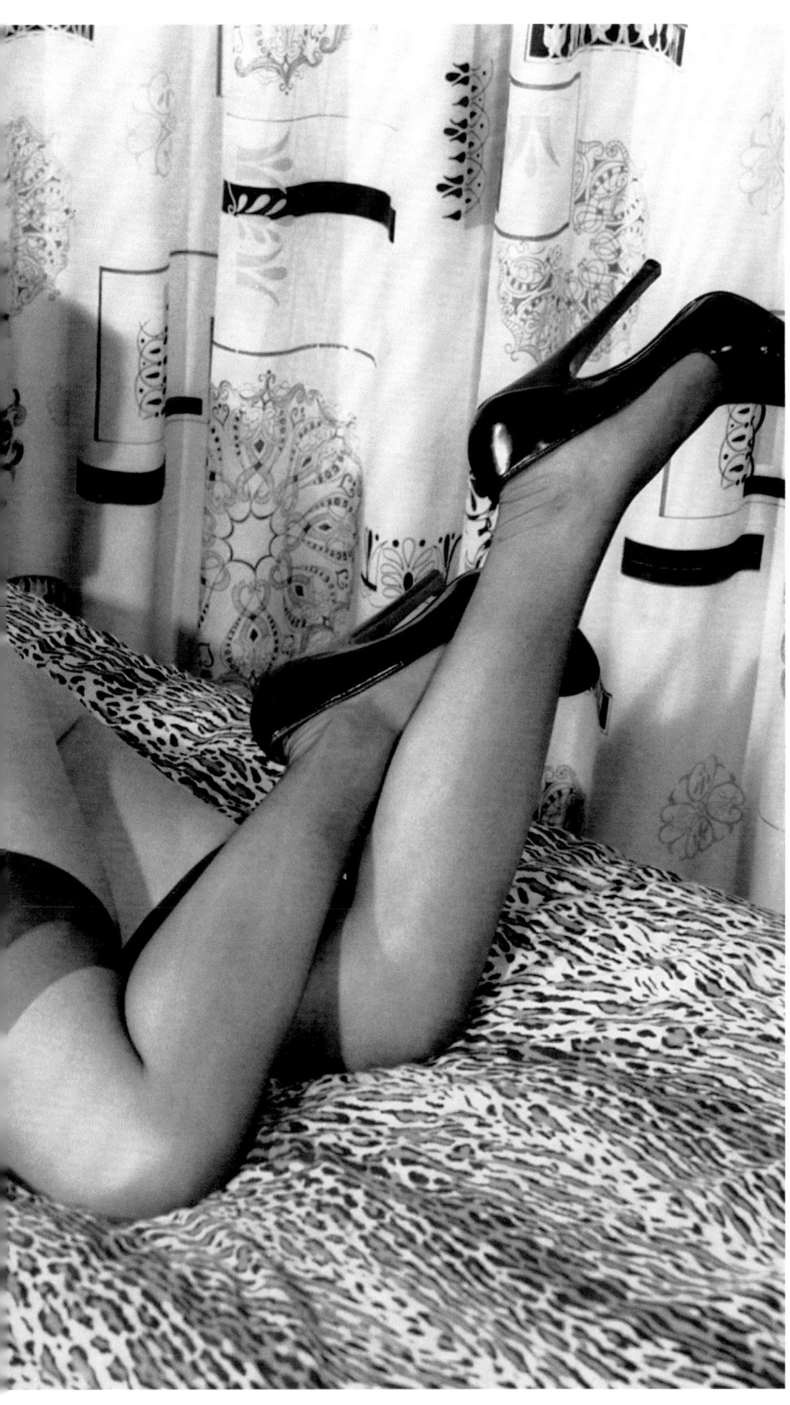

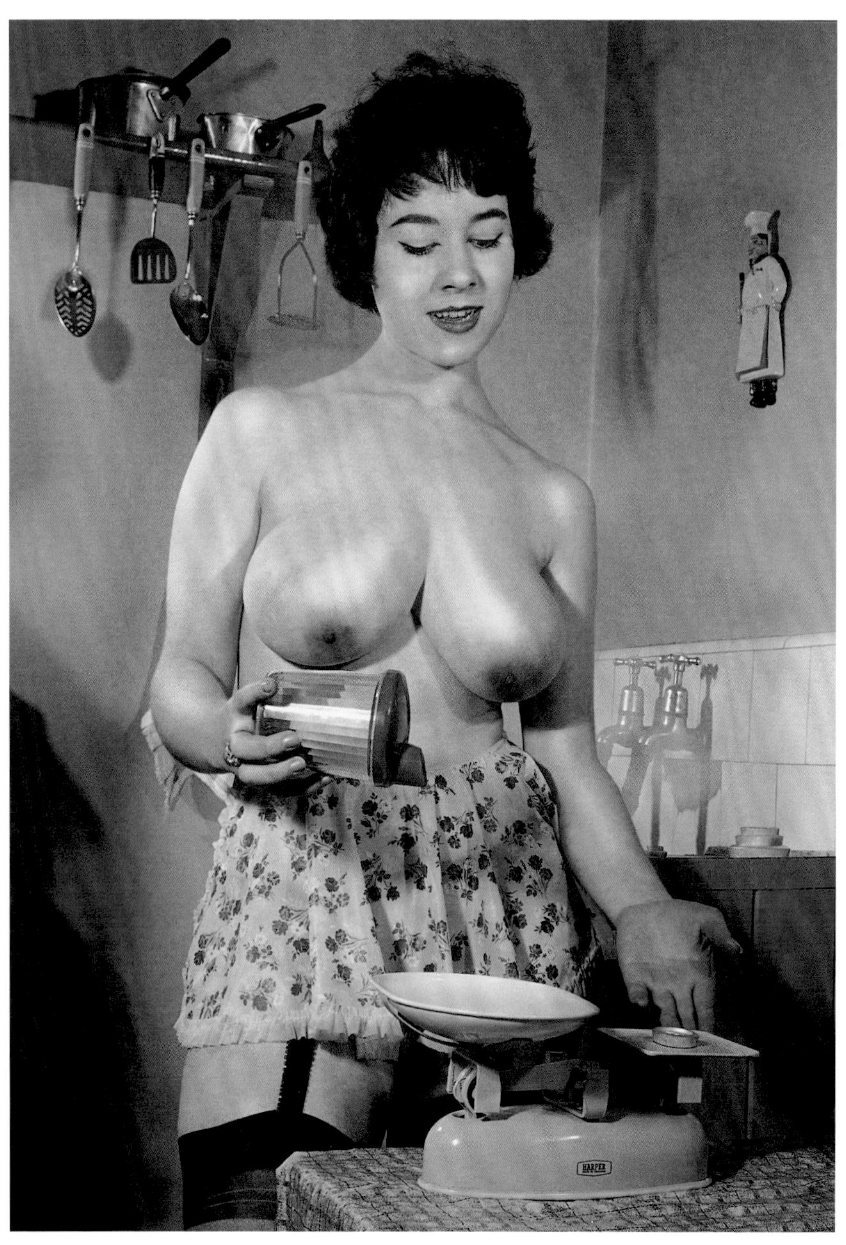

ABOVE Shane Lorrie OPPOSITE Gee Whiz PAGES 36-37 Terri Wigmore

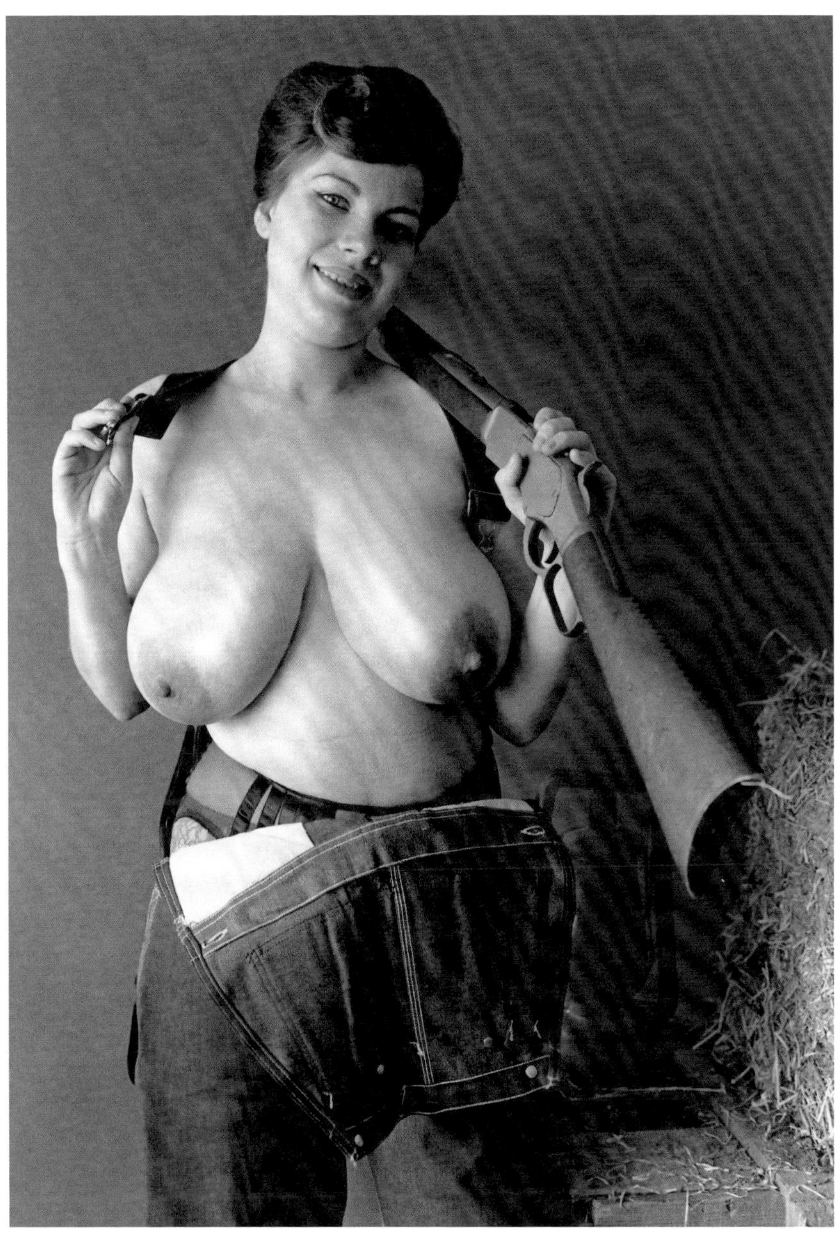

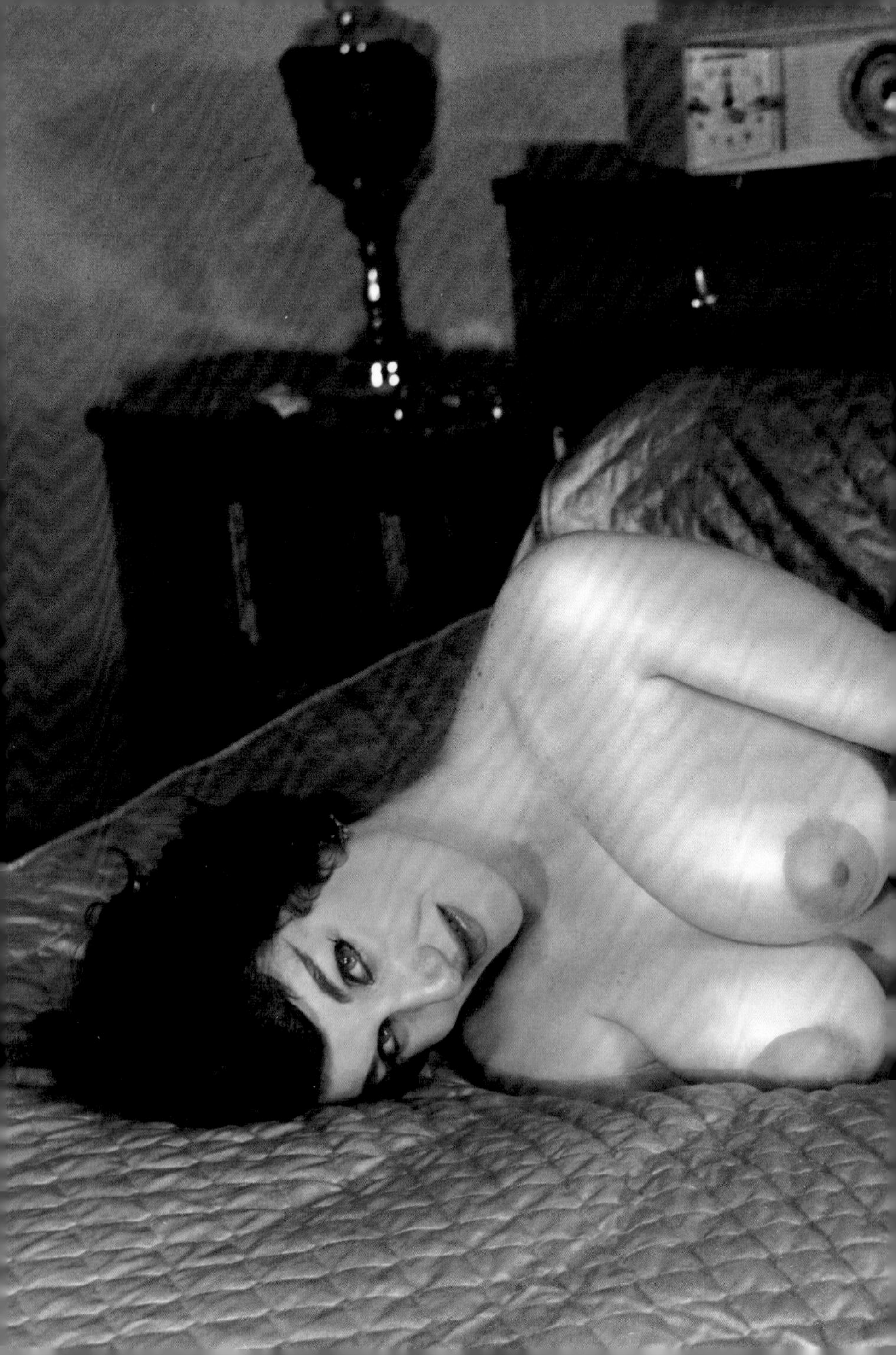

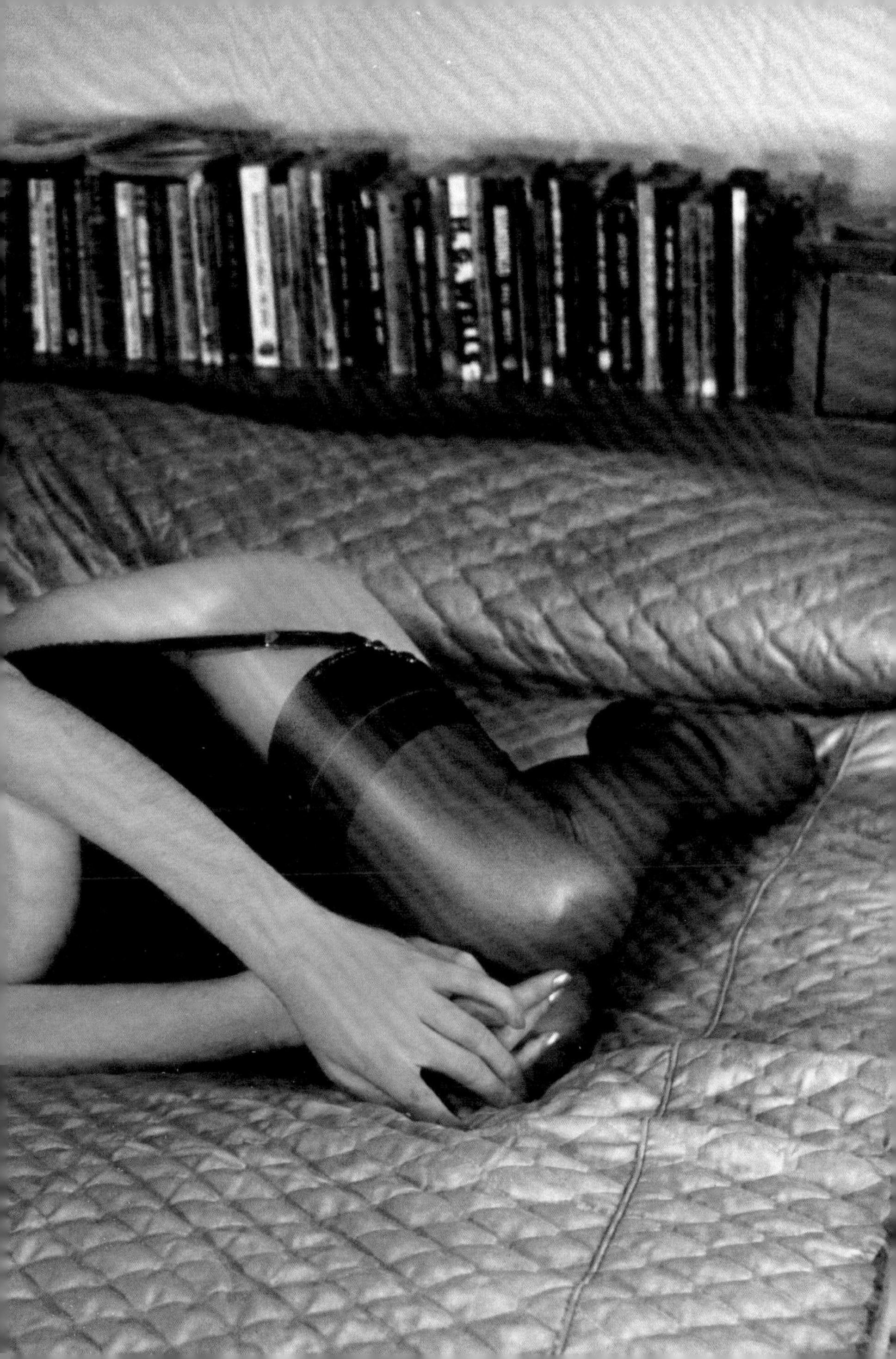

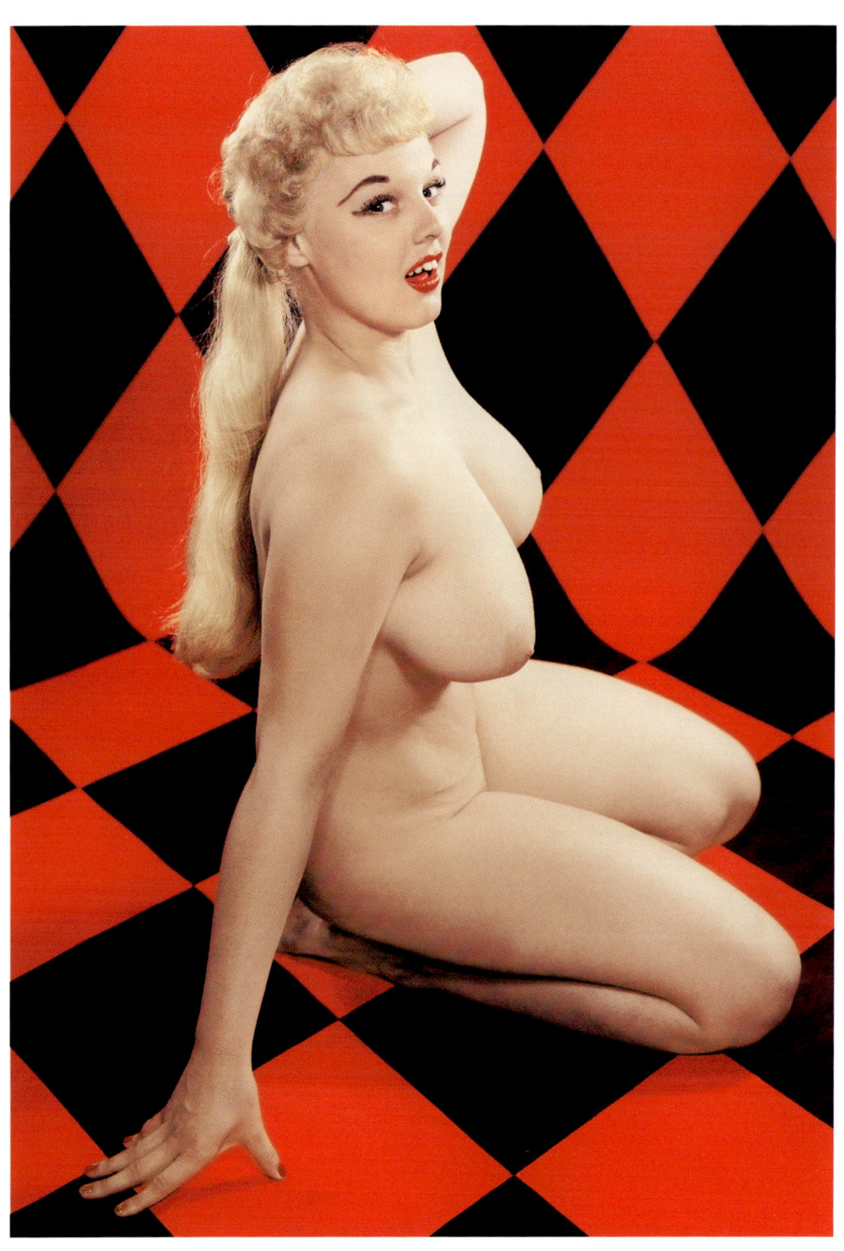

ABOVE Lorraine Burnett OPPOSITE Virgina Bell PAGES 40-41 Rosina Revelle

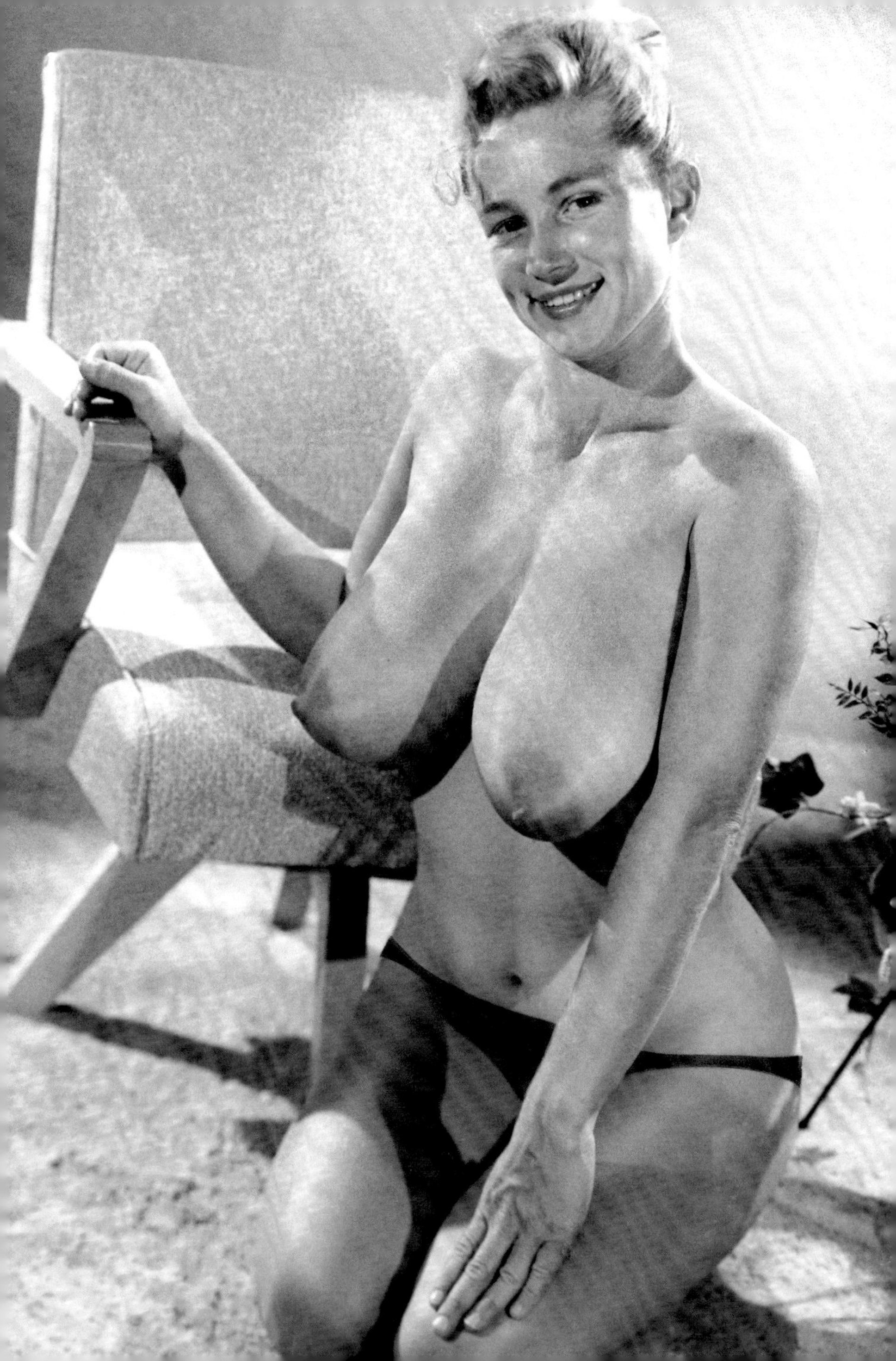

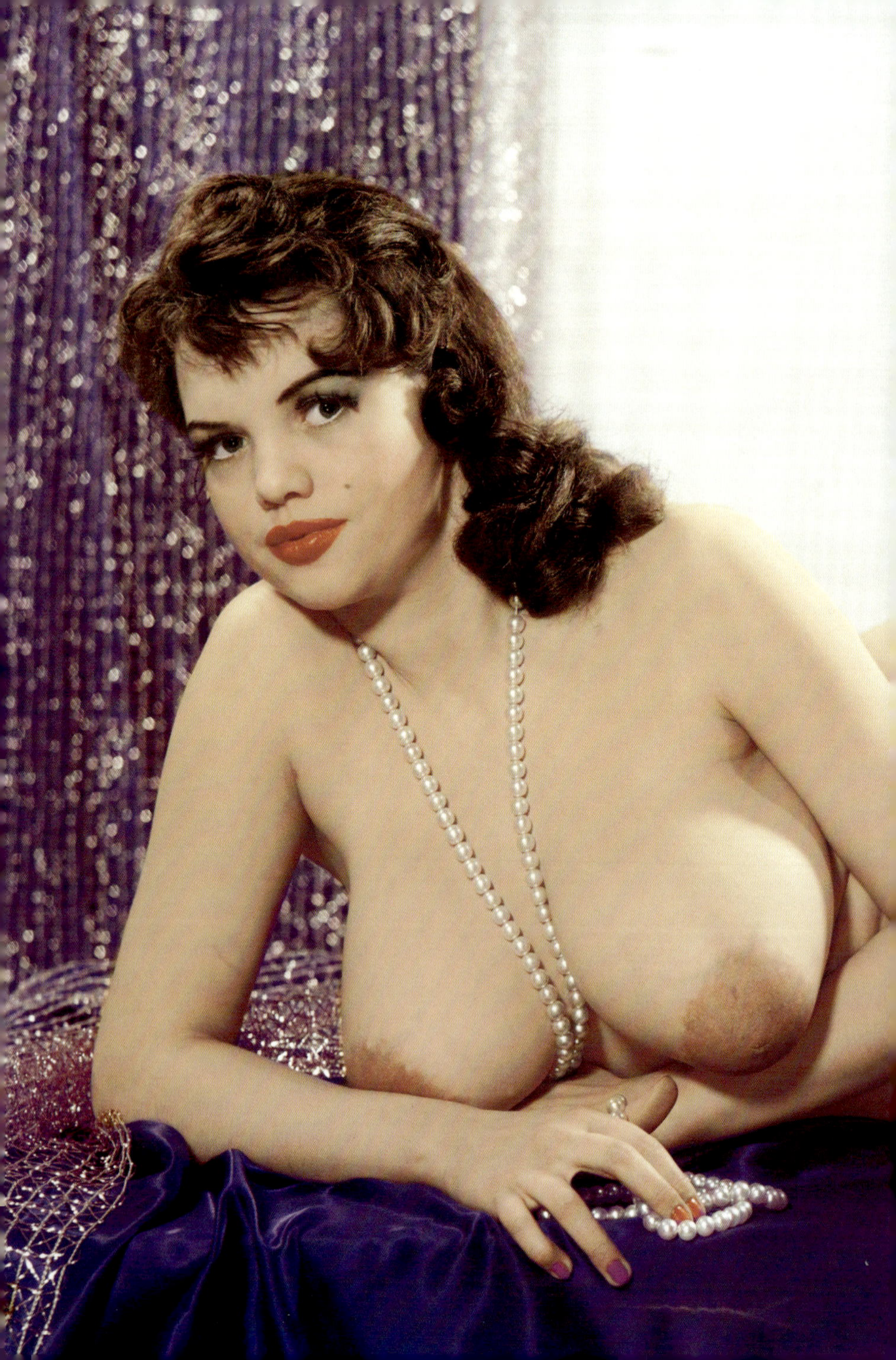

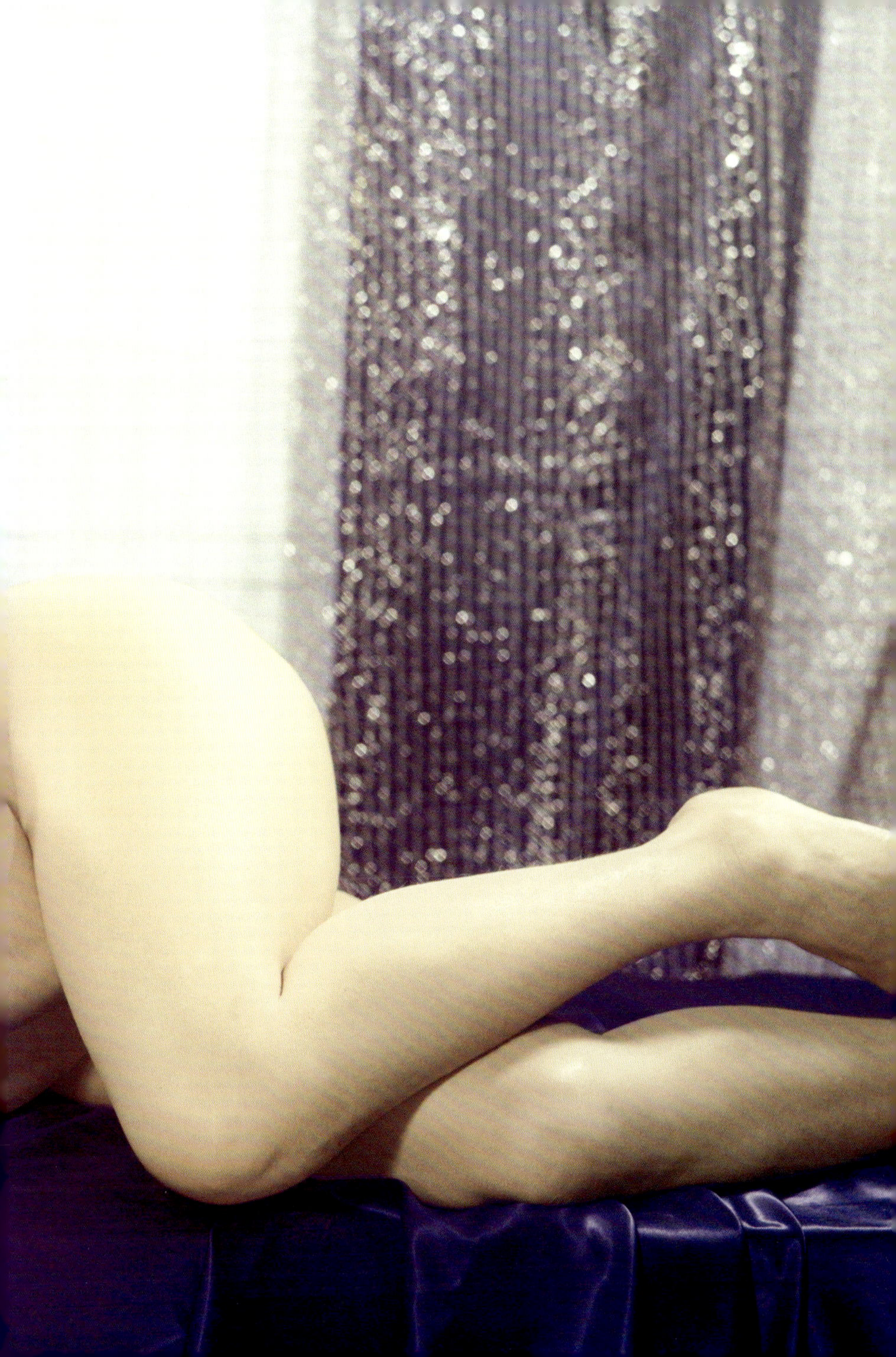

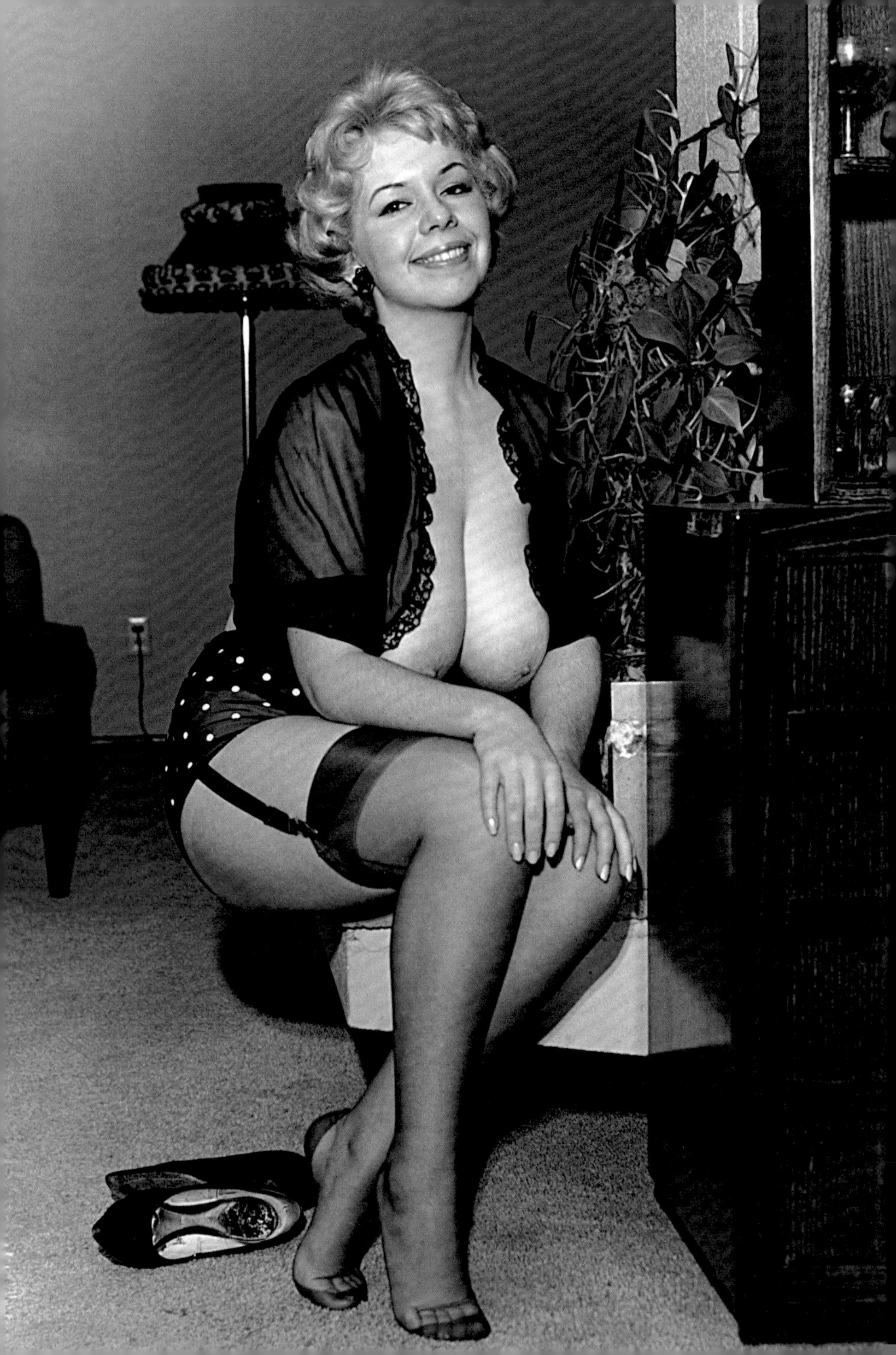

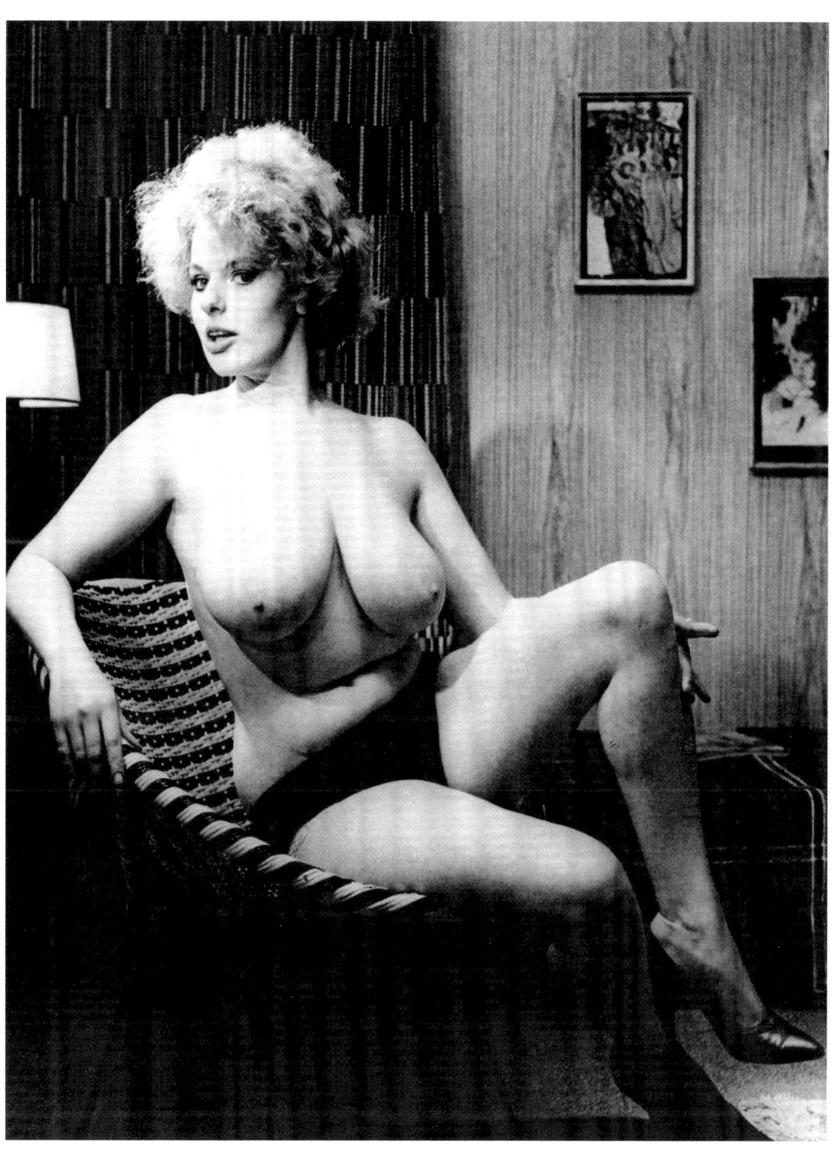

OPPOSITE Laurie Lippe ABOVE Unknown PAGES 44-45 Maria Stinger

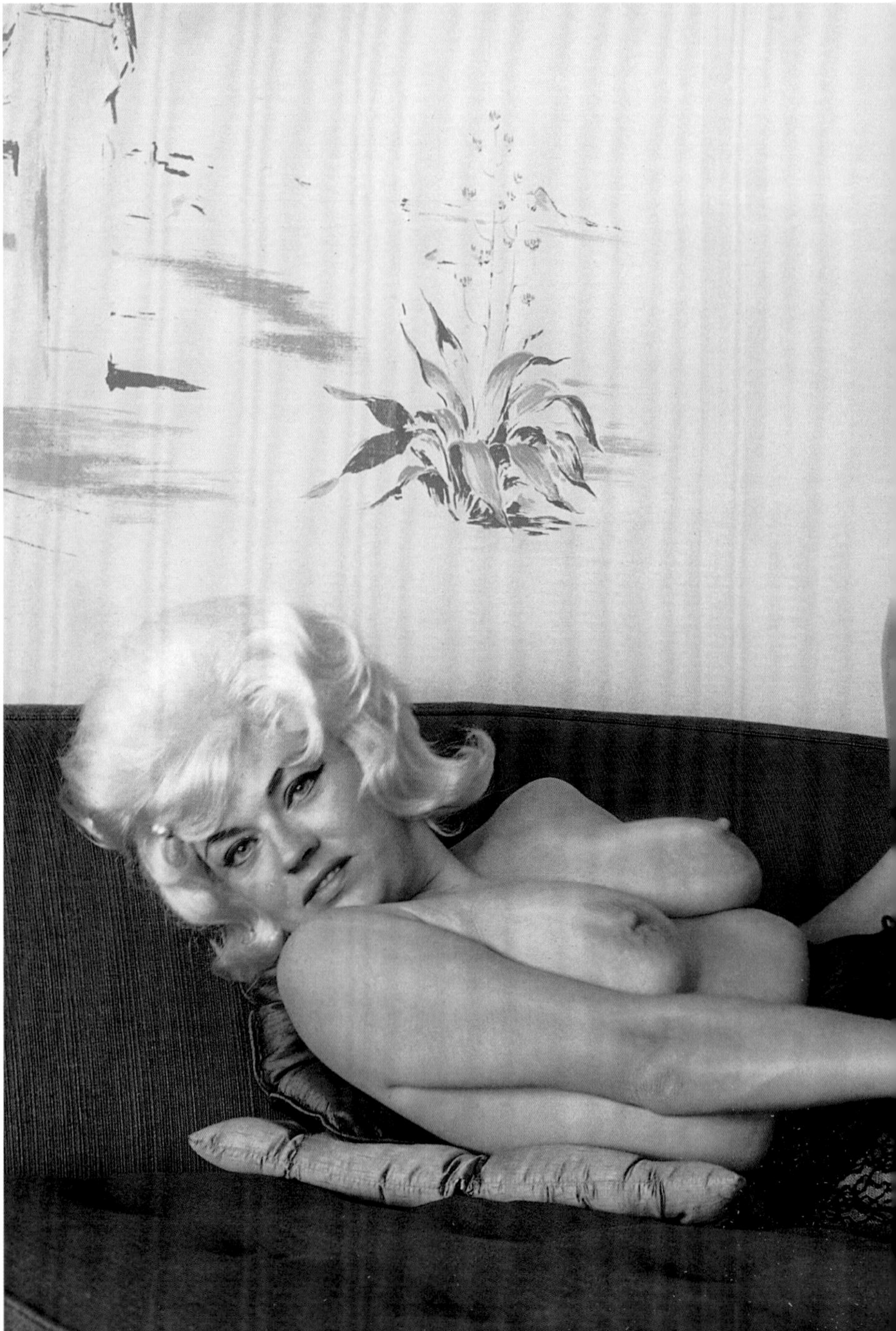

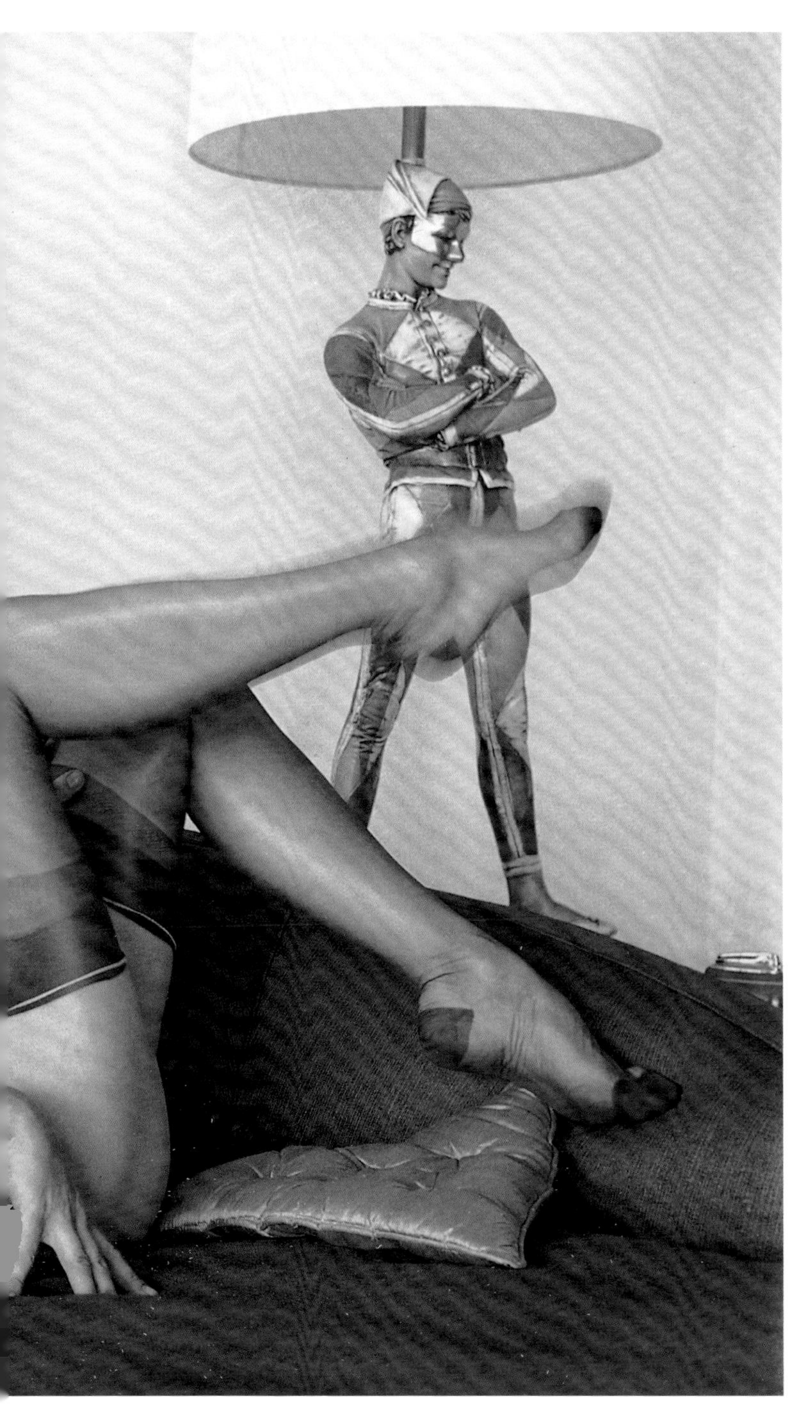

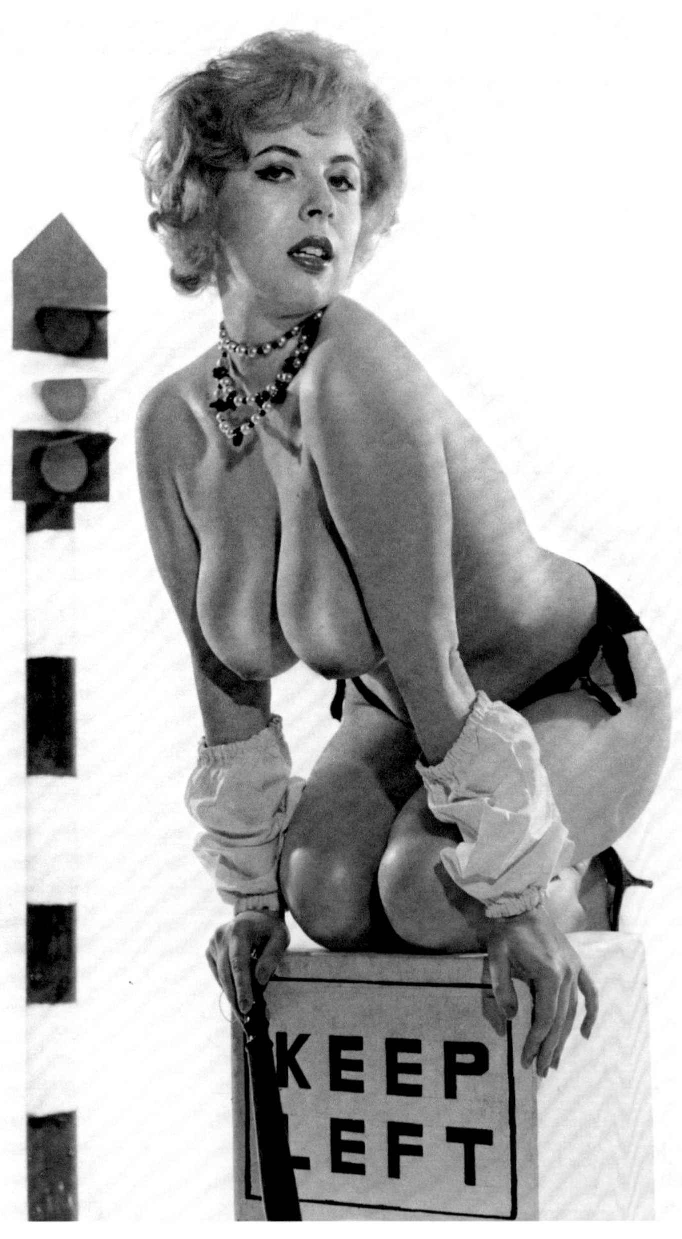

ABOVE Marie Davis OPPOSITE Paula Page PAGES 48-49 Unknown

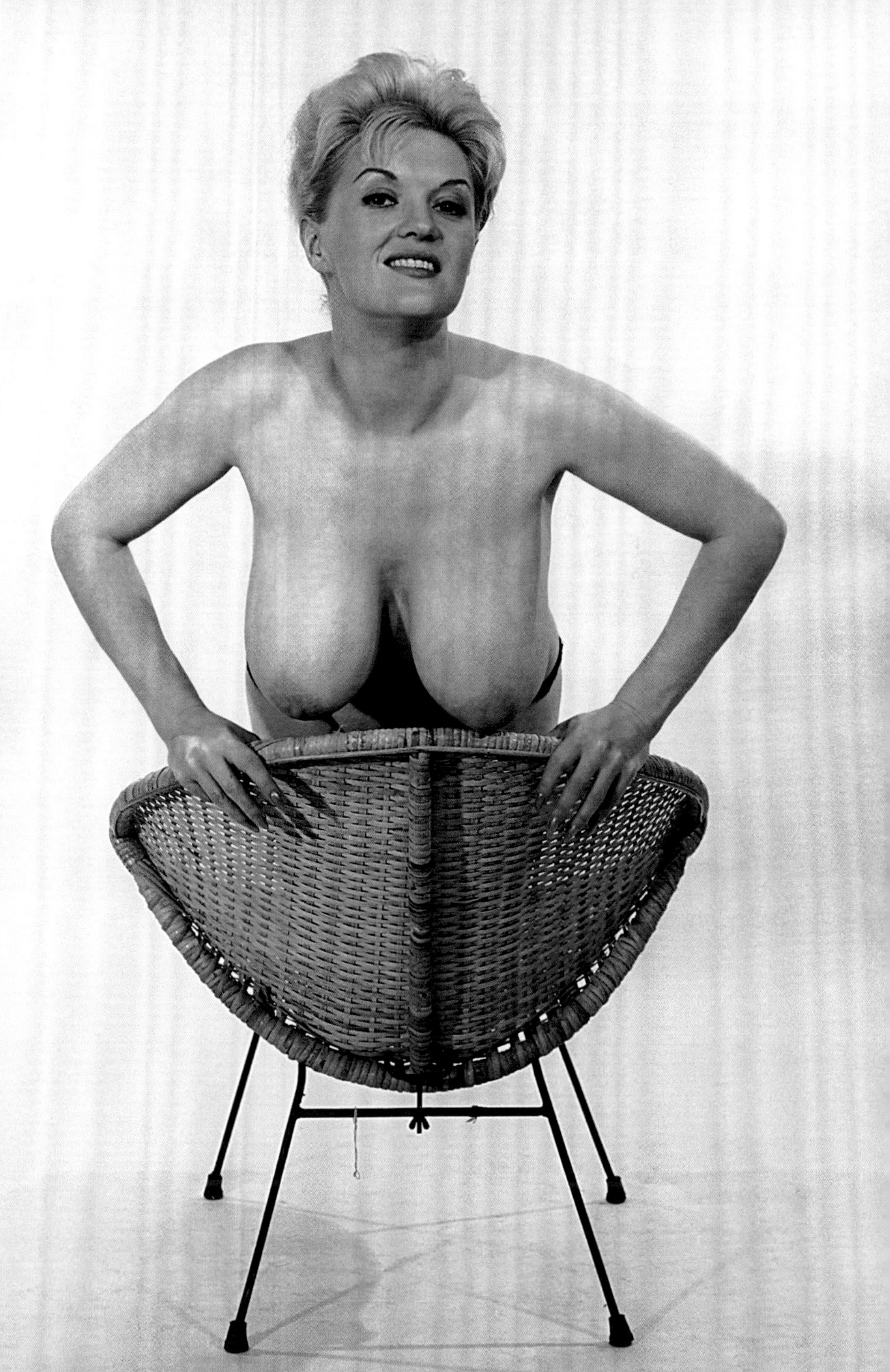

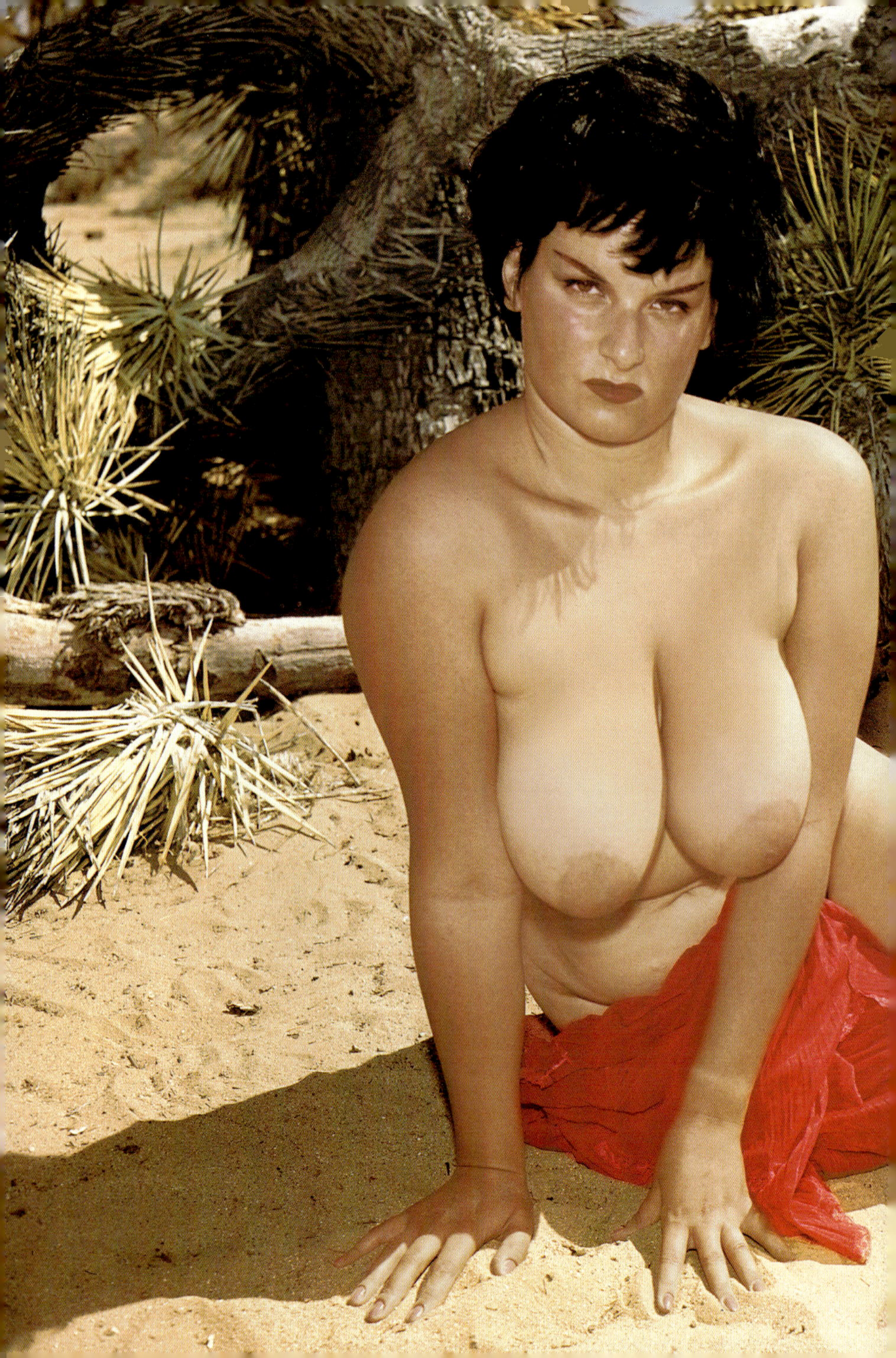

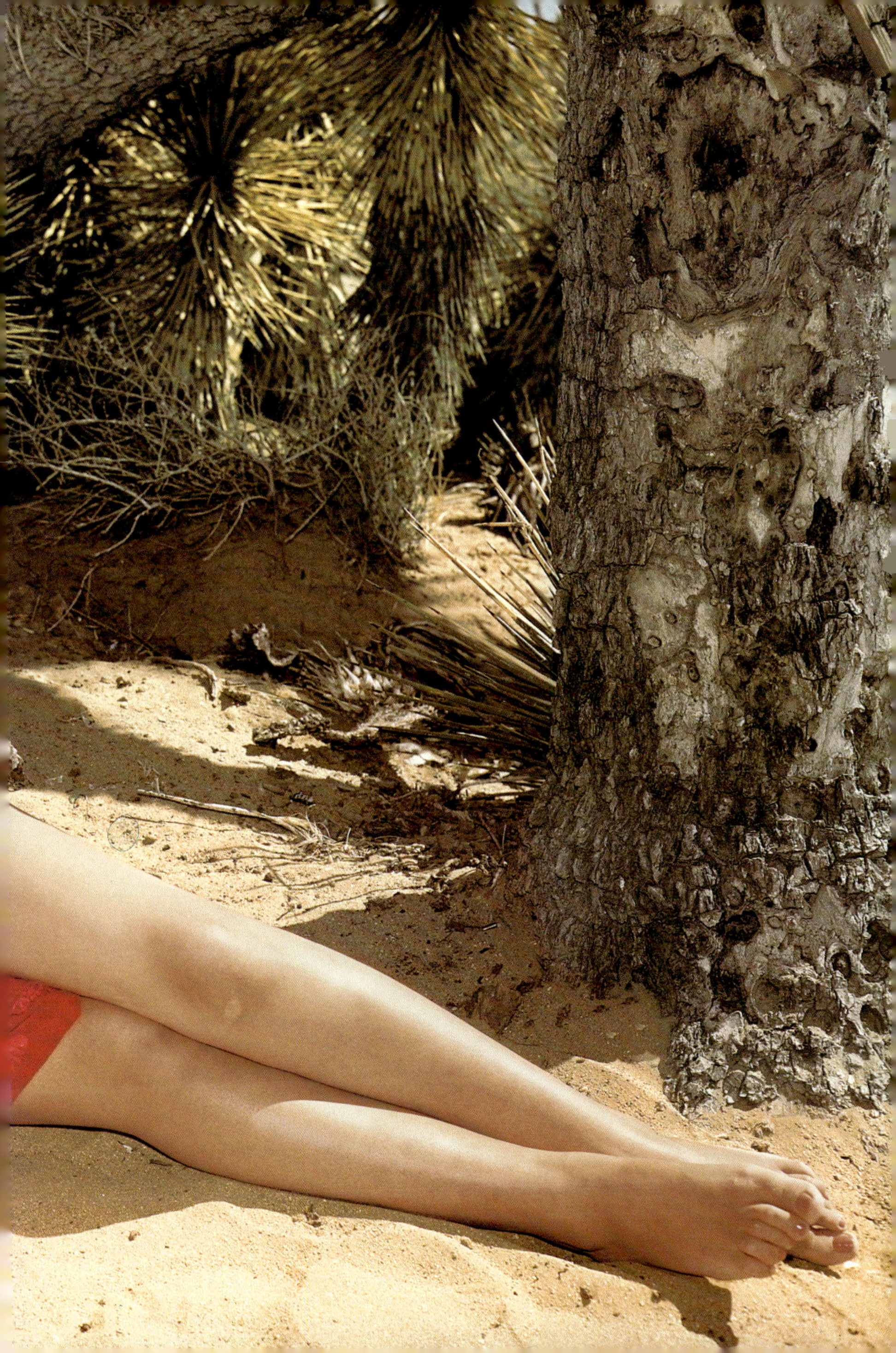

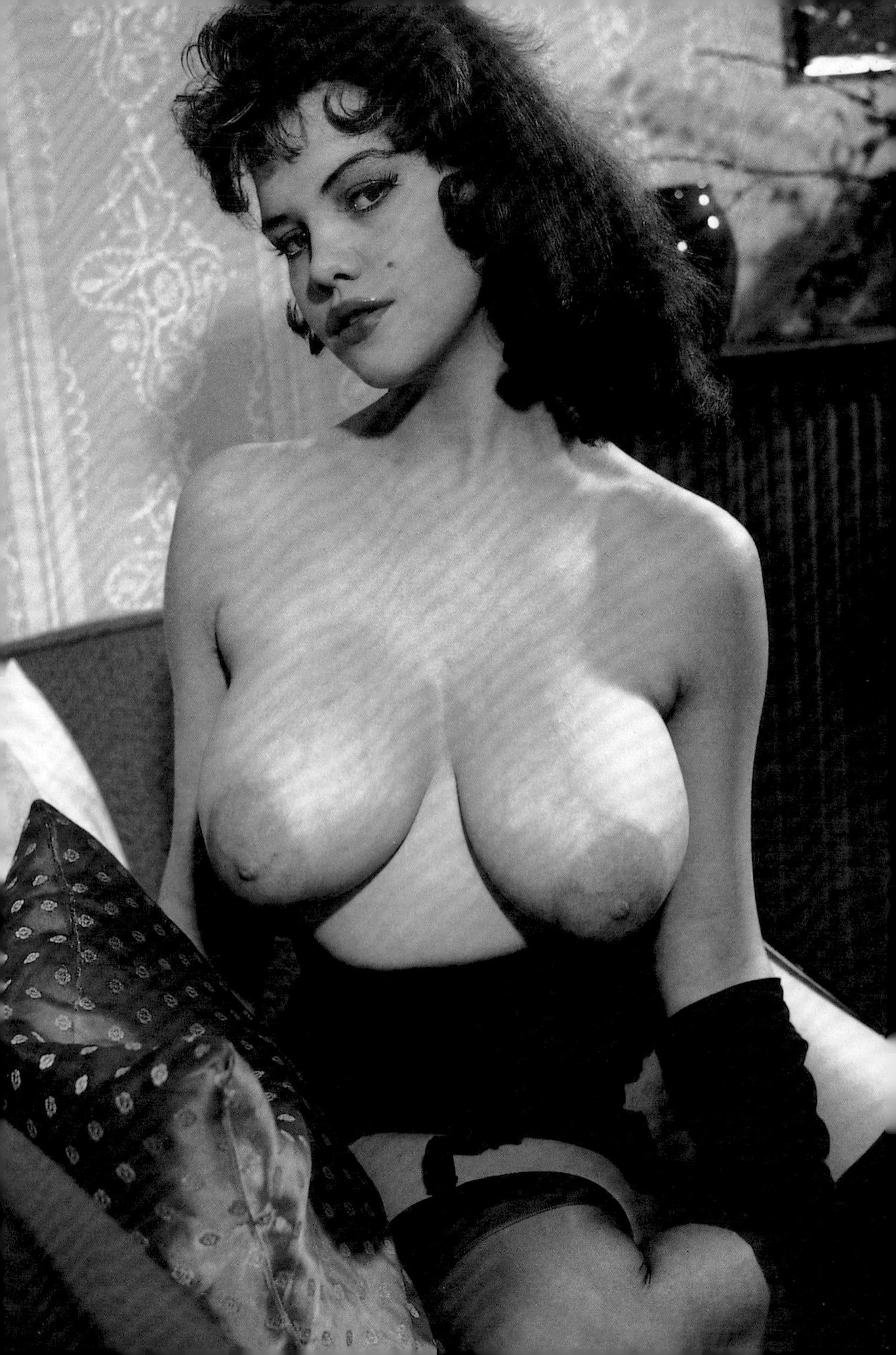

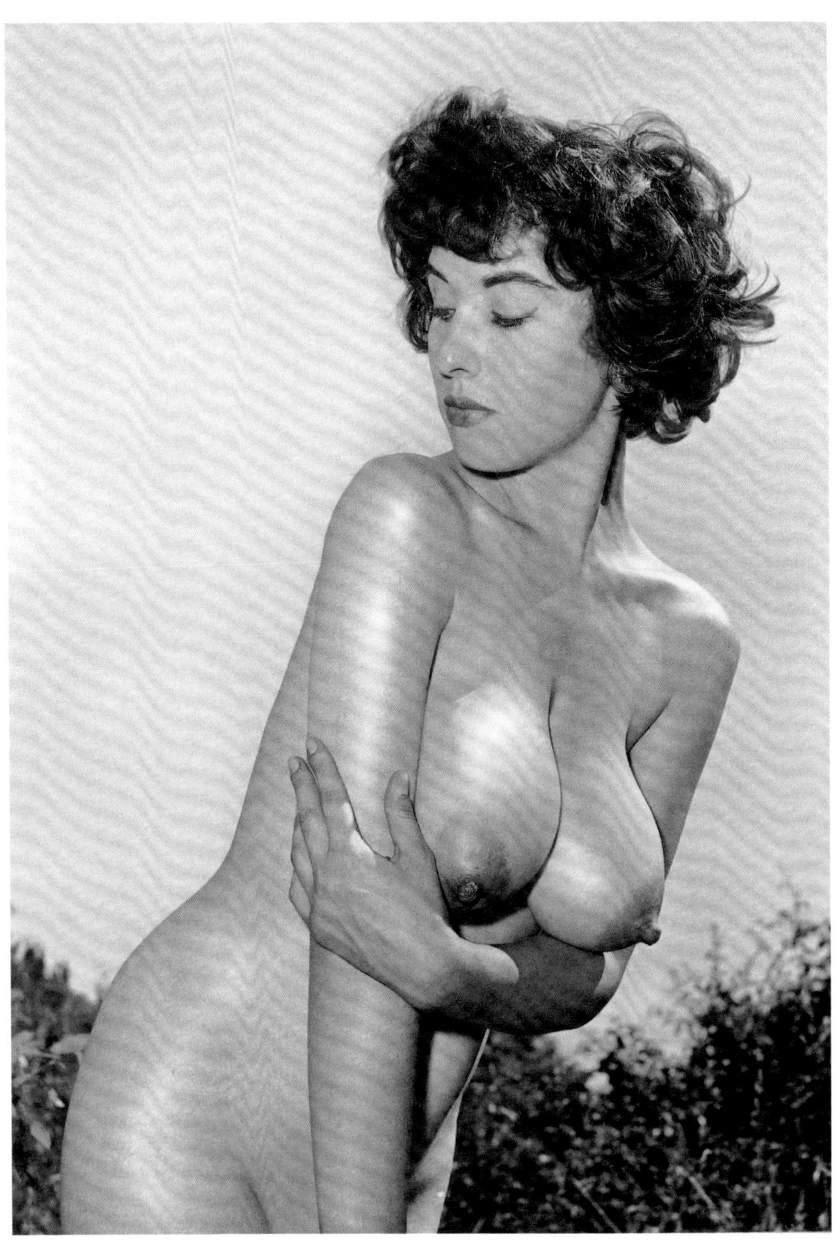

OPPOSITE Rosina Revelle ABOVE Roma Scott

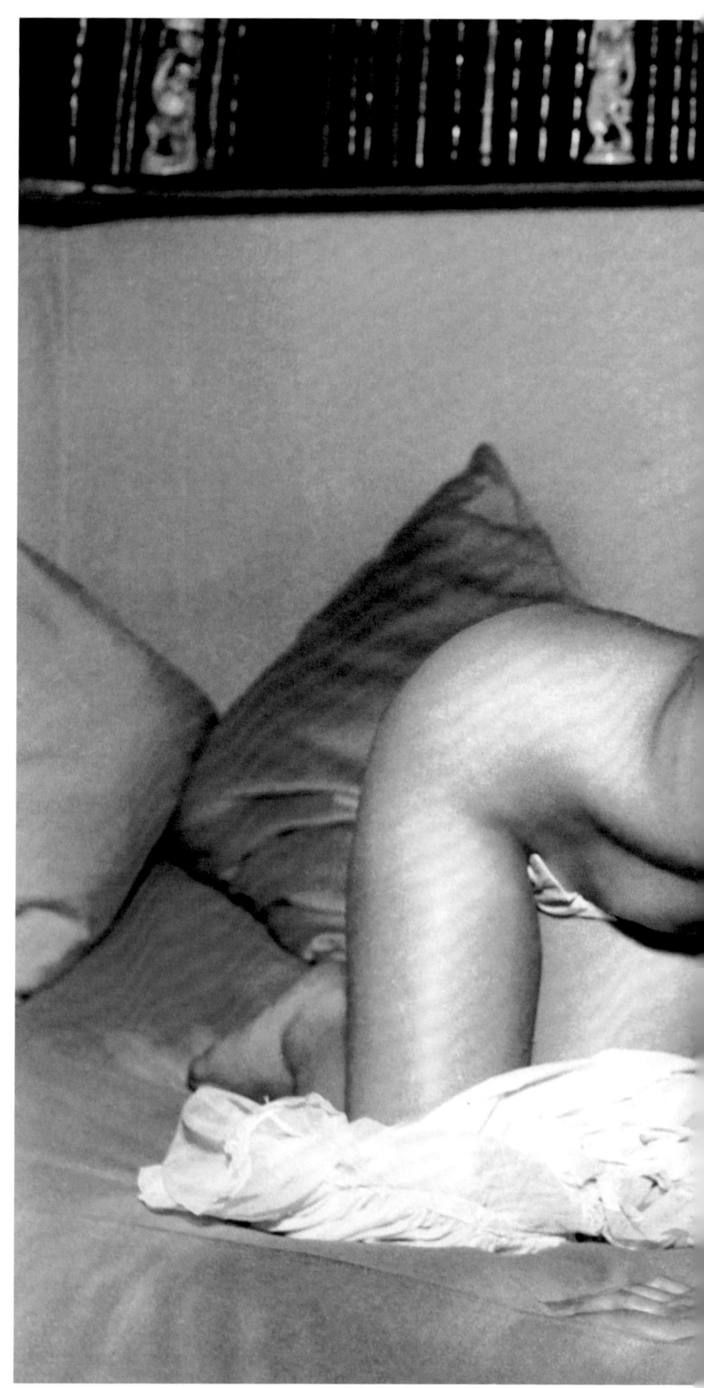

Unknown

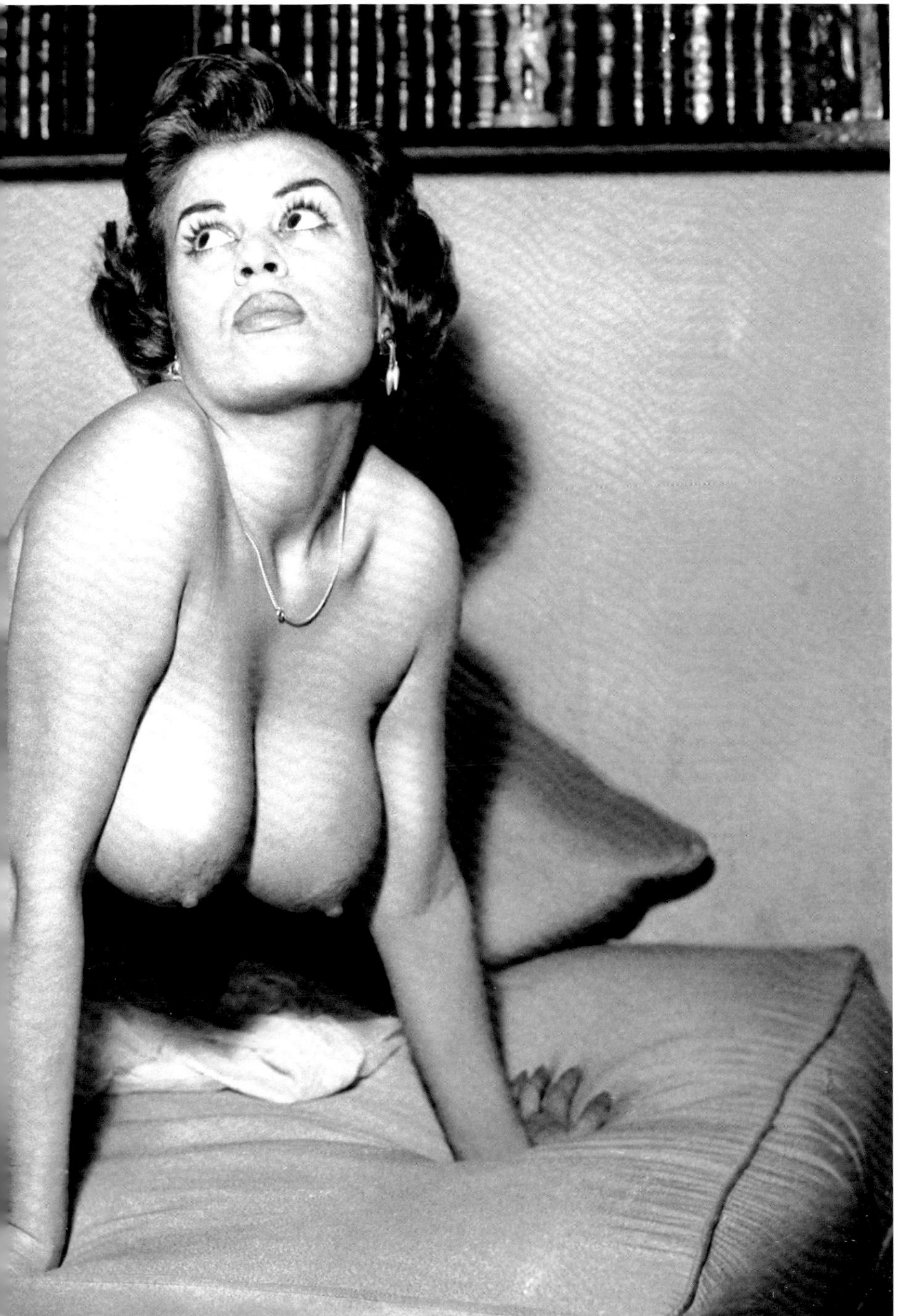

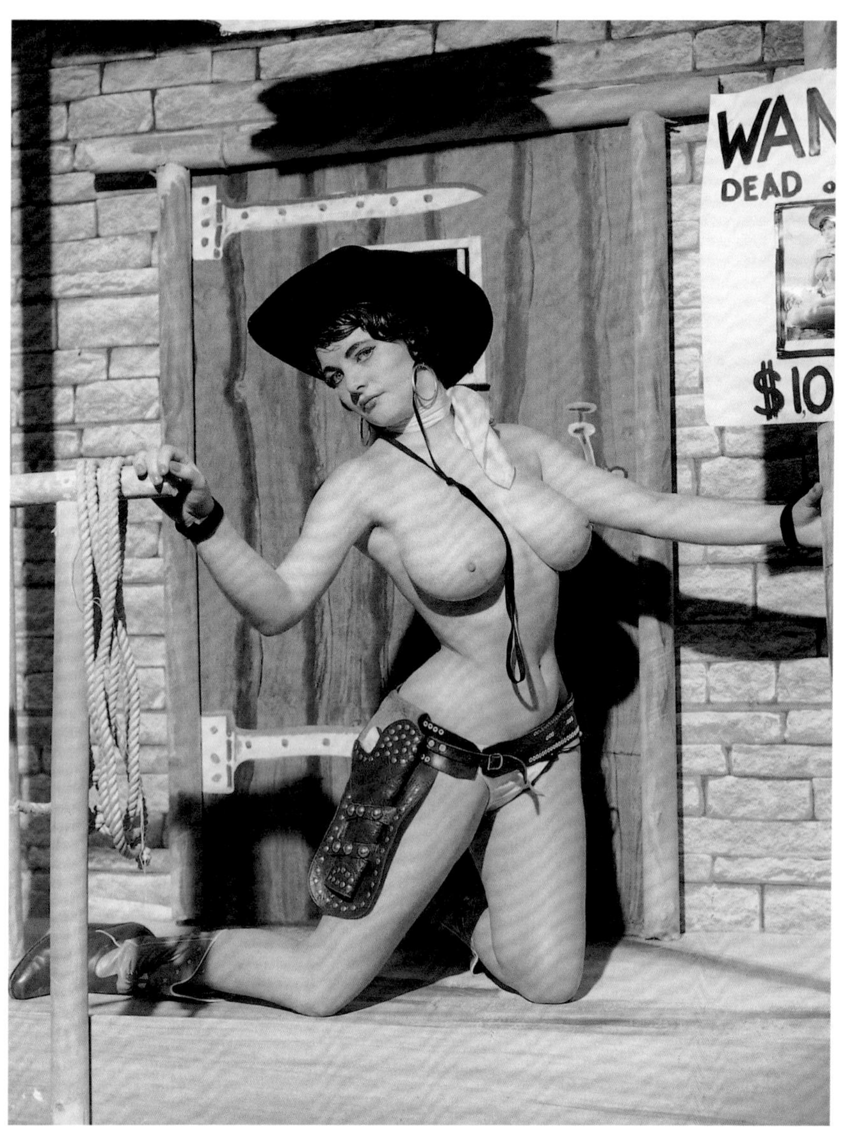

Unknown

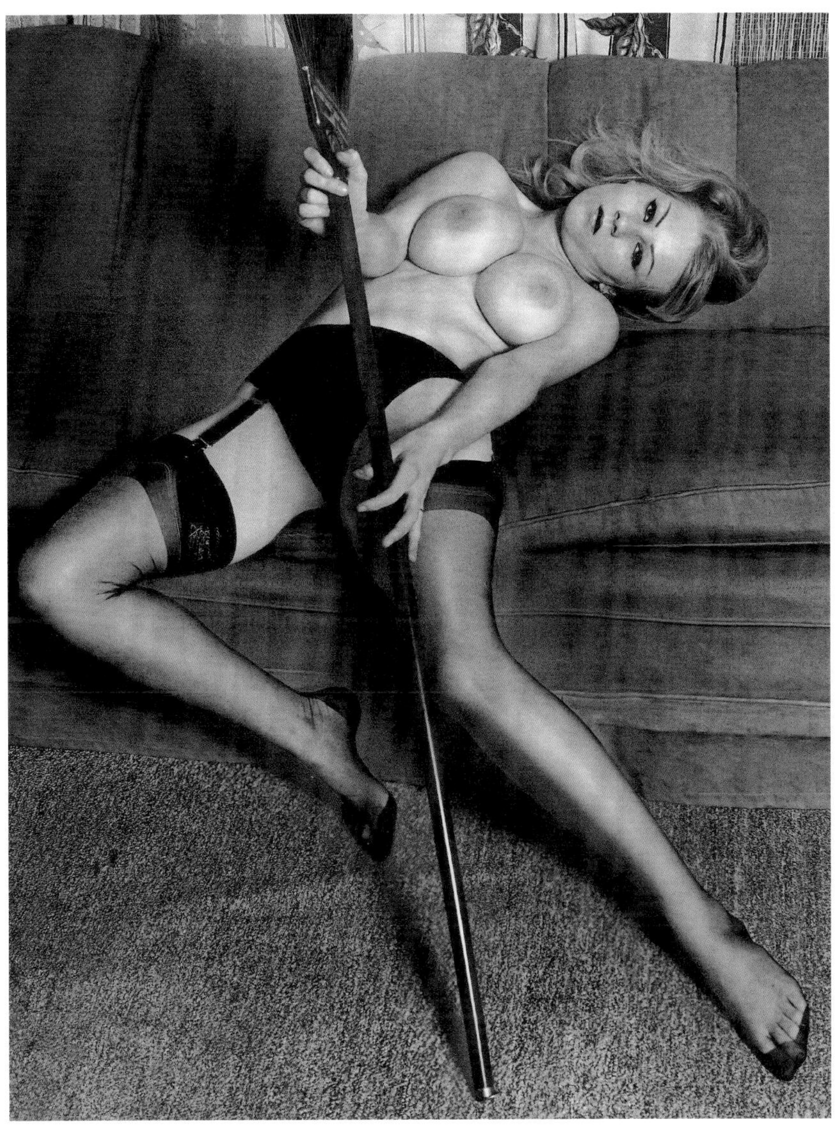

Starr Murphy

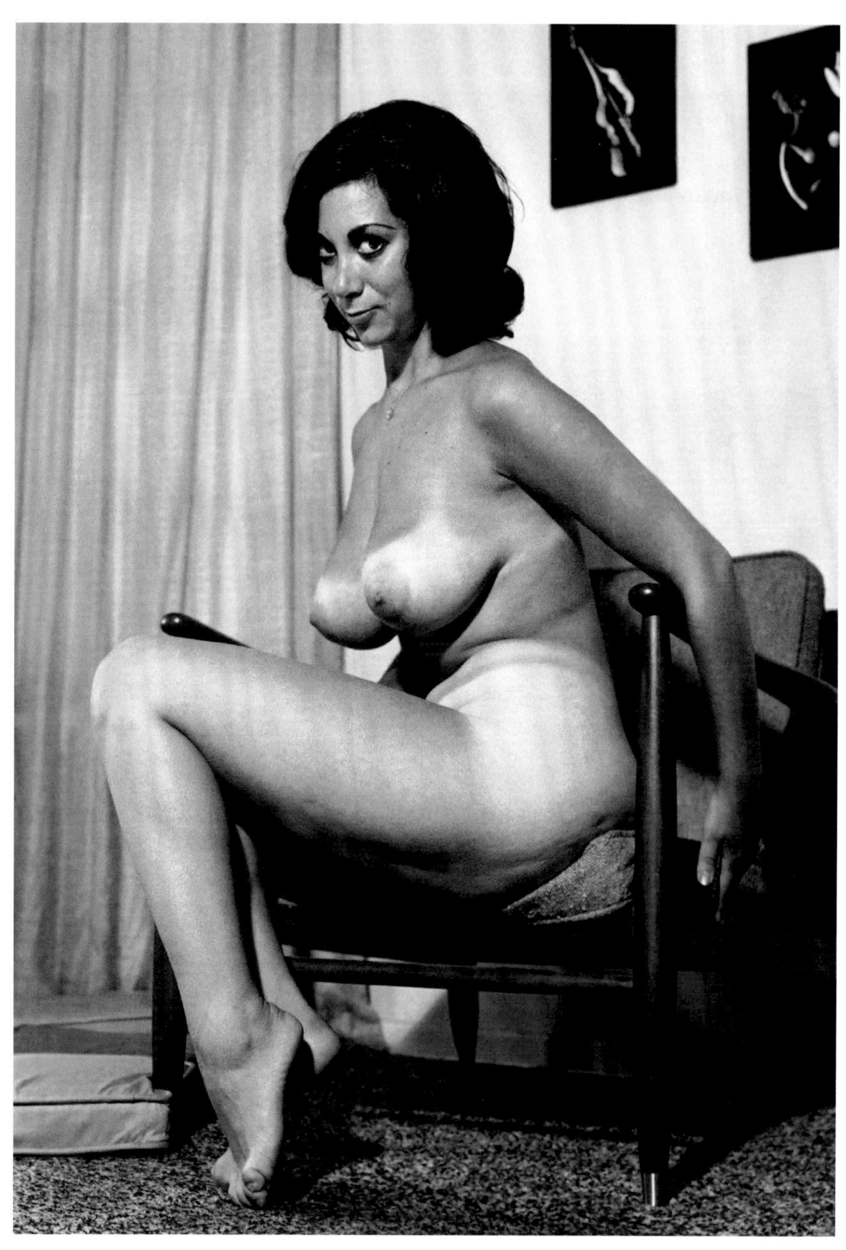

ABOVE Unknown OPPOSITE Joan Brinkman PAGES 58-59 Honey Bee

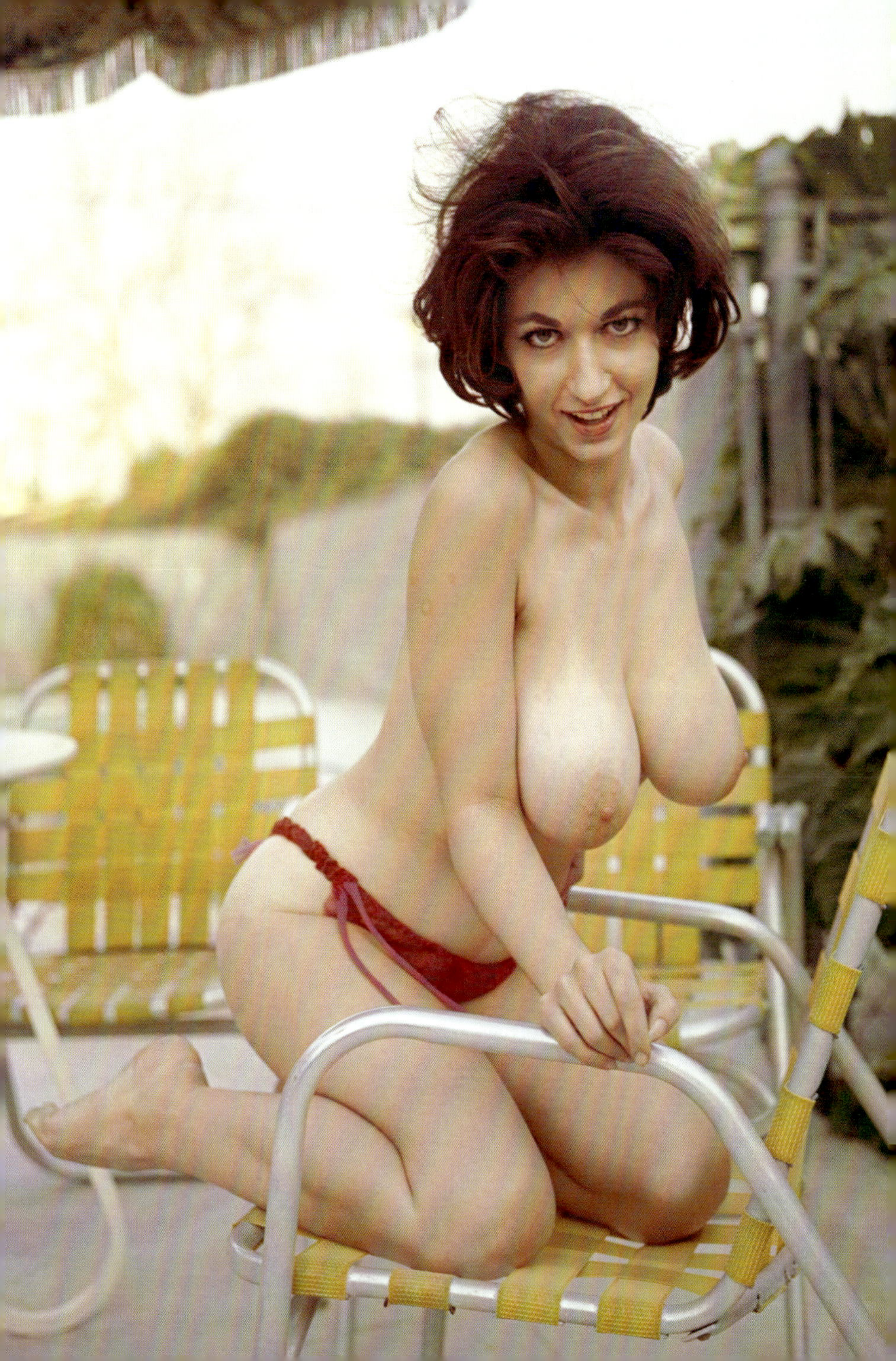

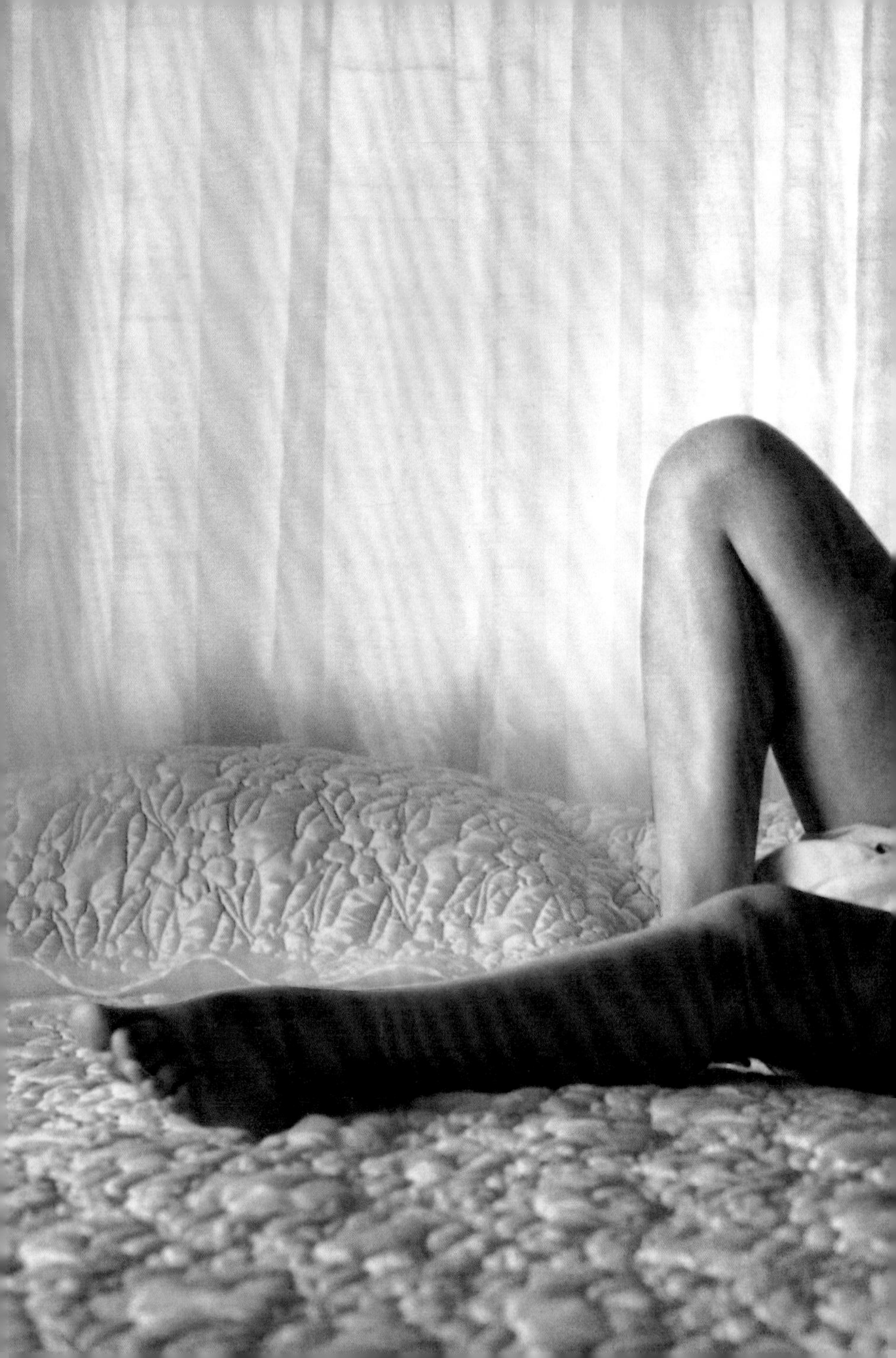

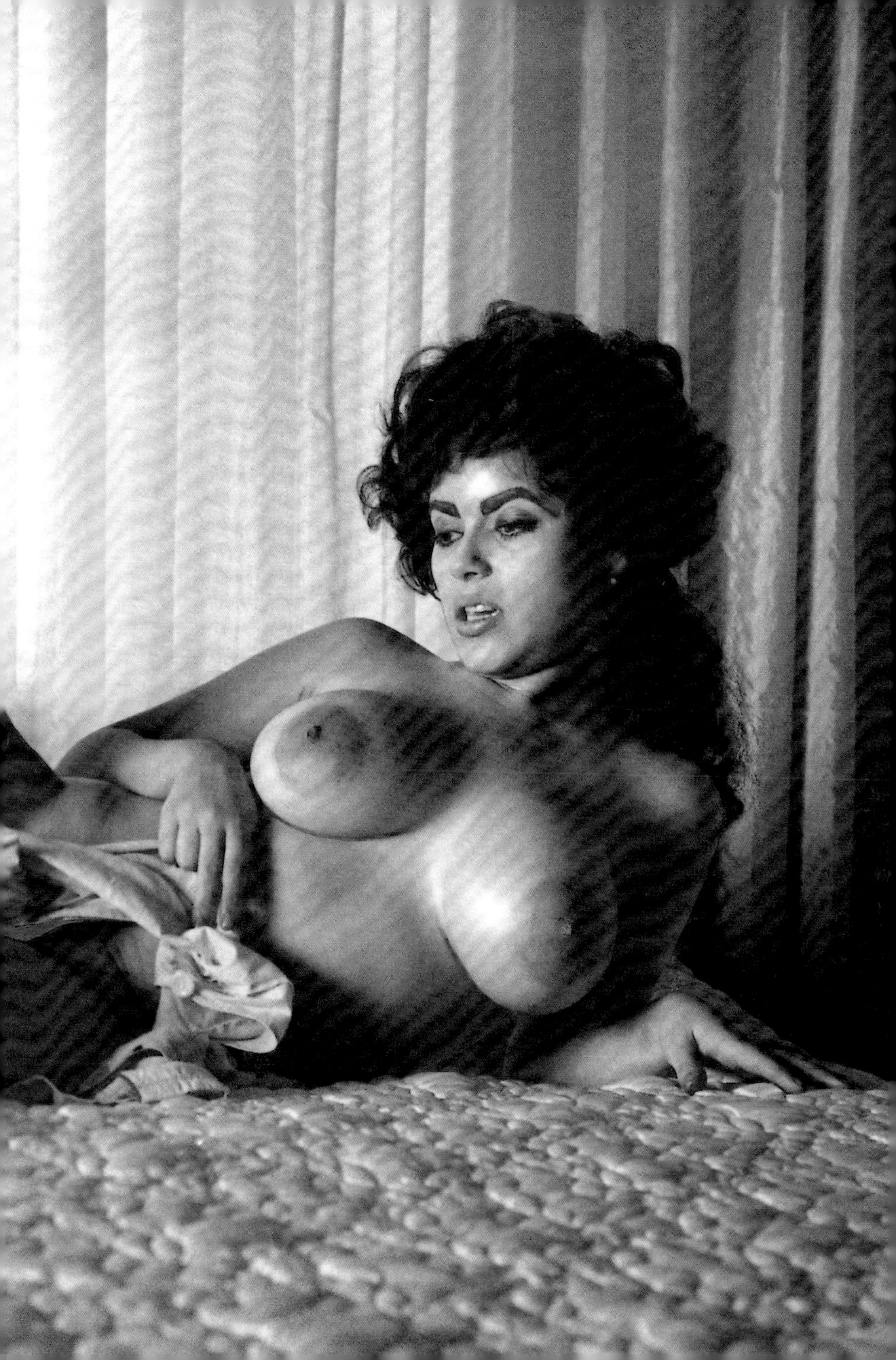

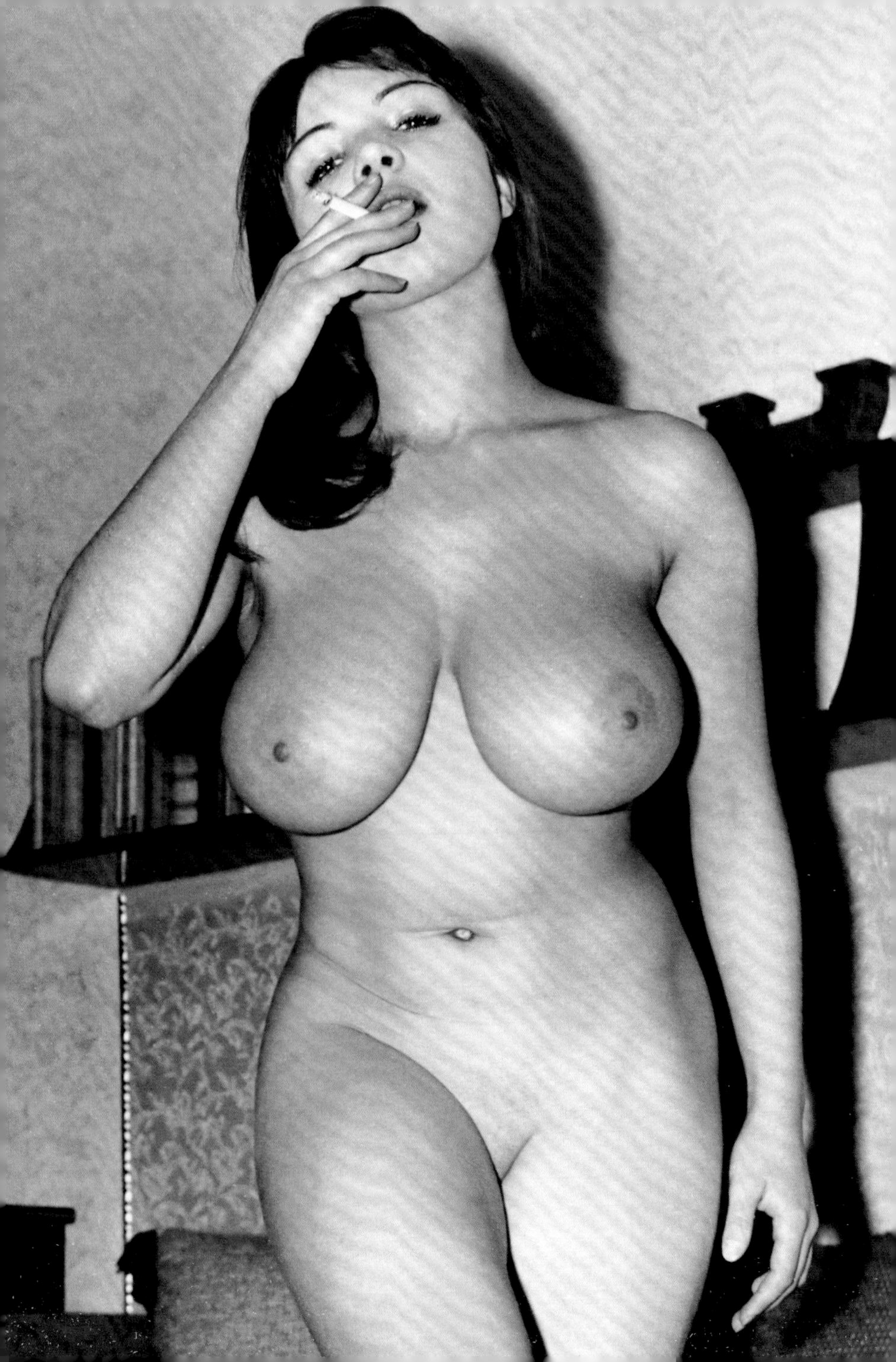

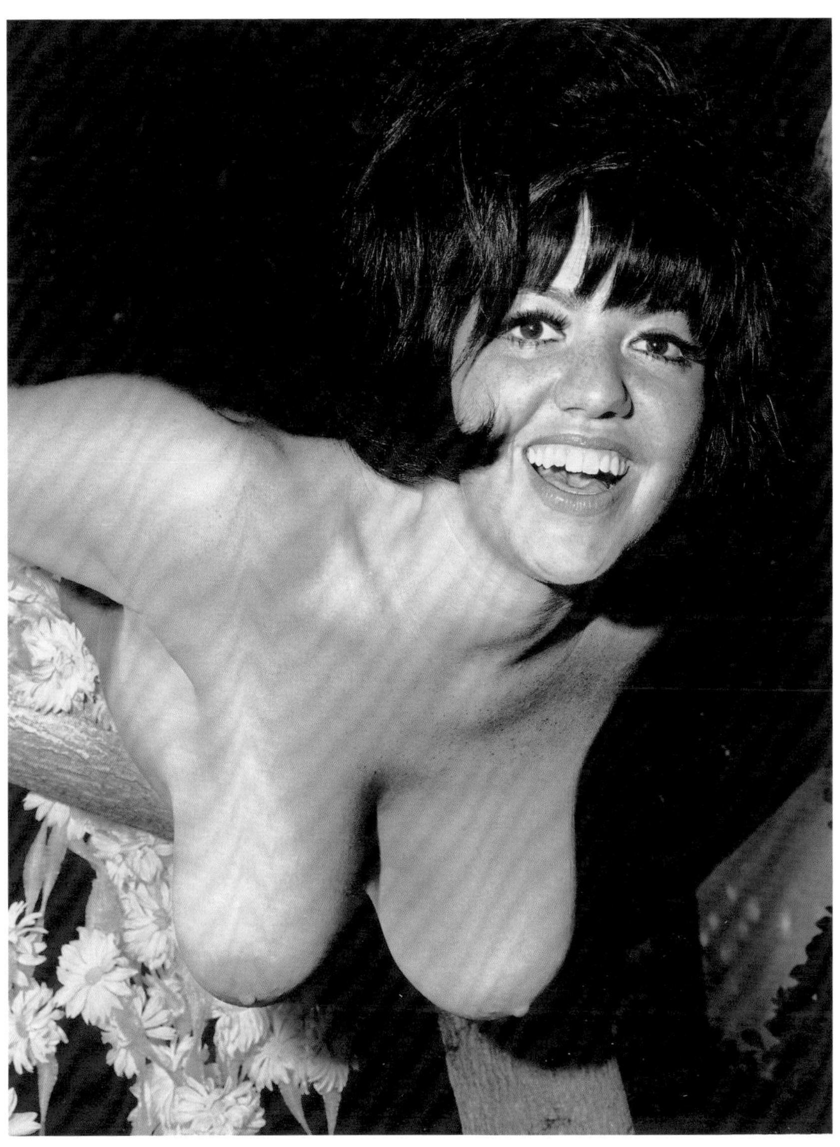

OPPOSITE Regina Andsrer ABOVE Shawn Deveraux

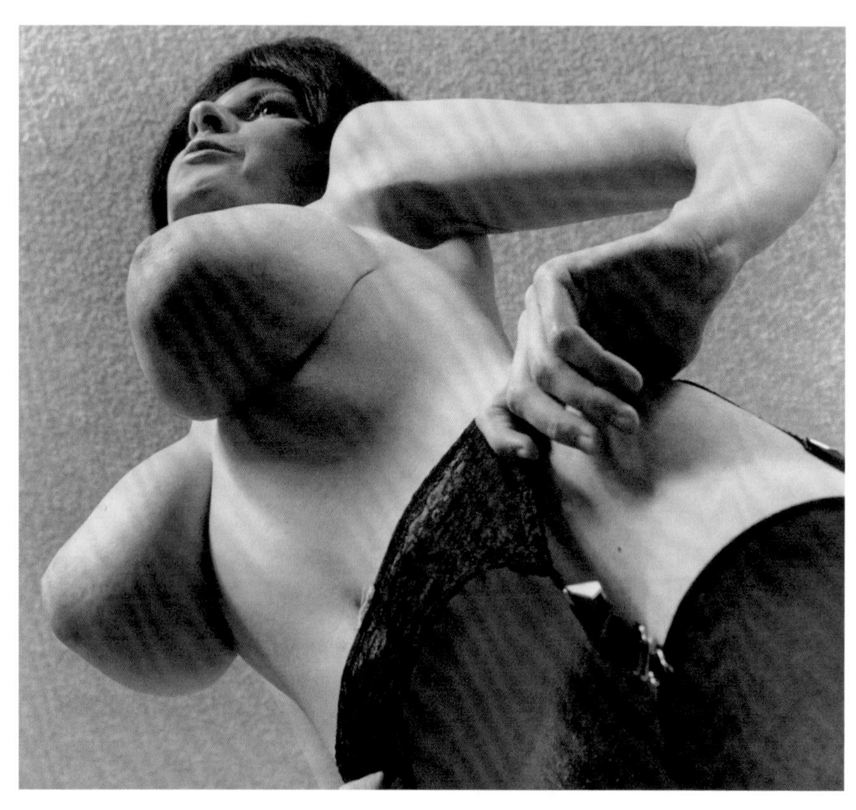

Janice Orames

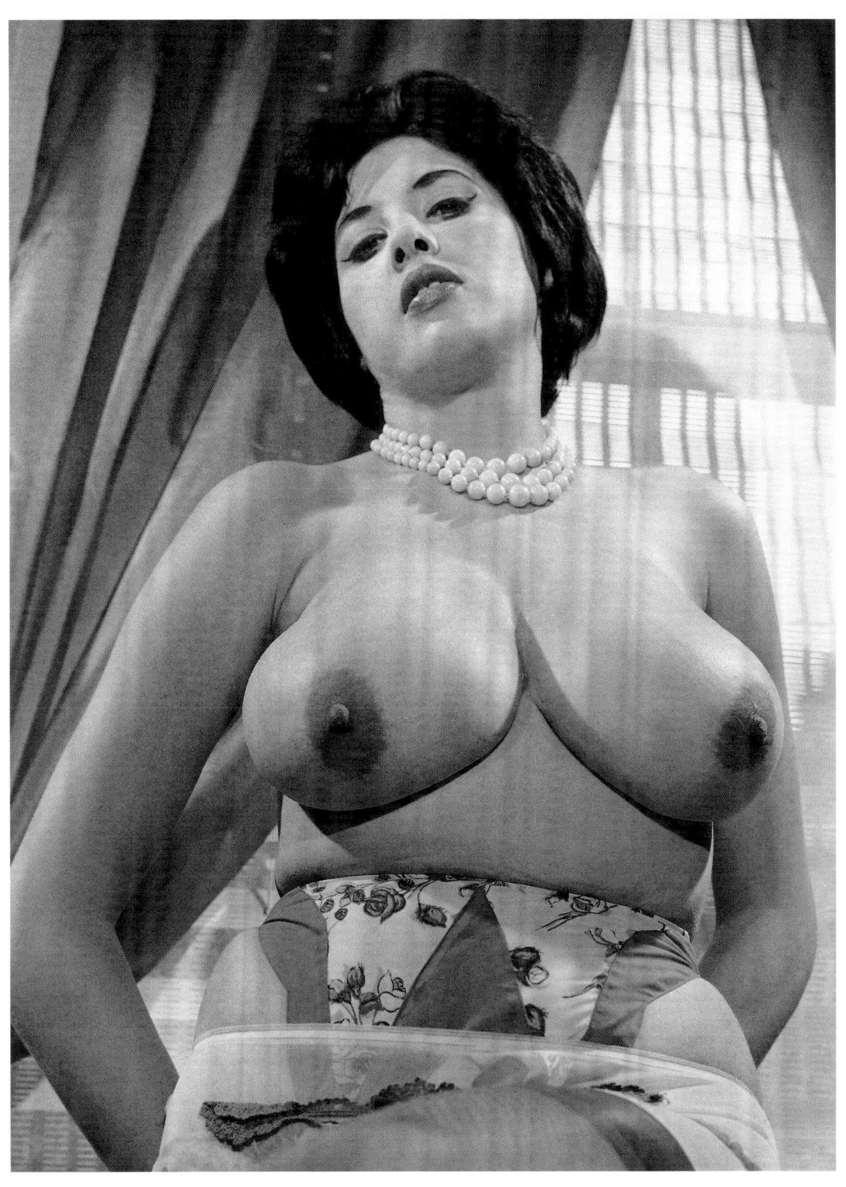

ABOVE Margaret Middleton PAGES 64-65 Michelle Angelo

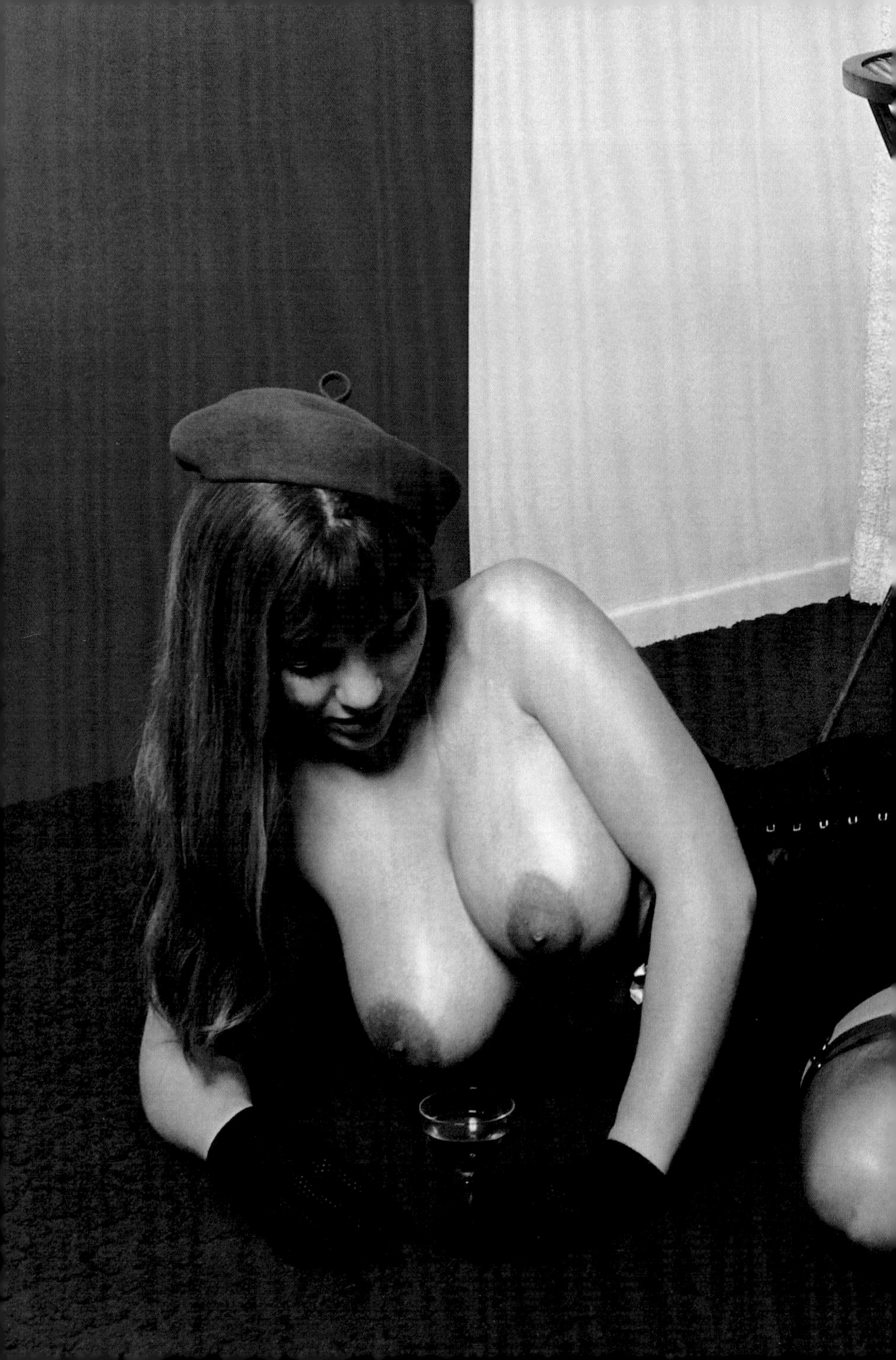

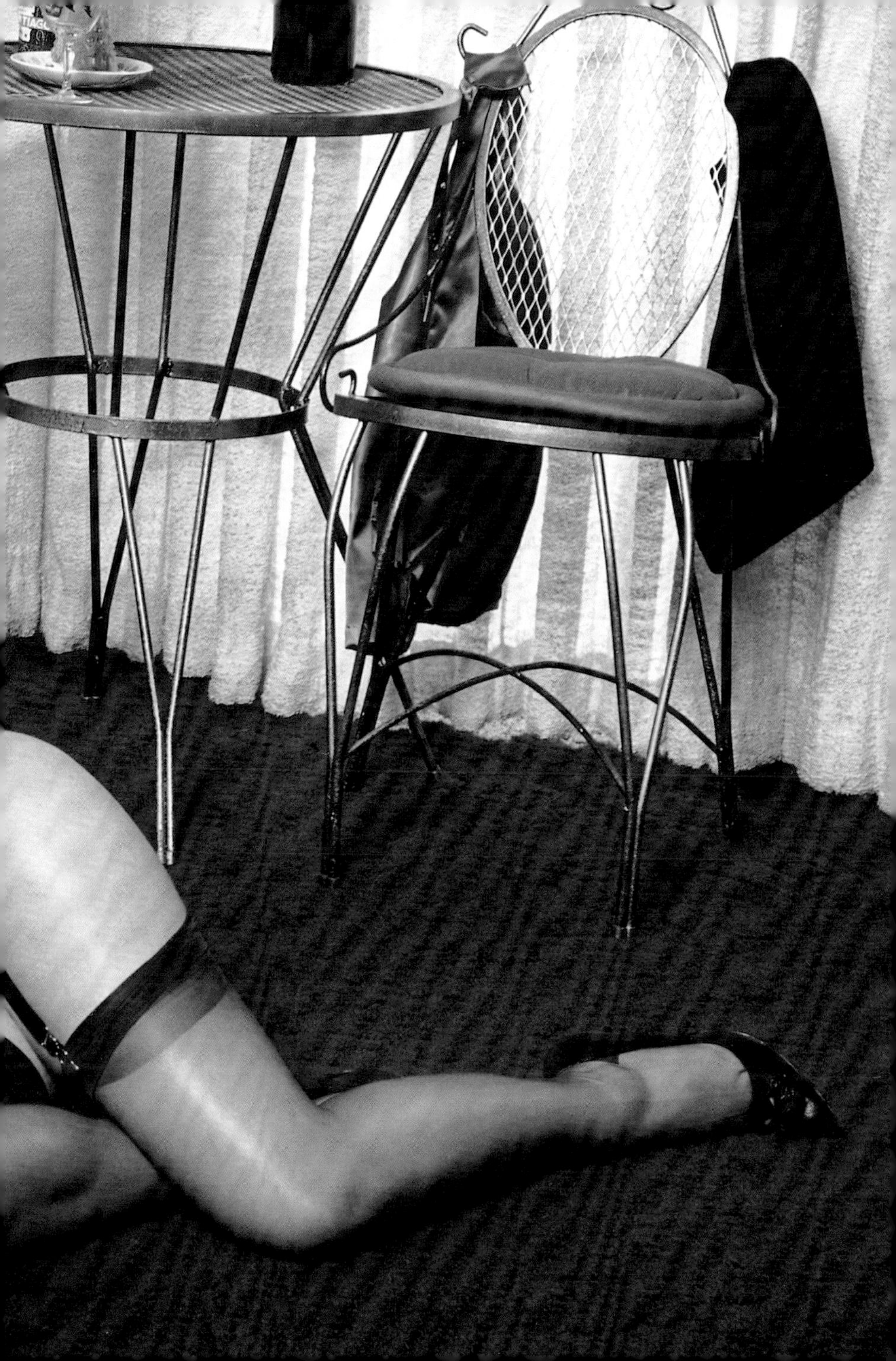

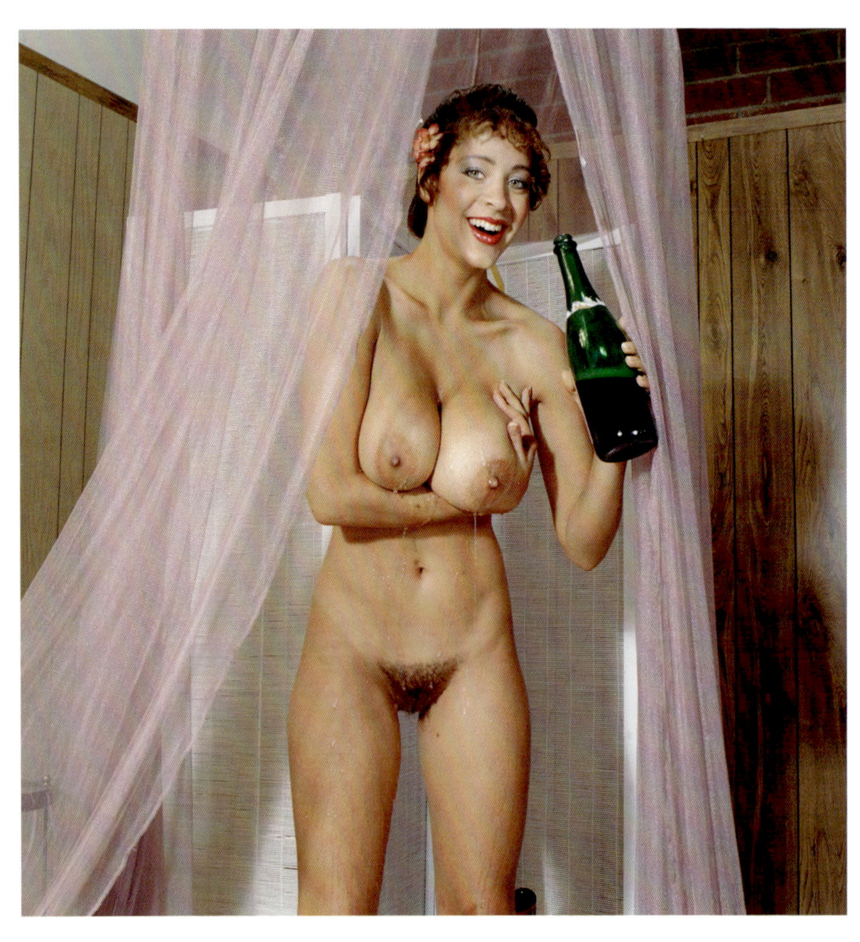

ABOVE Janice Orames OPPOSITE Unknown

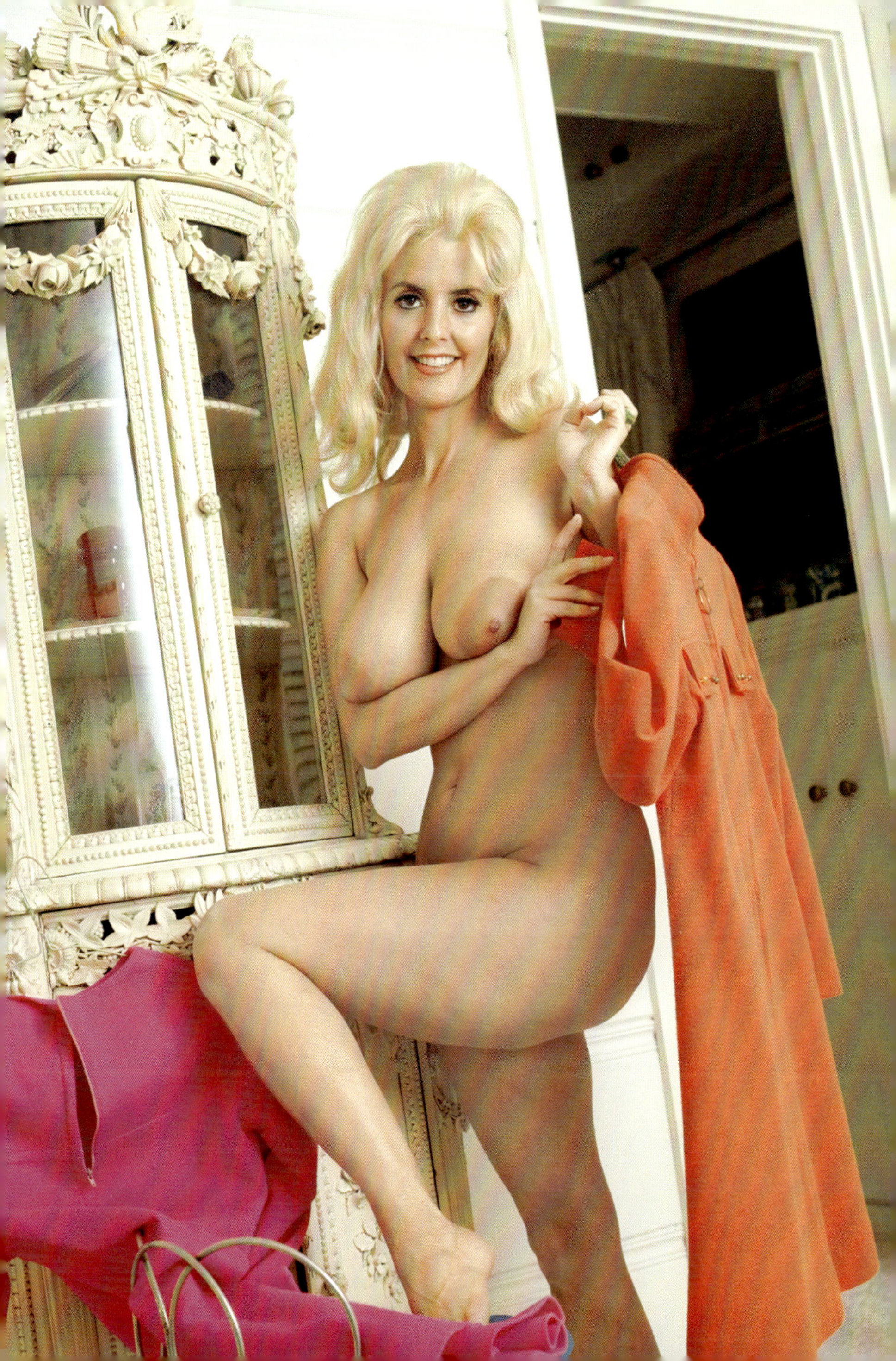

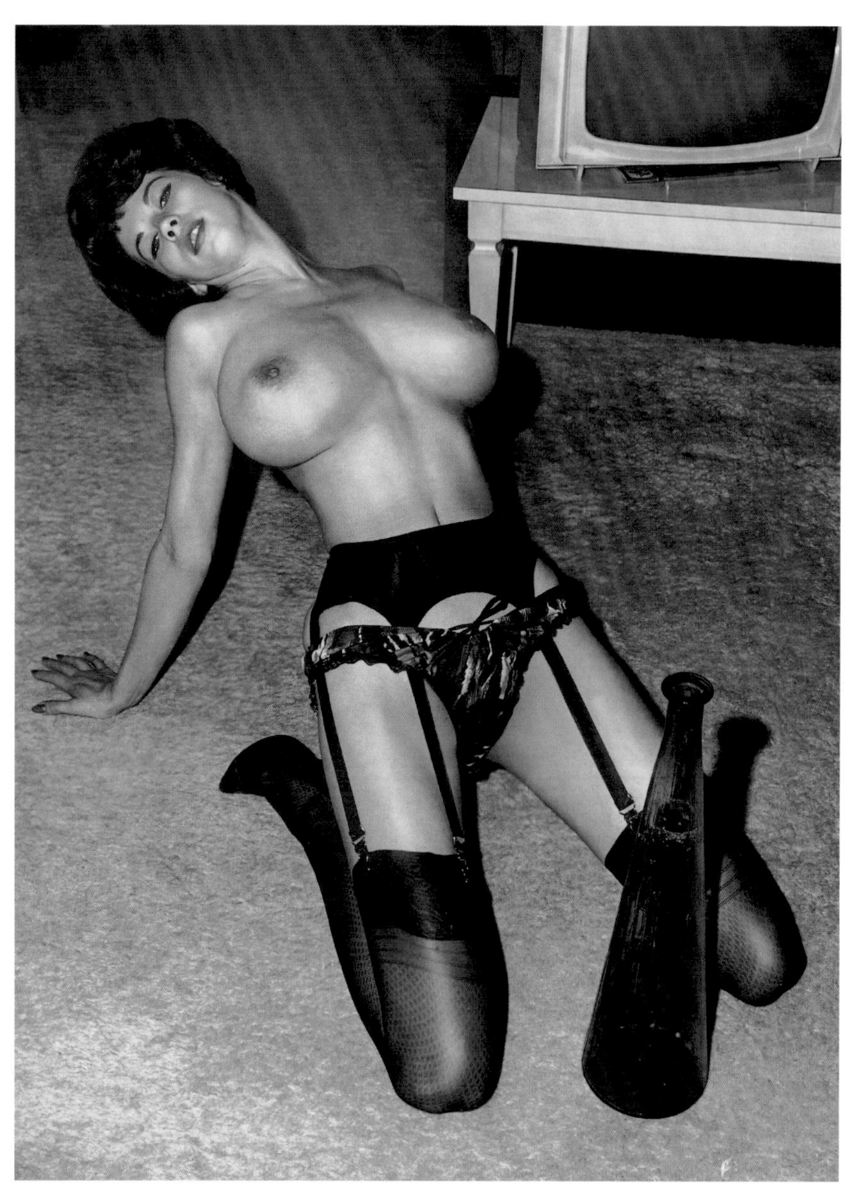

ABOVE Linda McClung OPPOSITE Unknown

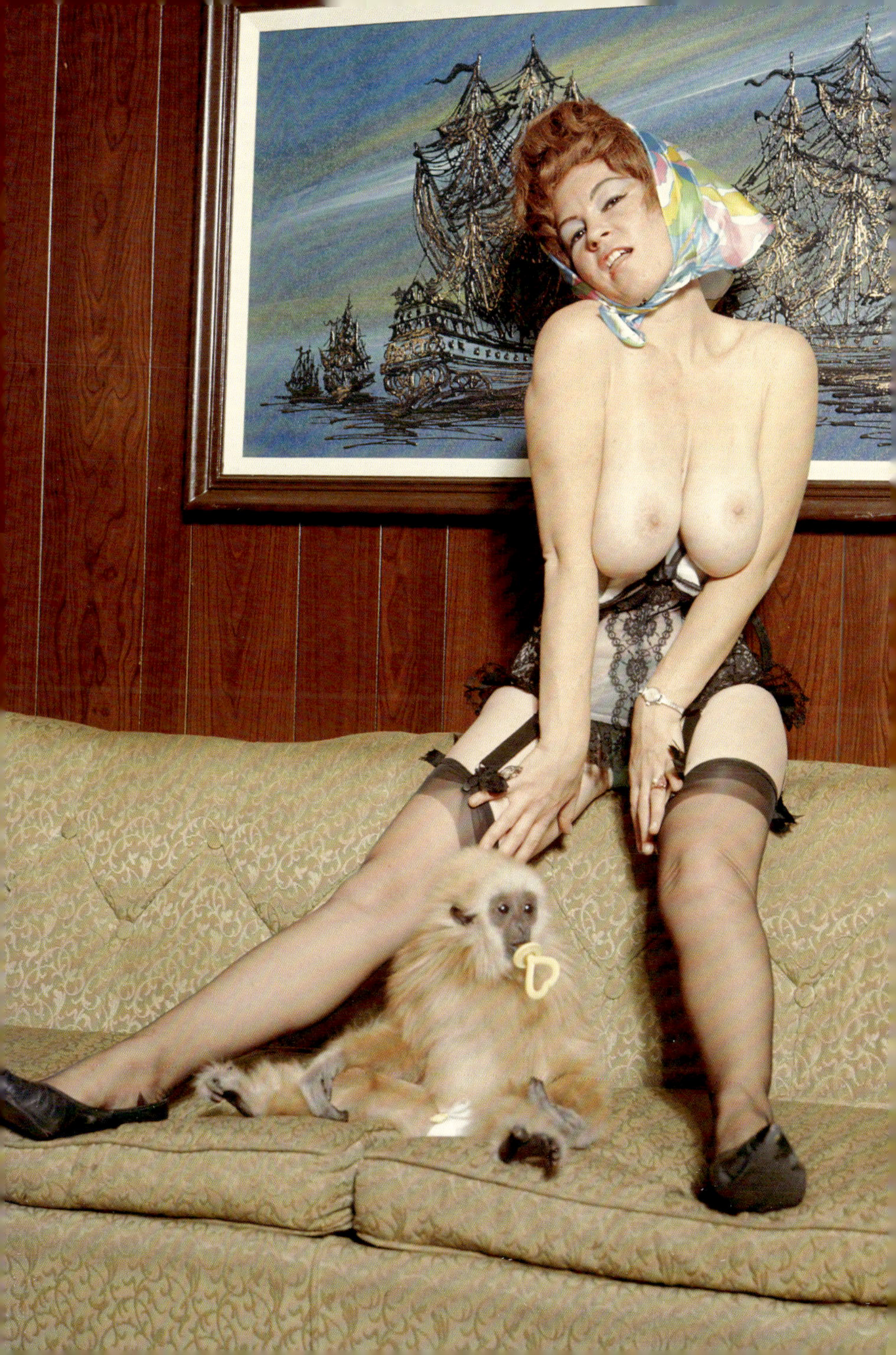

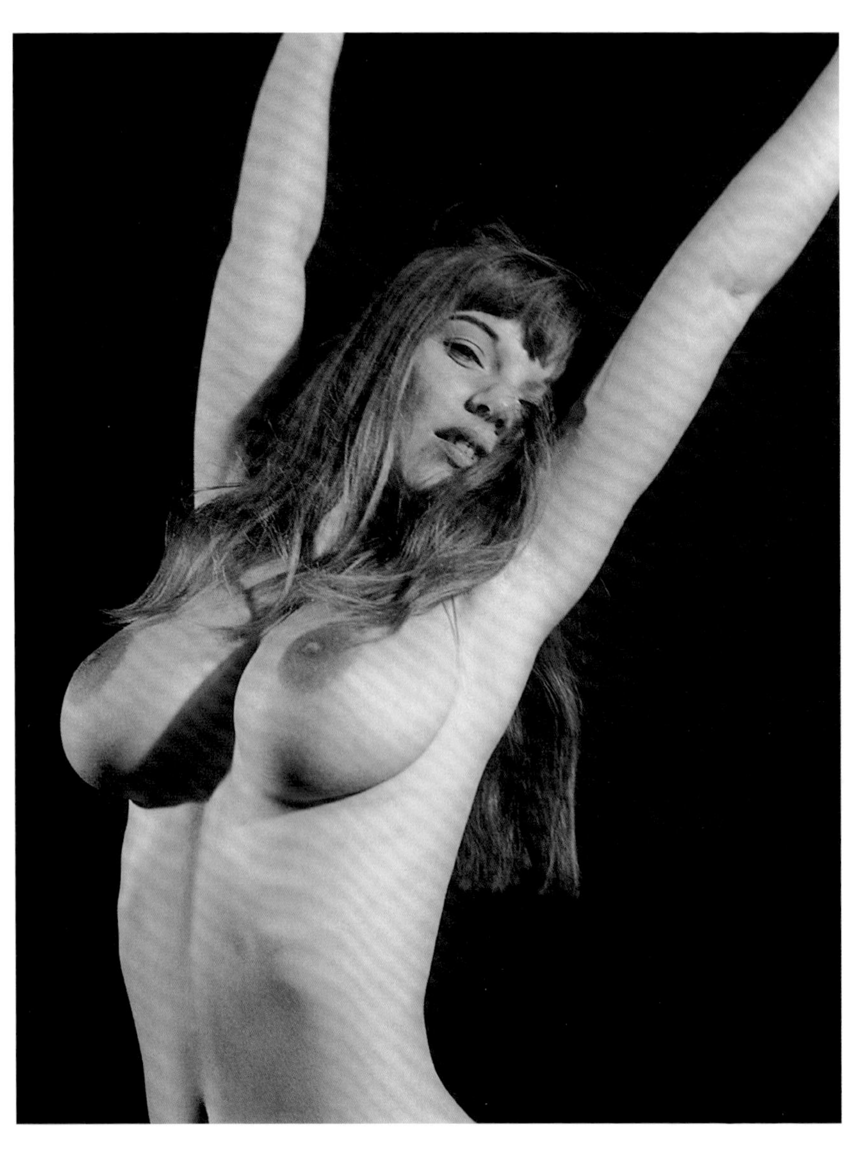

ABOVE Michelle Angelo OPPOSITE Julie Wills PAGES 72-73 Janie Reynolds

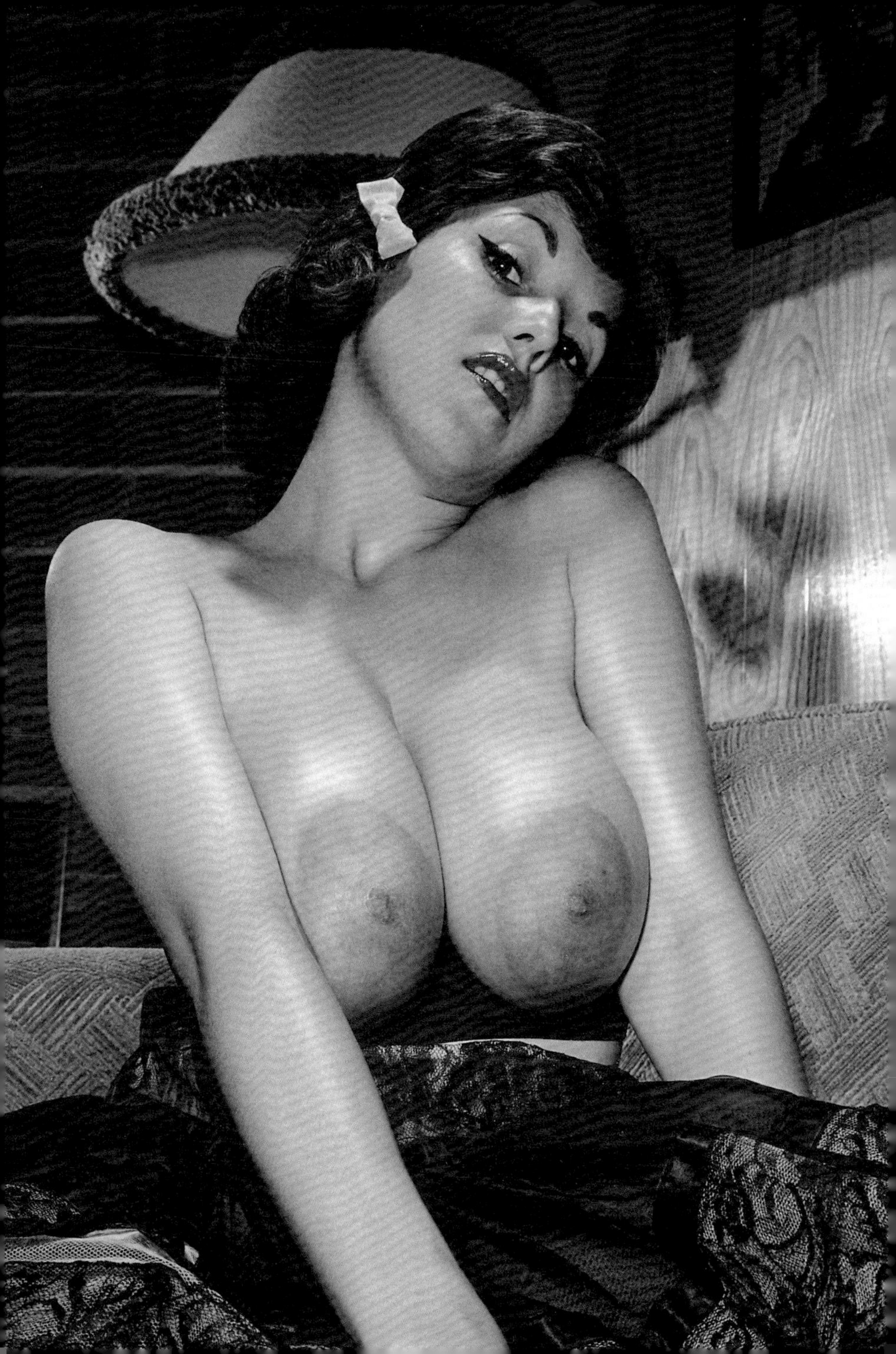

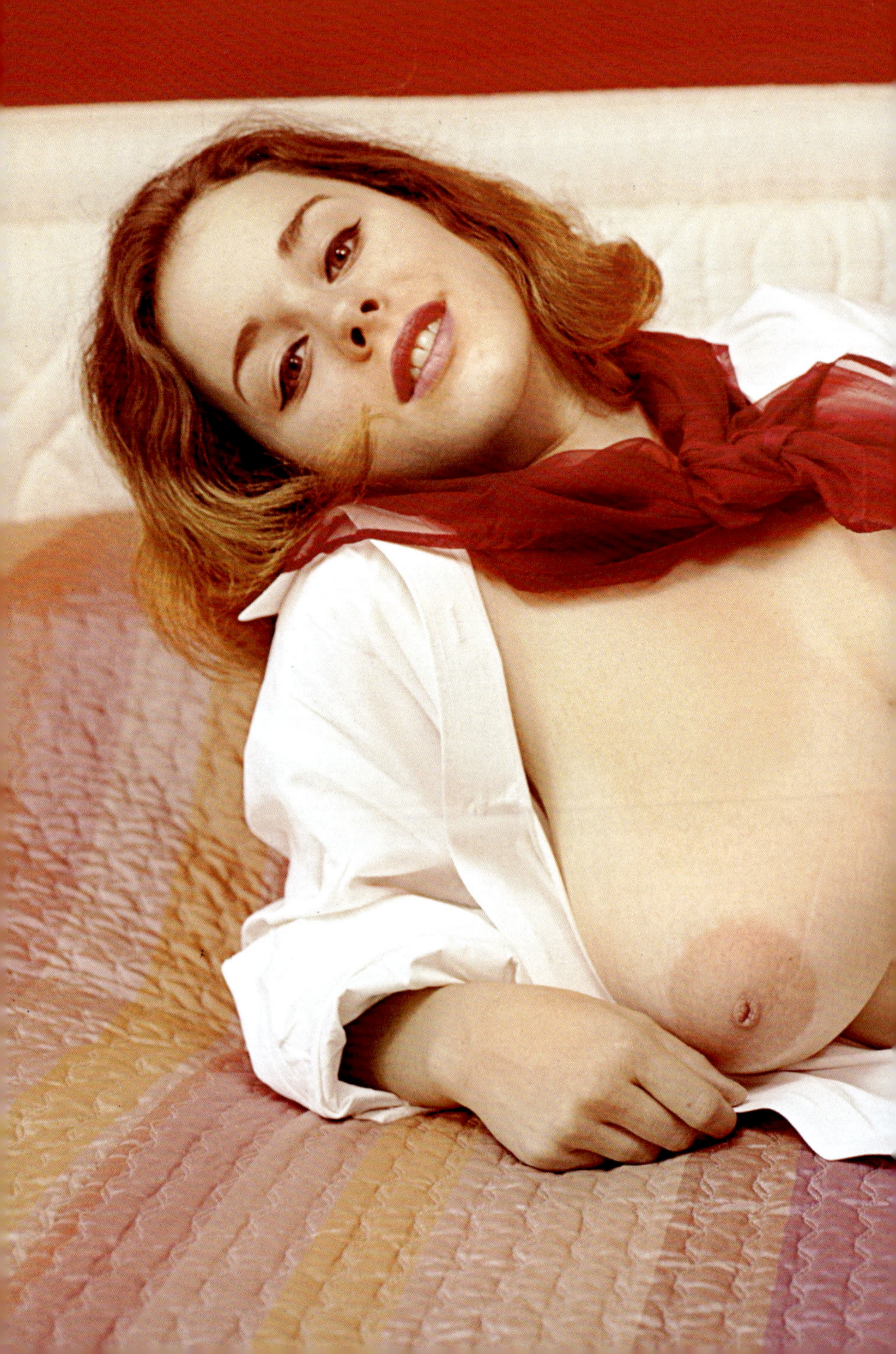

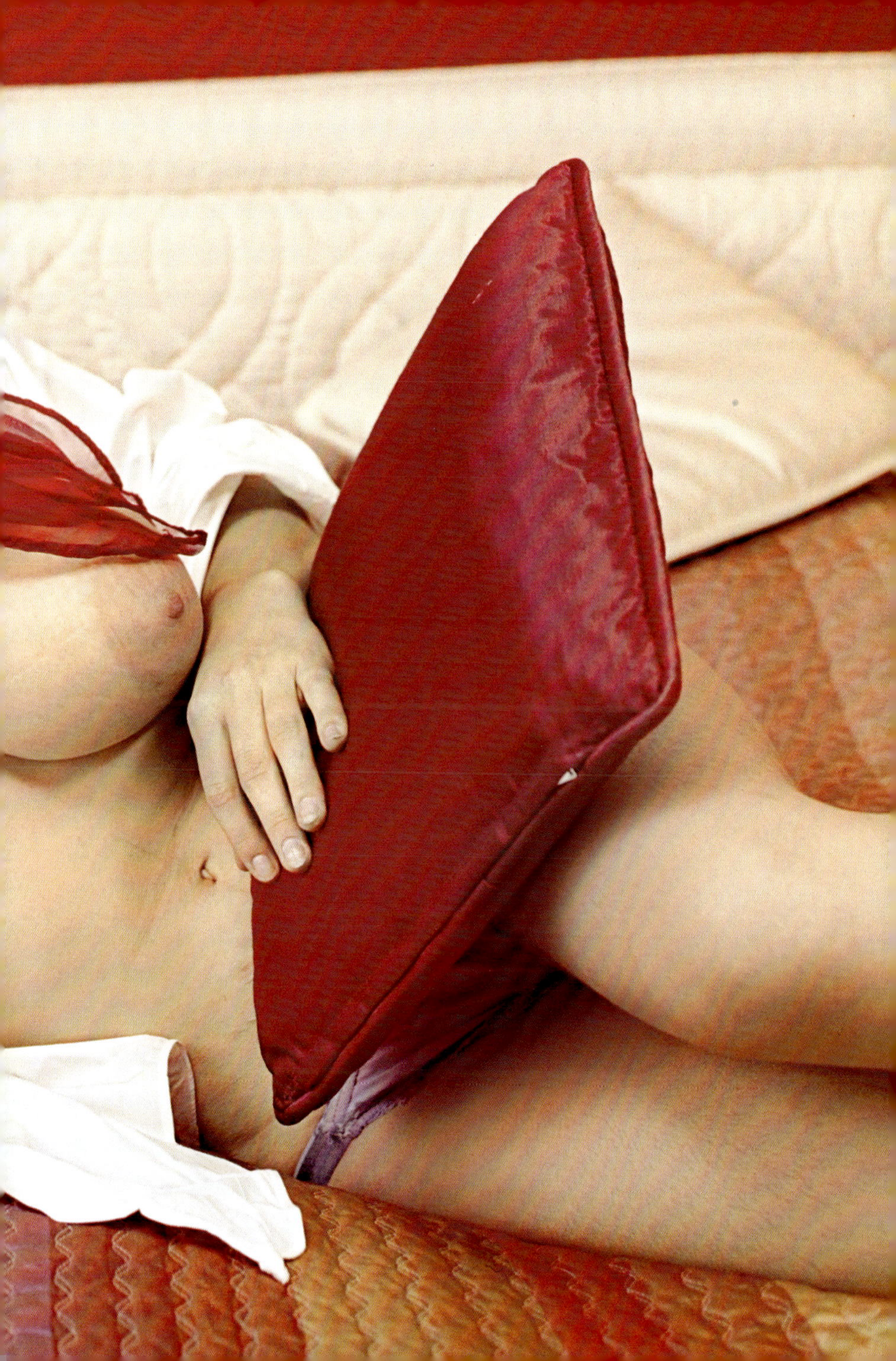

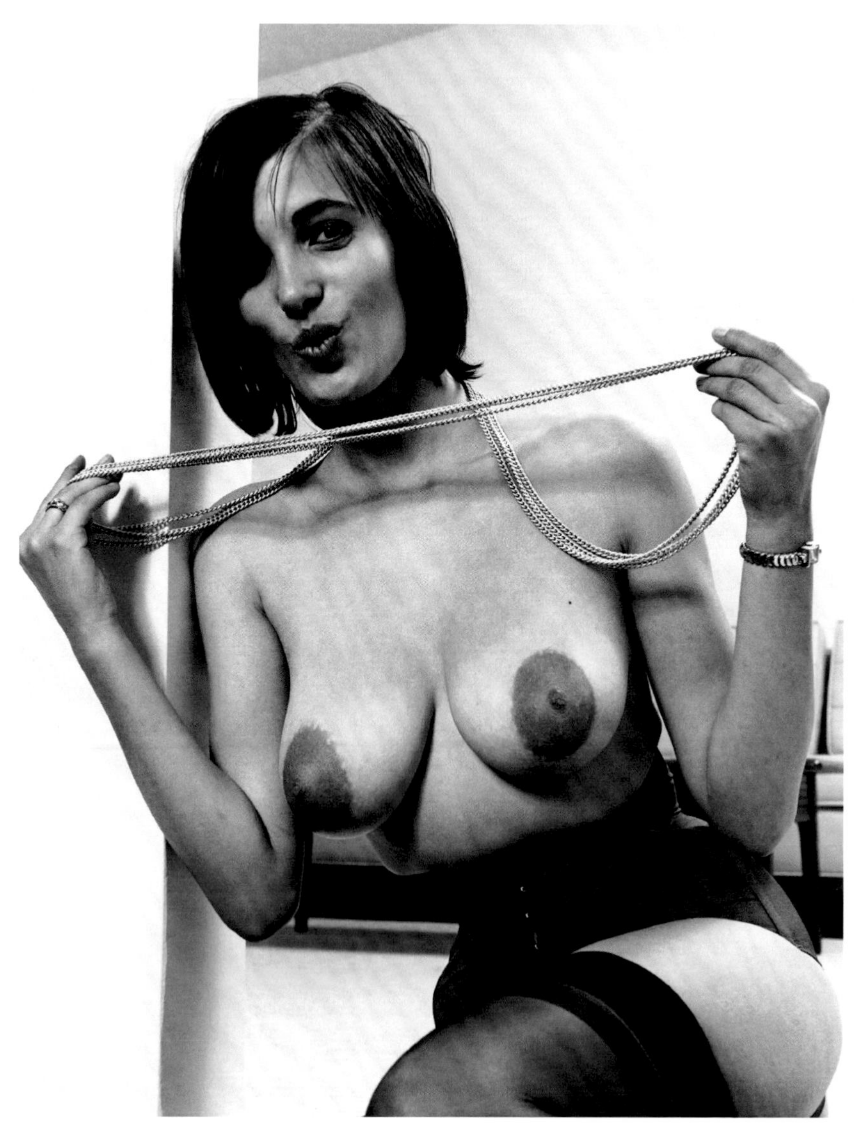

ABOVE Madeline Elliot OPPOSITE Diane Peters

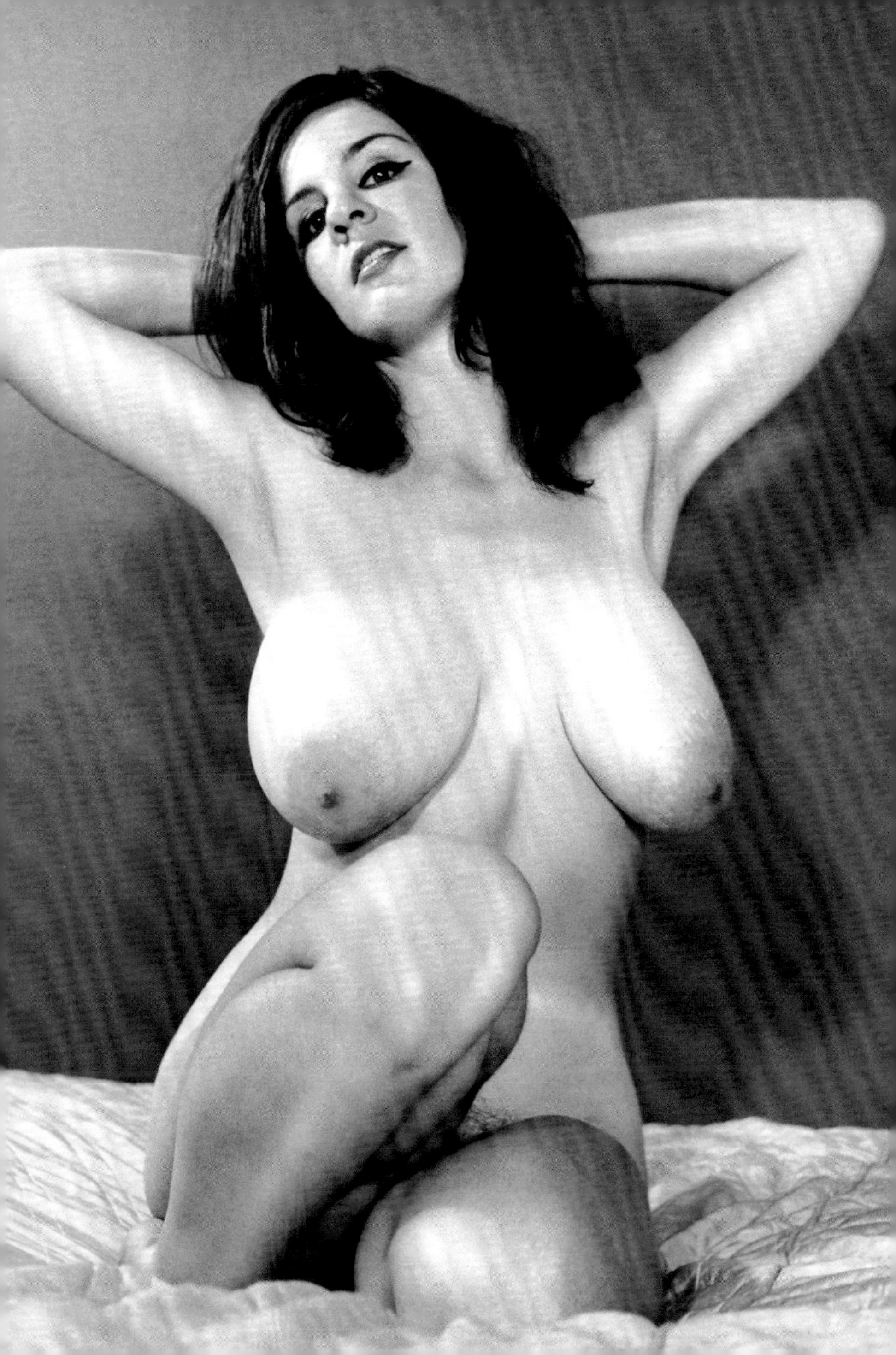

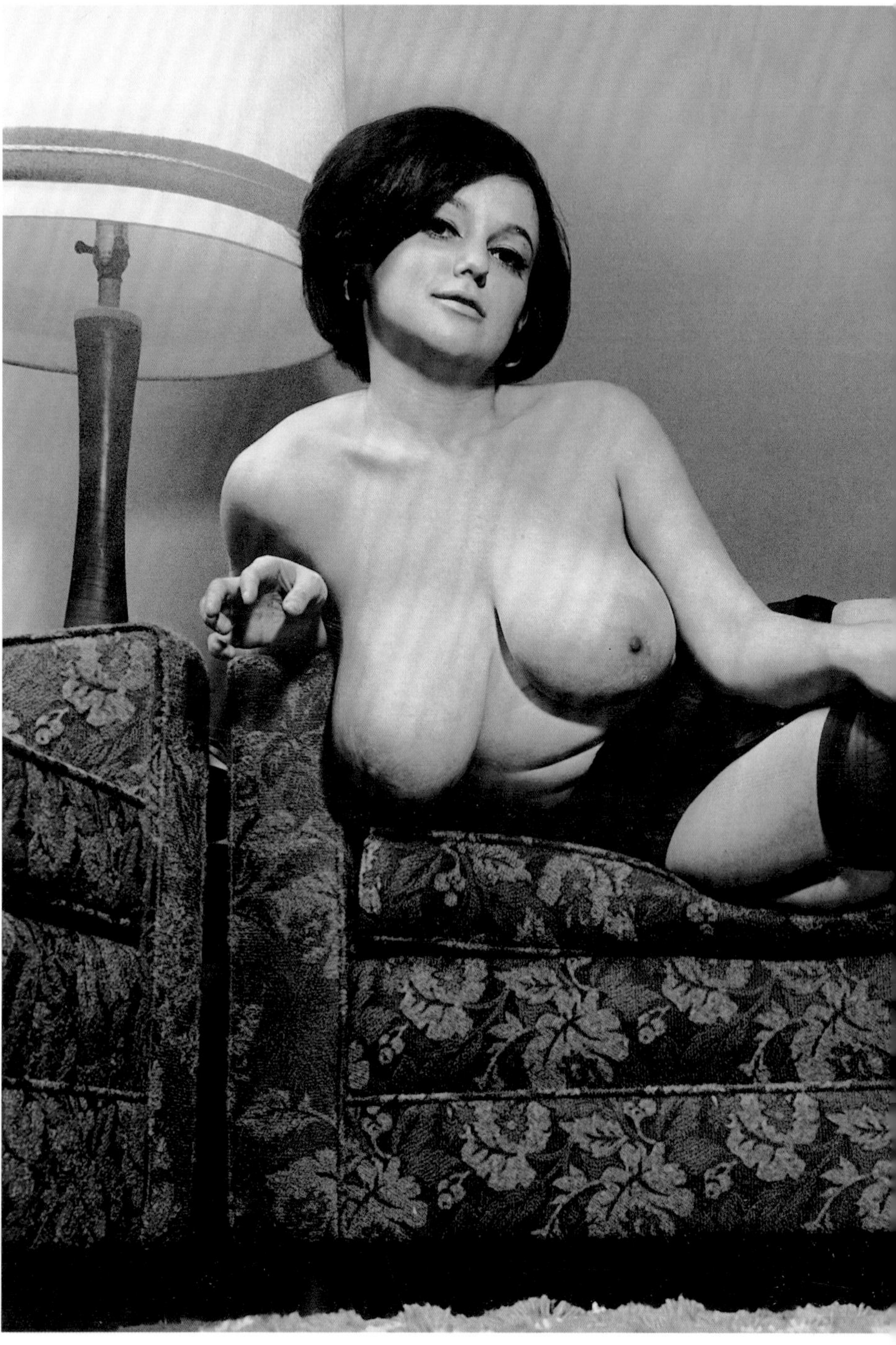

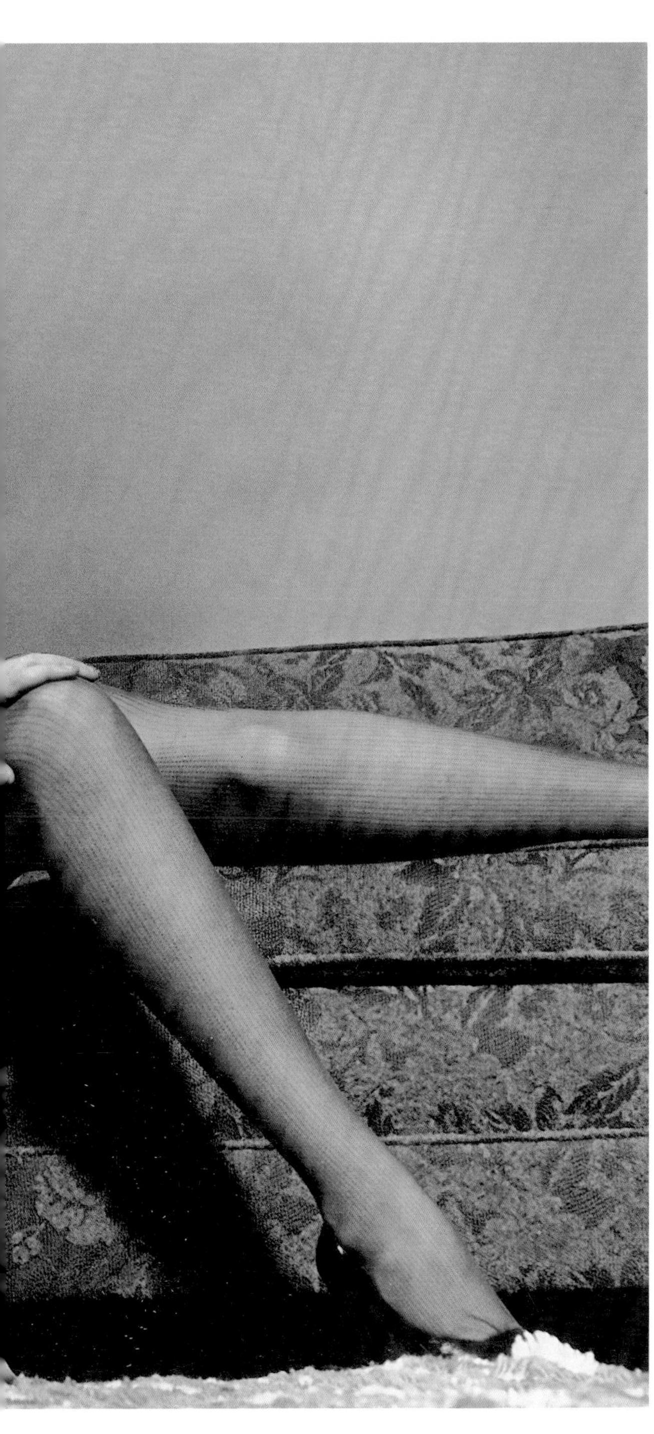

Mary Ellen Bowles

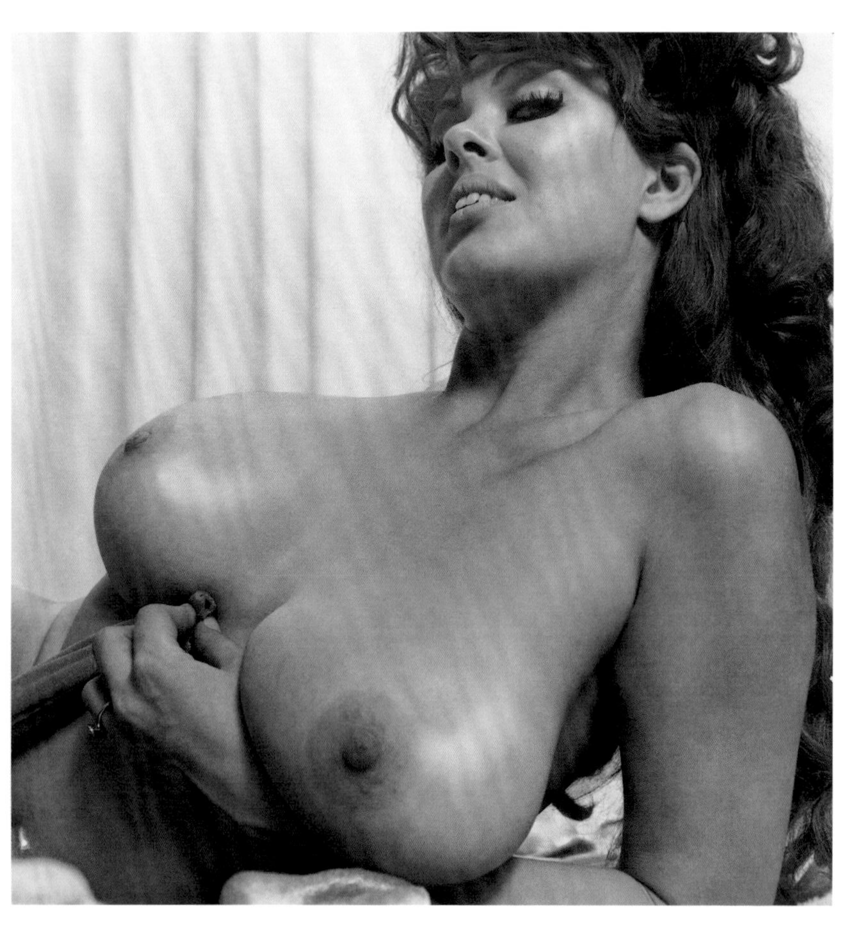

Roxanne Brewer

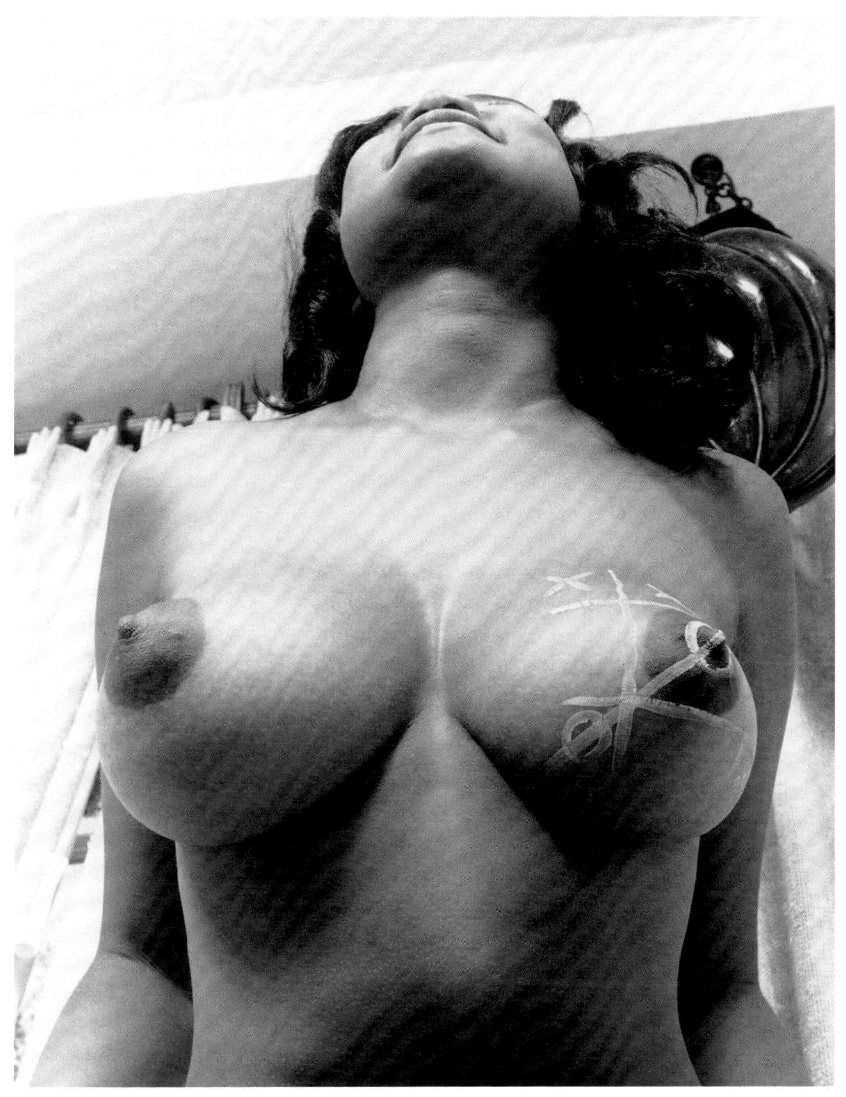

Mia Coco

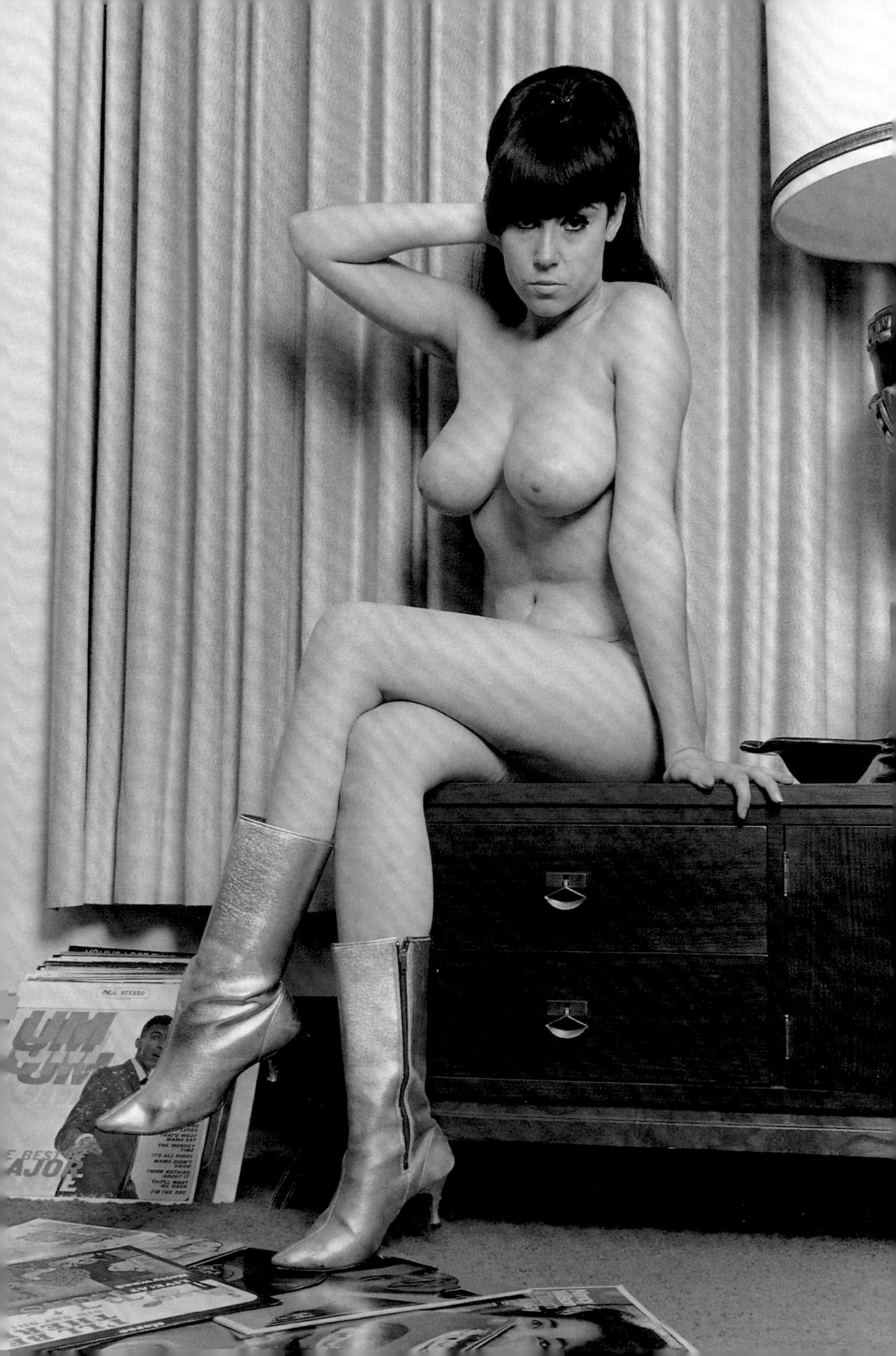
UM
THAT'S WHAT MAMA SAY
THE MONKEY TIME
IT'S ALL RIGHT
MAMA DIDN'T KNOW
THINK NOTHING ABOUT IT
YOU'LL WANT ME BACK
I'M THE ONE

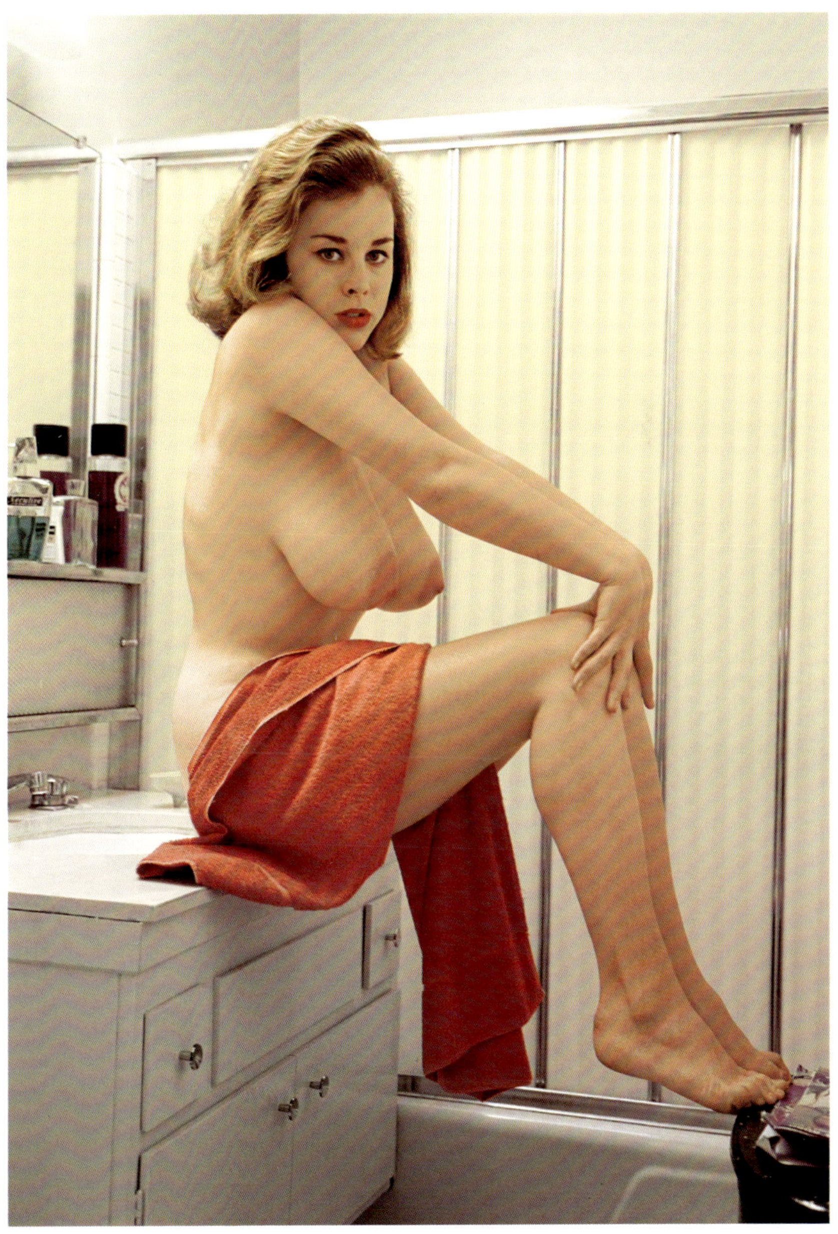

OPPOSITE Linde Freiderix ABOVE Janie Reynolds

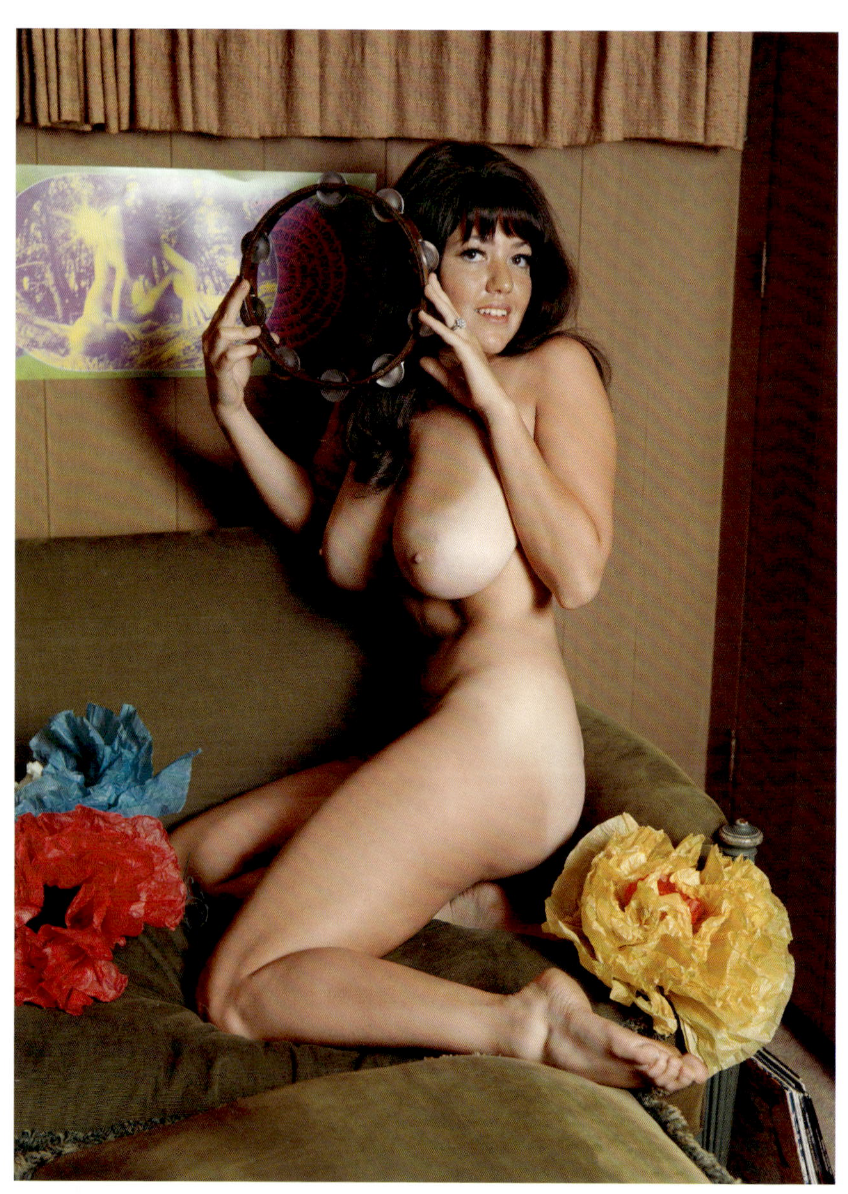

ABOVE Shawn Devereaux OPPOSITE Lisa Matthews

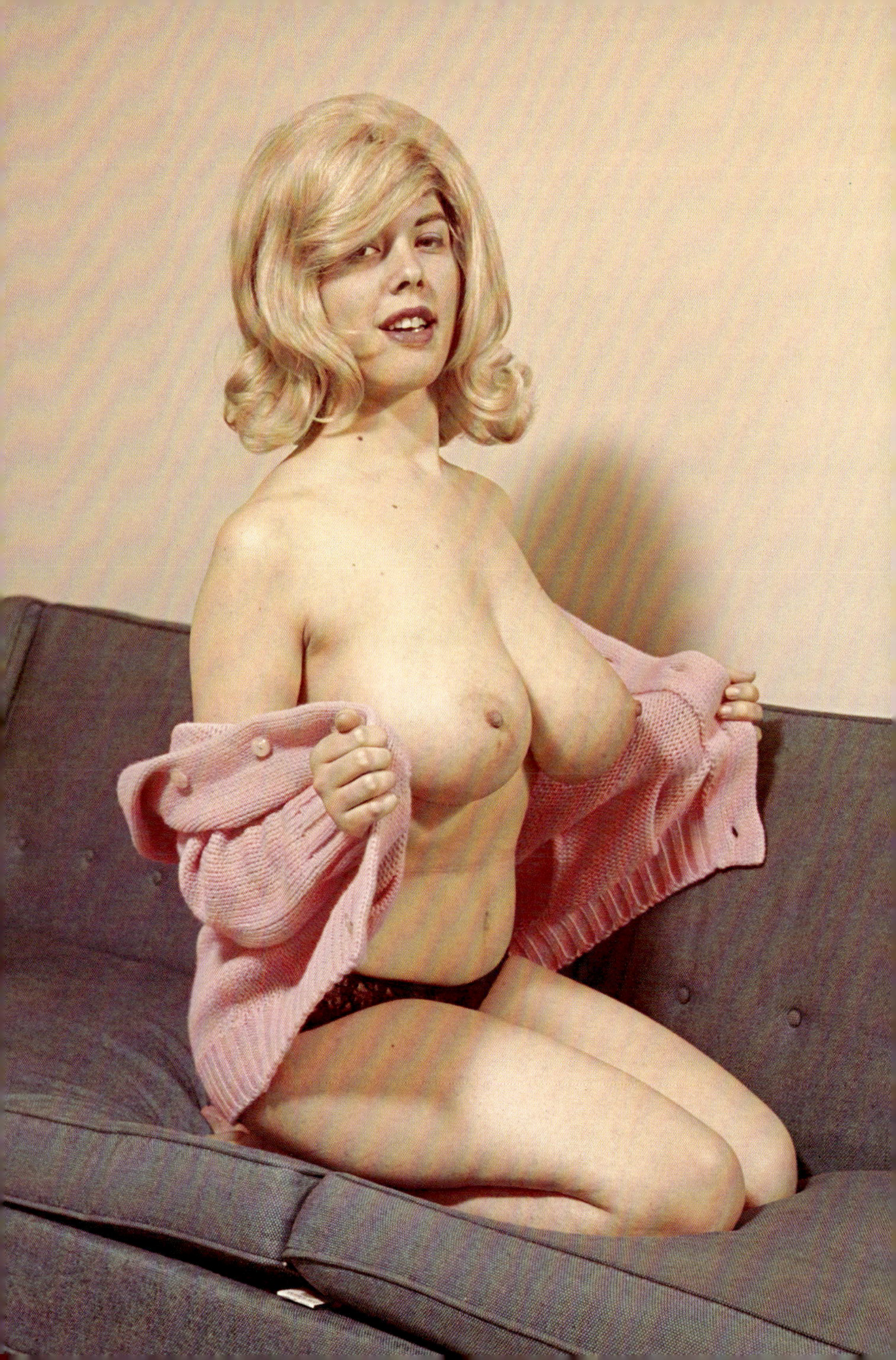

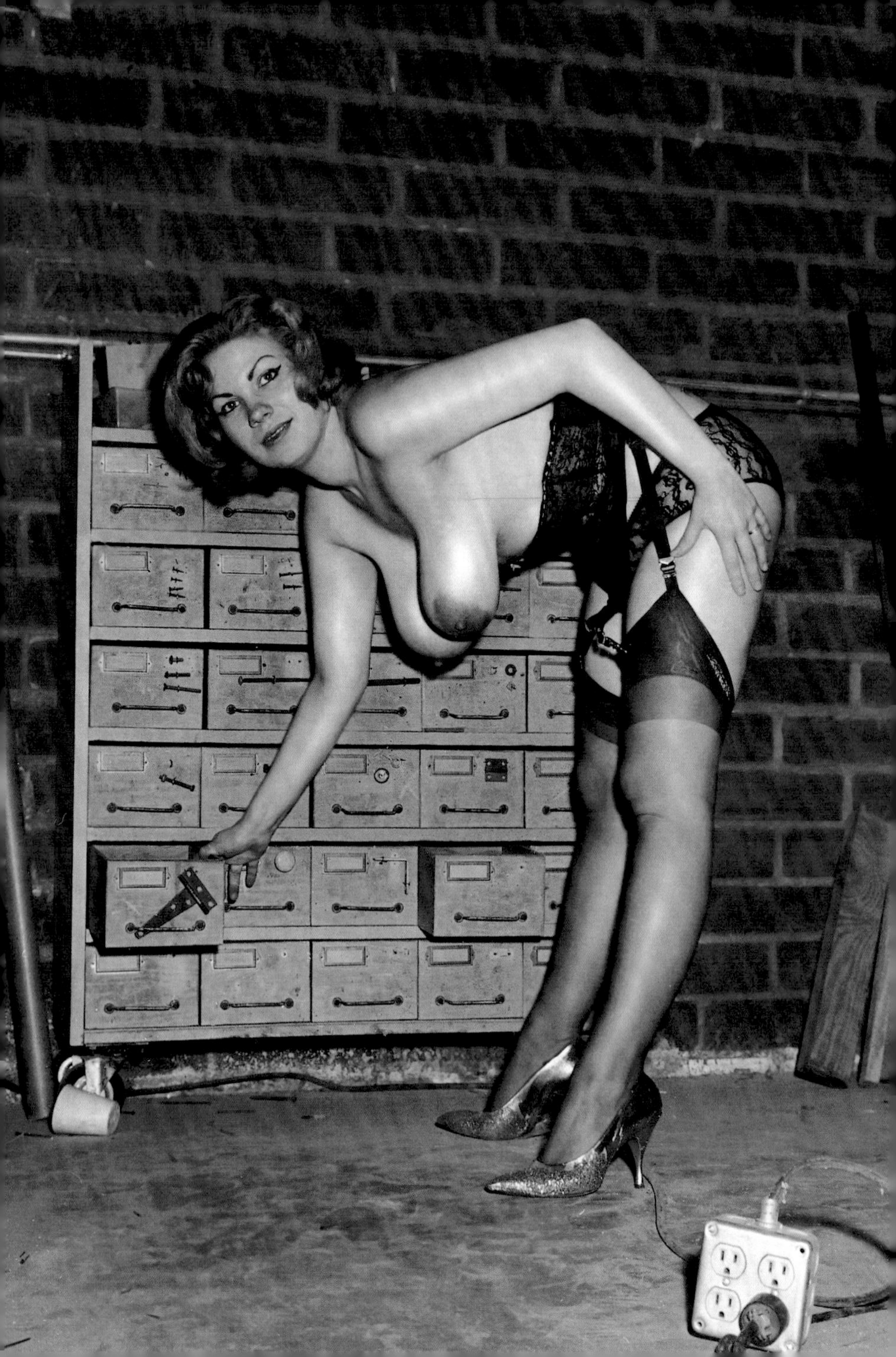

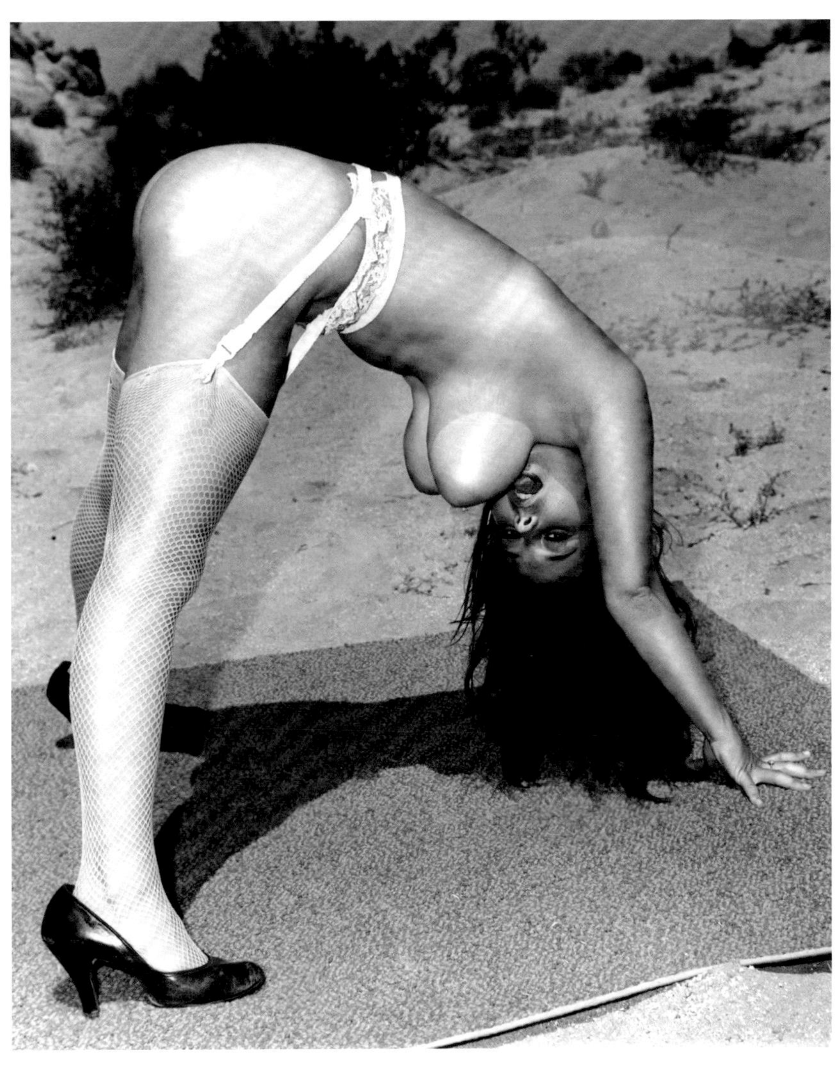

OPPOSITE Gee Whiz ABOVE Barbara Miller

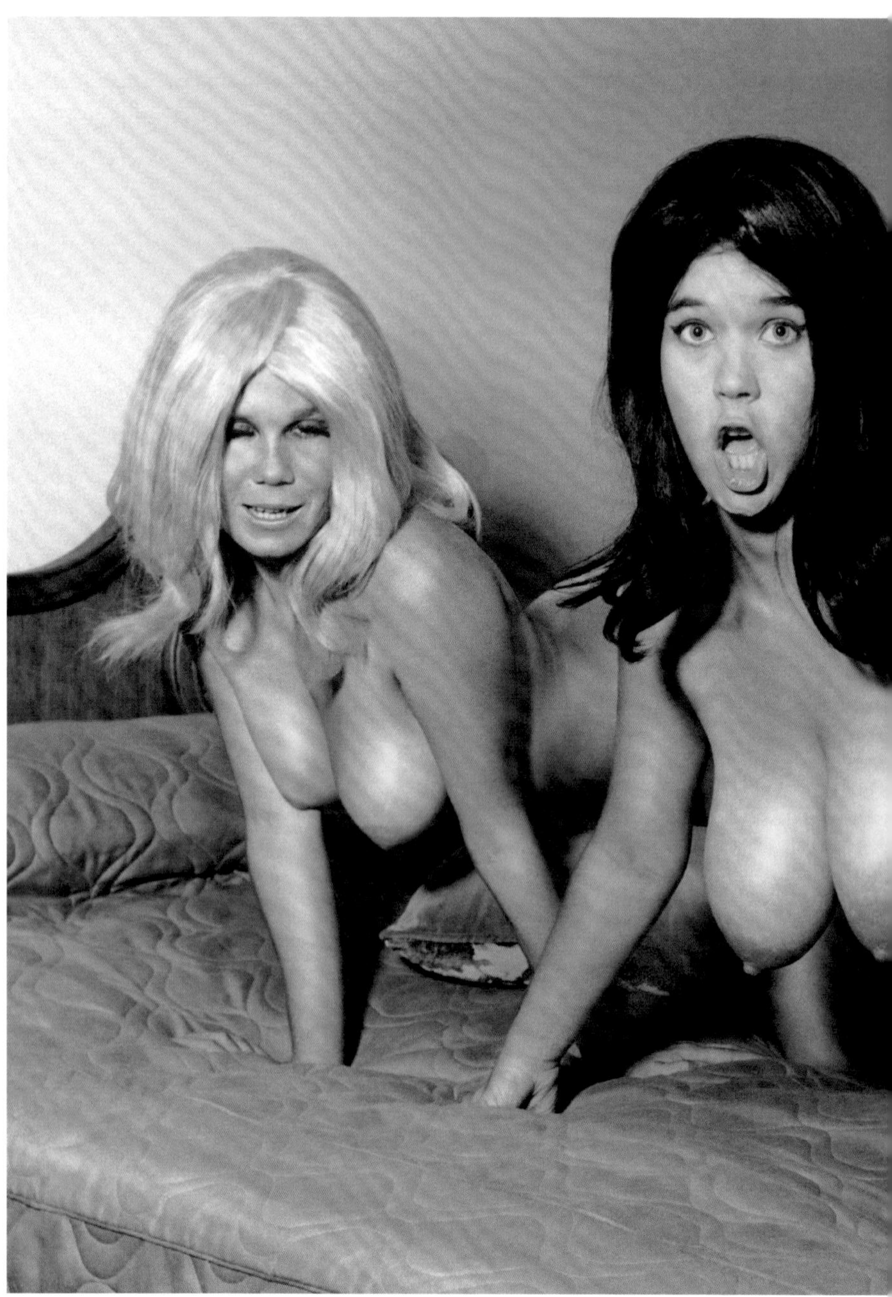

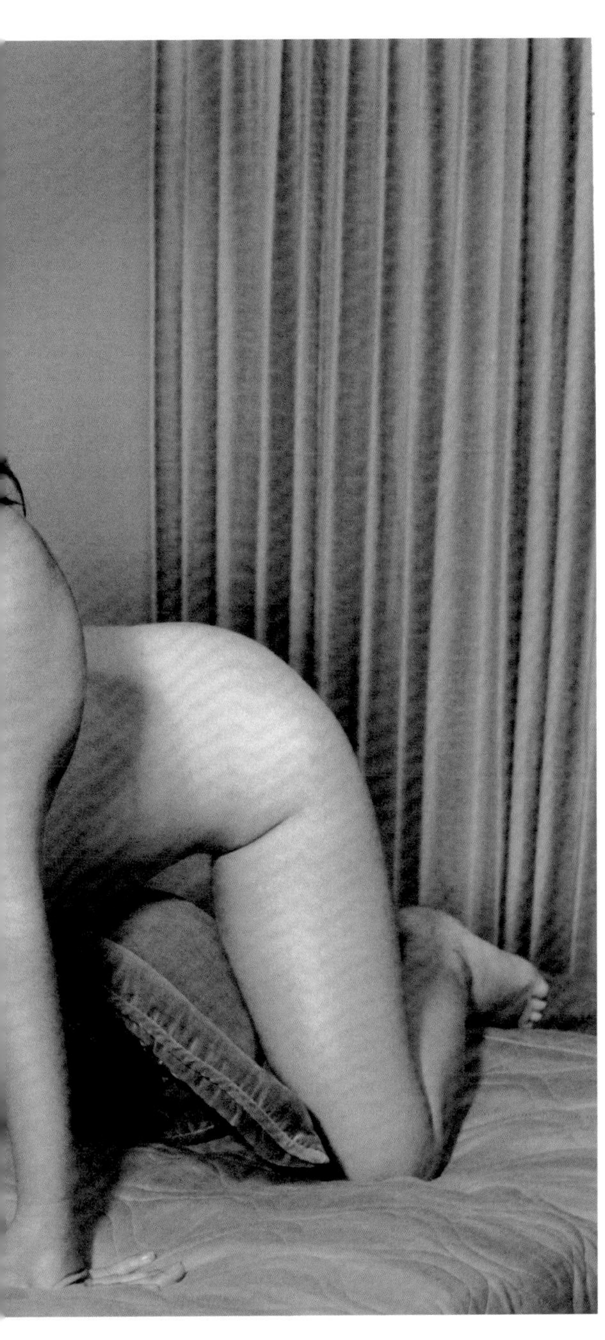

Ann Day and
Suzanne Pritchard

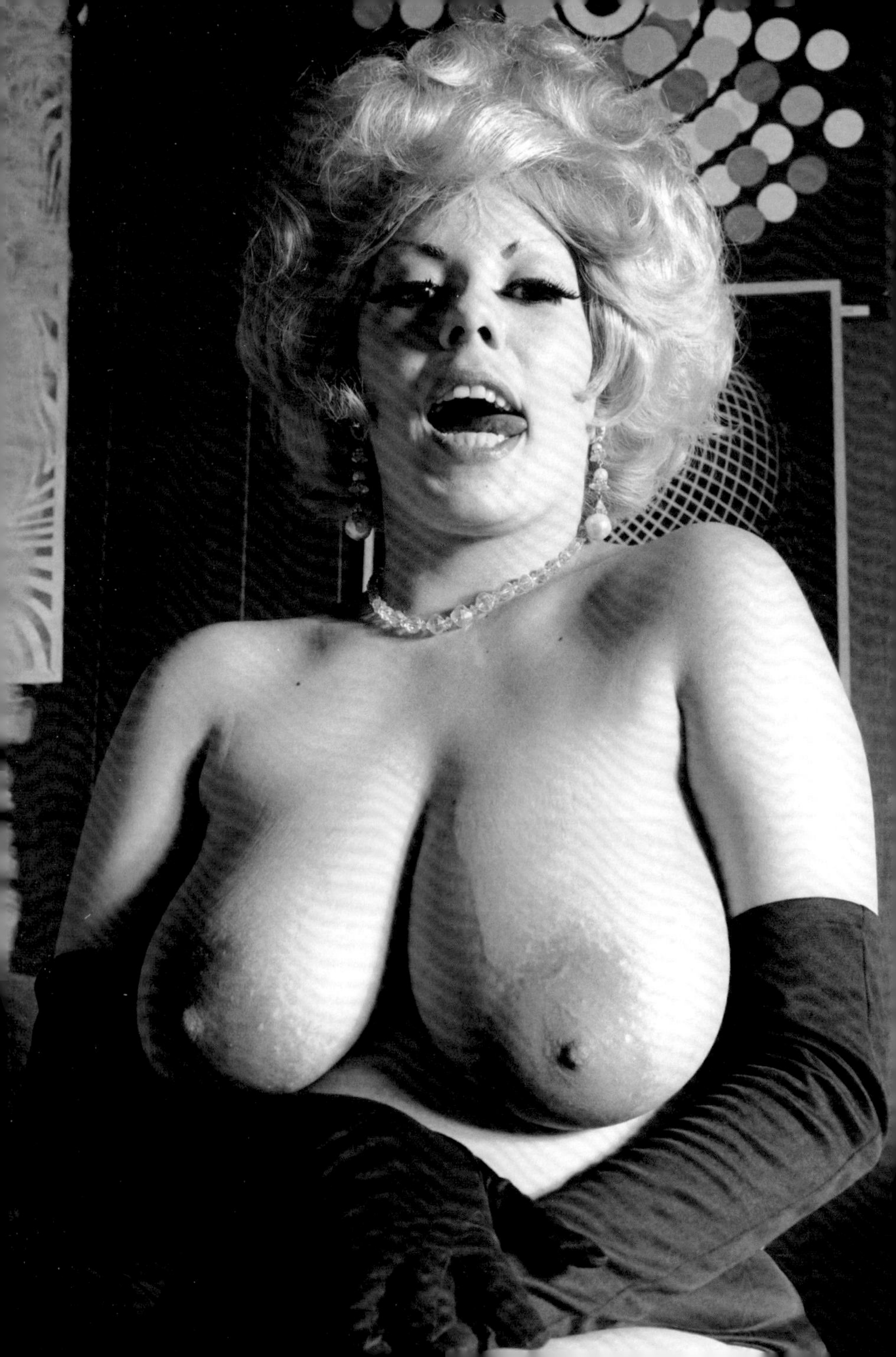

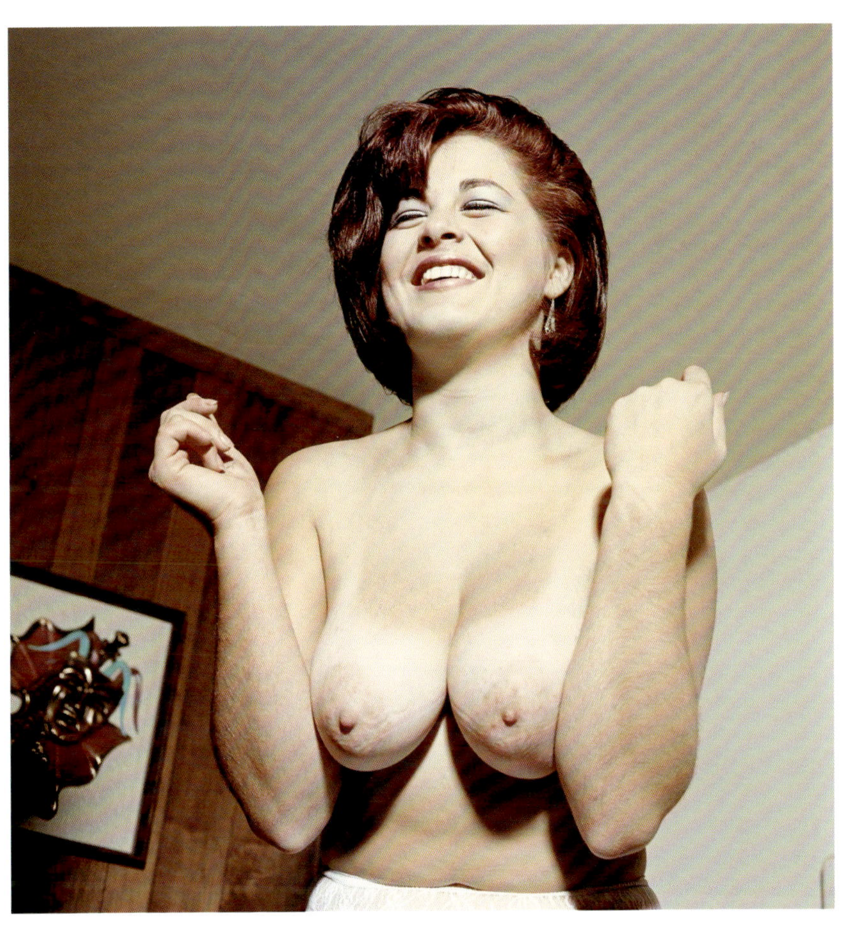

OPPOSITE Crystal Clear ABOVE Unknown

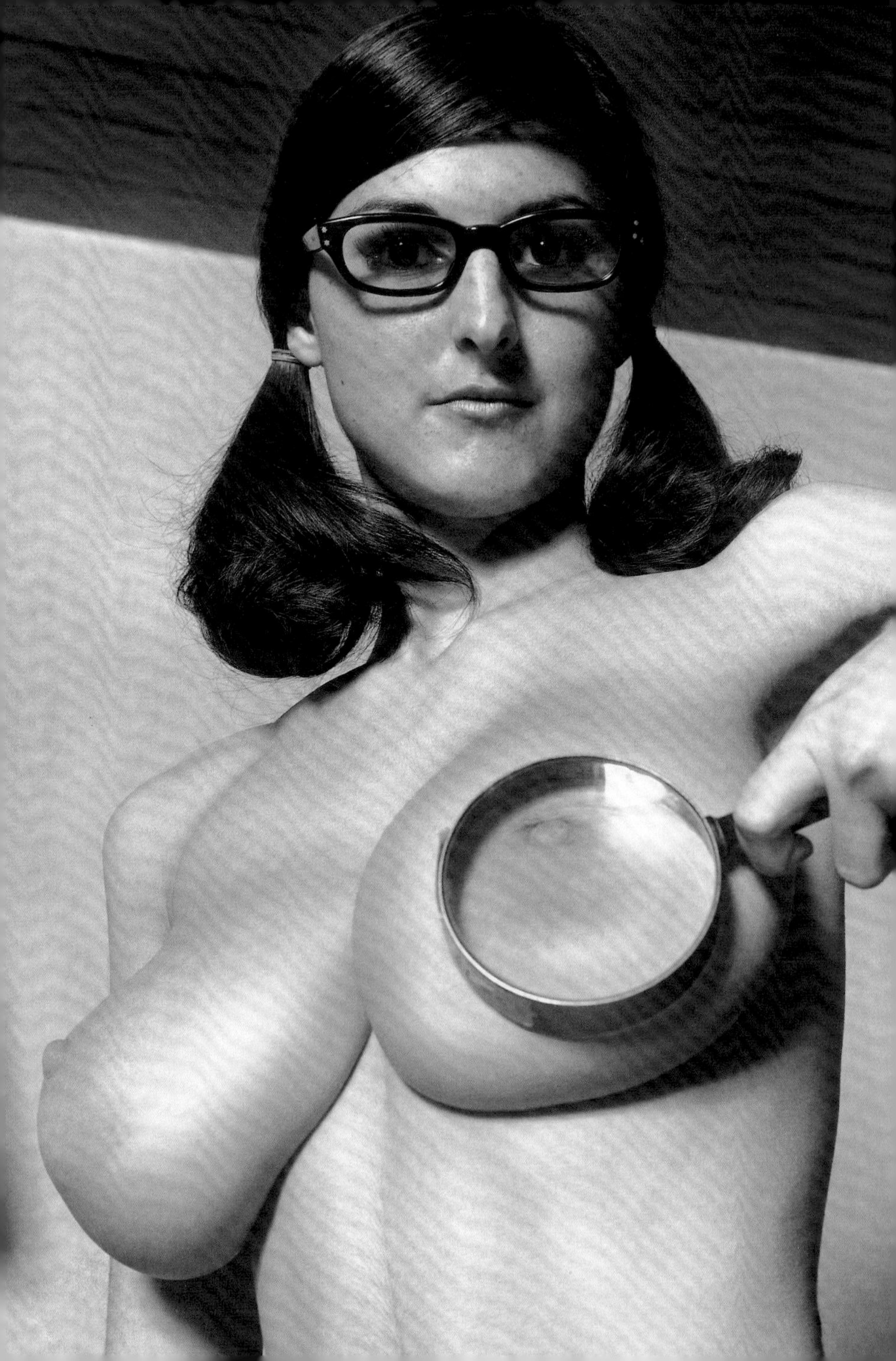

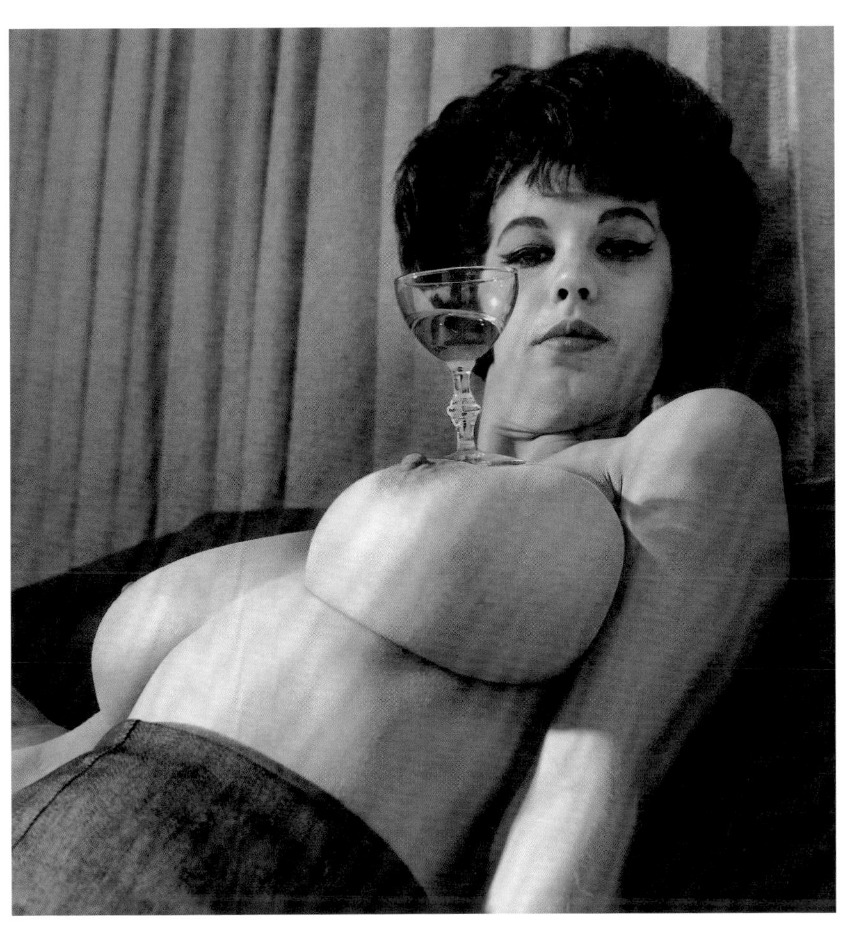

OPPOSITE Lillian Parker ABOVE Linda McClung PAGES 92-93 Uschi Digard

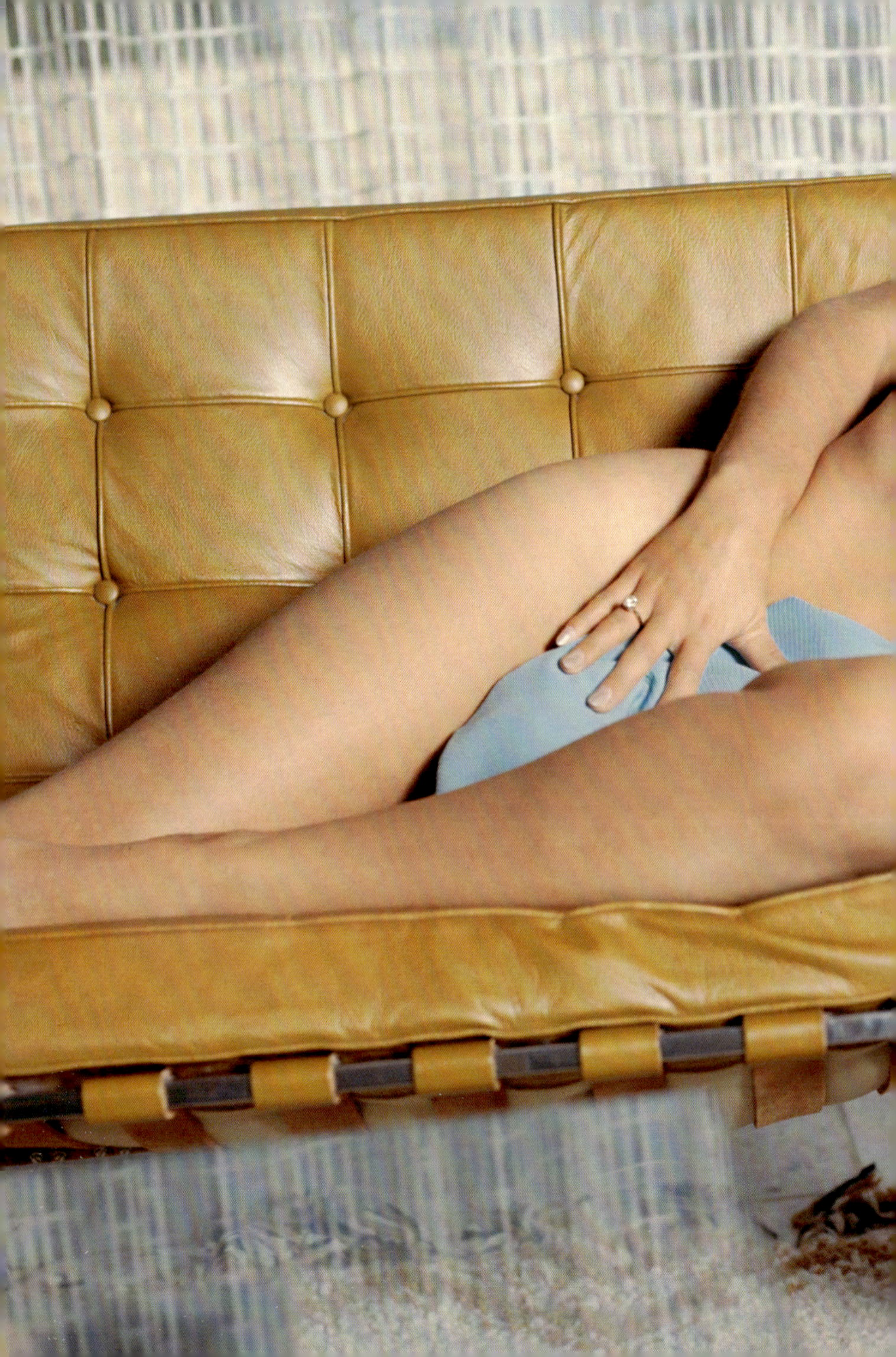

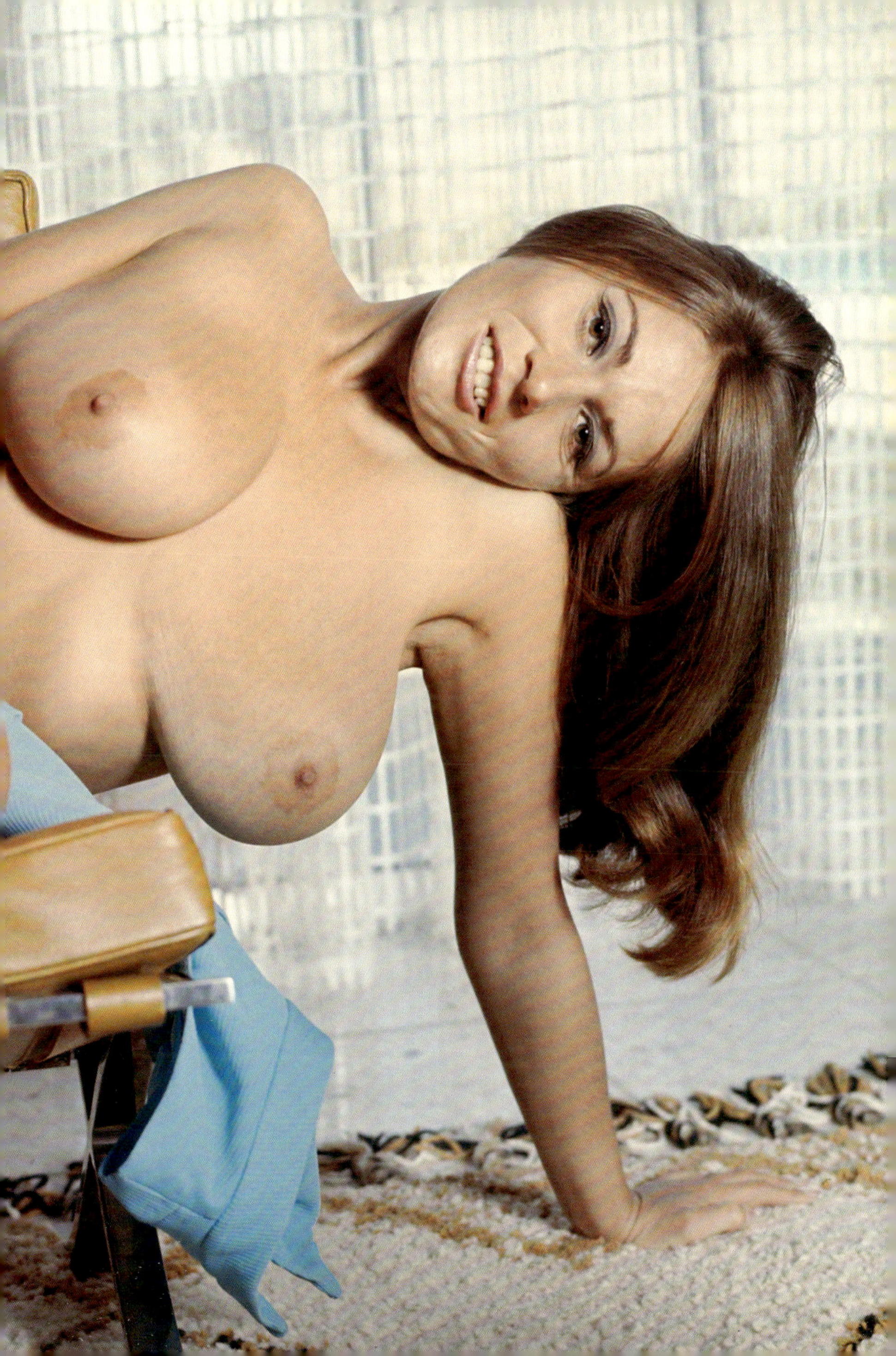

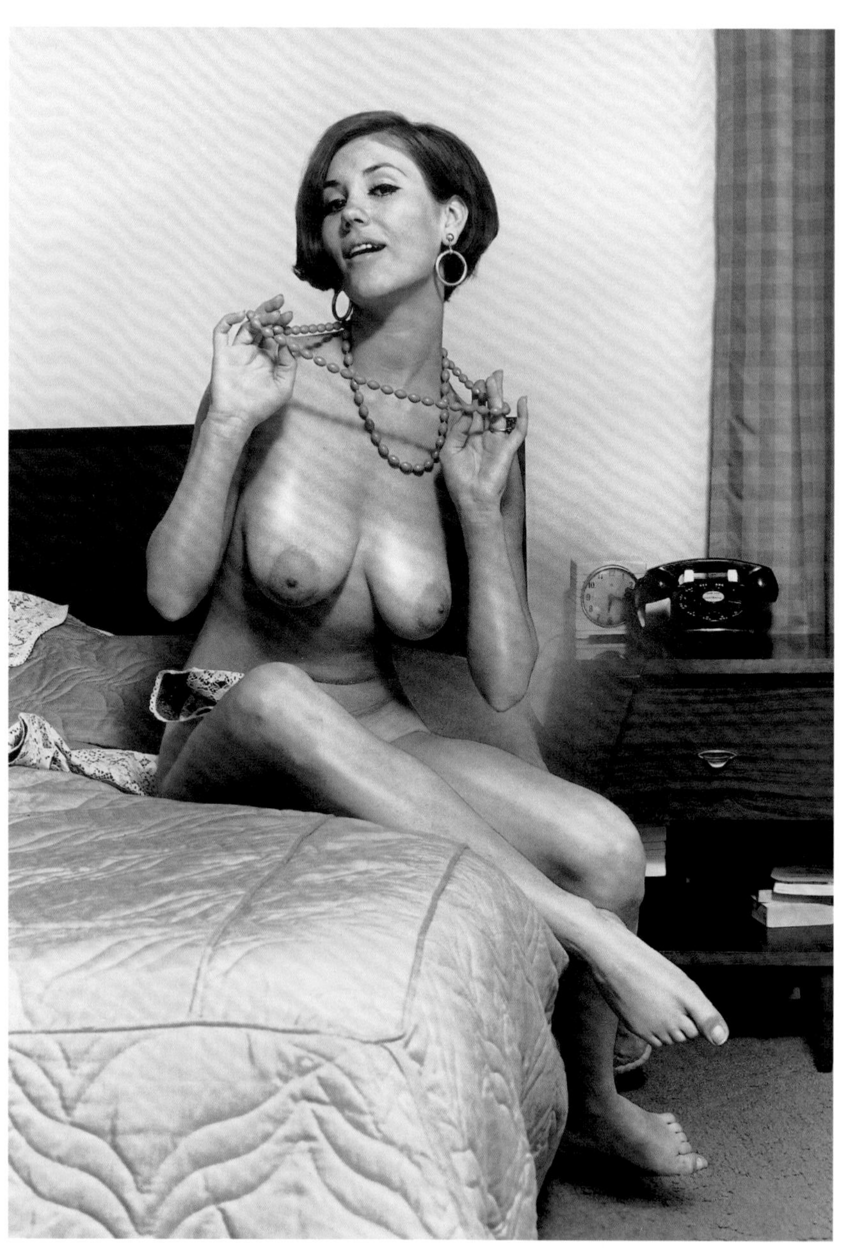

ABOVE Candy Earl OPPOSITE Patricia Meise

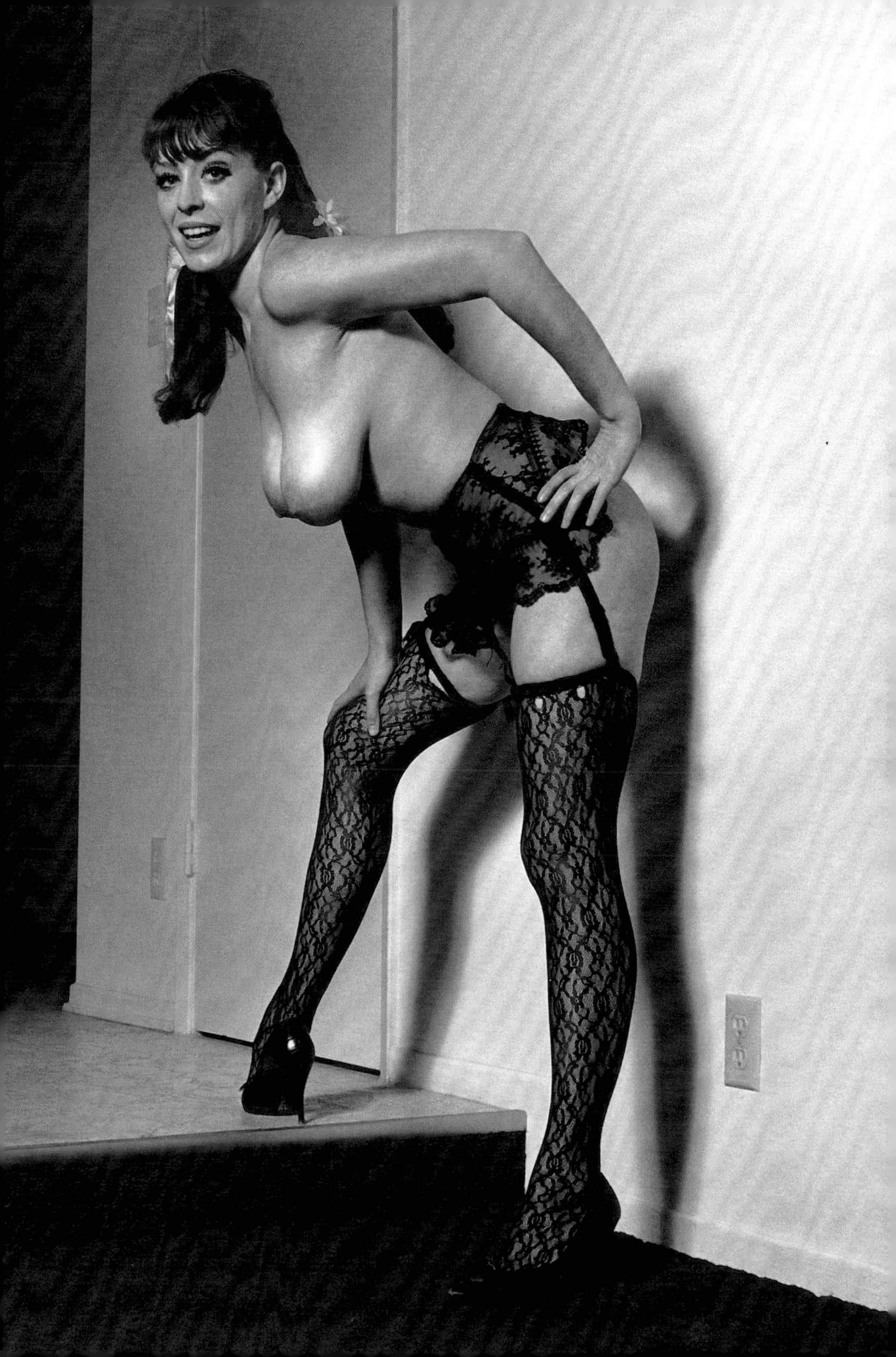

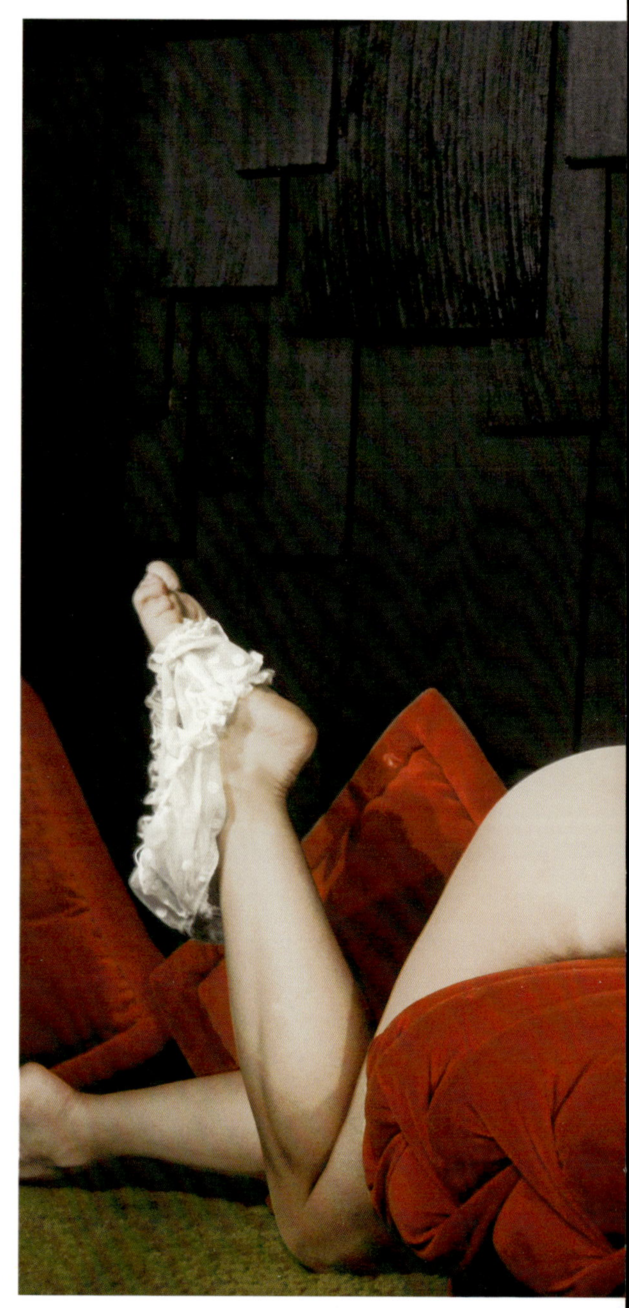

Diane Curtis

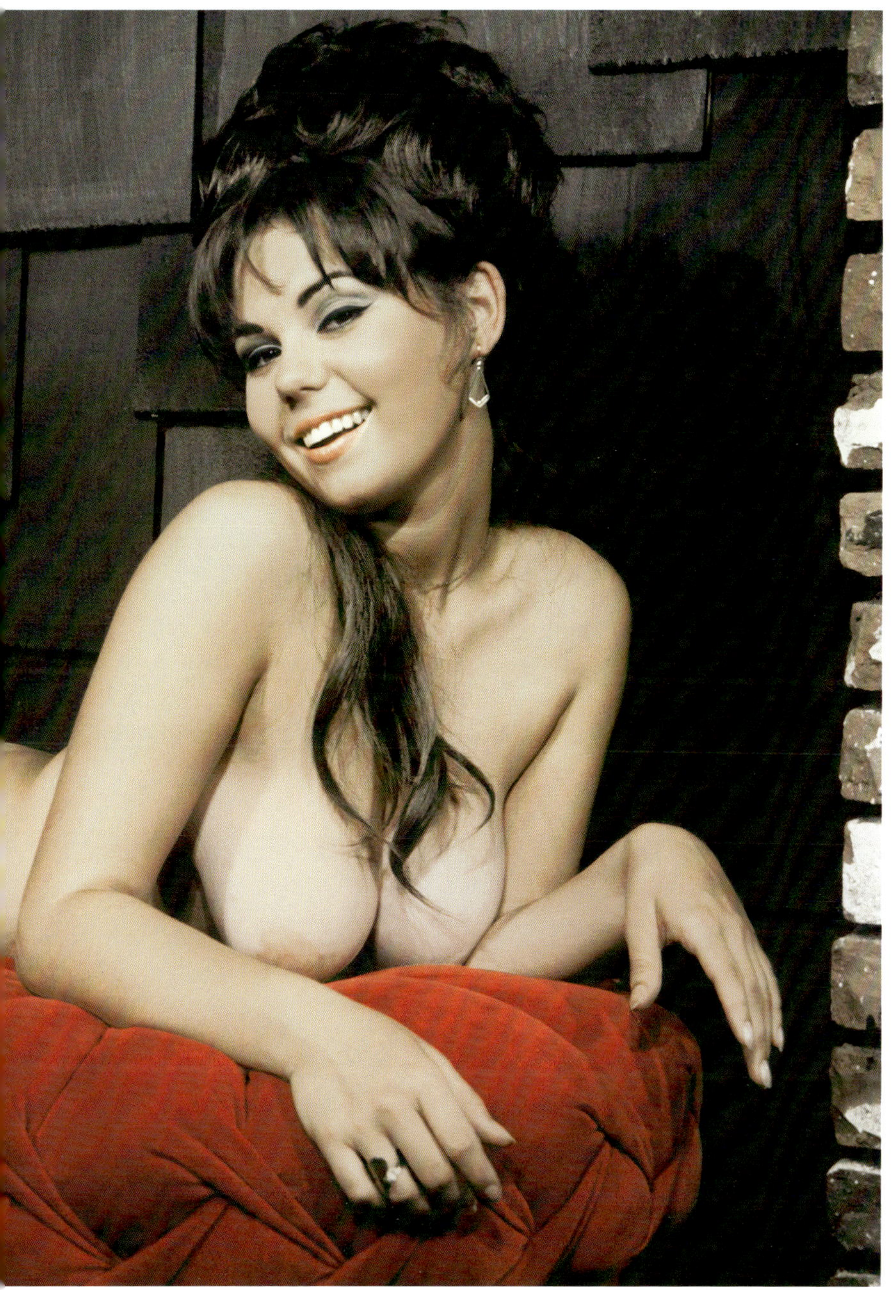

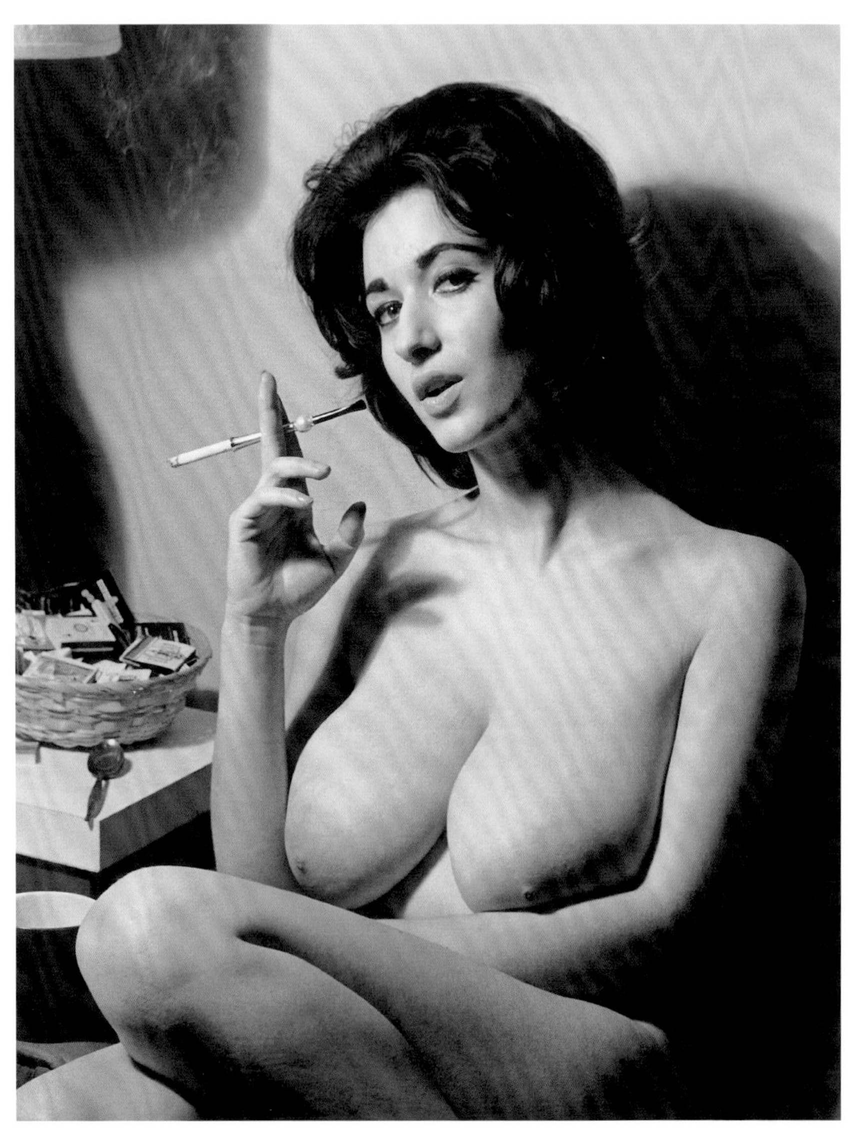

Joan Brinkman

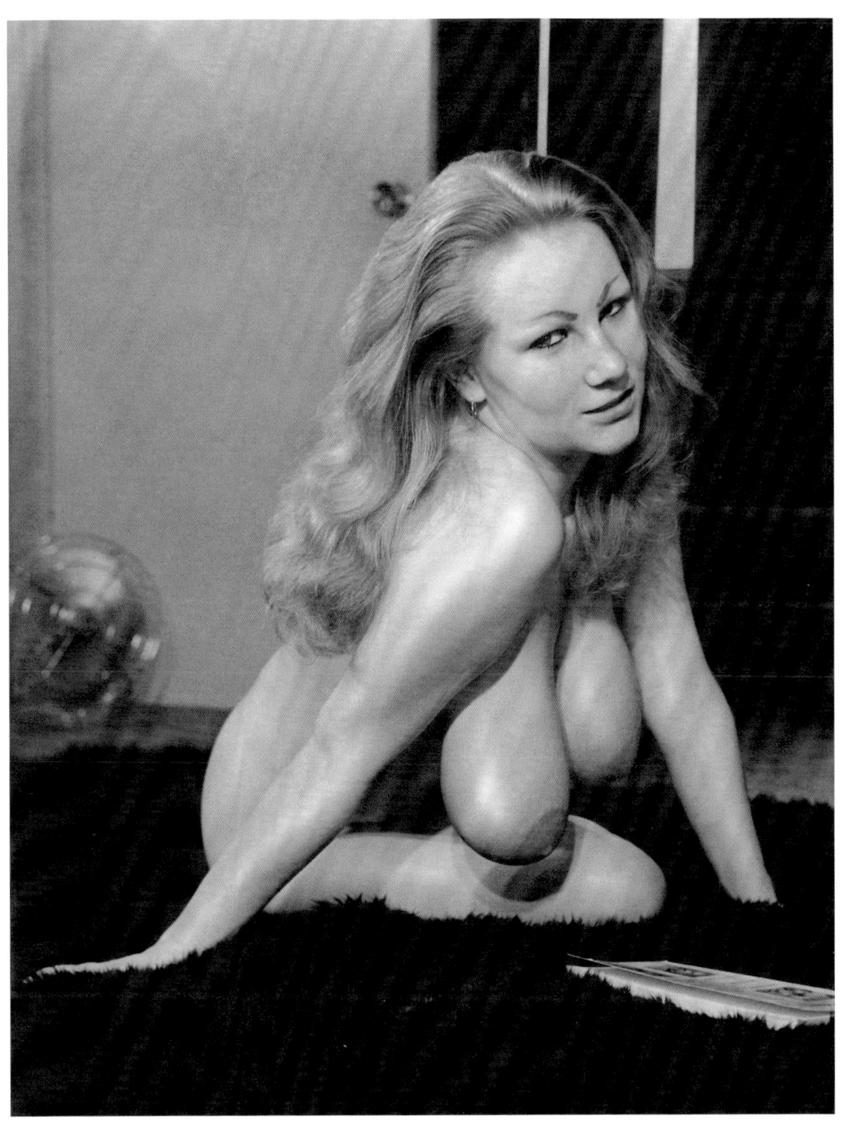

ABOVE Starr Murphy PAGES 100-101 Suzanne Pritchard

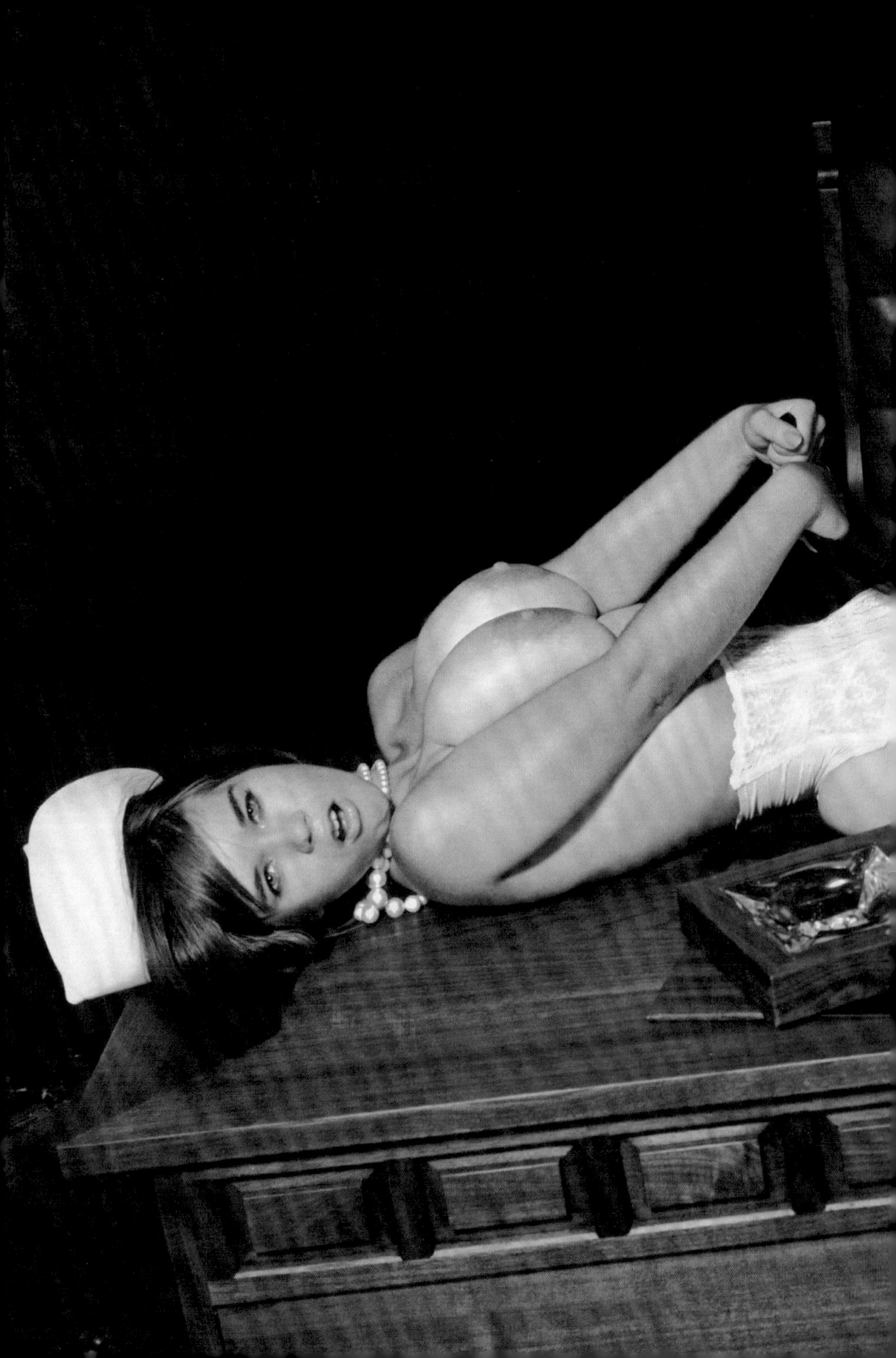

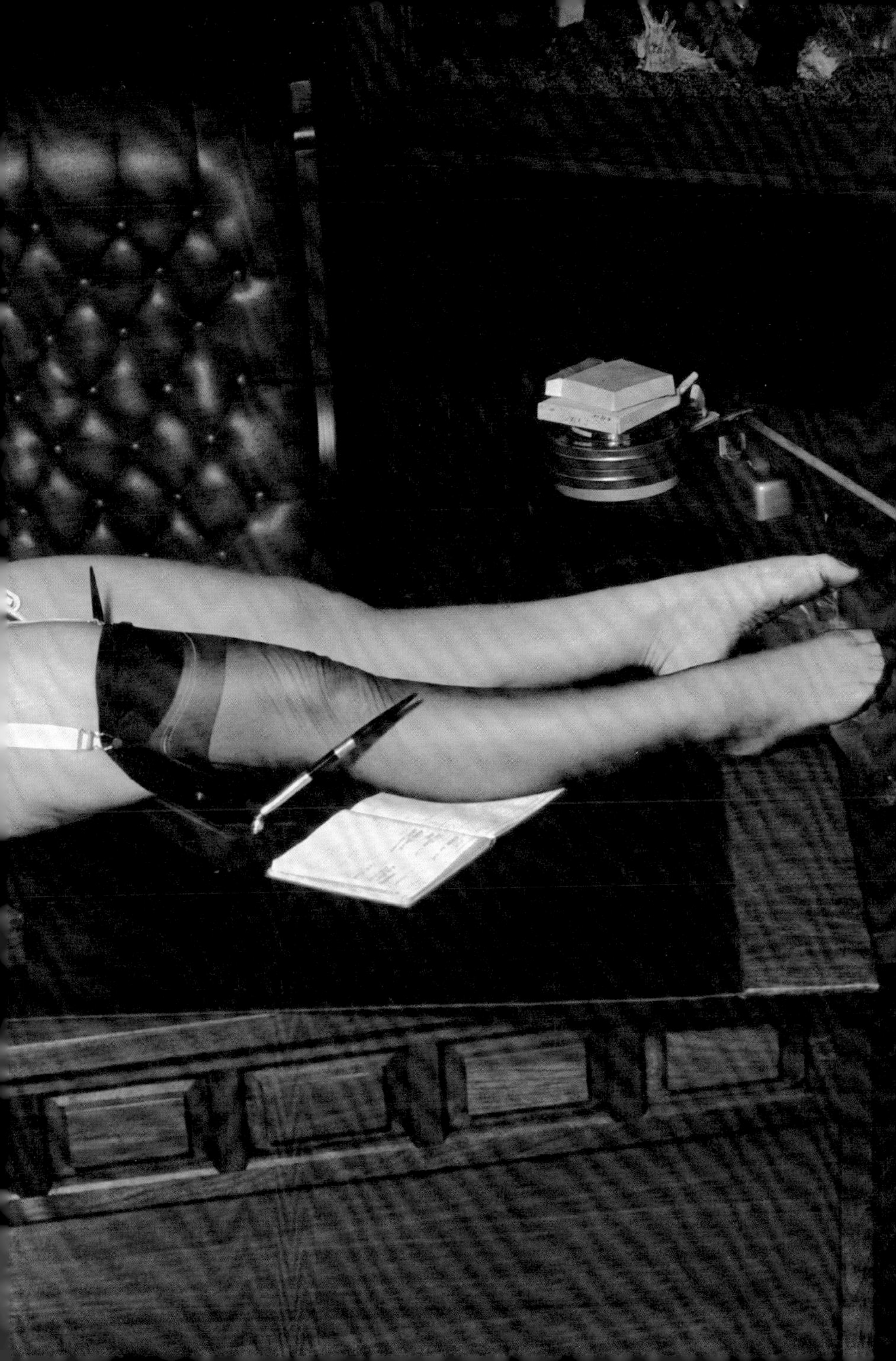

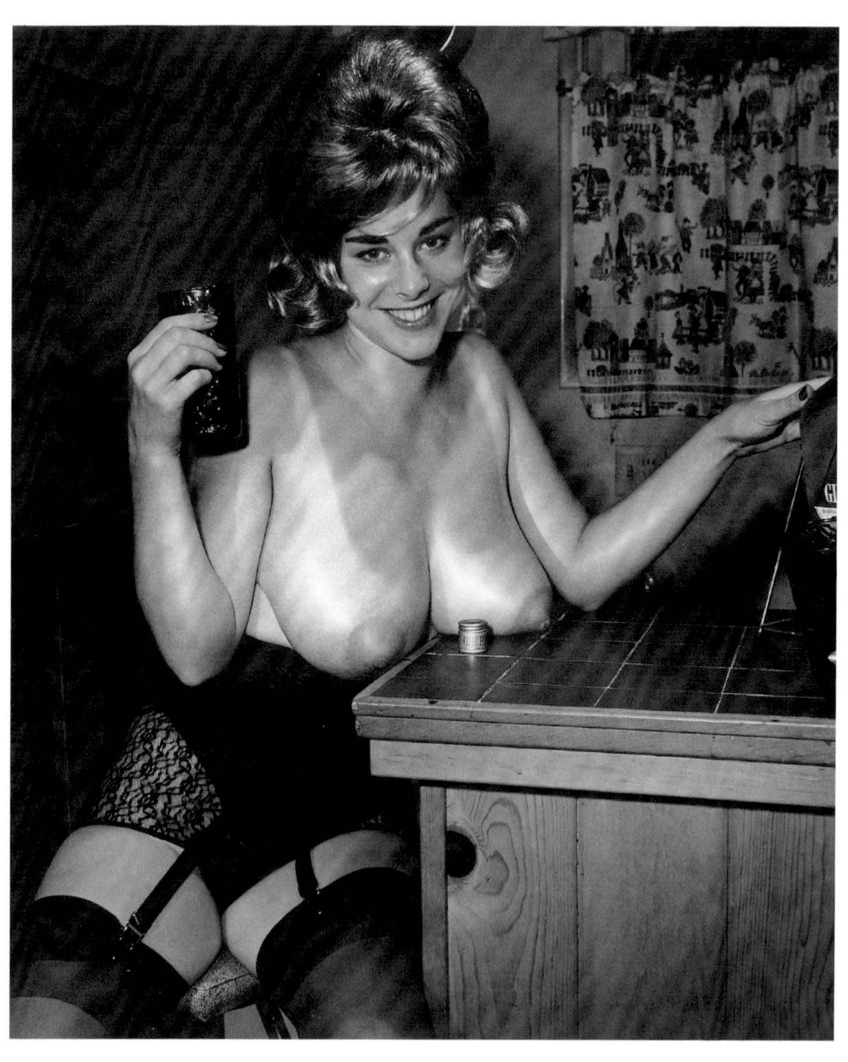

ABOVE Janie Renolds OPPOSITE Uschi Digard

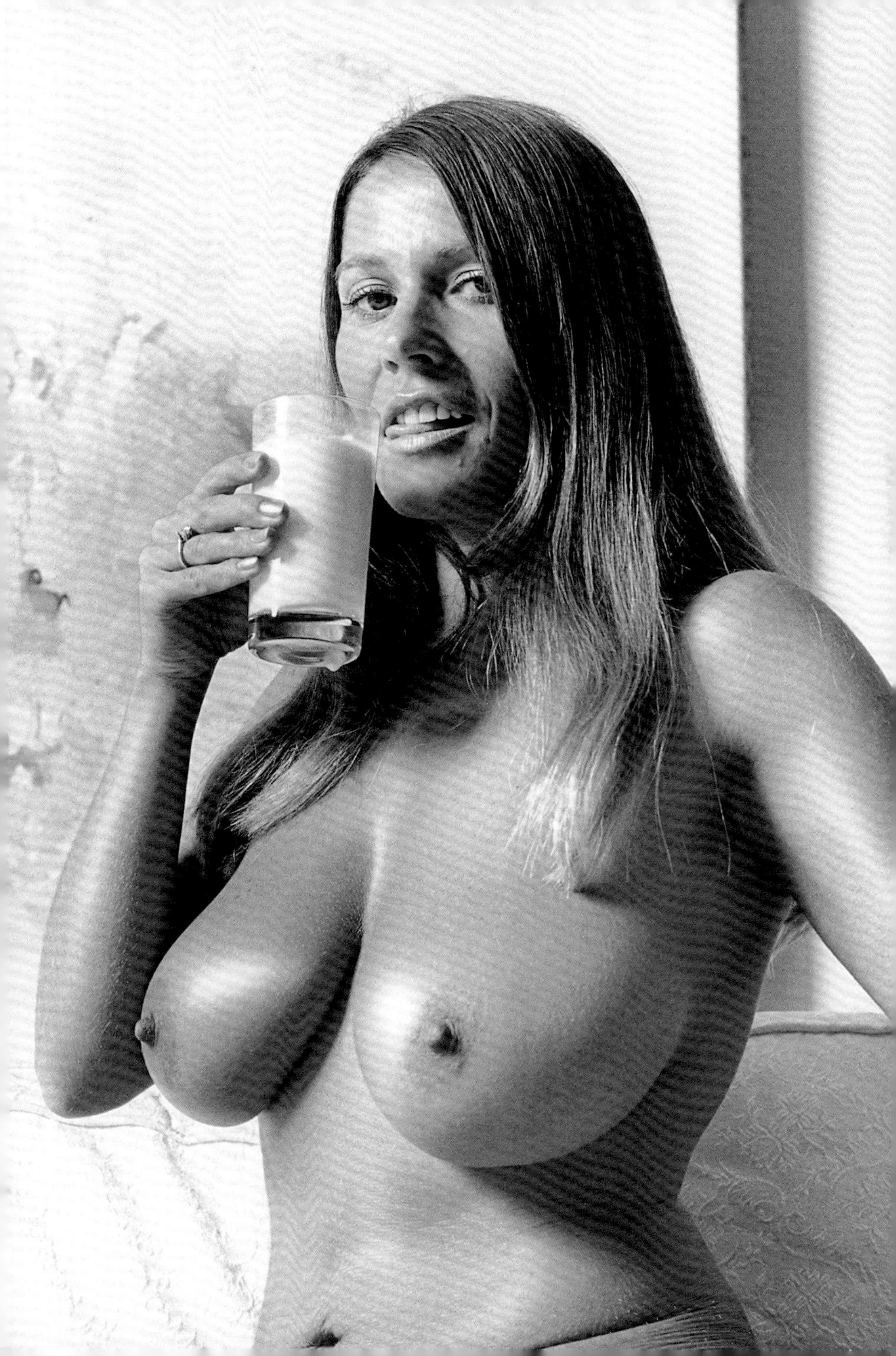

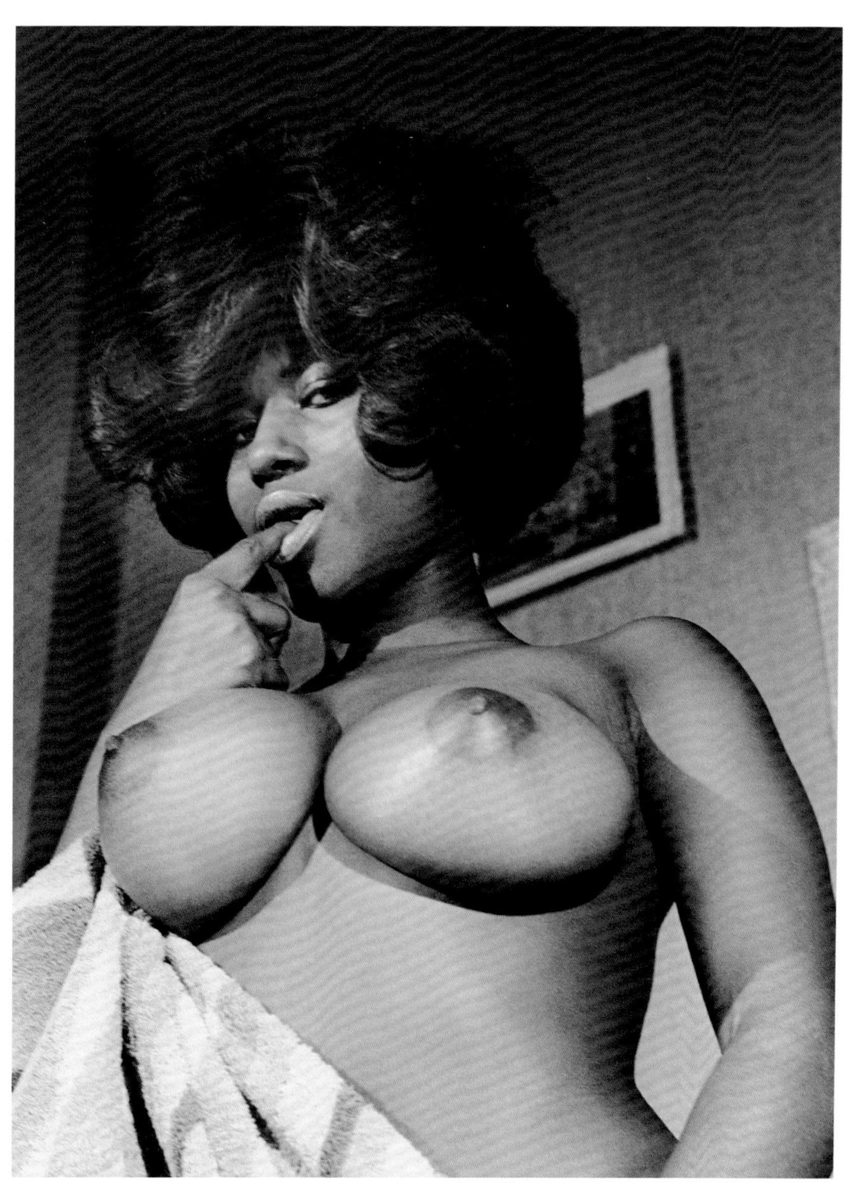

ABOVE Unknown OPPOSITE Lisa Matthews

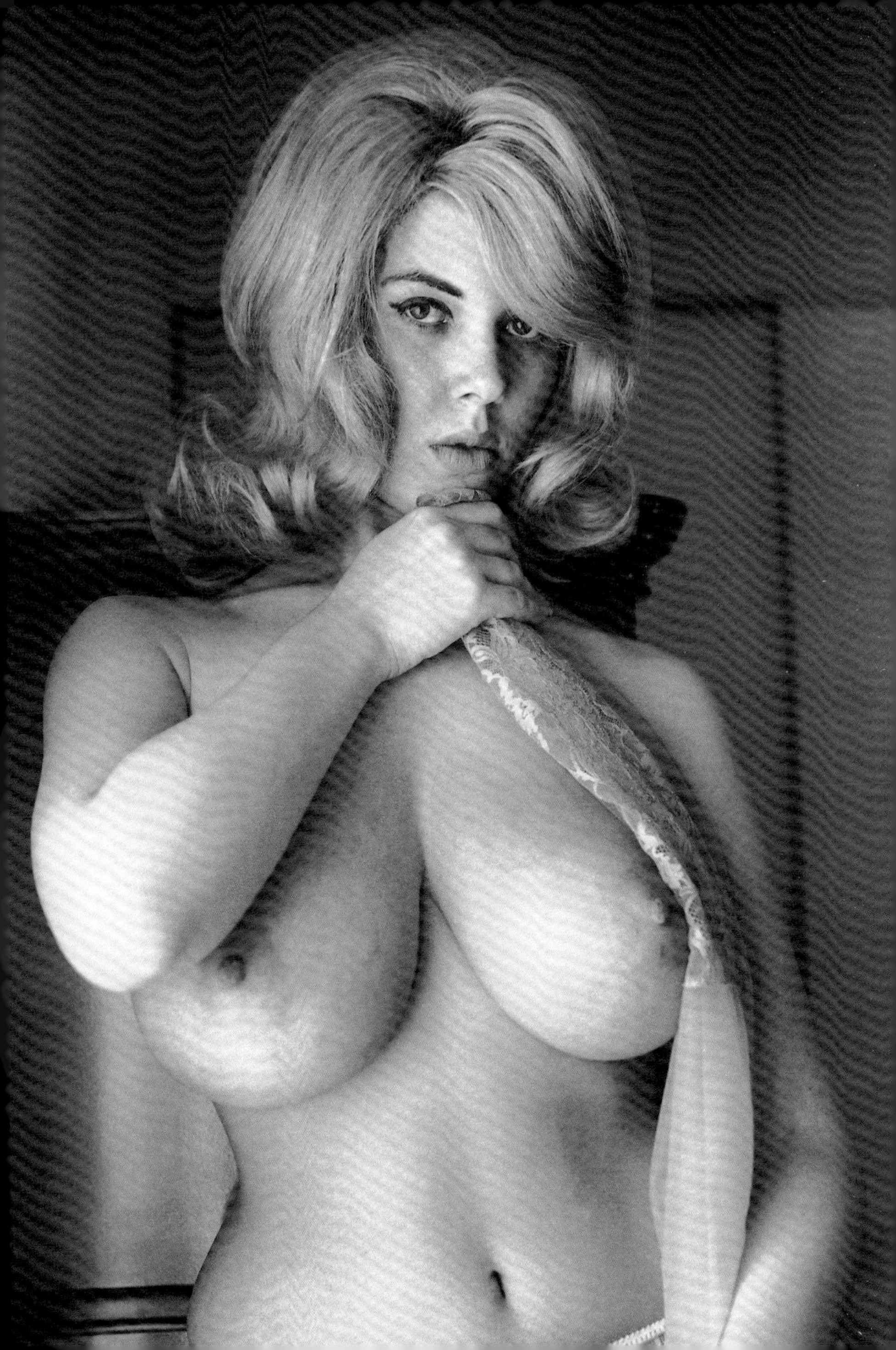

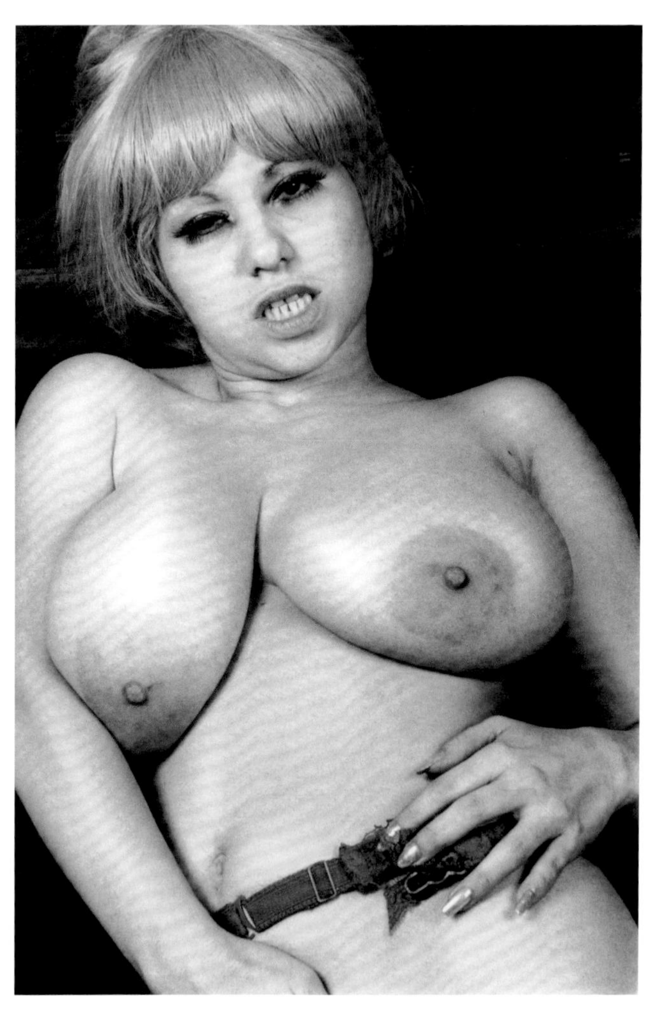

ABOVE Danielle Dawson OPPOSITE Shawn Devereaux

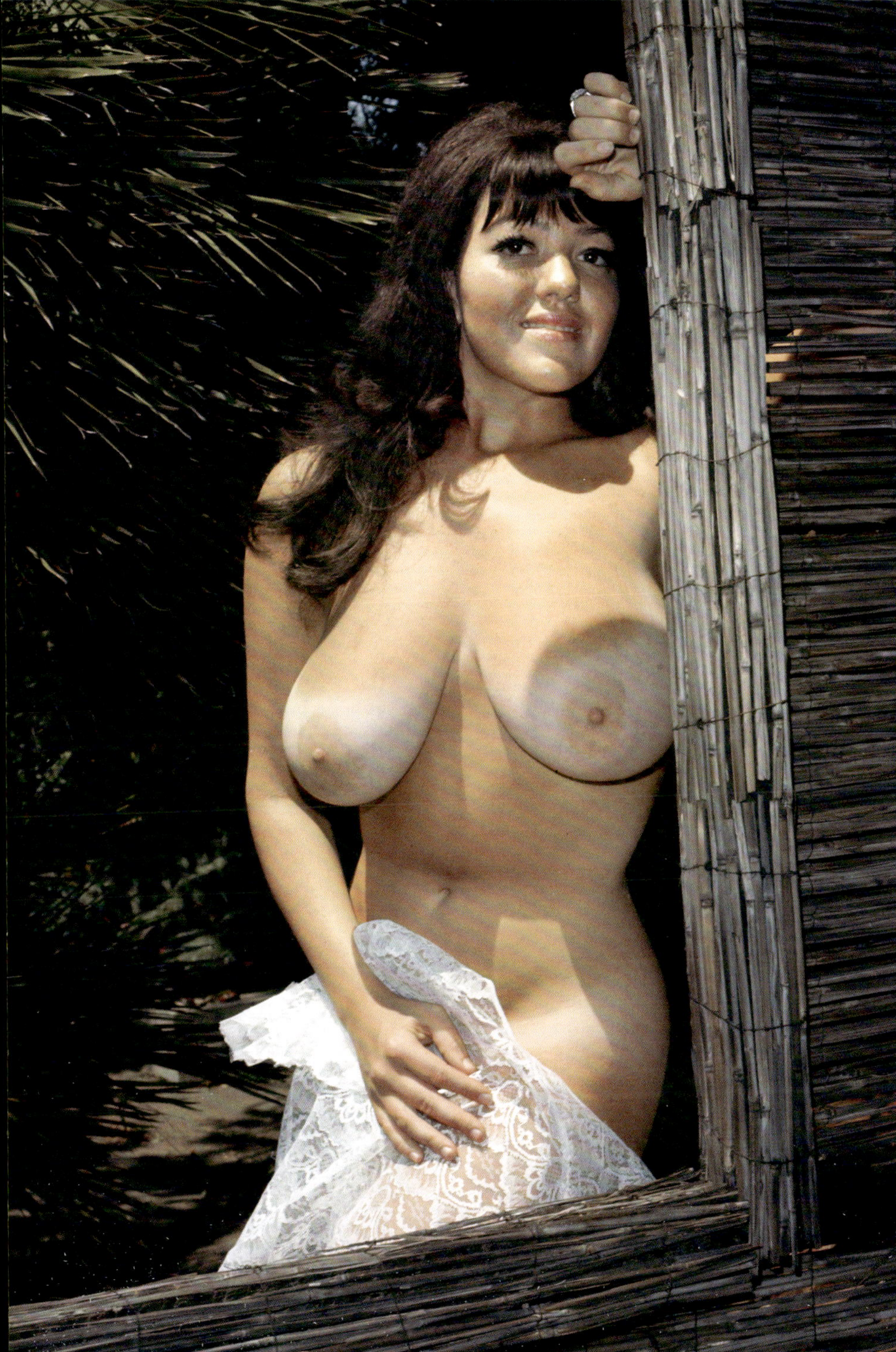

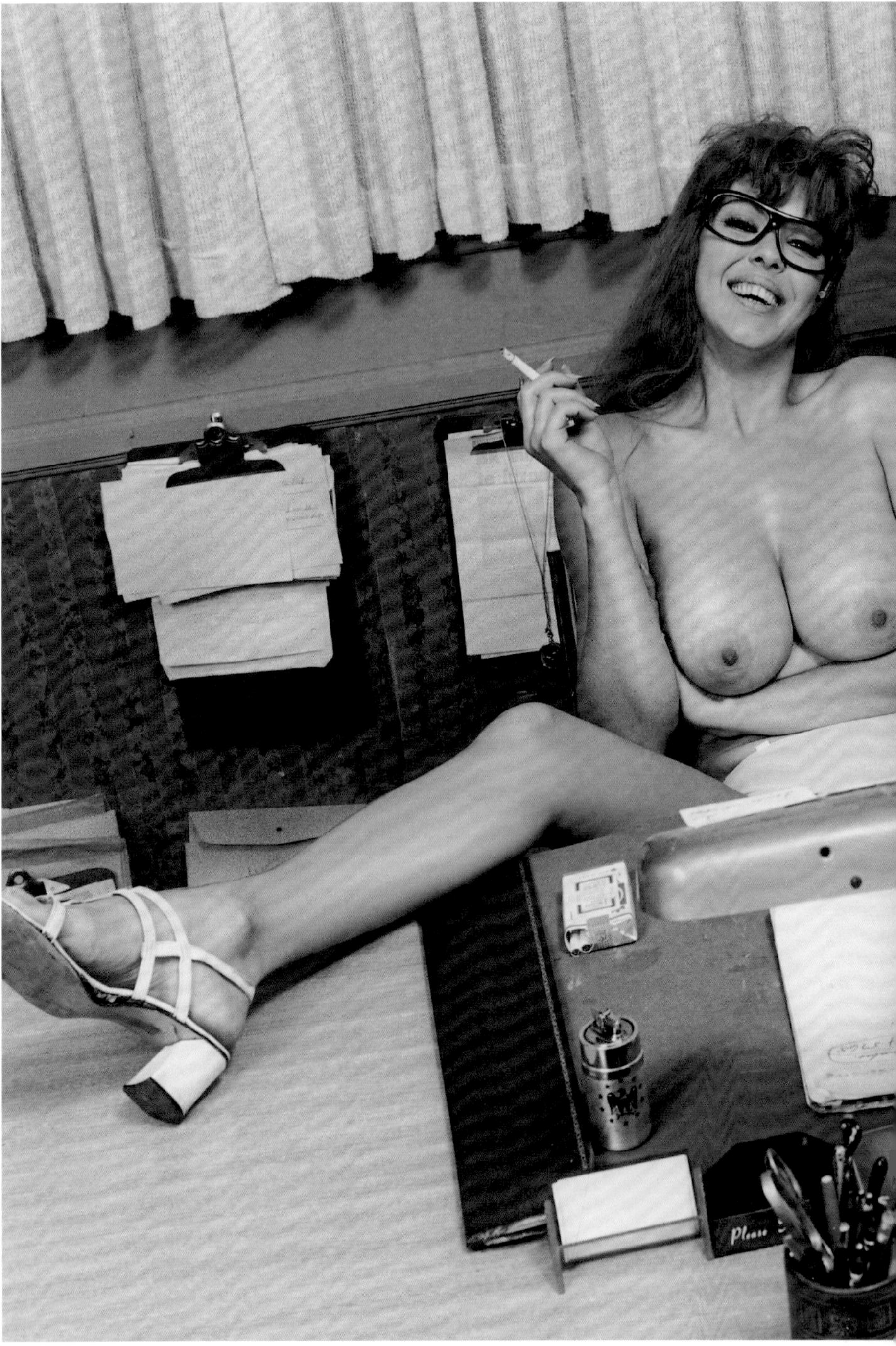
Please

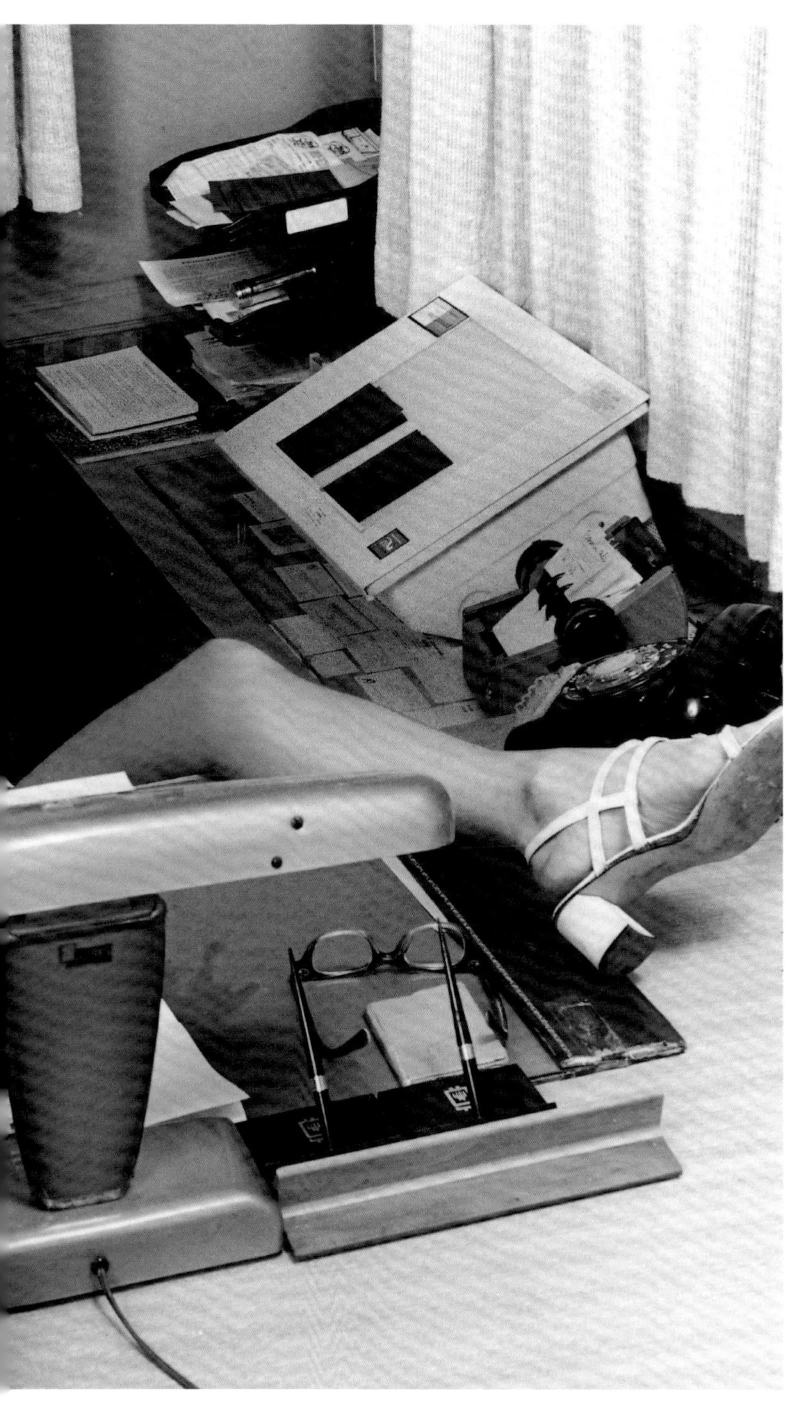

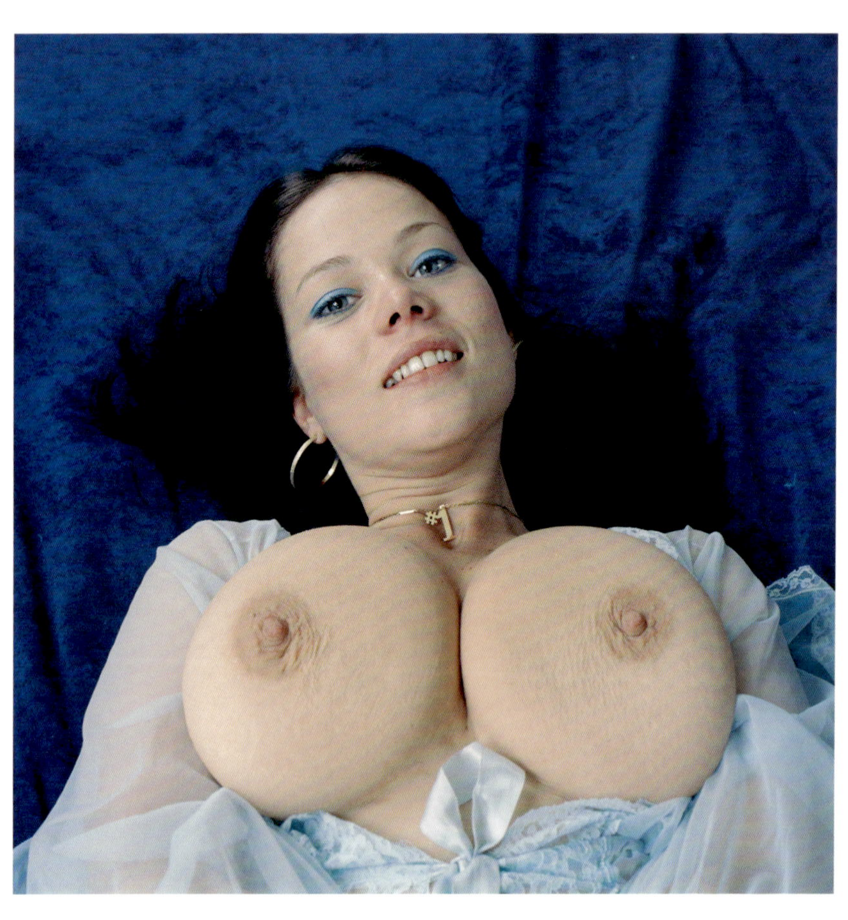

PAGES 108-109 Roxanne Brewer ABOVE Unknown

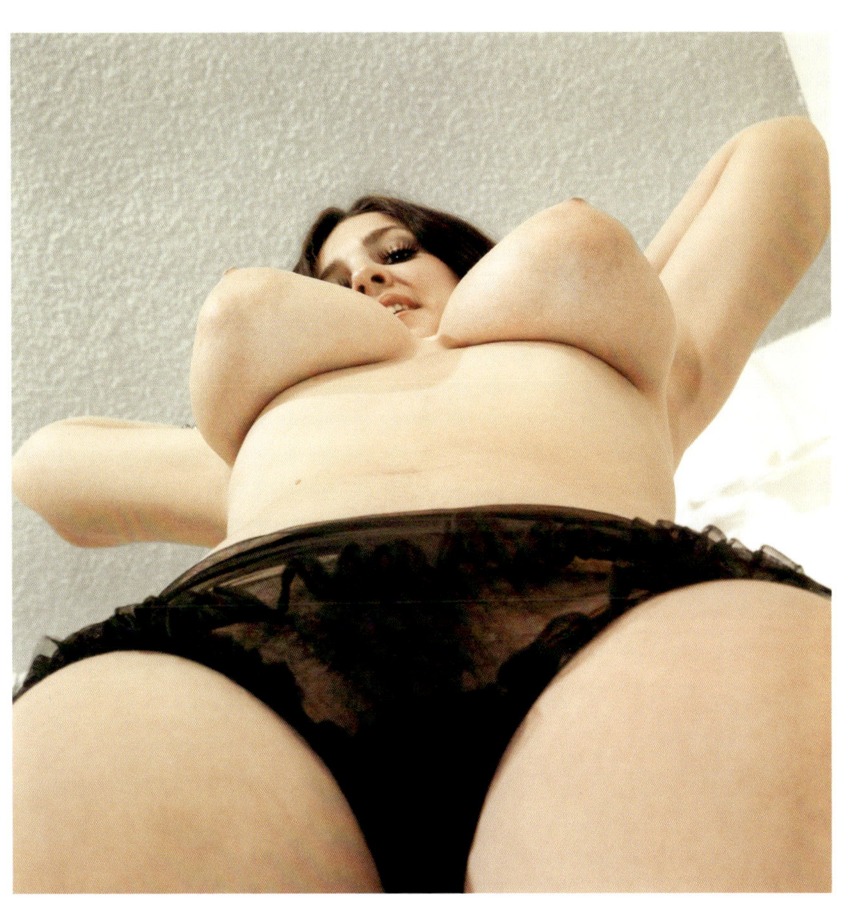

Unknown

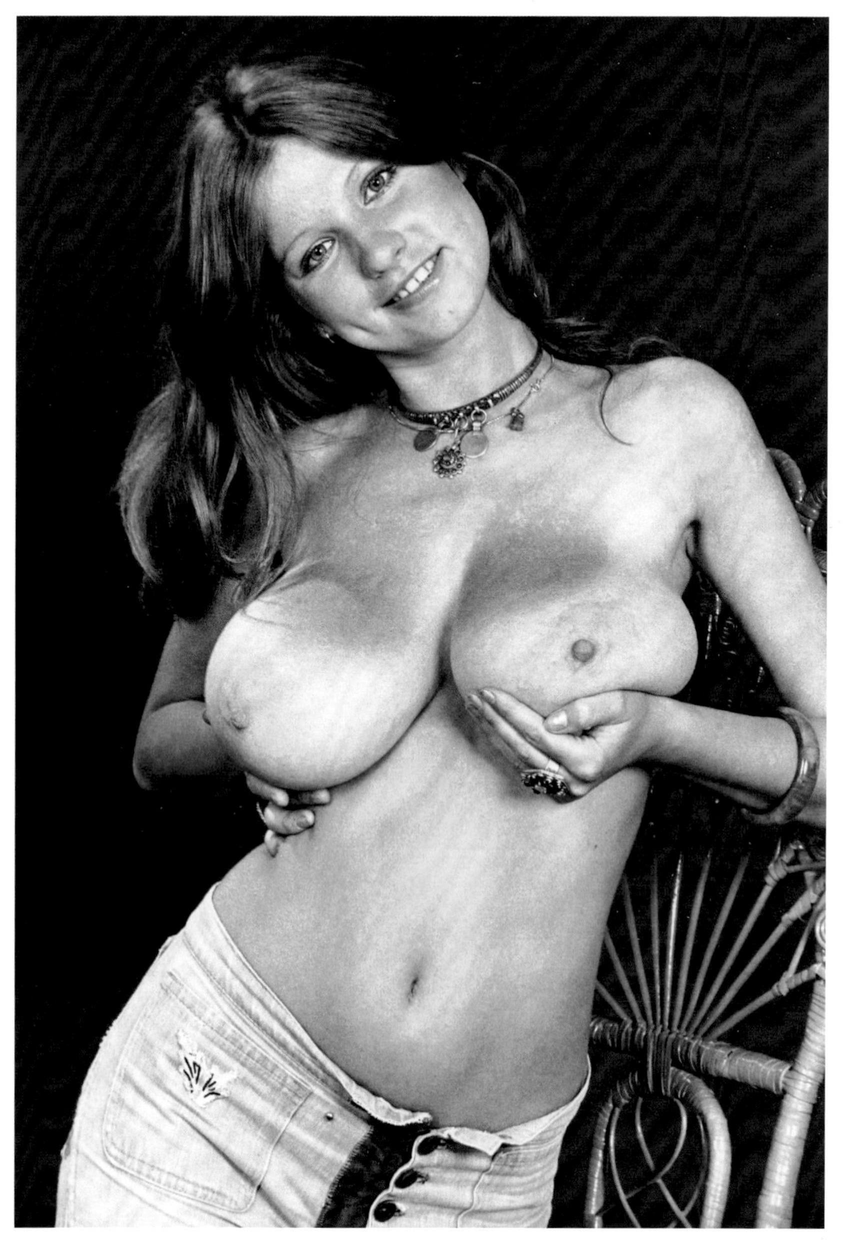

Roberta Pedon

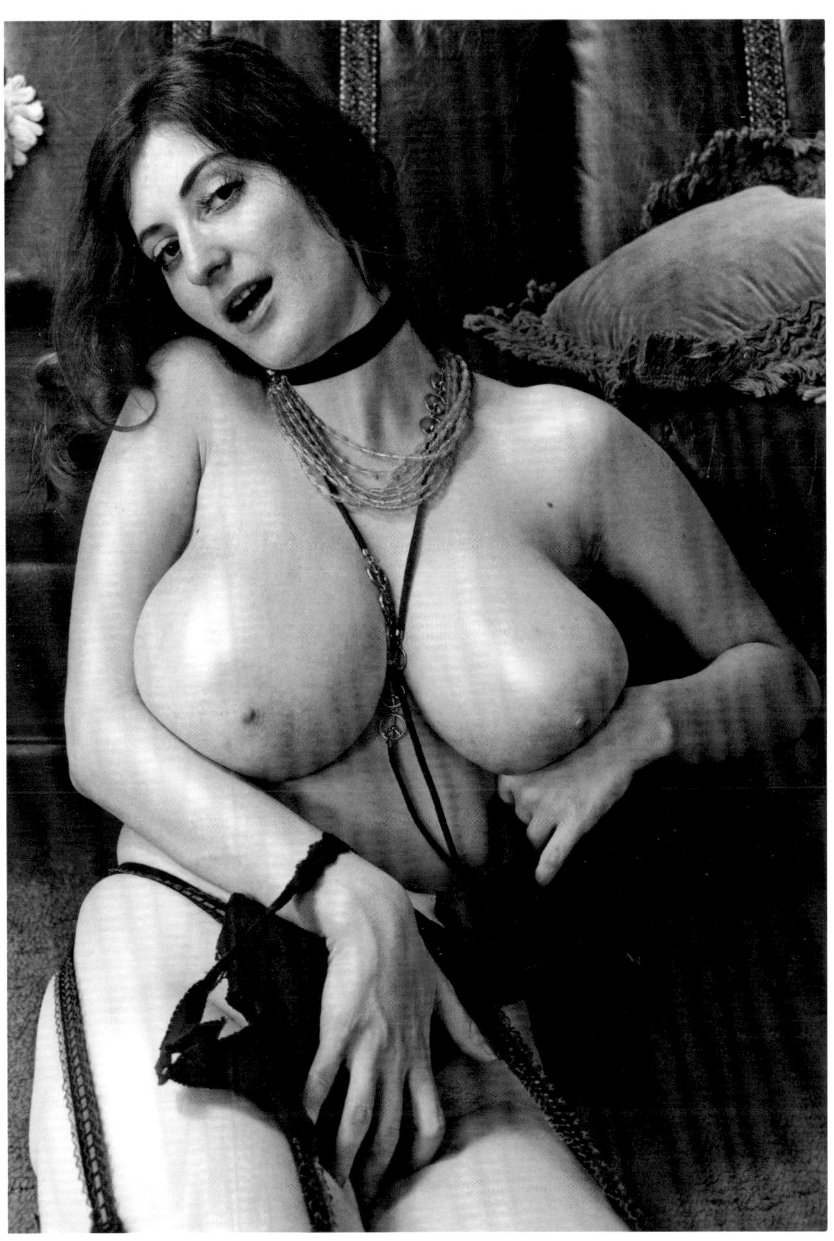

ABOVE Michelle Weiner PAGES 114-115 Linda Corrigan

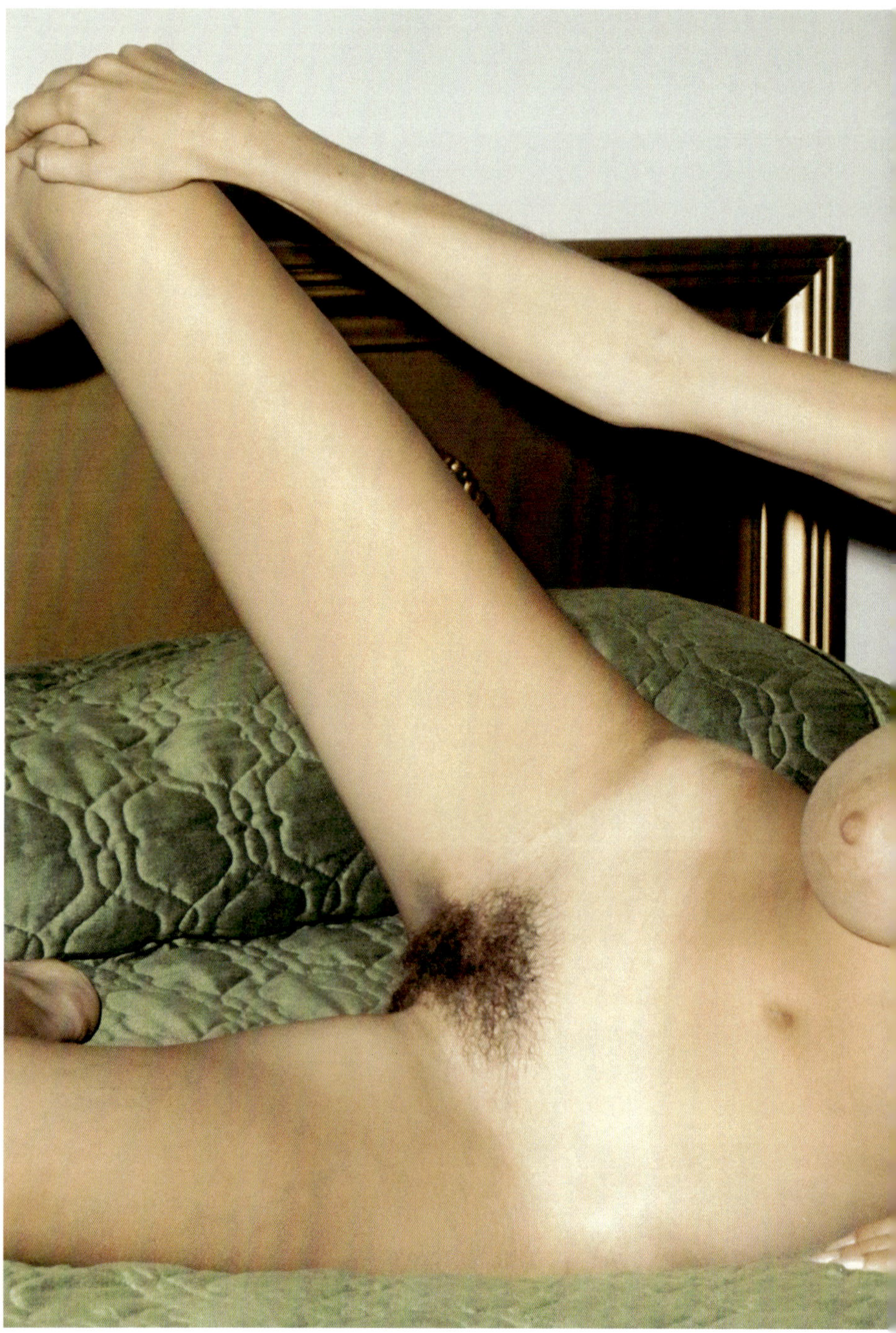

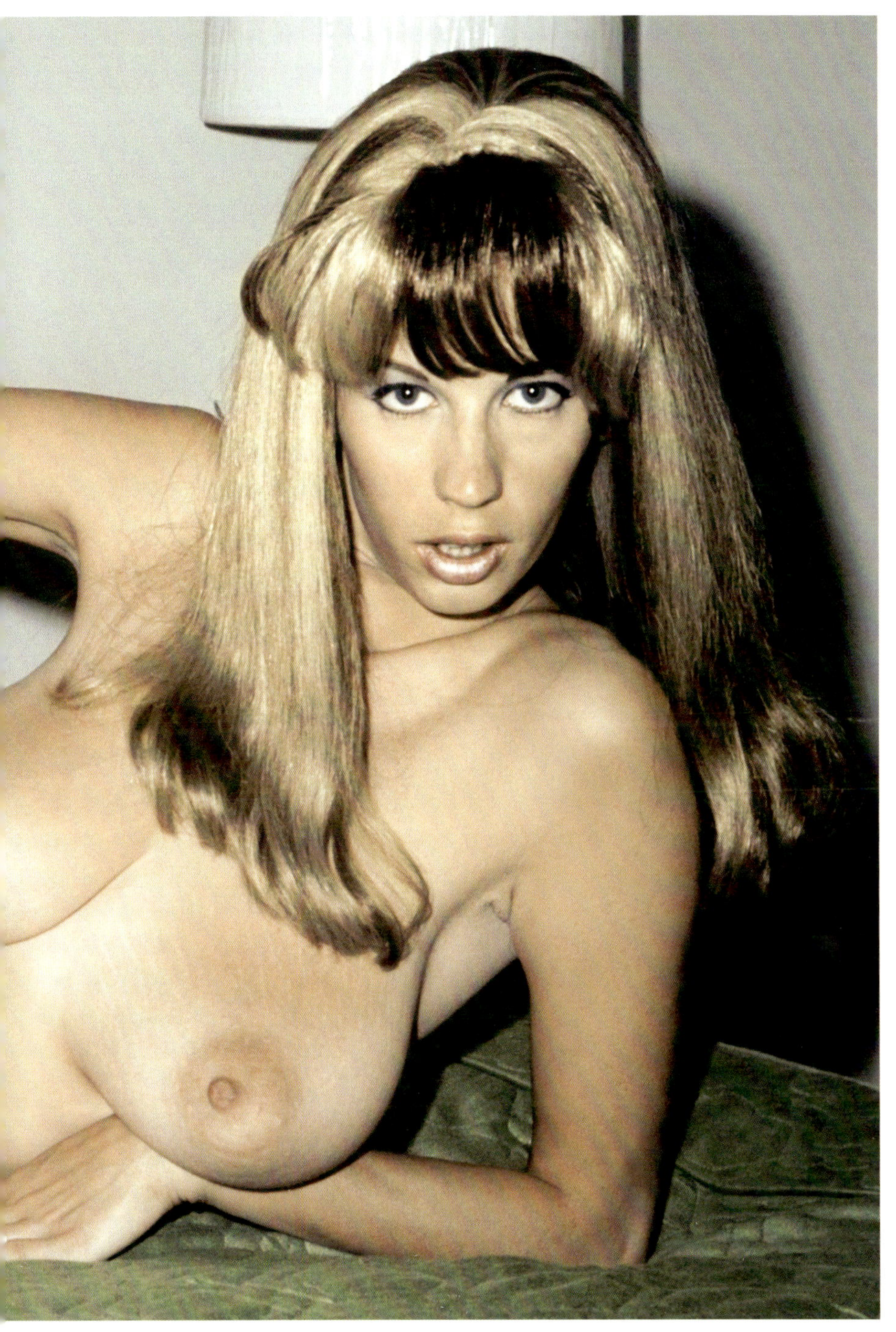

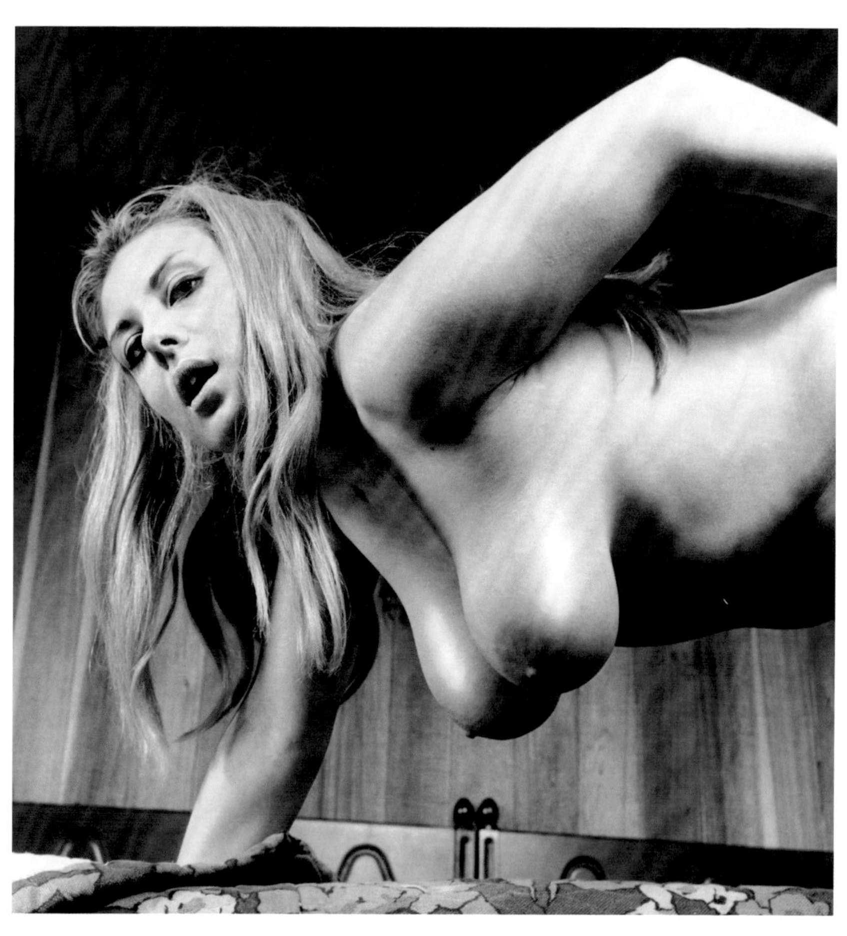

Sherry Lane

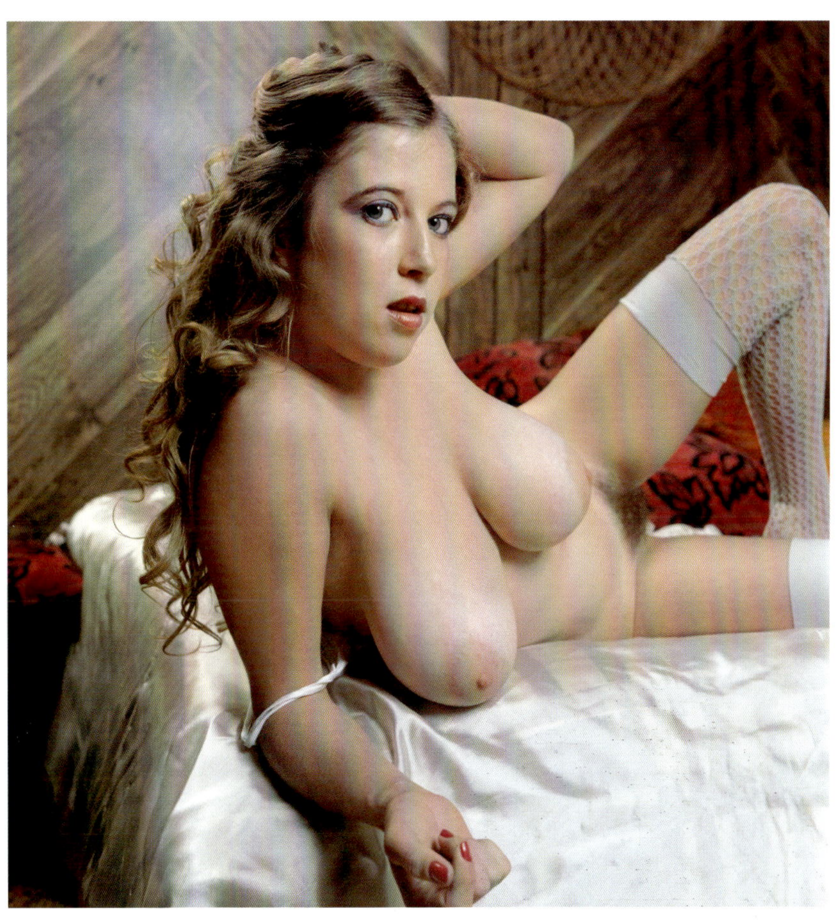

Unknown

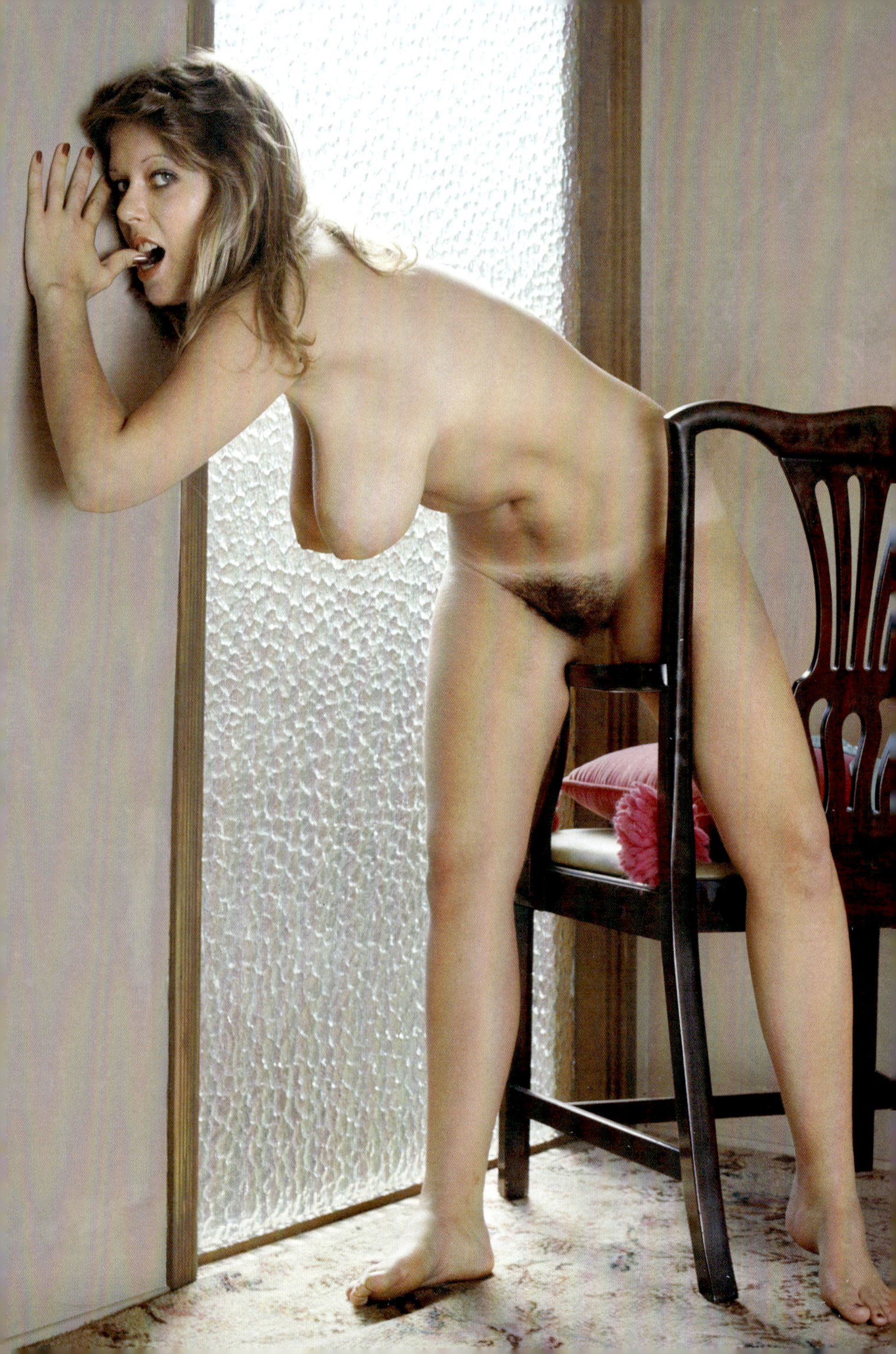

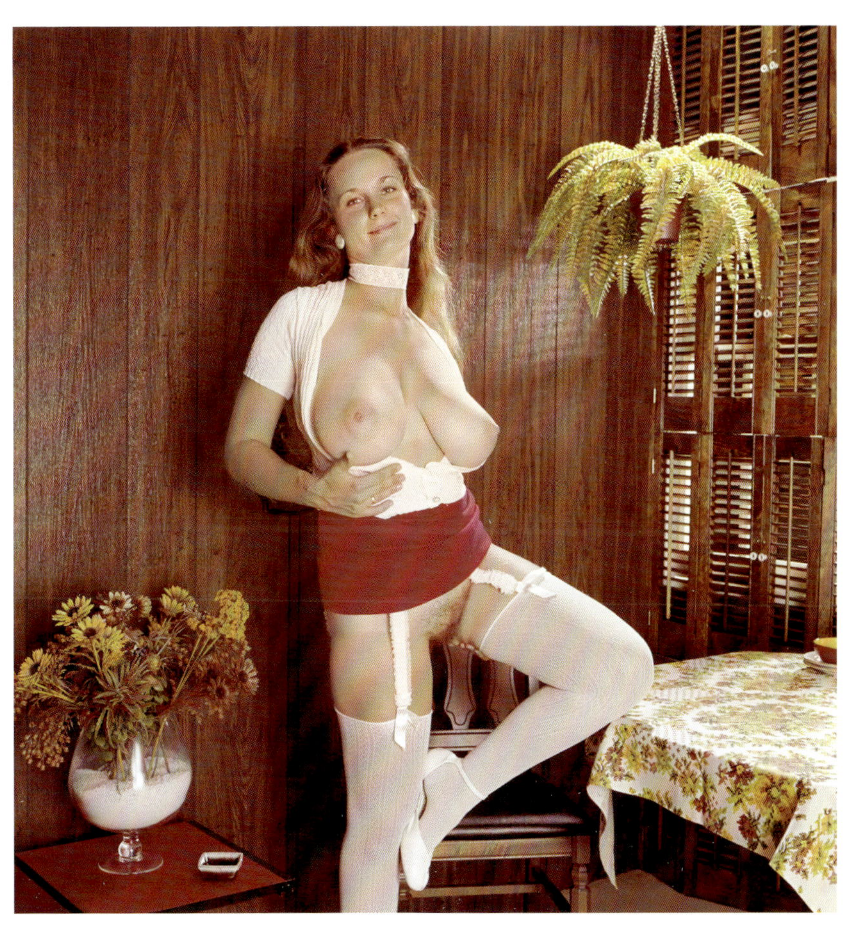

OPPOSITE Unknown ABOVE Sheryl Lipsohn PAGES 120-121 Theresa Jackman

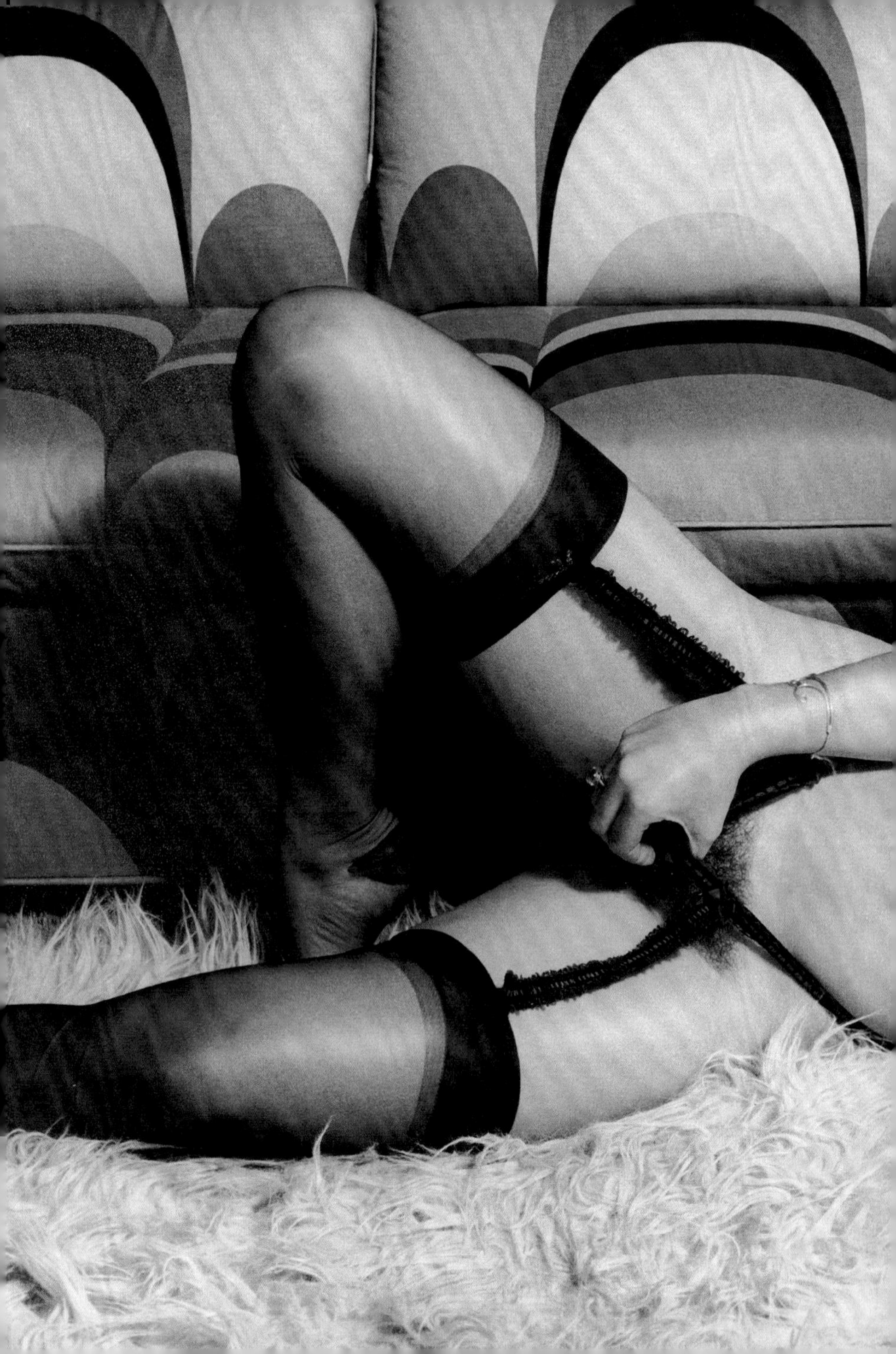

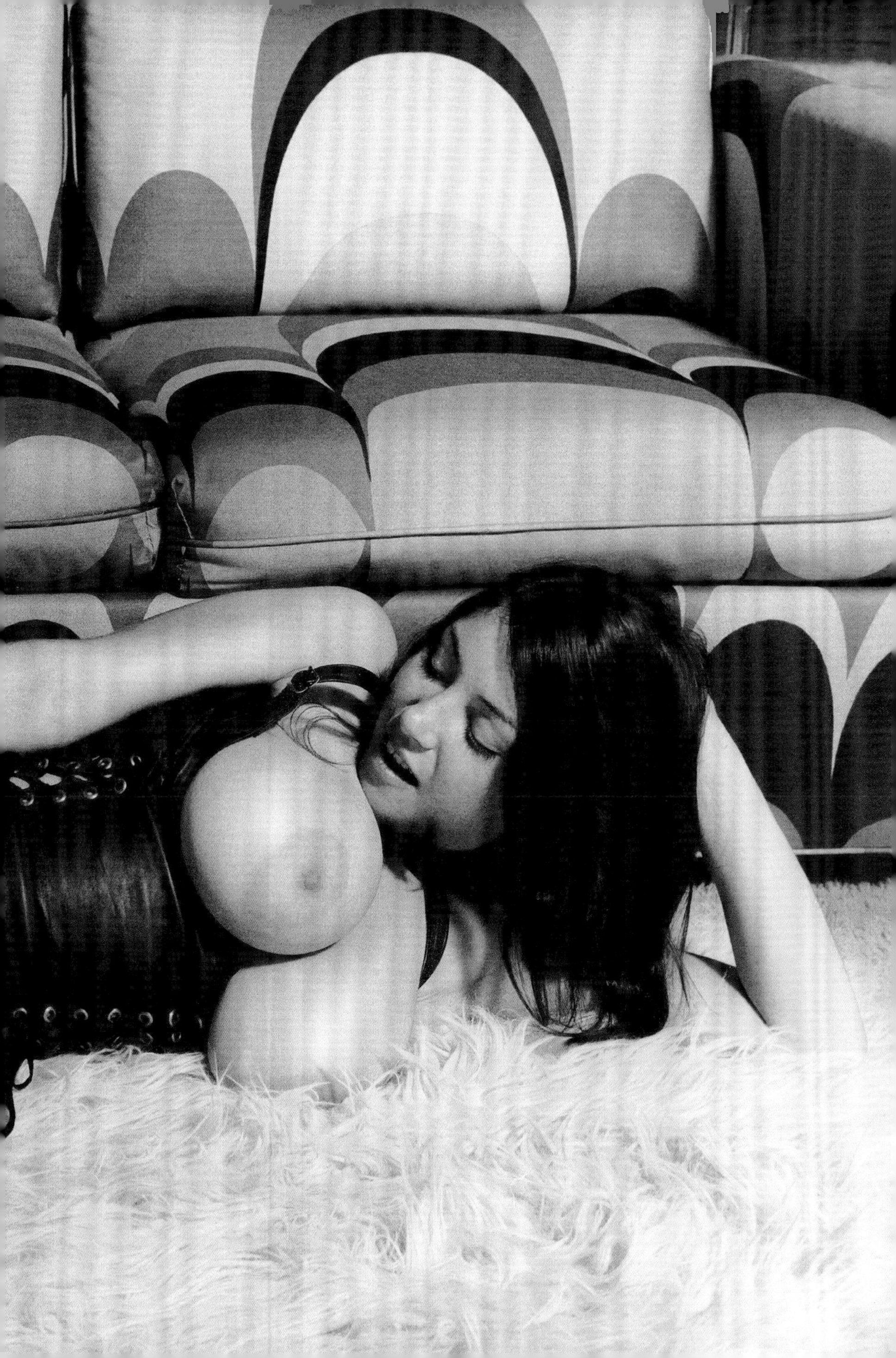

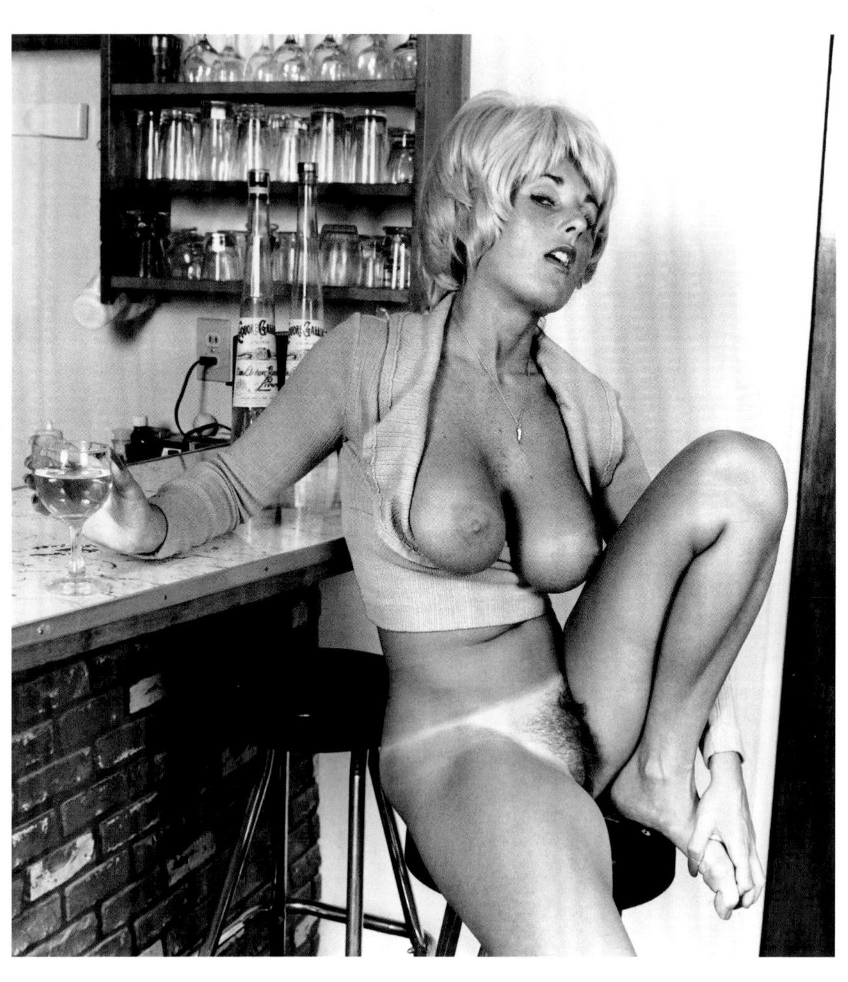

Wren Wreynolds

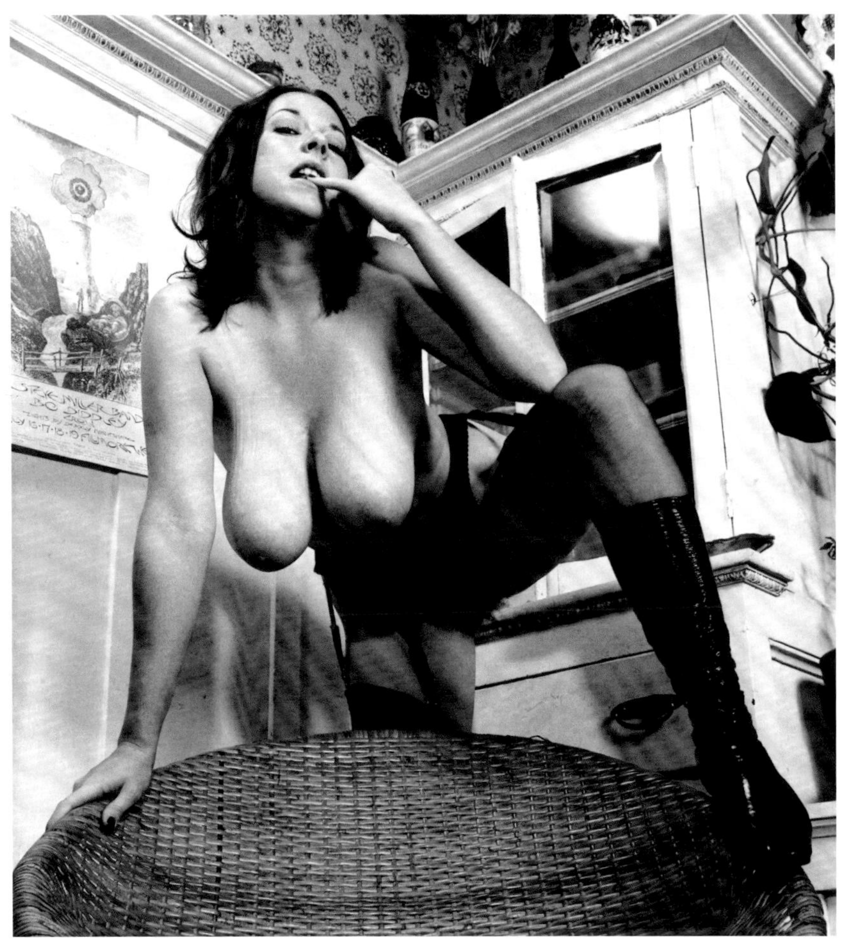

Unknown

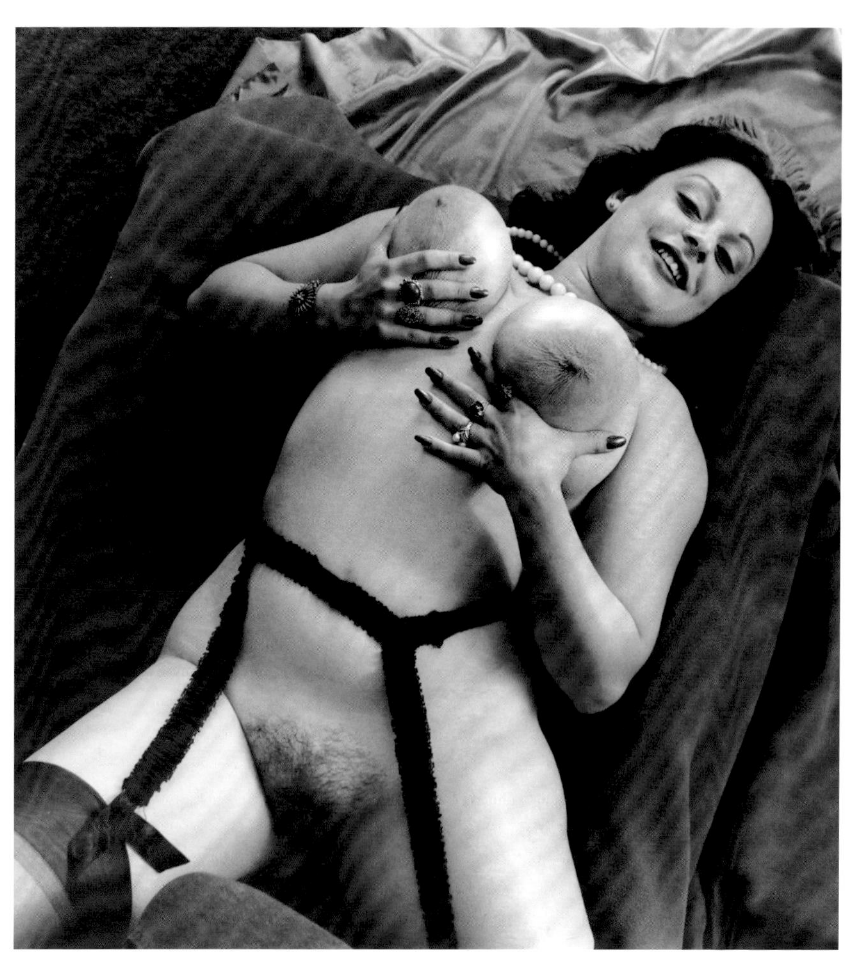

ABOVE Caroline Arroyo OPPOSITE Kristen Anderson

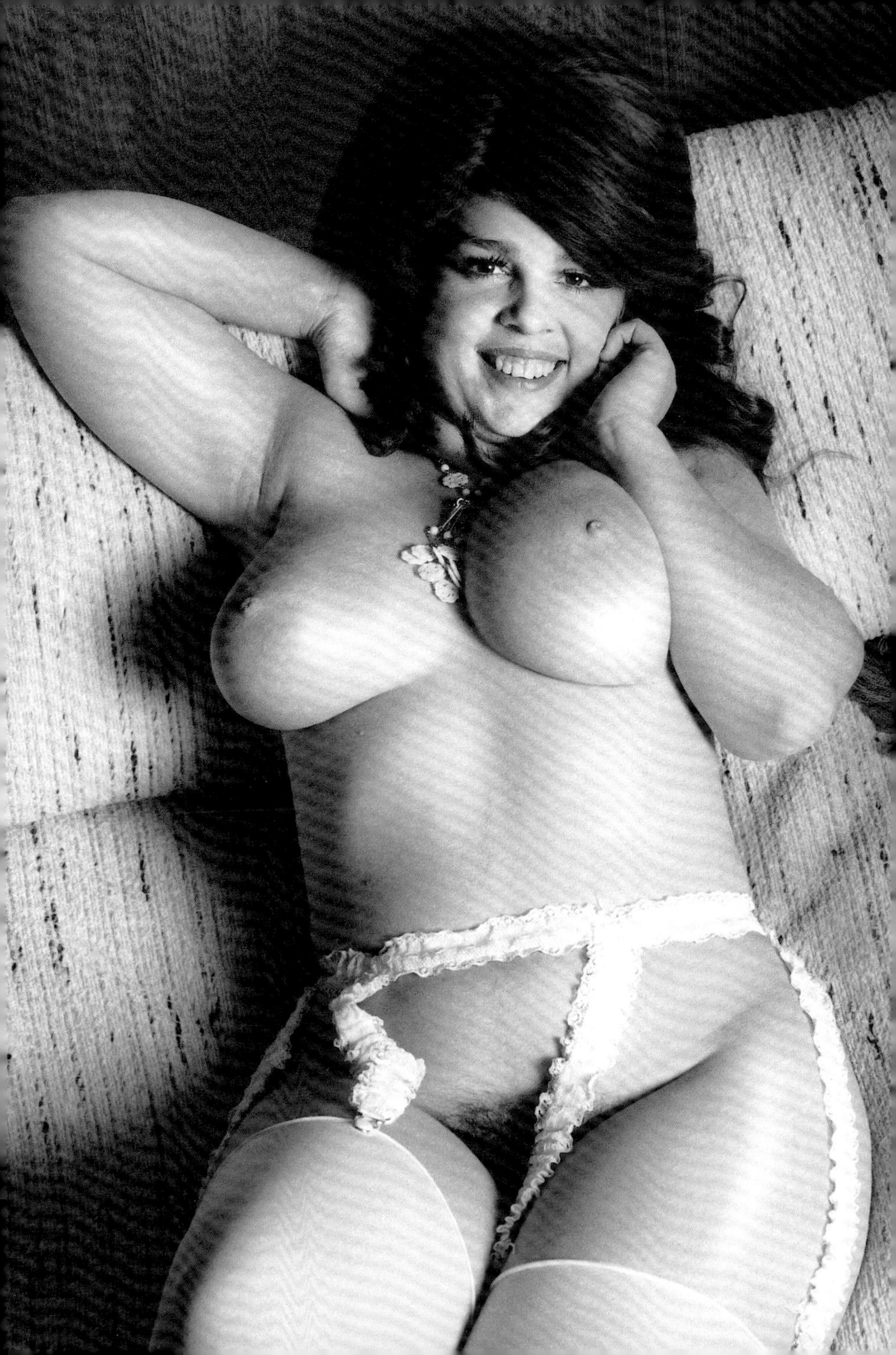

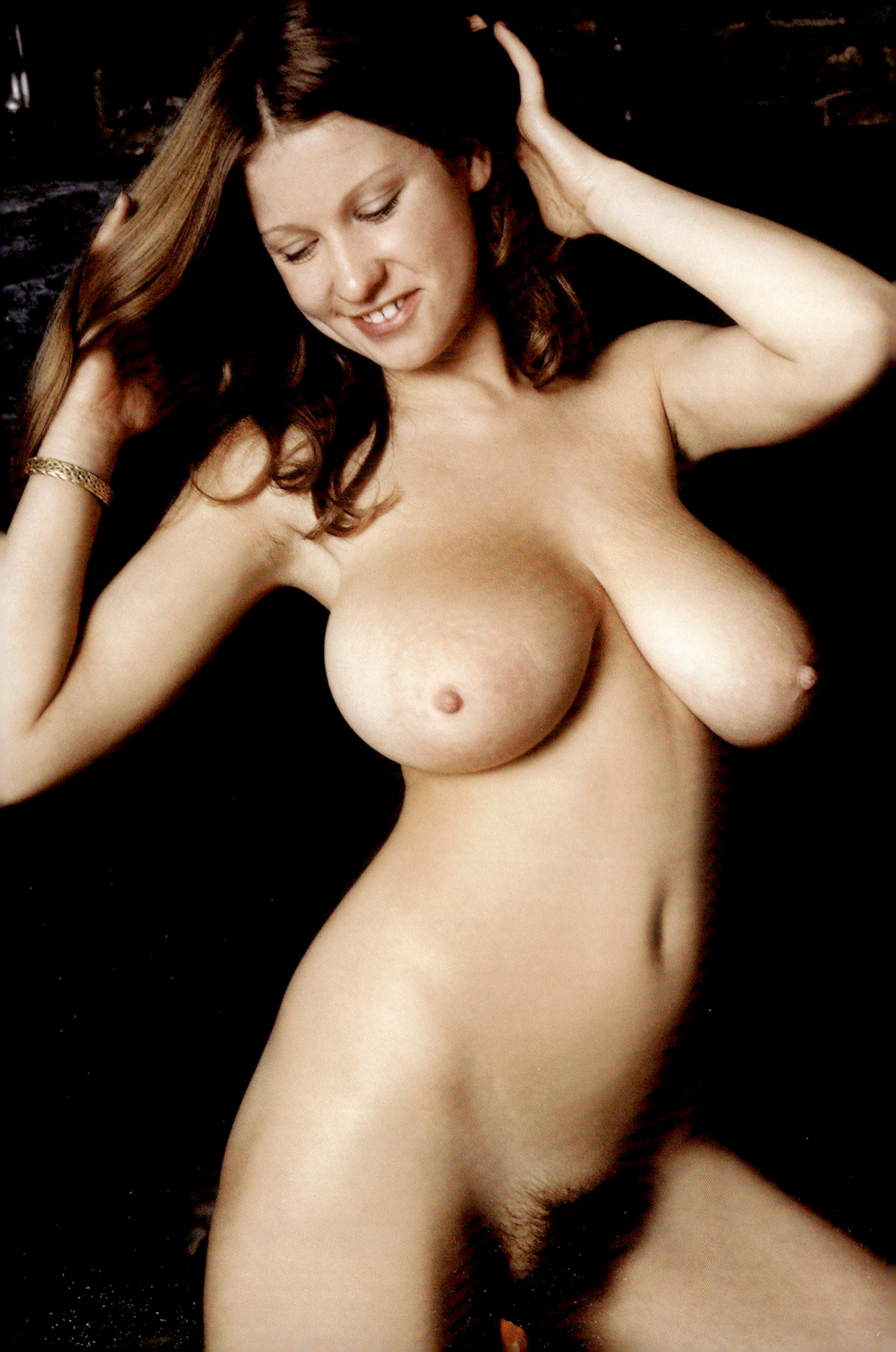

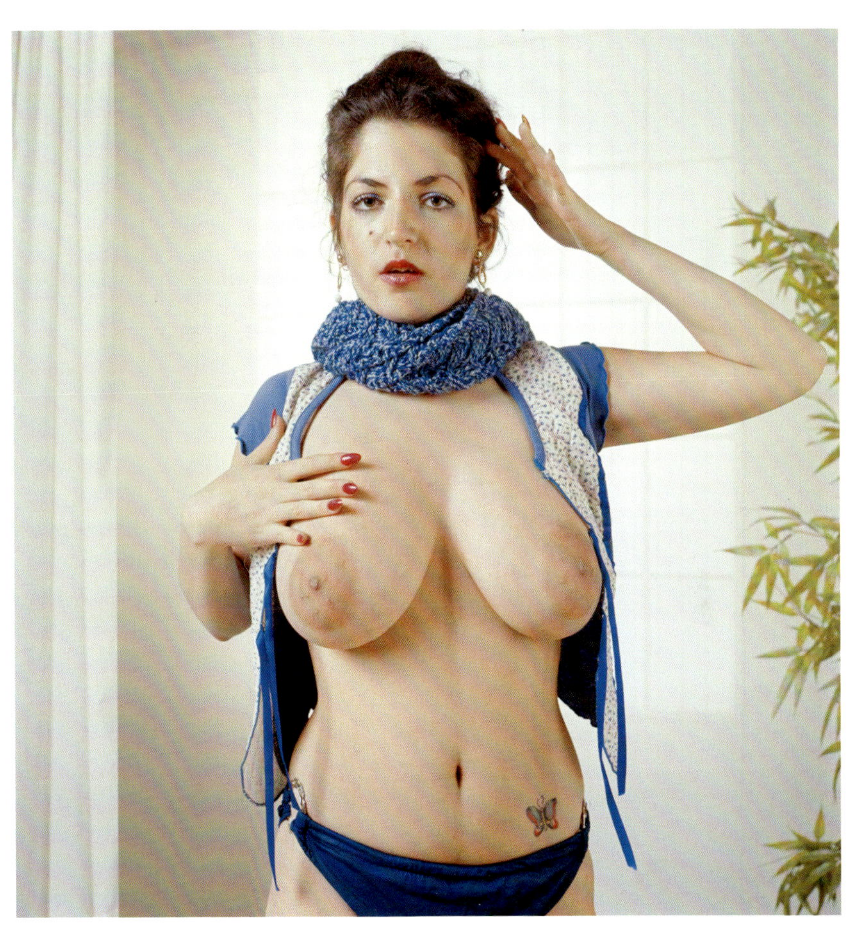

OPPOSITE Roberta Pedon ABOVE Unknown

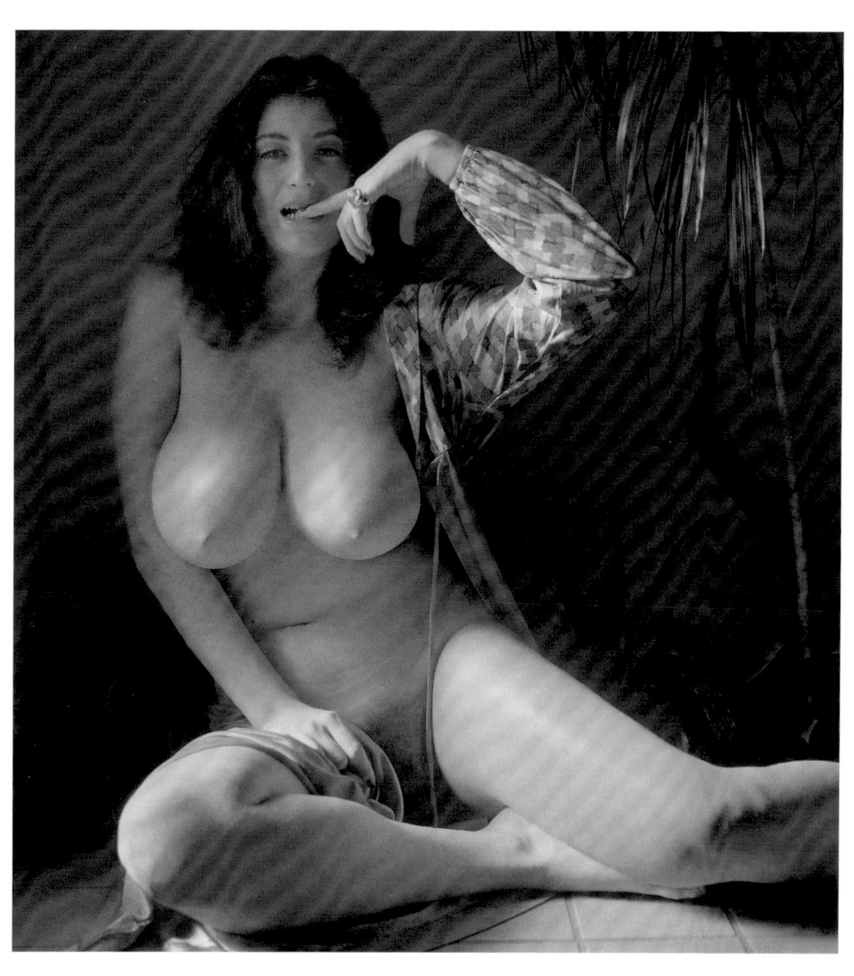

Michelle Weiner

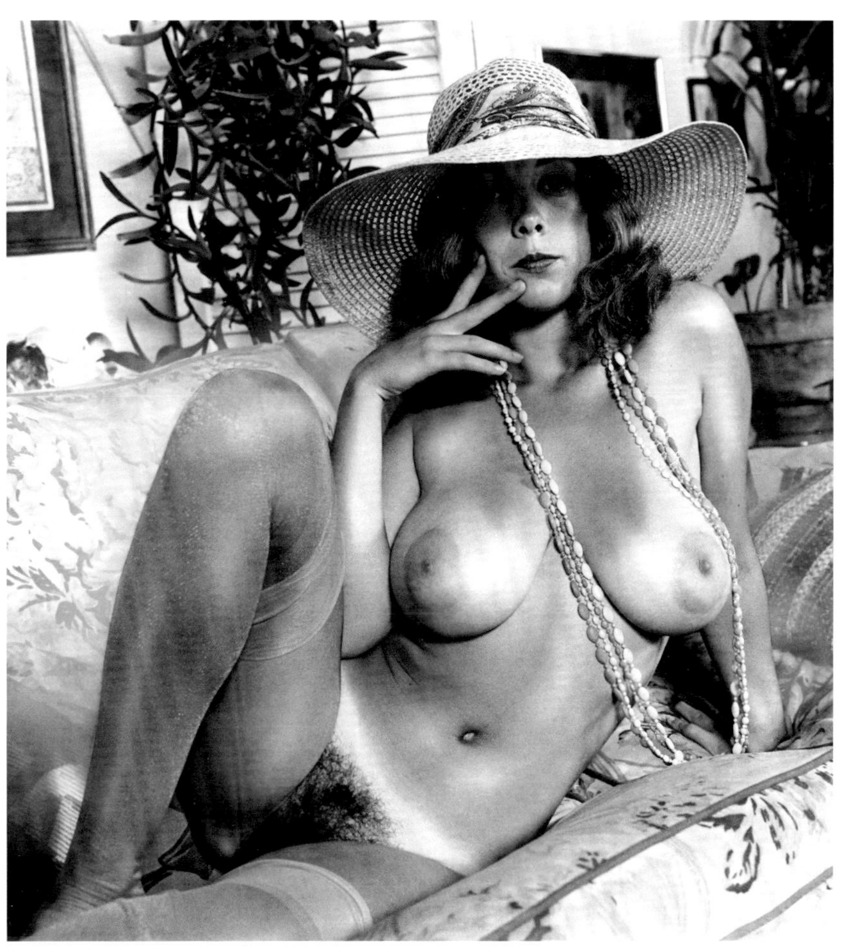

Christine DeShaffer

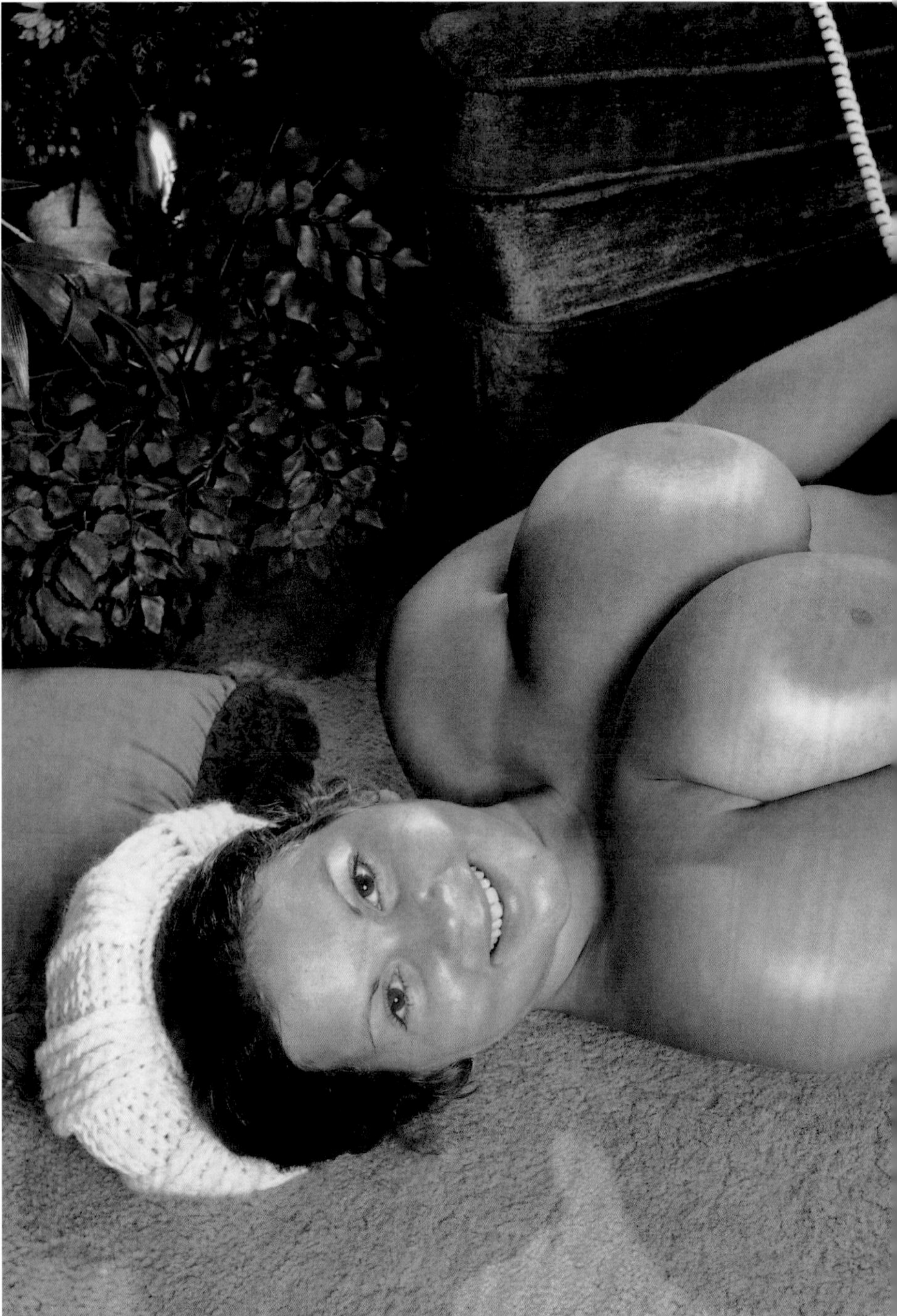

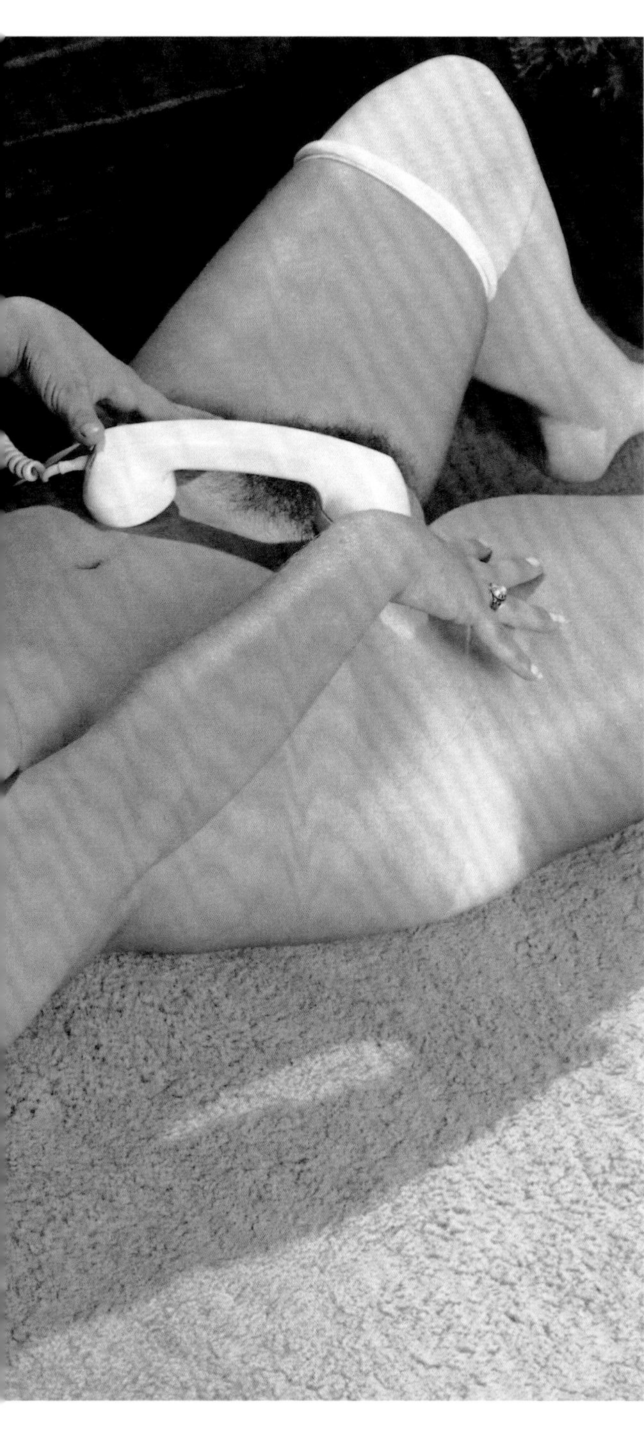

Karen Brown

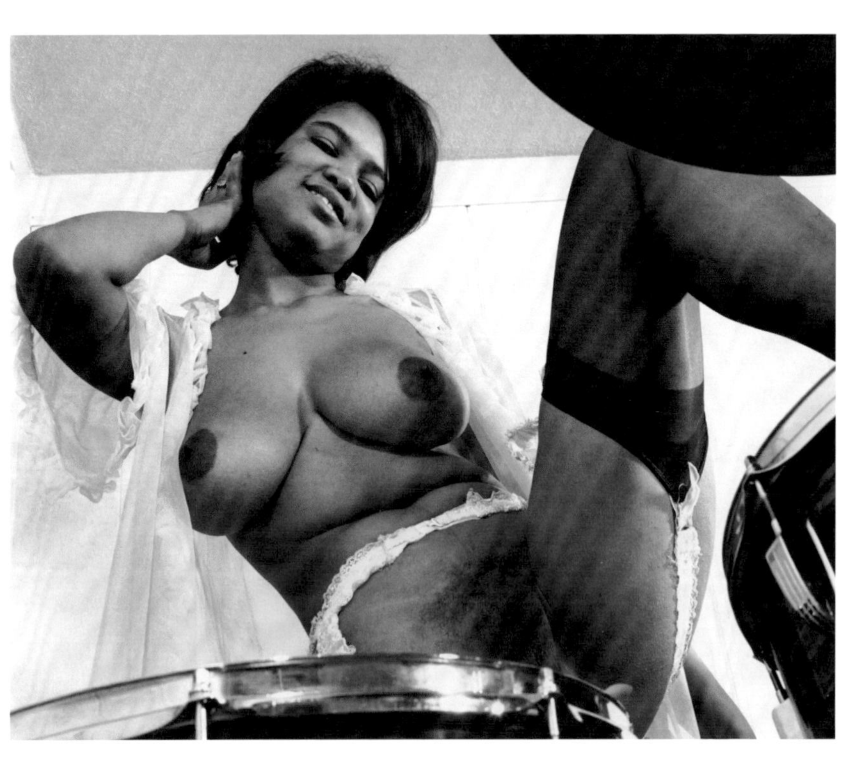

ABOVE Mia Coco OPPOSITE Sari Saevitz

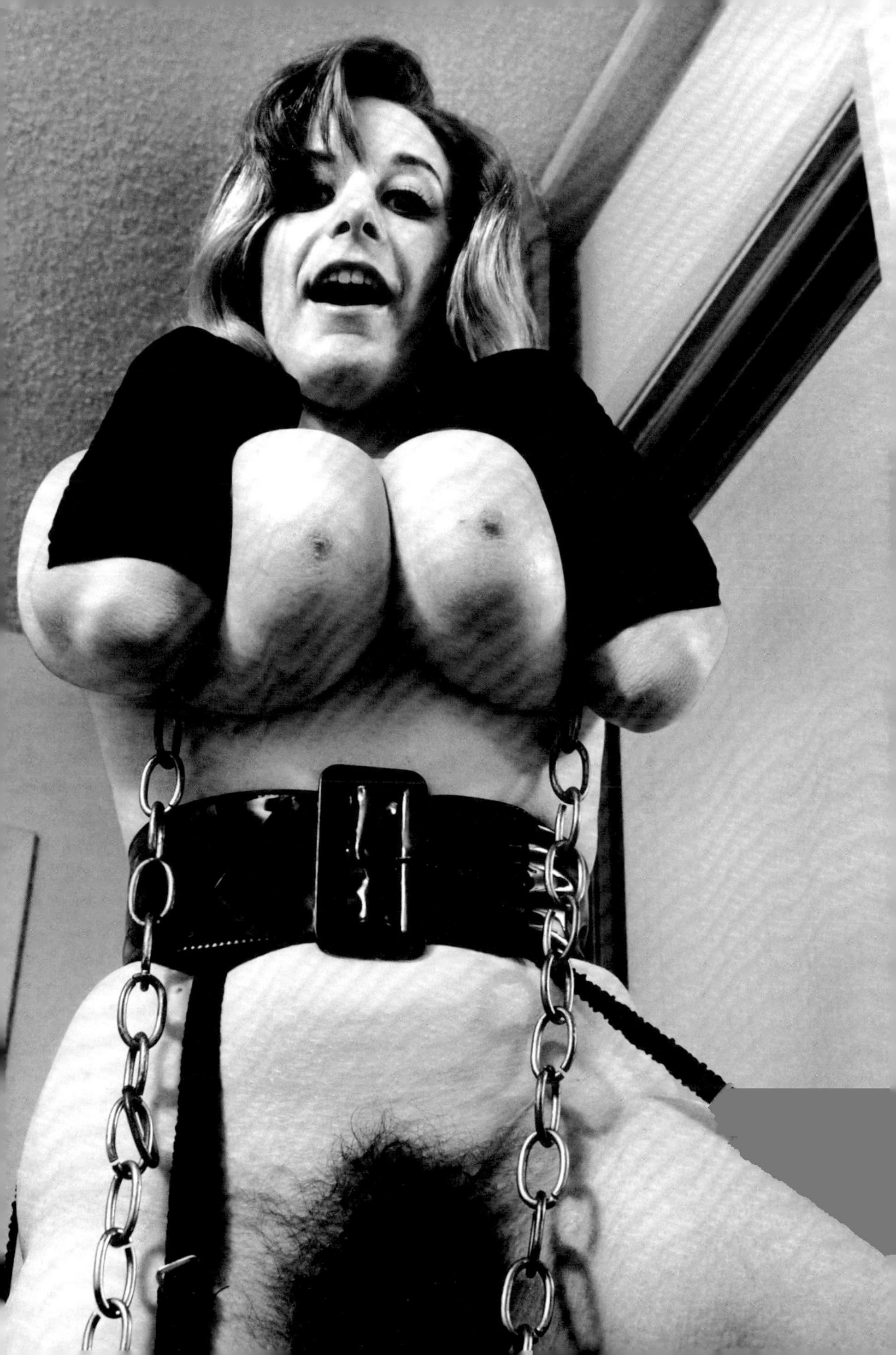

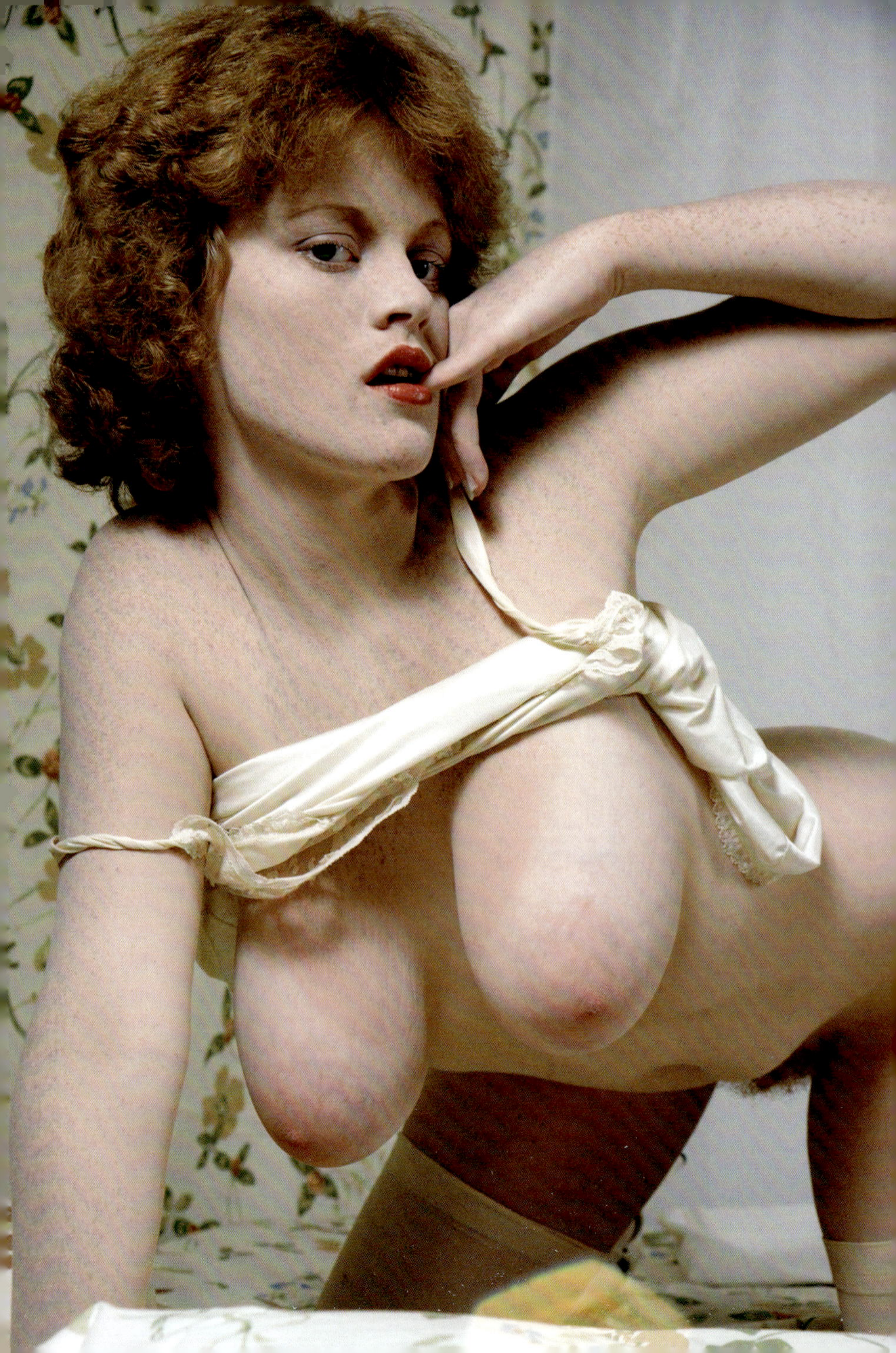

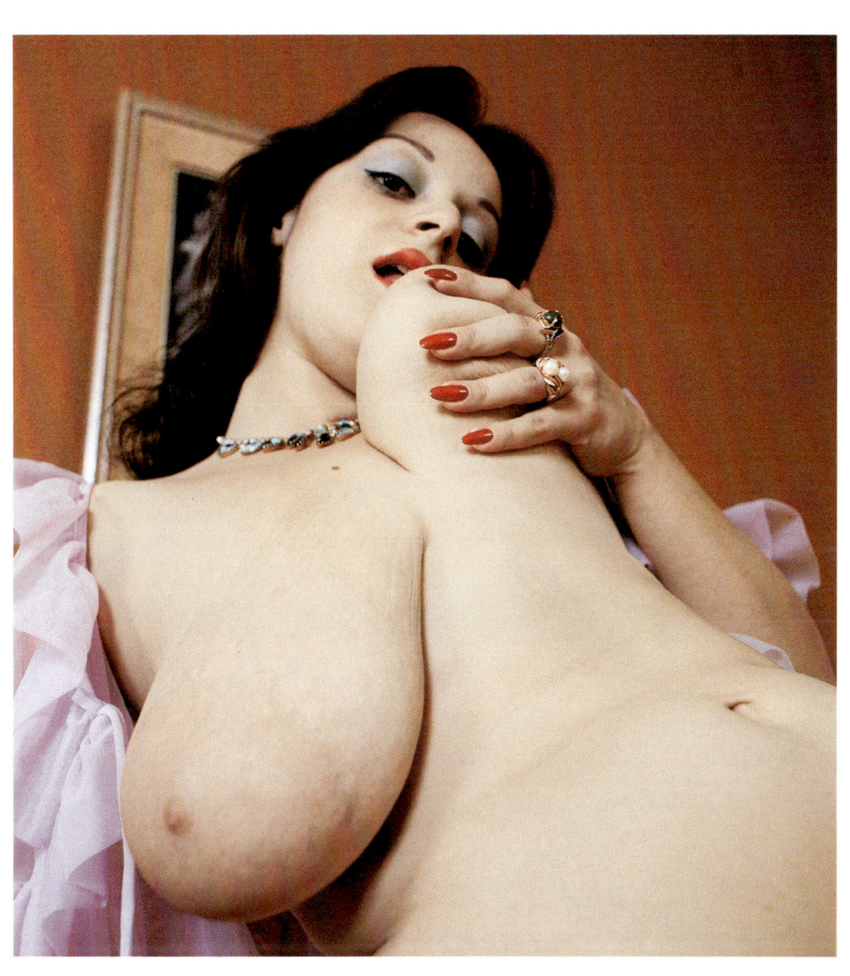

OPPOSITE Lisa DeLeeuw ABOVE Unknown PAGES 136-137 Sylvia McFarland

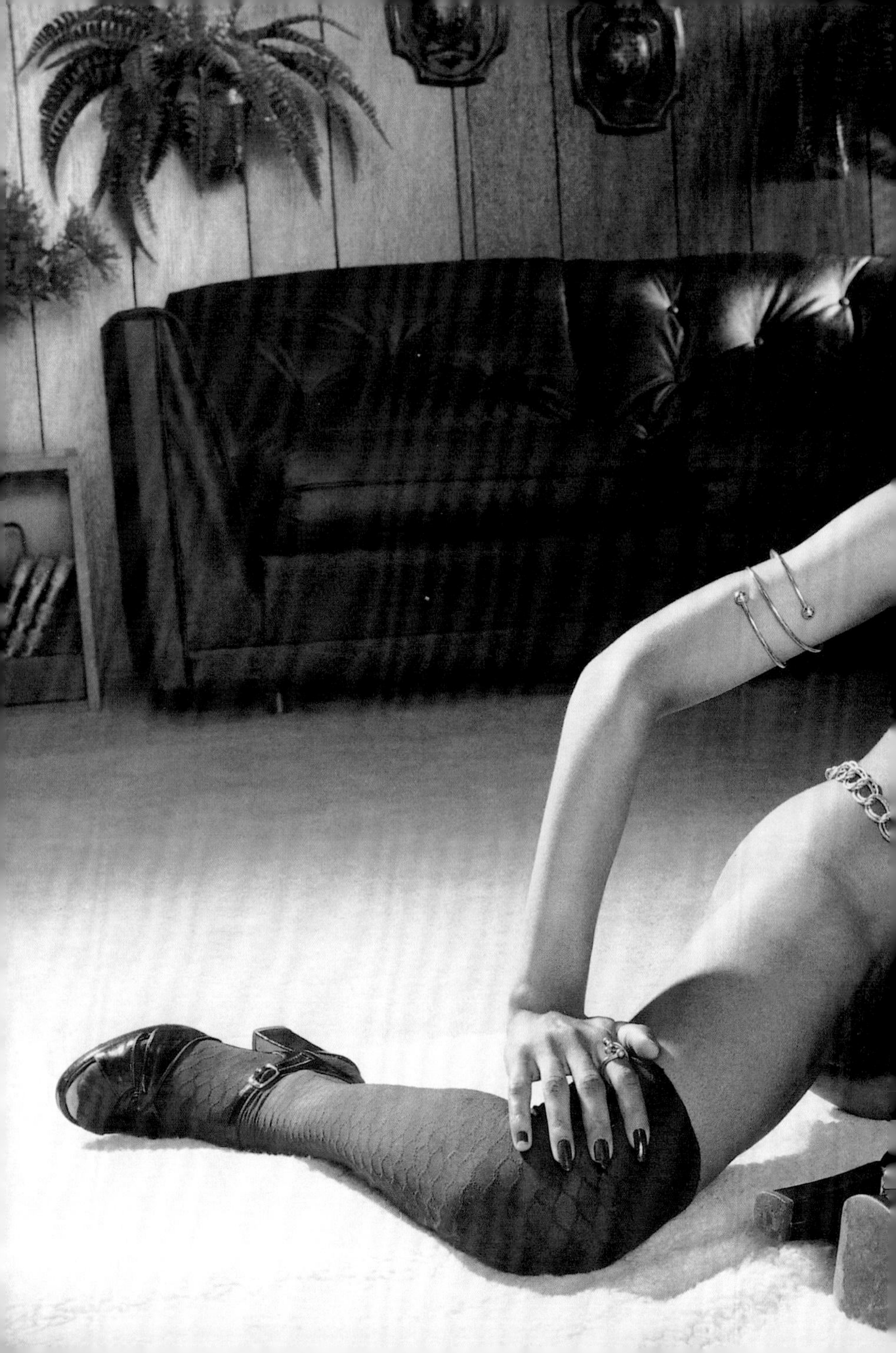

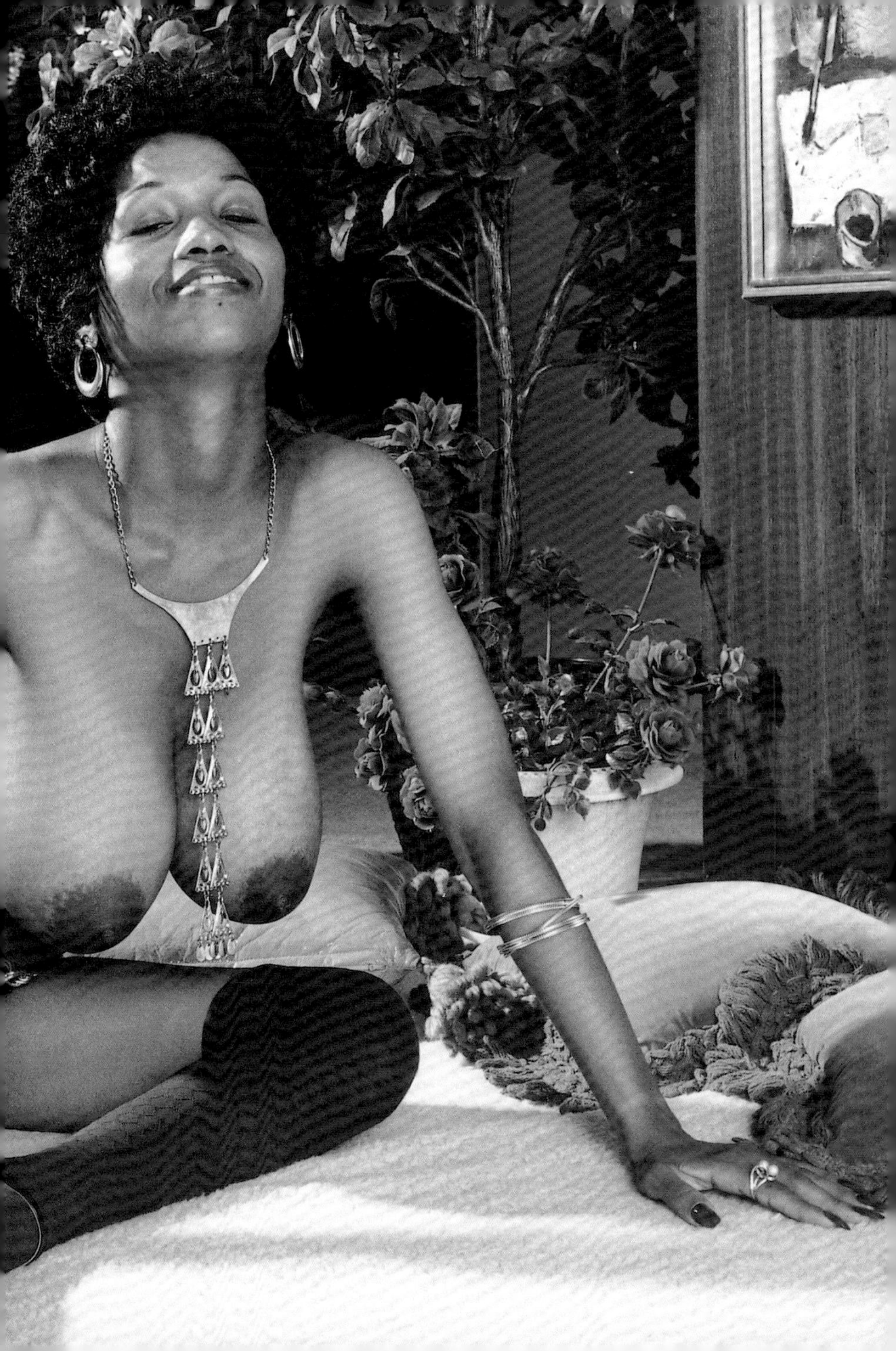

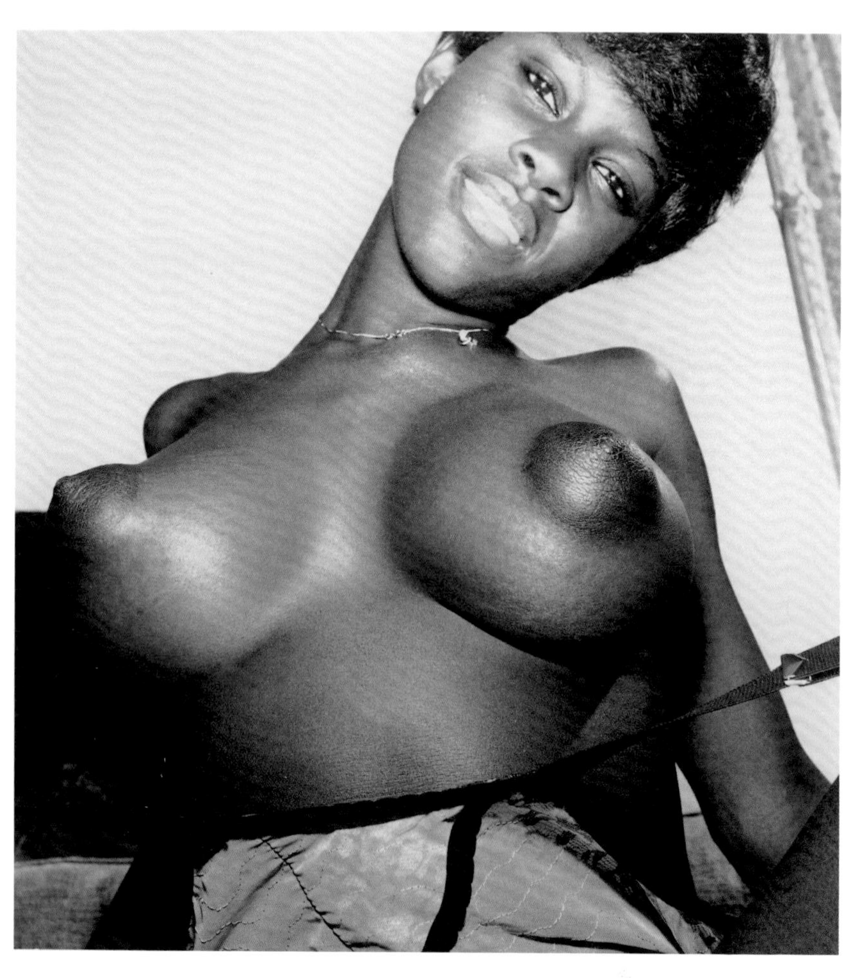

Regina Christian

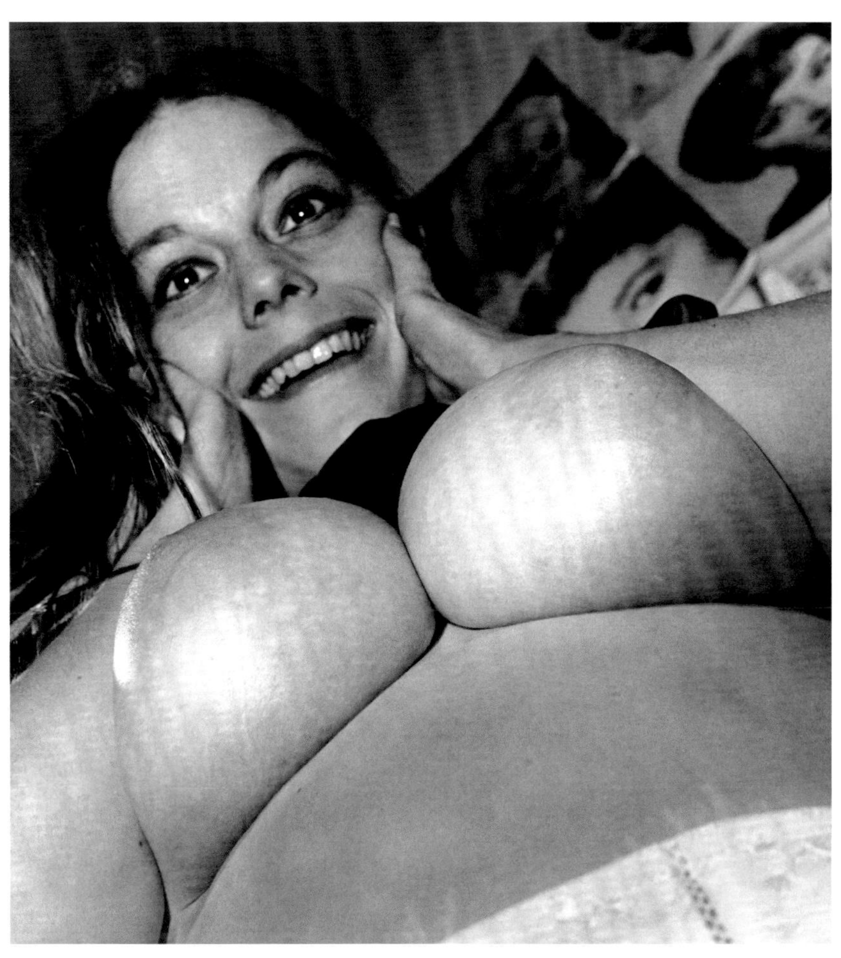

Carol Habberly

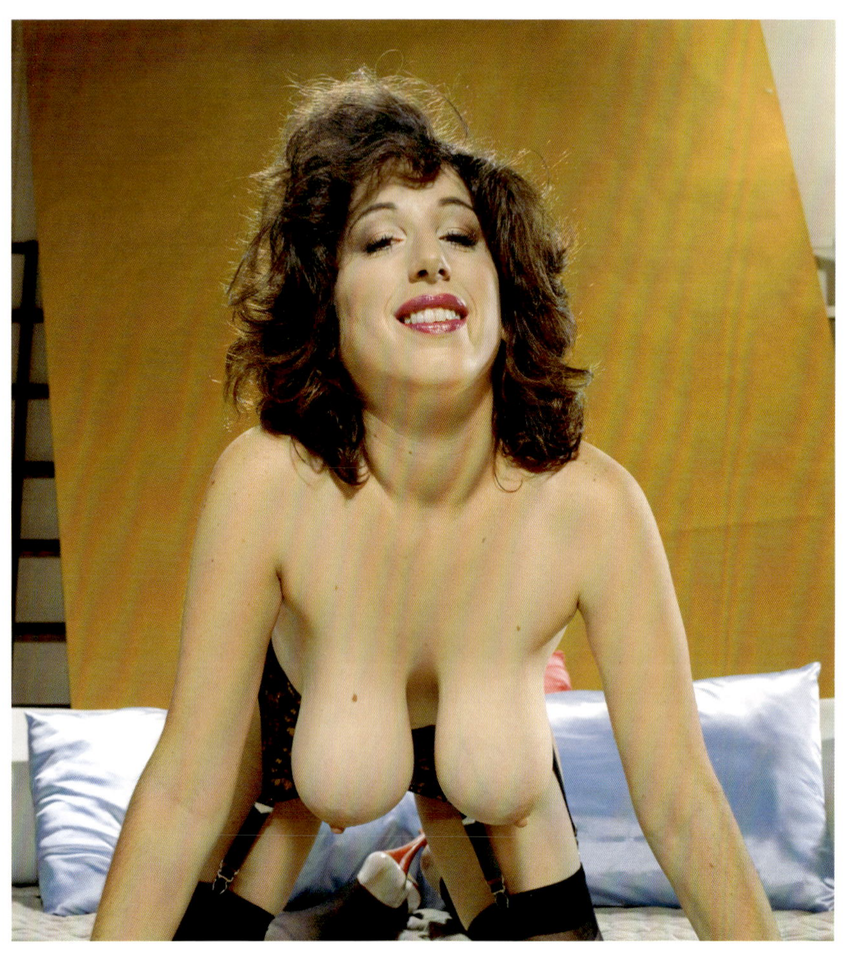

Unknown

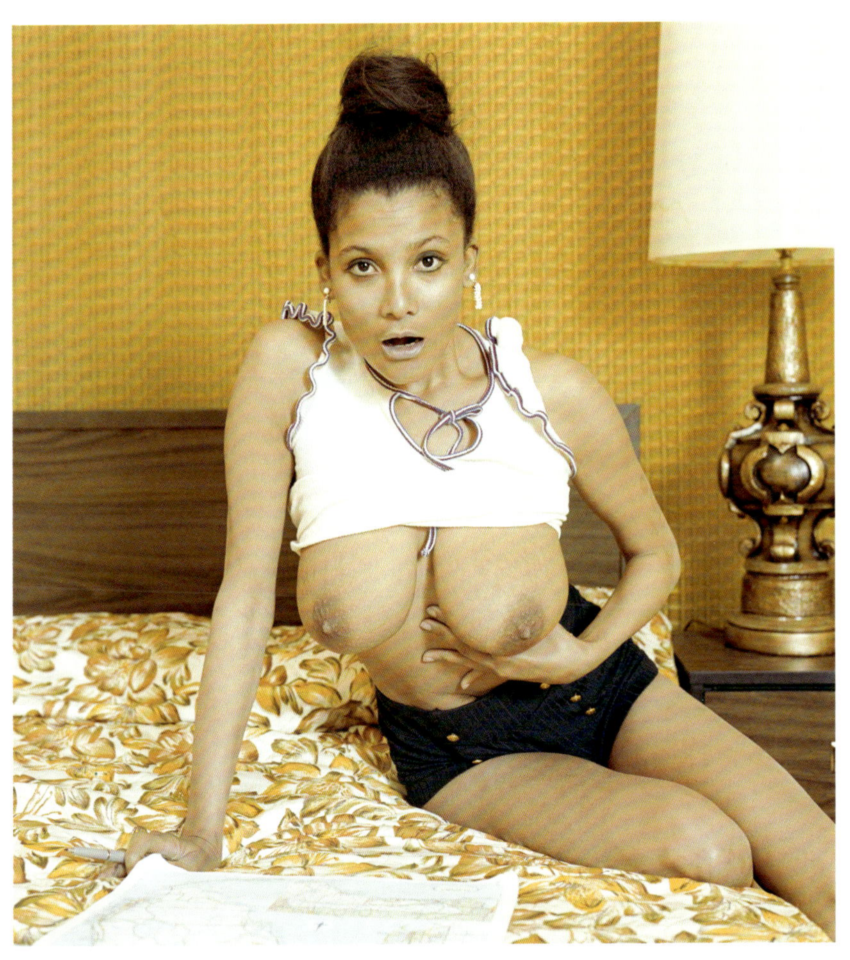

Unknown

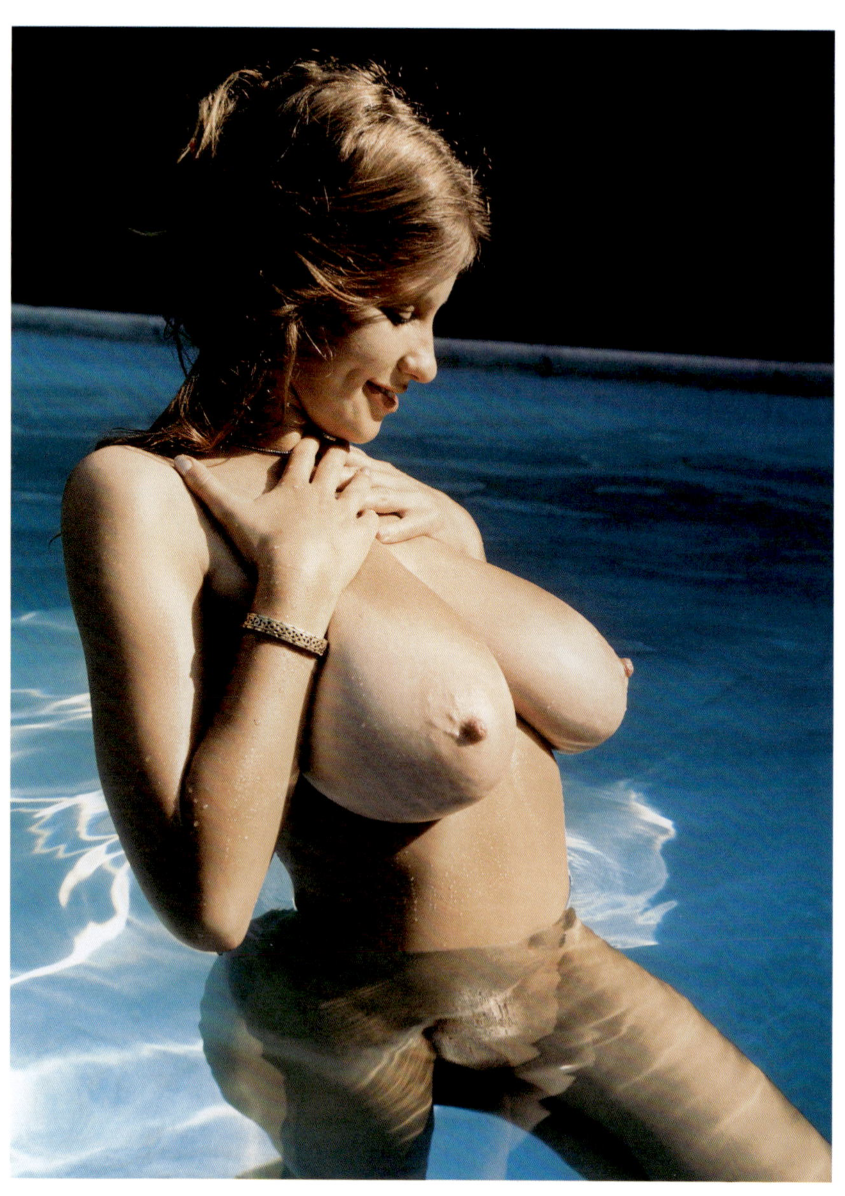

ABOVE Roberta Pedon OPPOSITE Mary Jane Wolfson PAGES 144-145 Sam

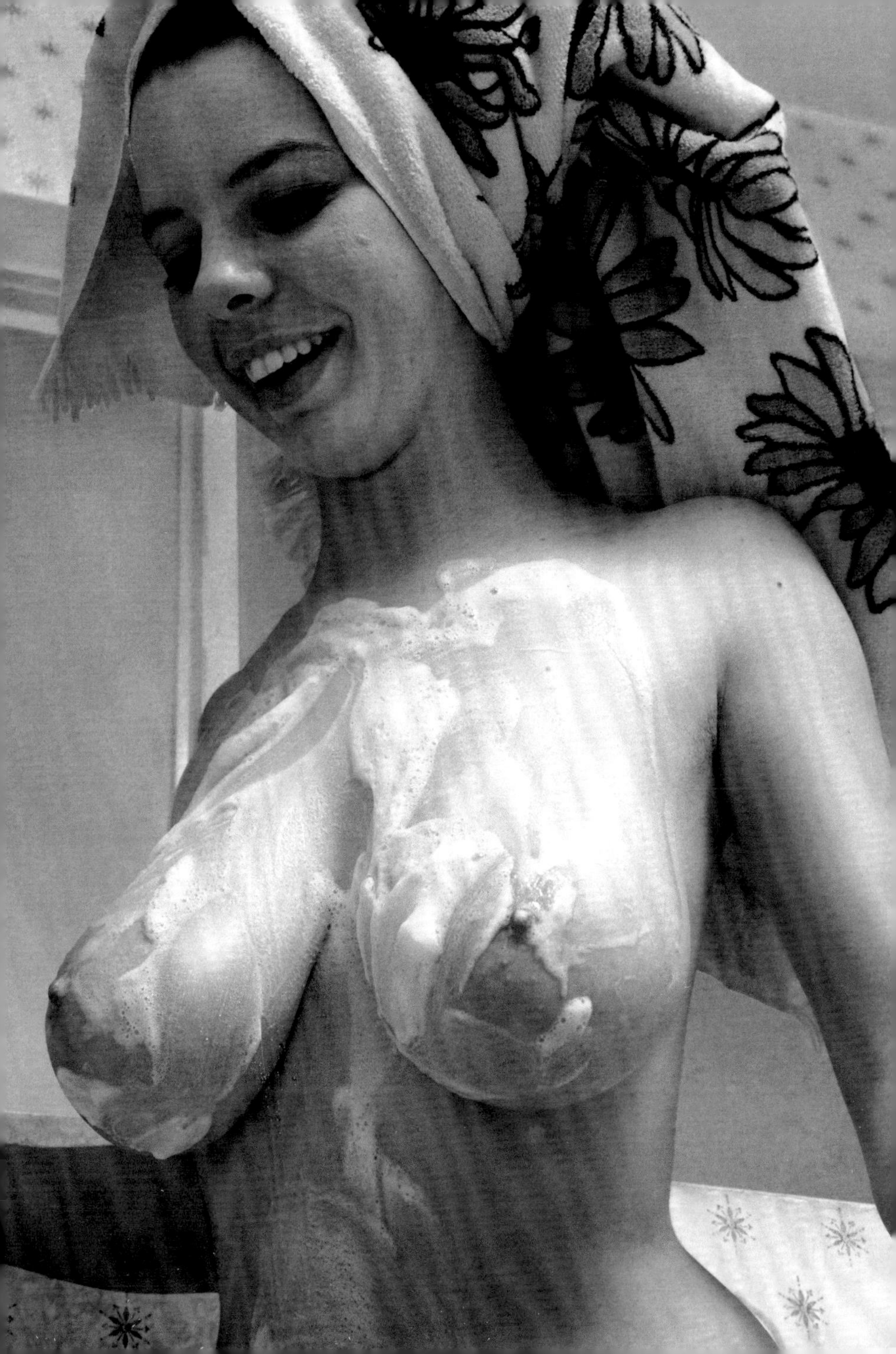

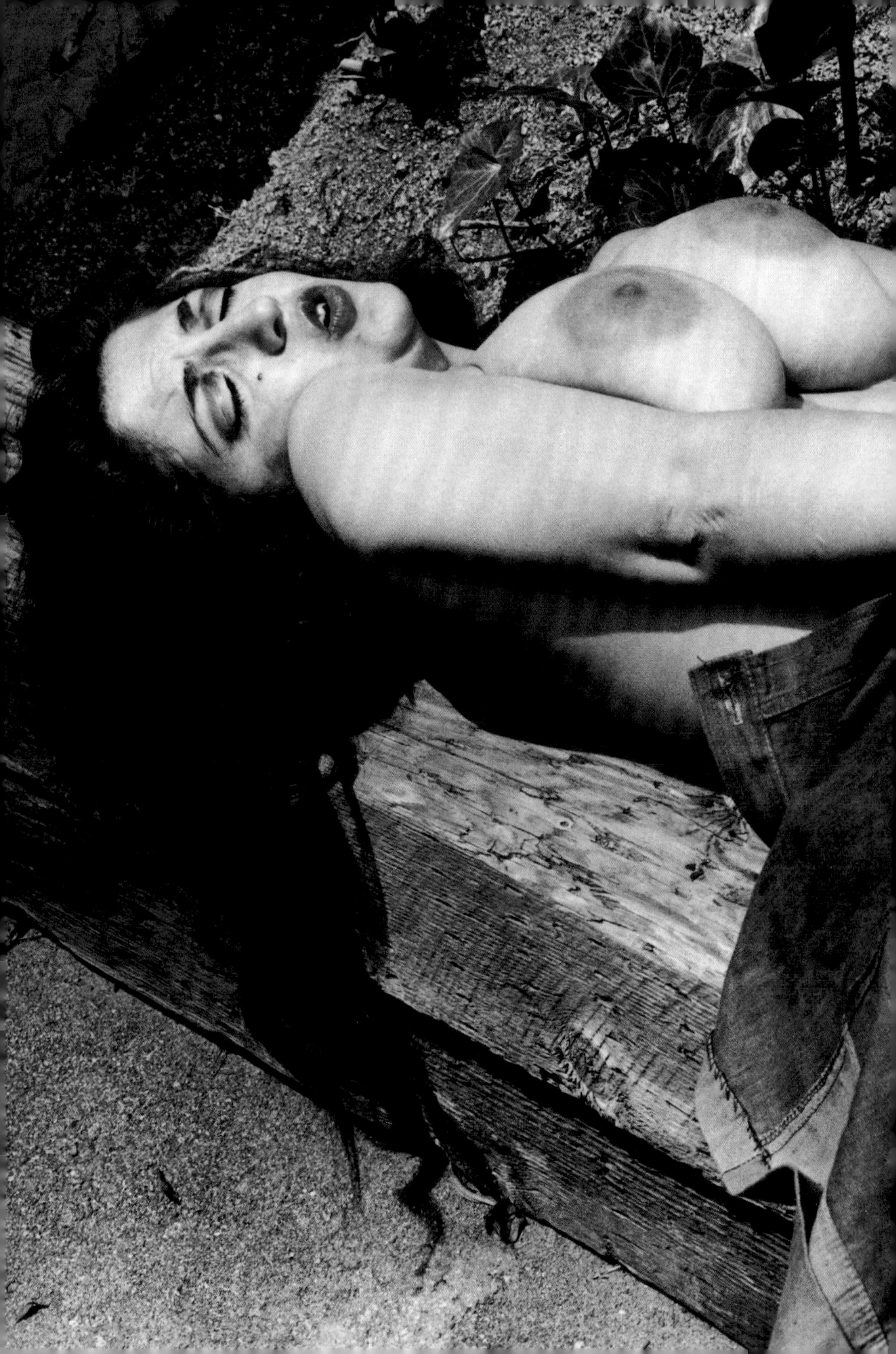

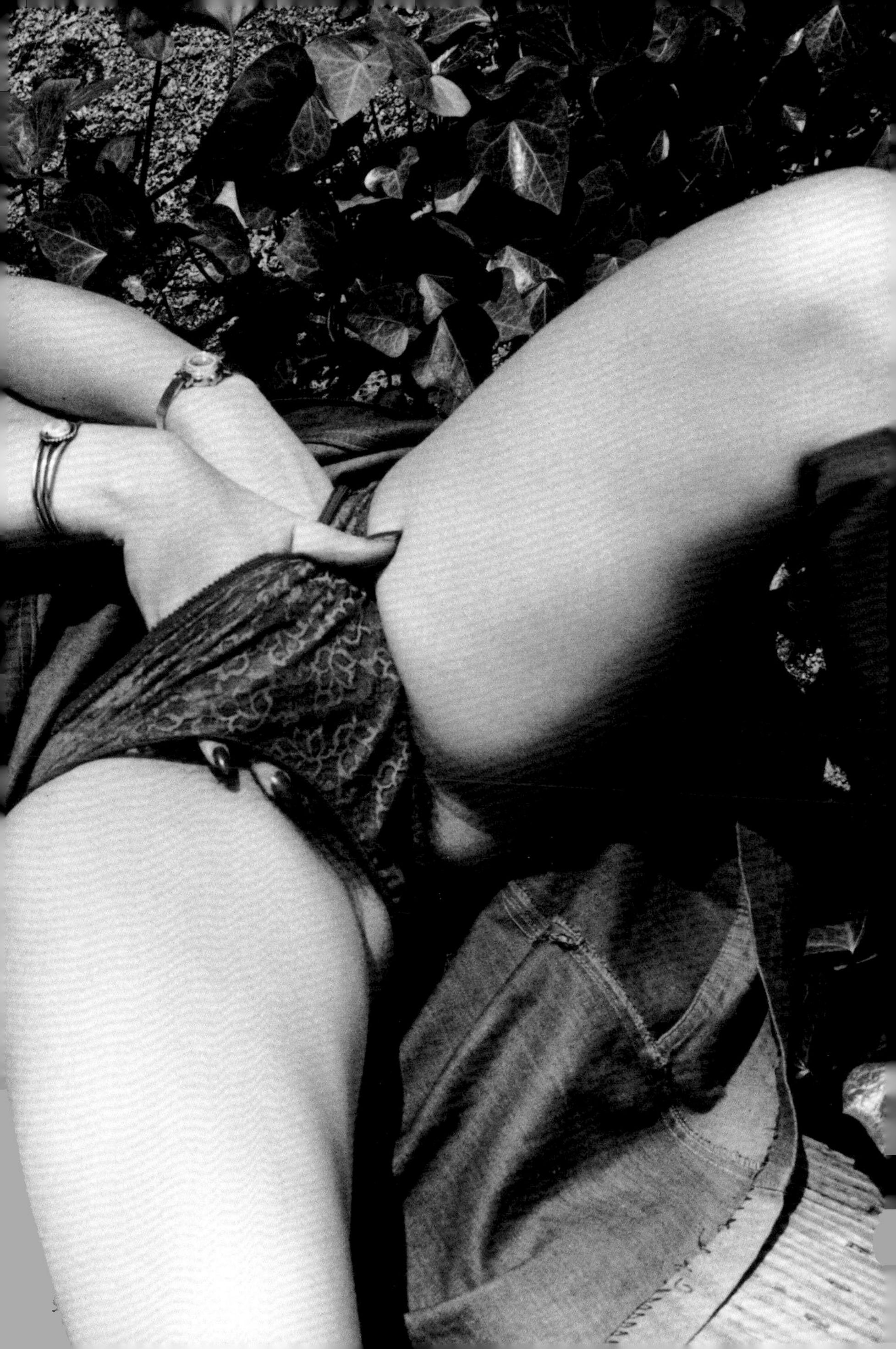

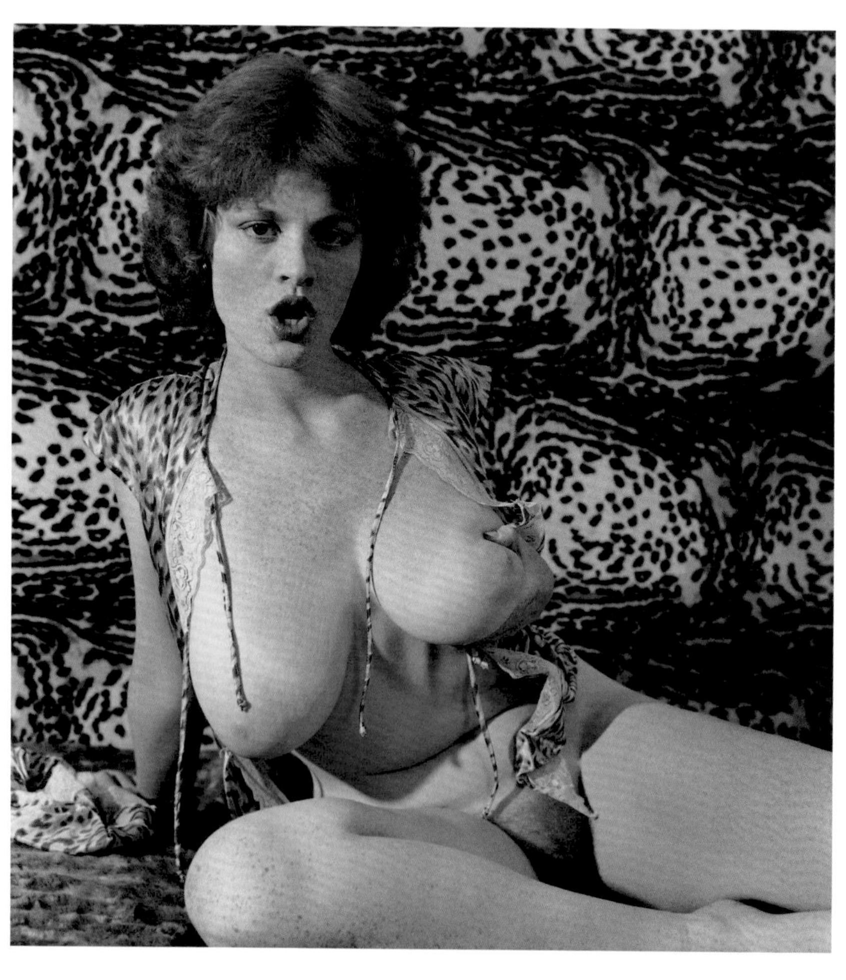

ABOVE Lisa DeLeeuw OPPOSITE Janis Hurst

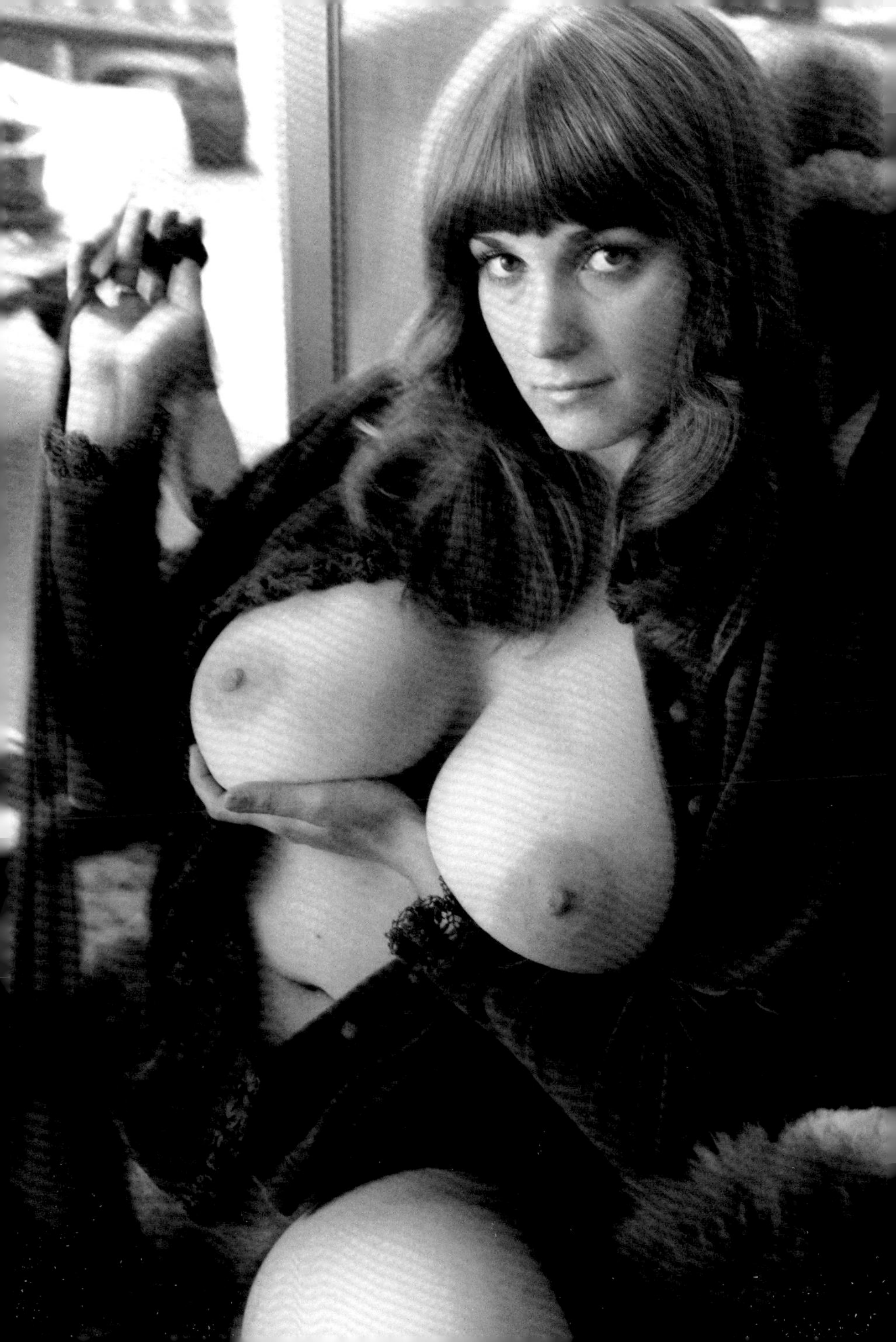

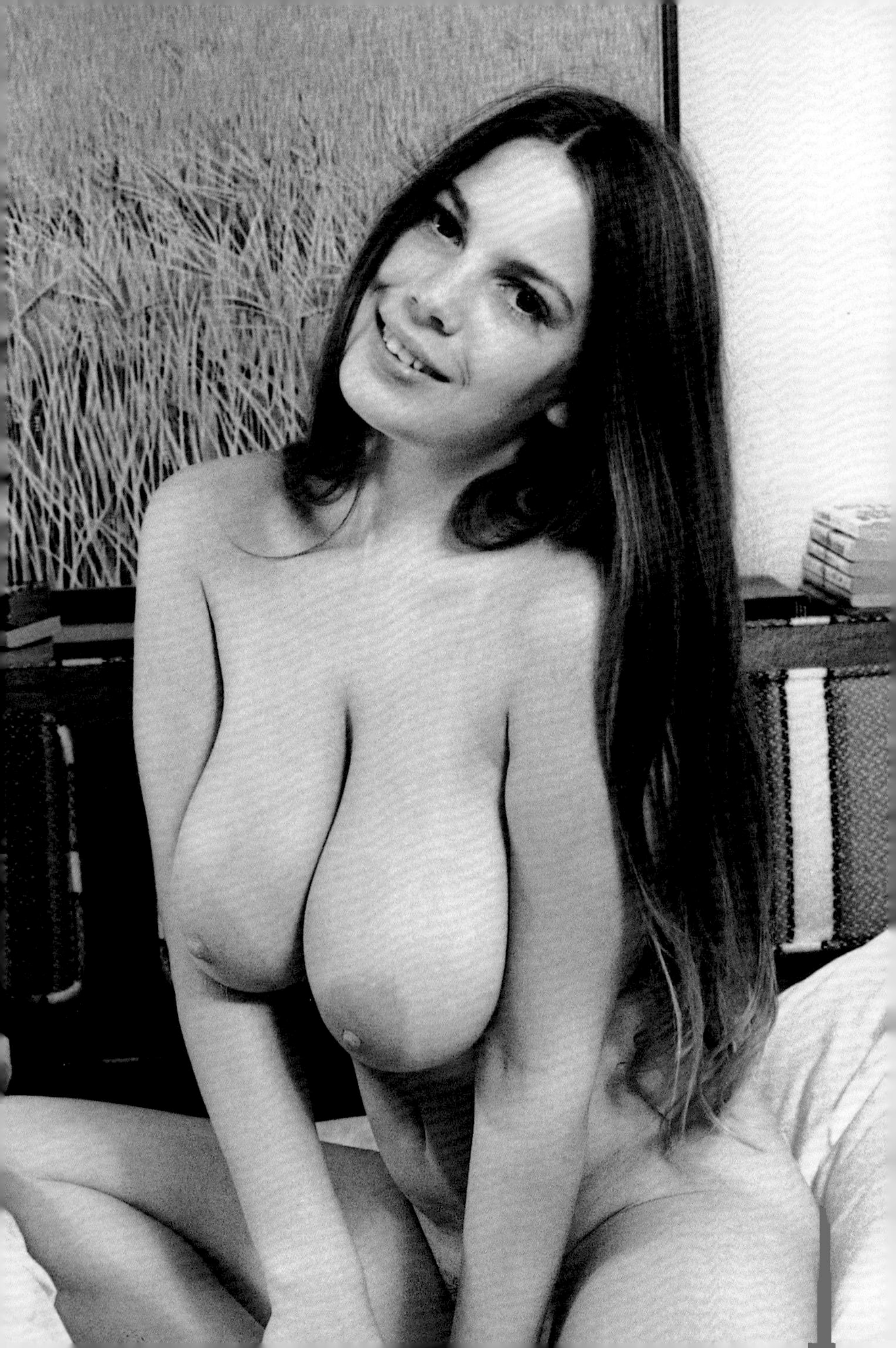

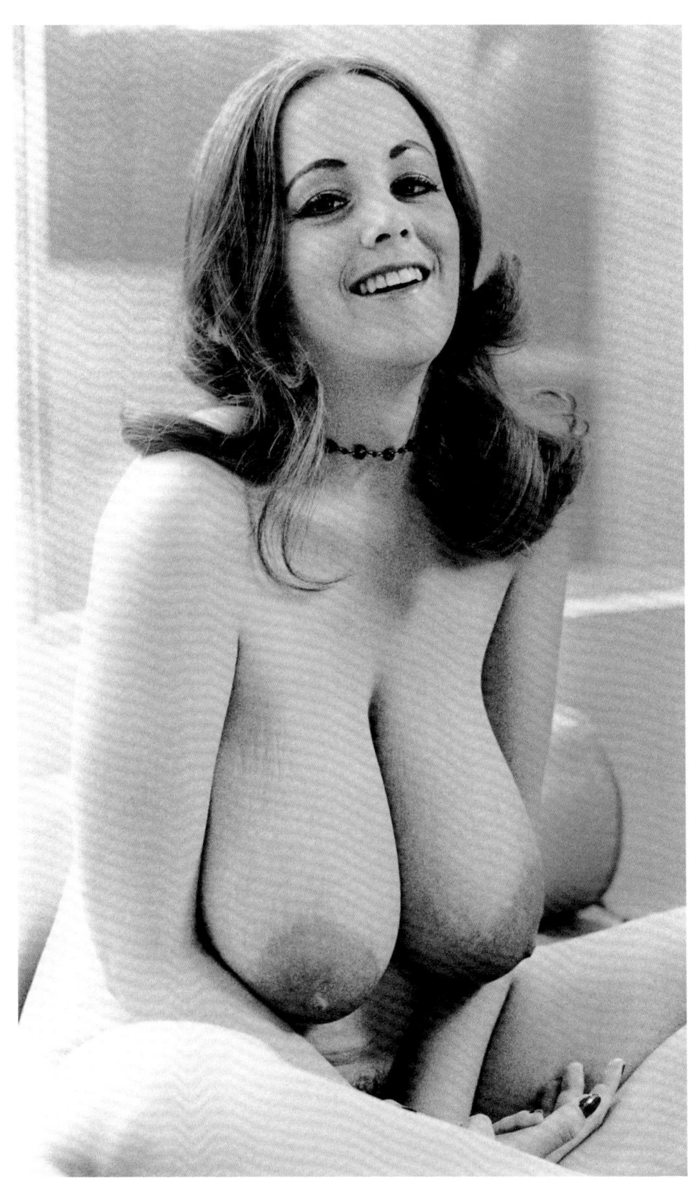

OPPOSITE Linda Schmidt ABOVE Penny Pontoons

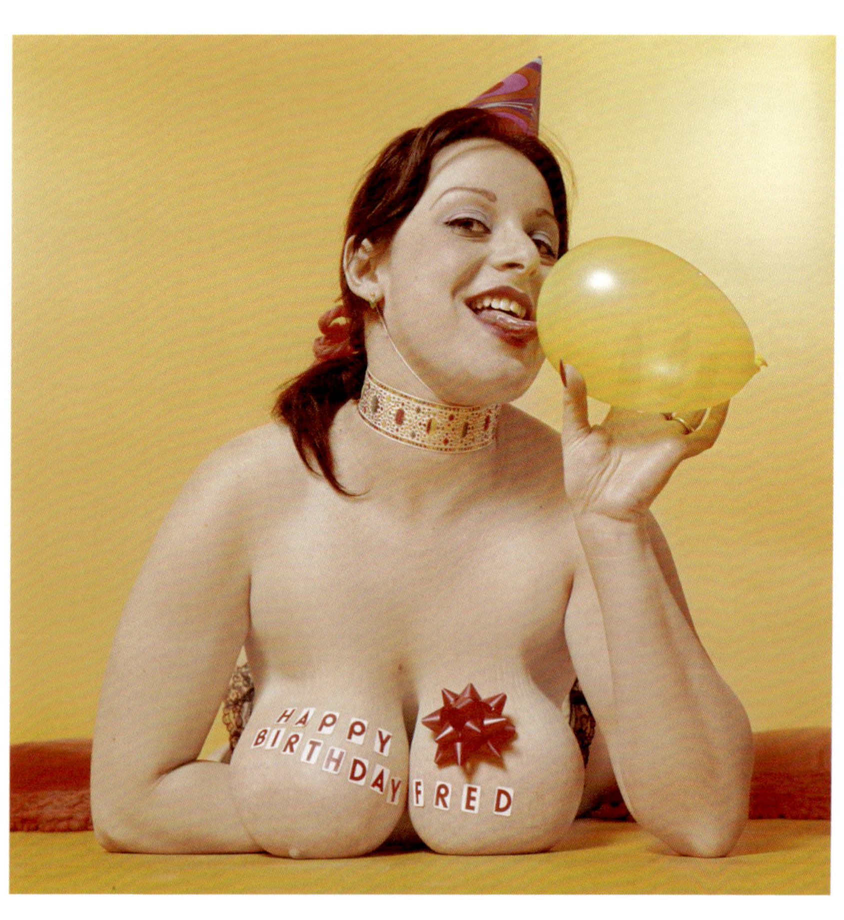

ABOVE Unknown OPPOSITE Candy Samples PAGES 152-153 Jill Pike

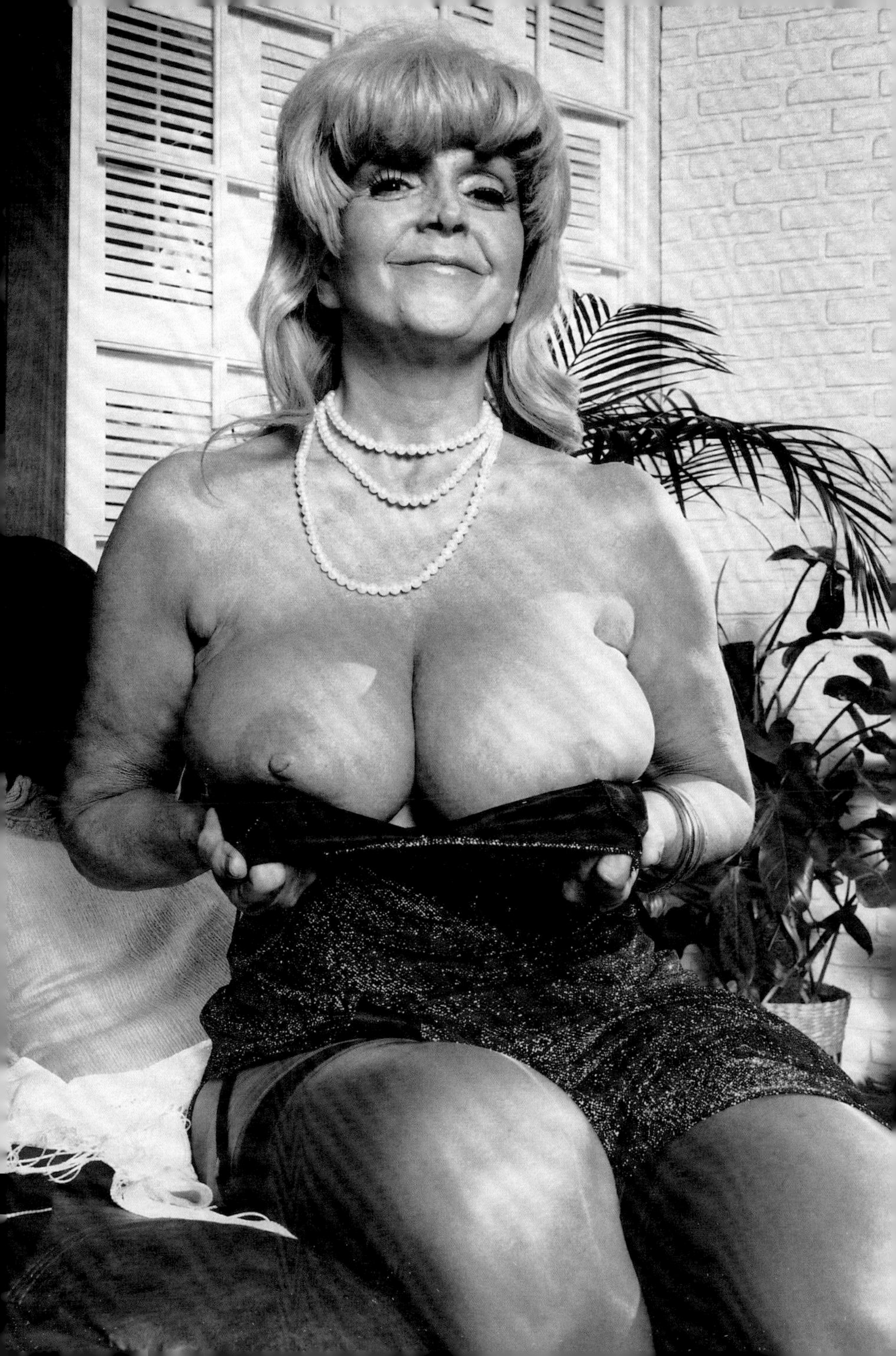

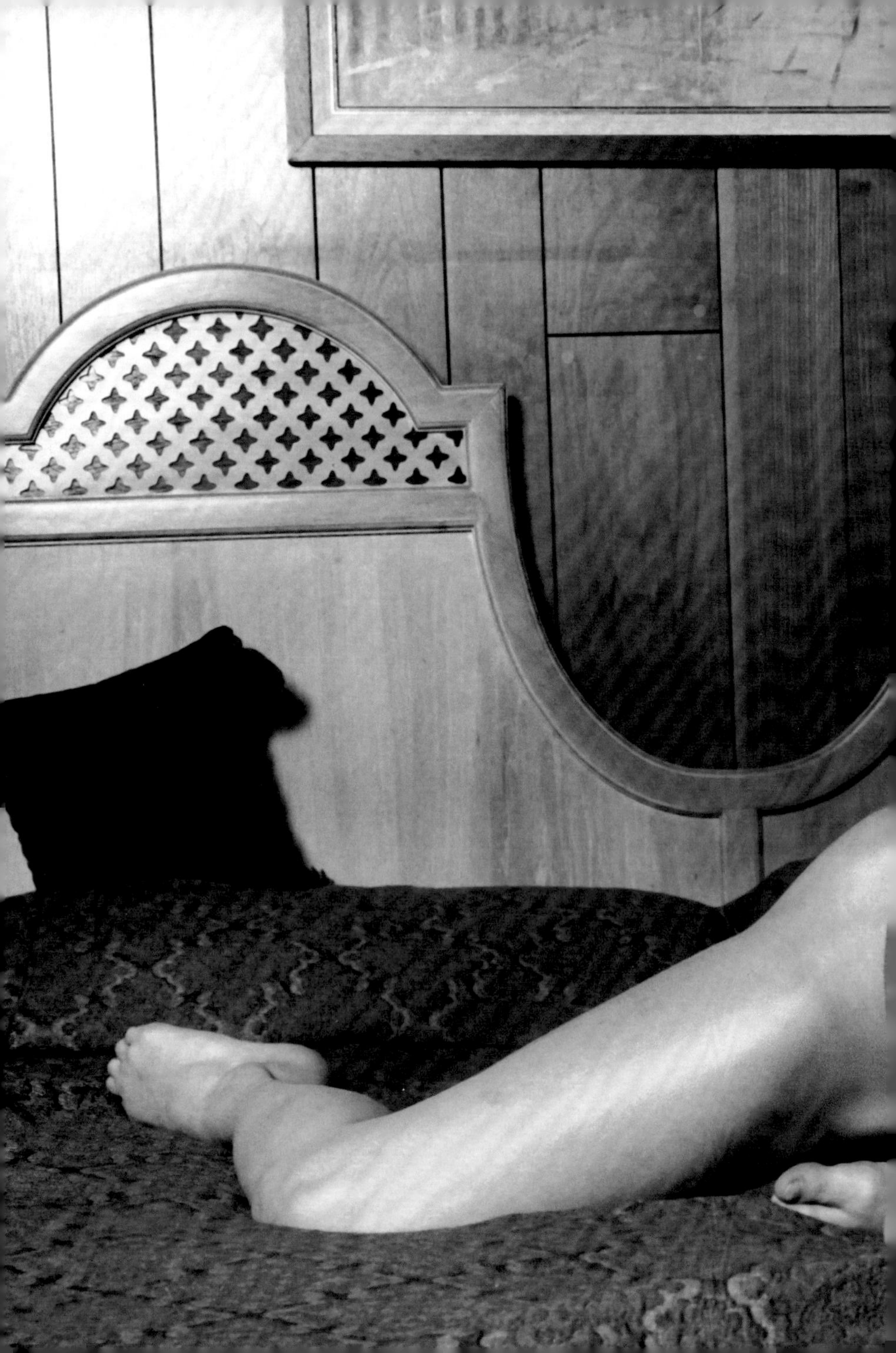

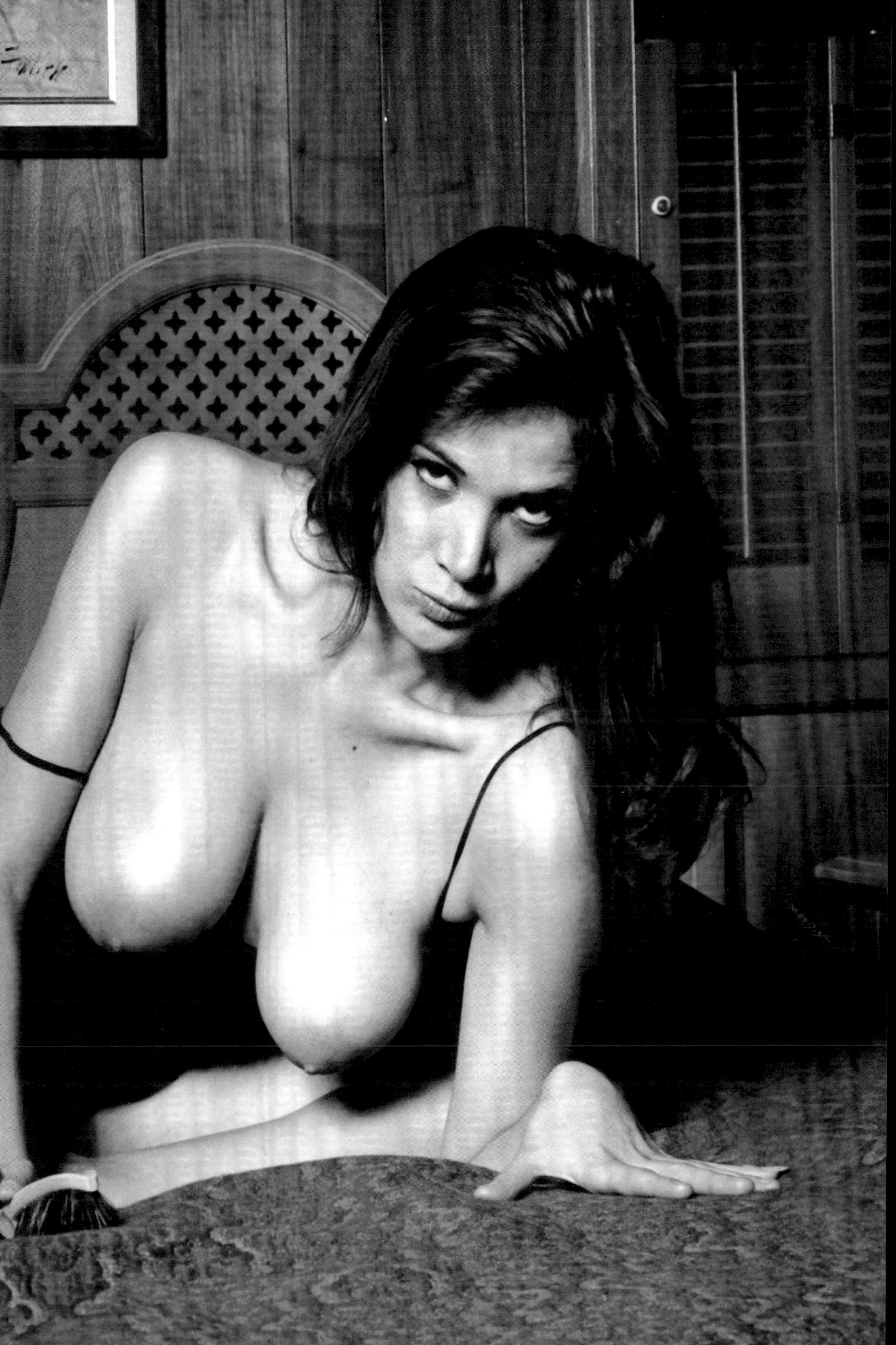

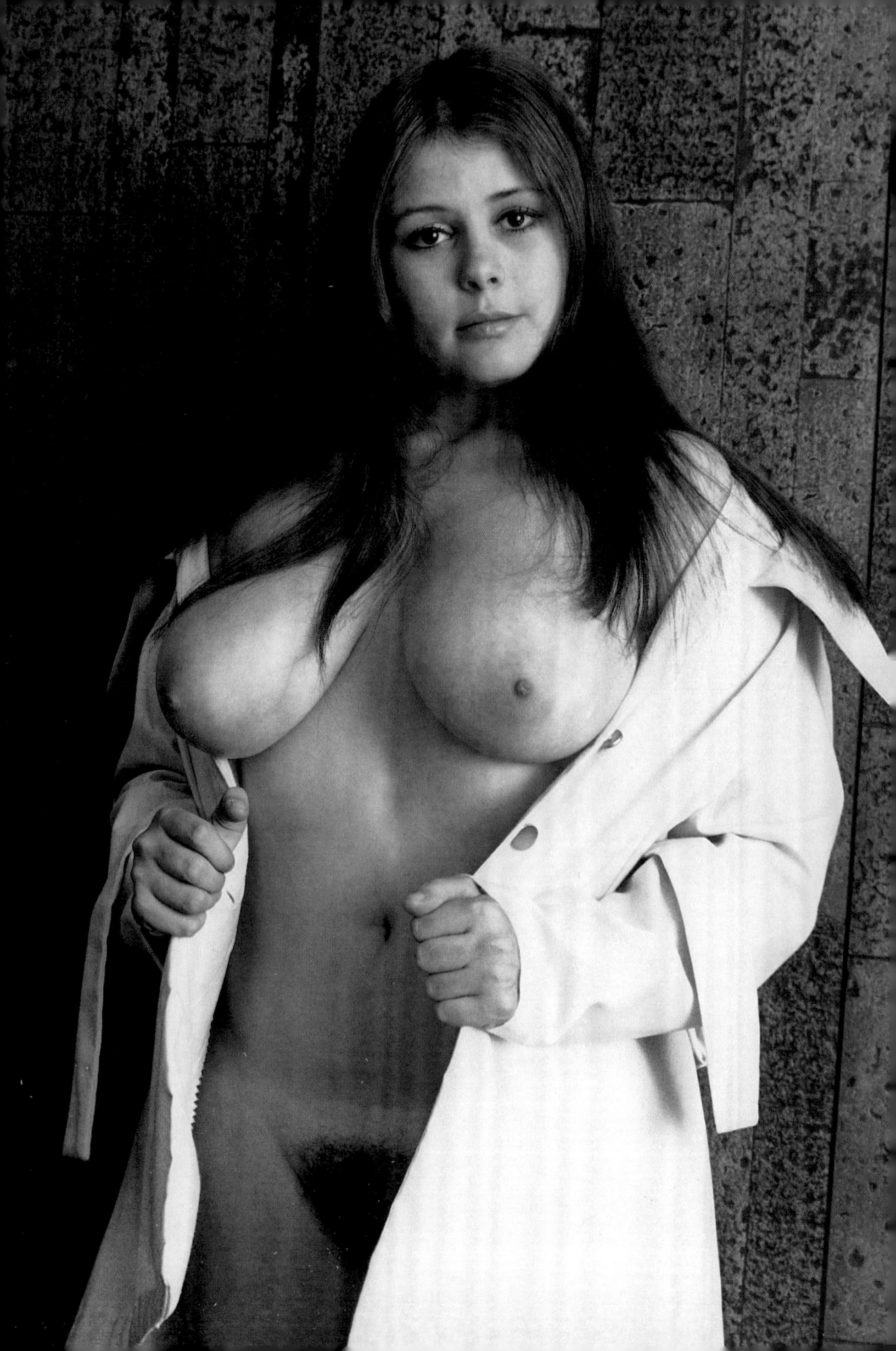

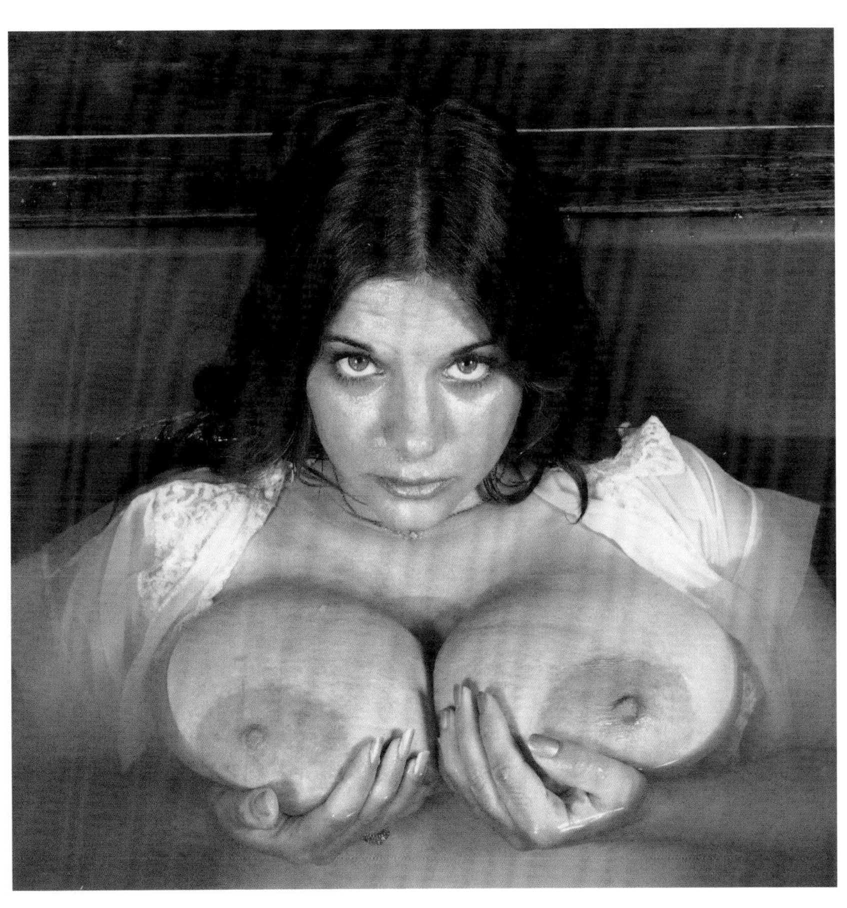

OPPOSITE Toni Olson ABOVE Mary Waters

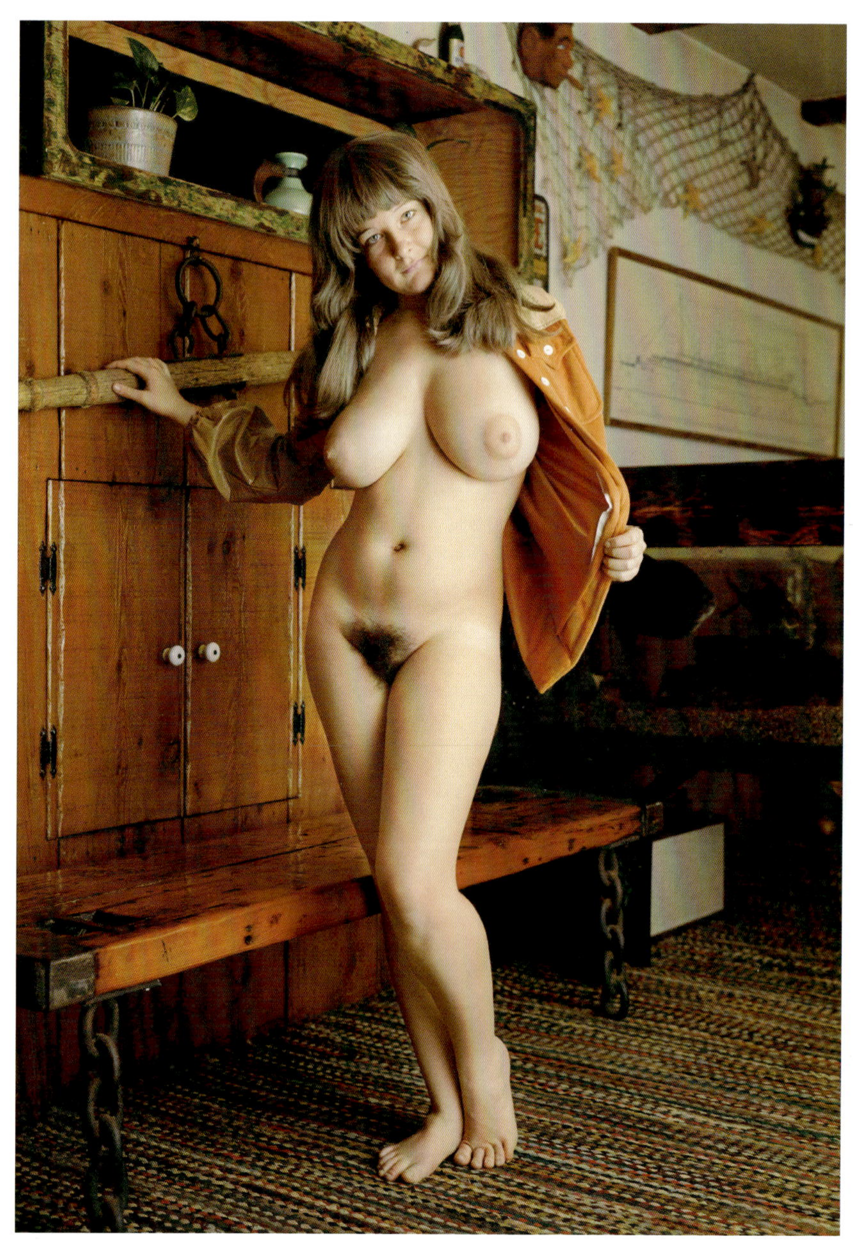

ABOVE Unknown OPPOSITE Sylvia McFarland PAGES 158-159 Joyce Spaeth

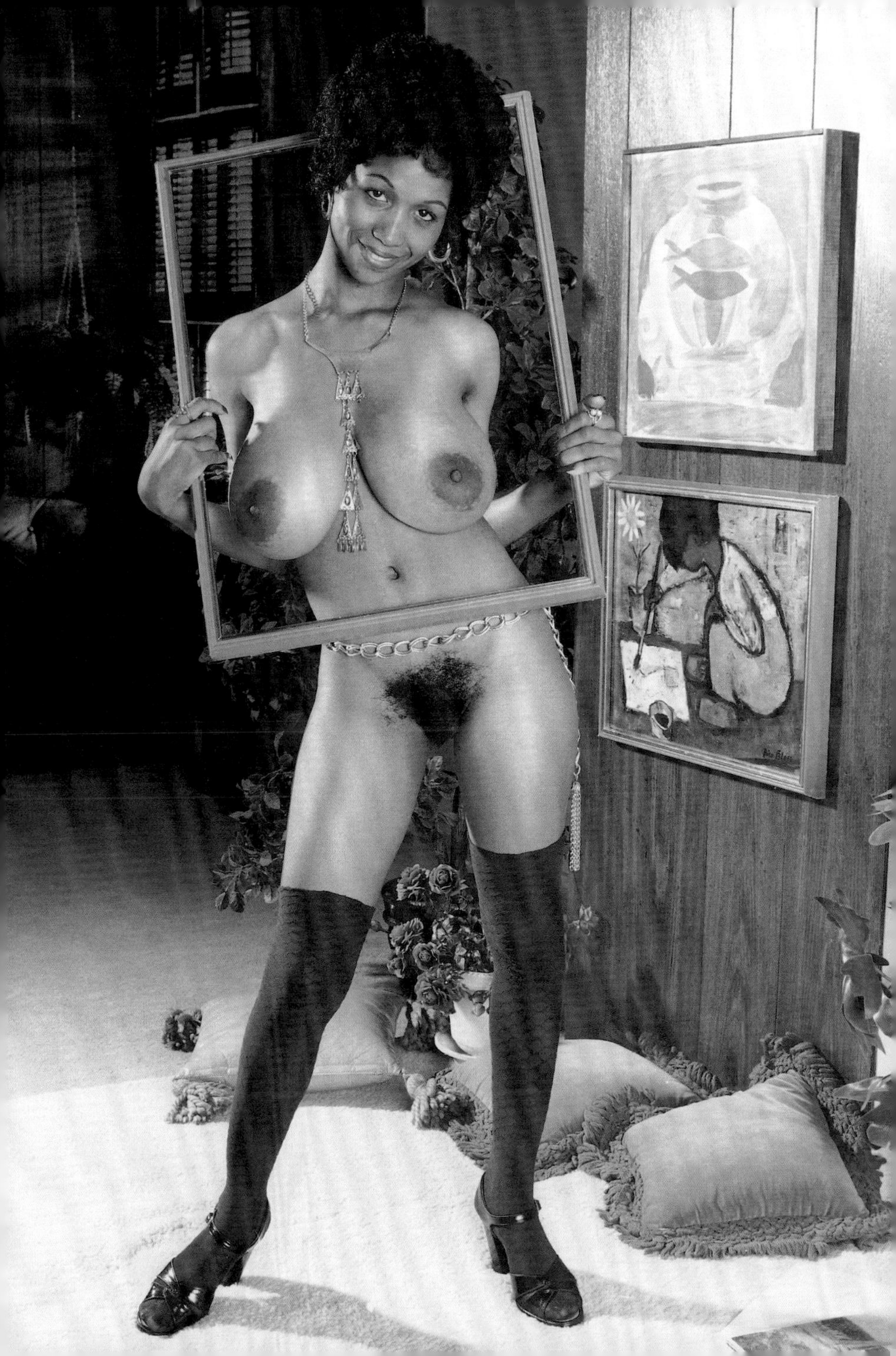

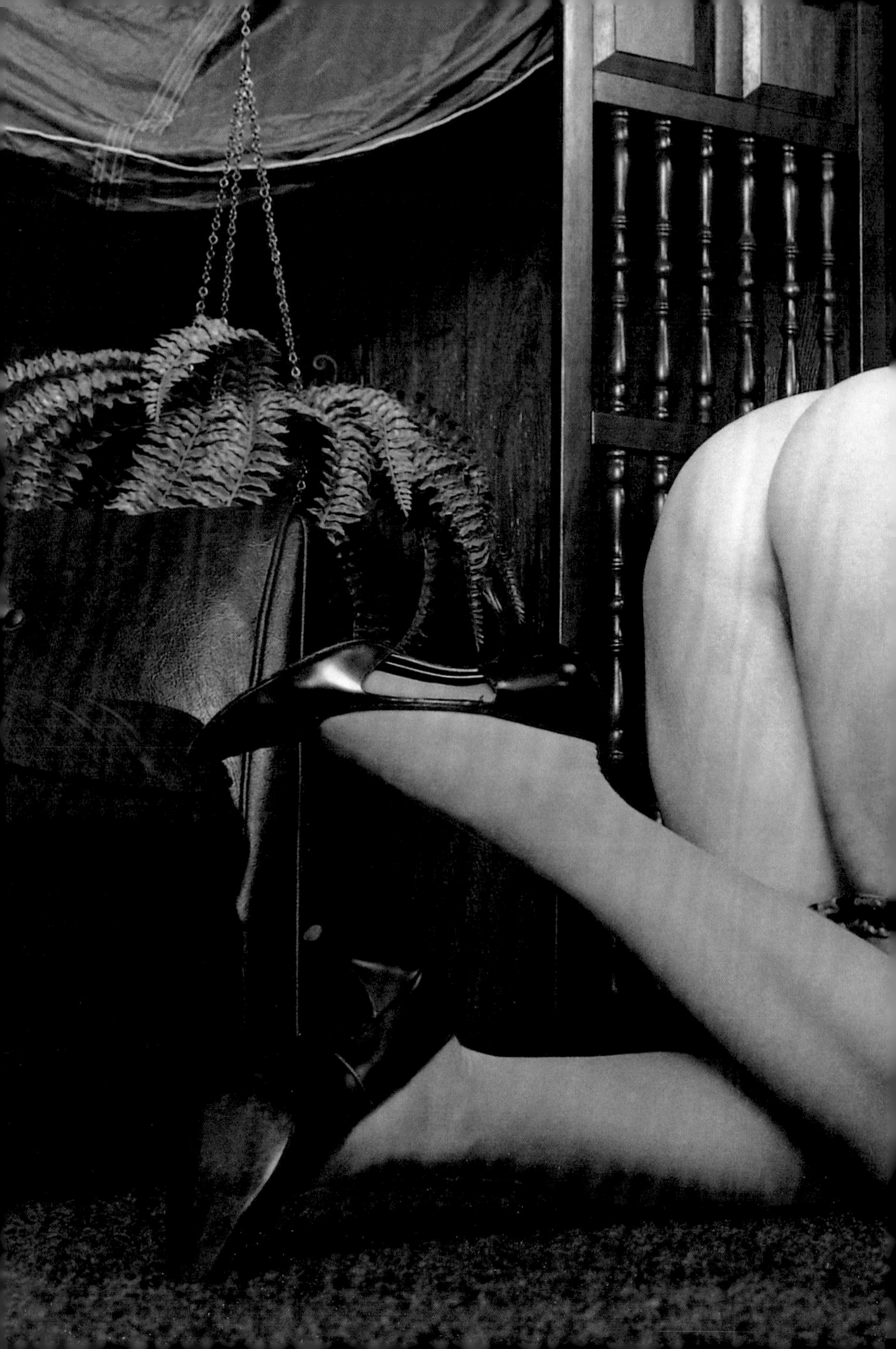

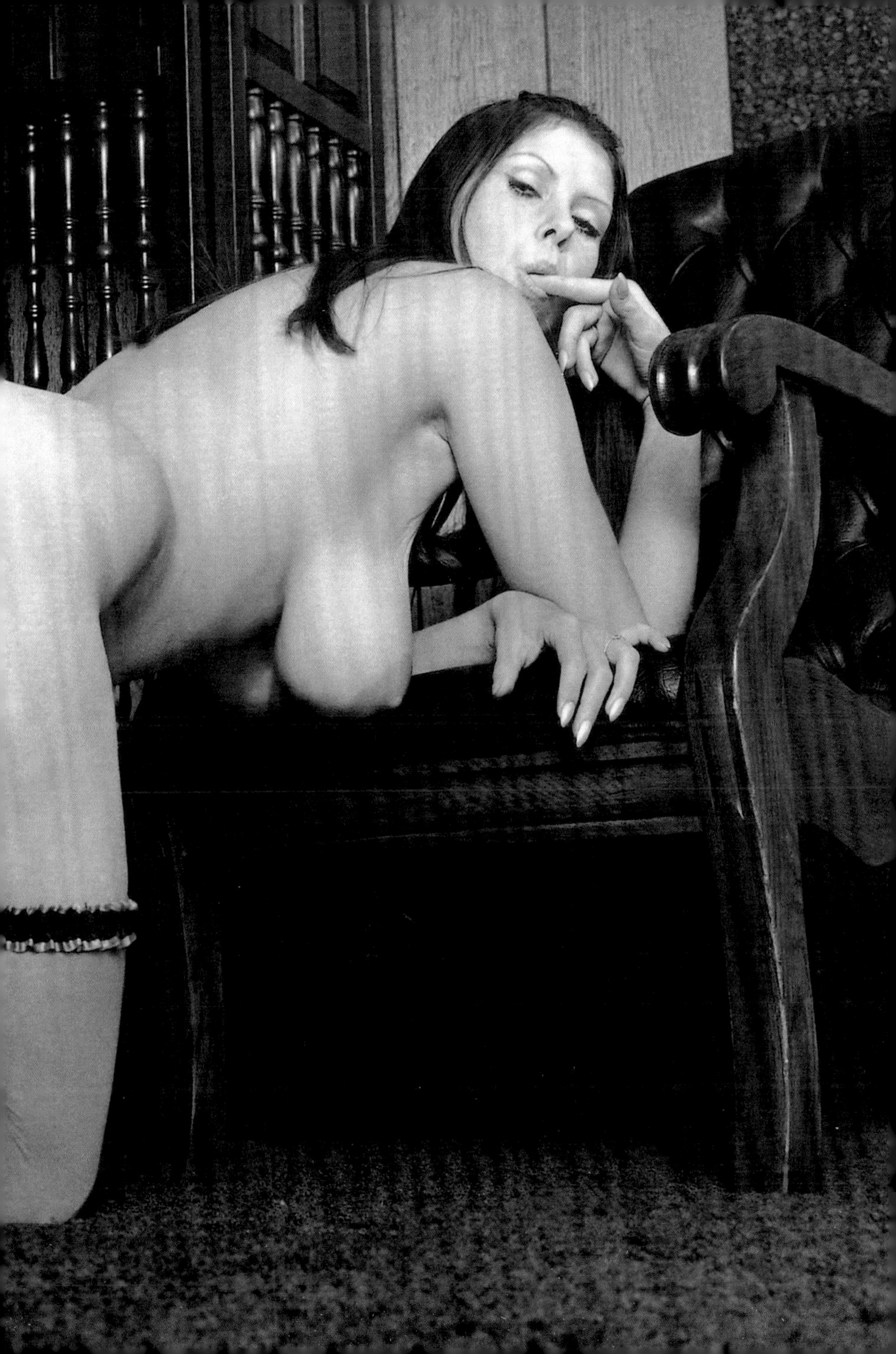

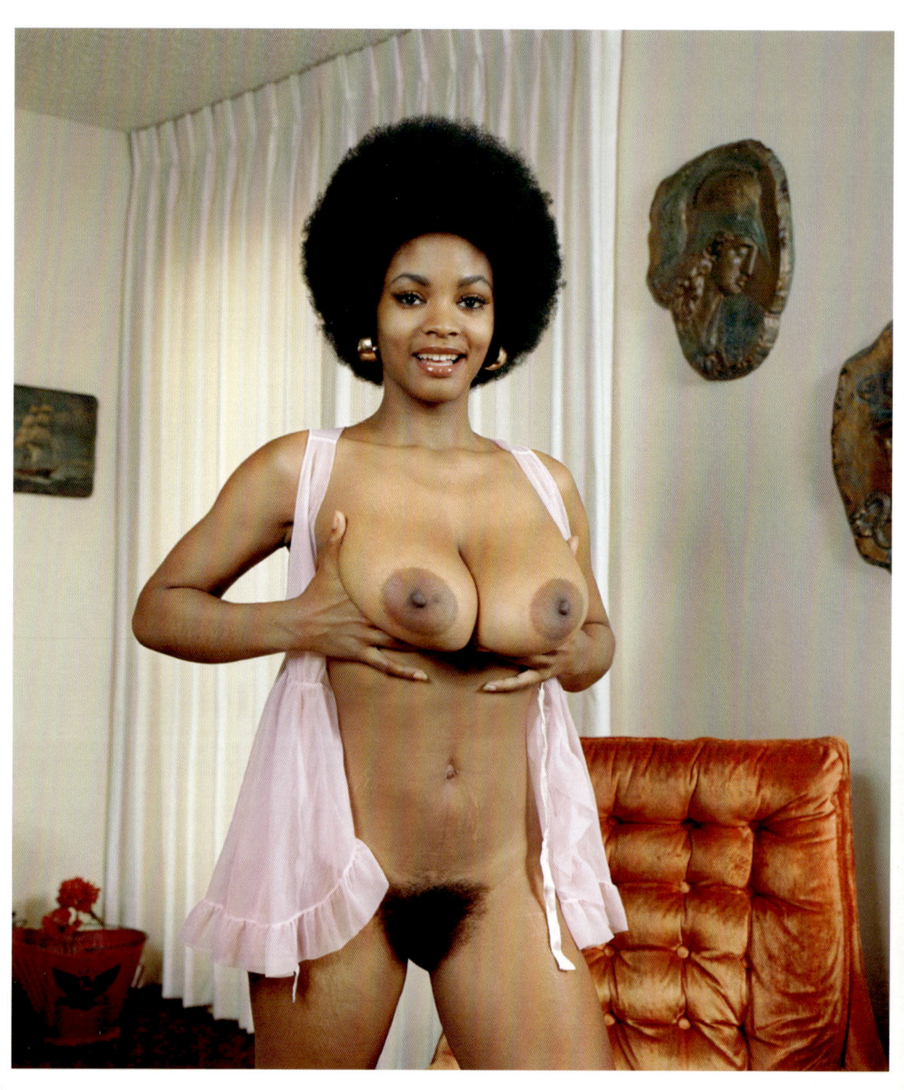

ABOVE Elaine Collins   OPPOSITE Kitten Natividad

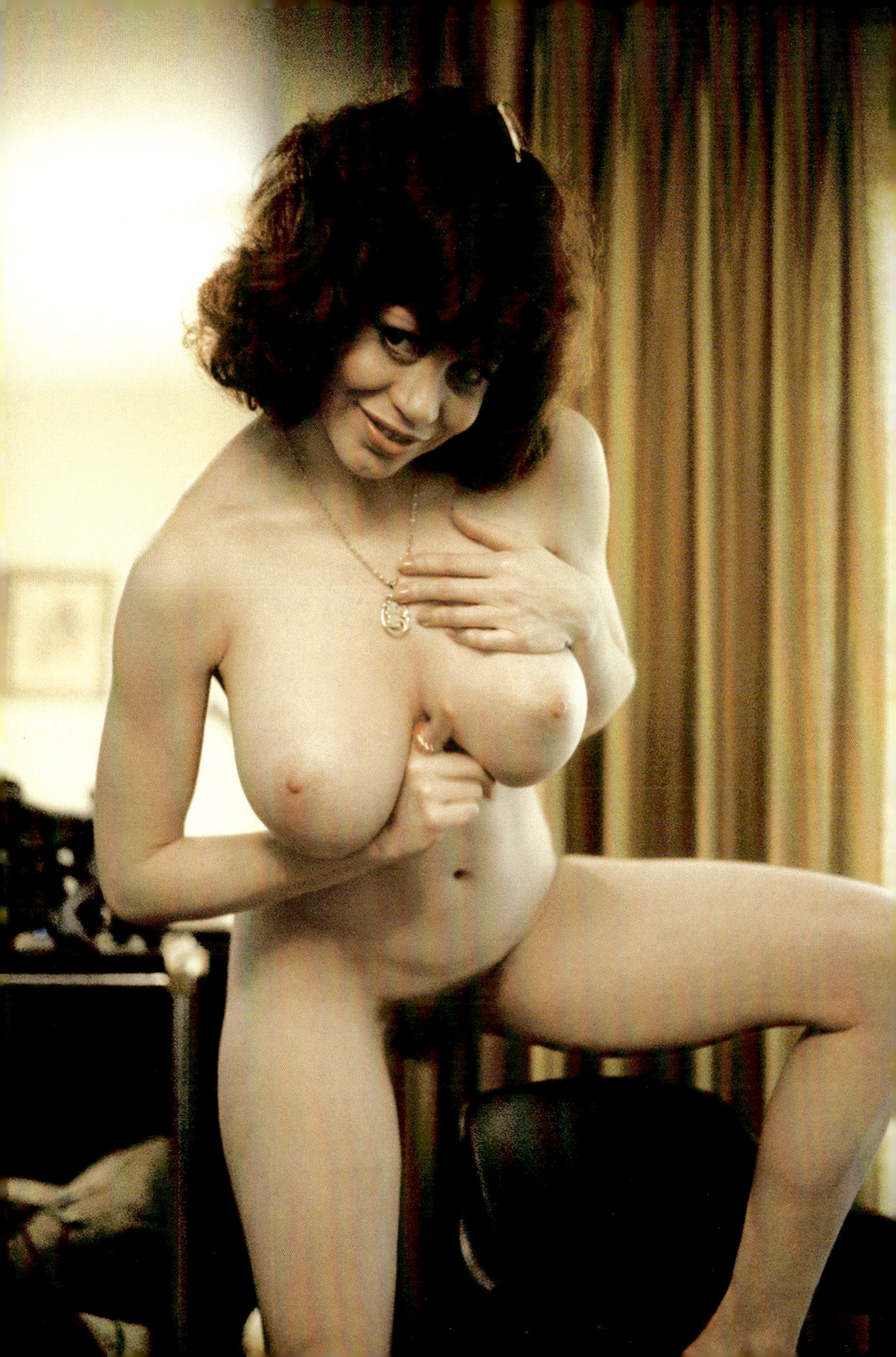

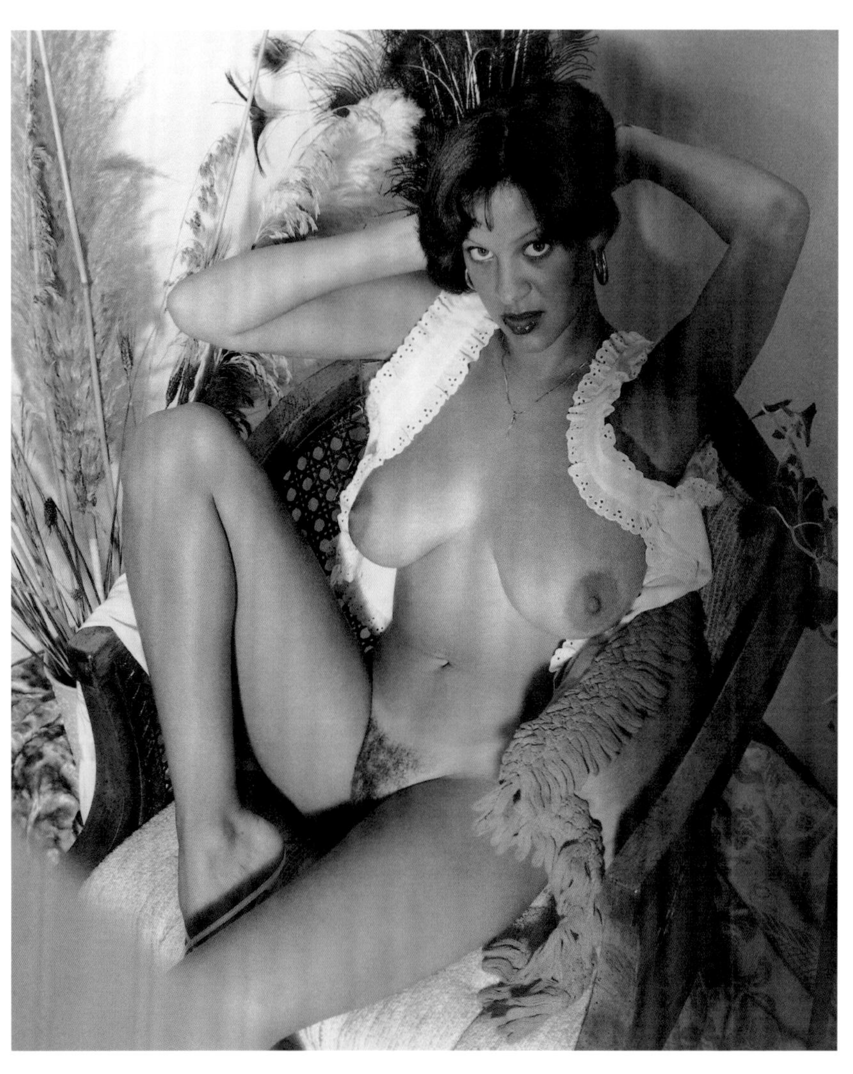

ABOVE Keli Stewart OPPOSITE Unknown PAGES 164-165 Michelle Weiner

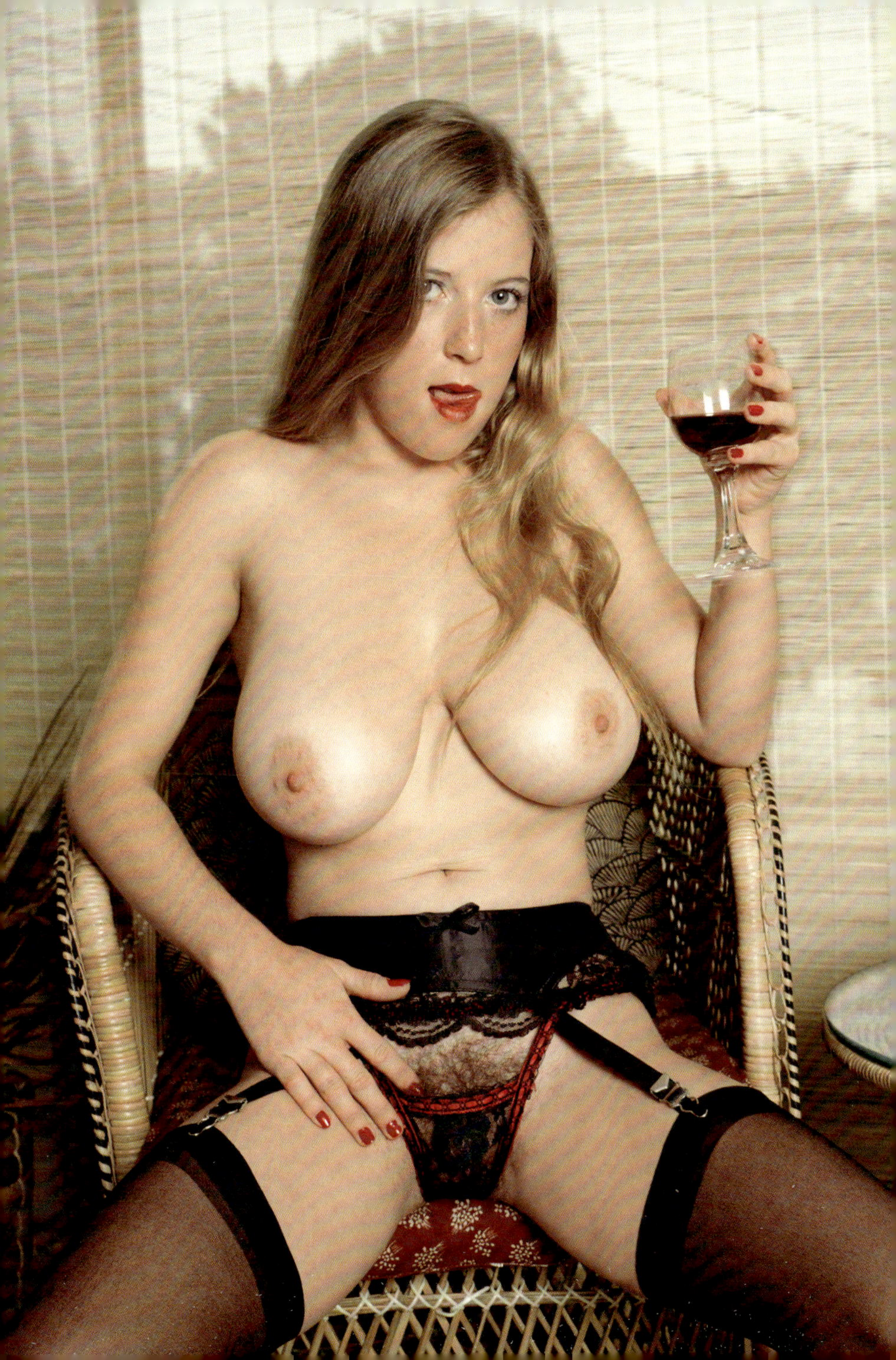

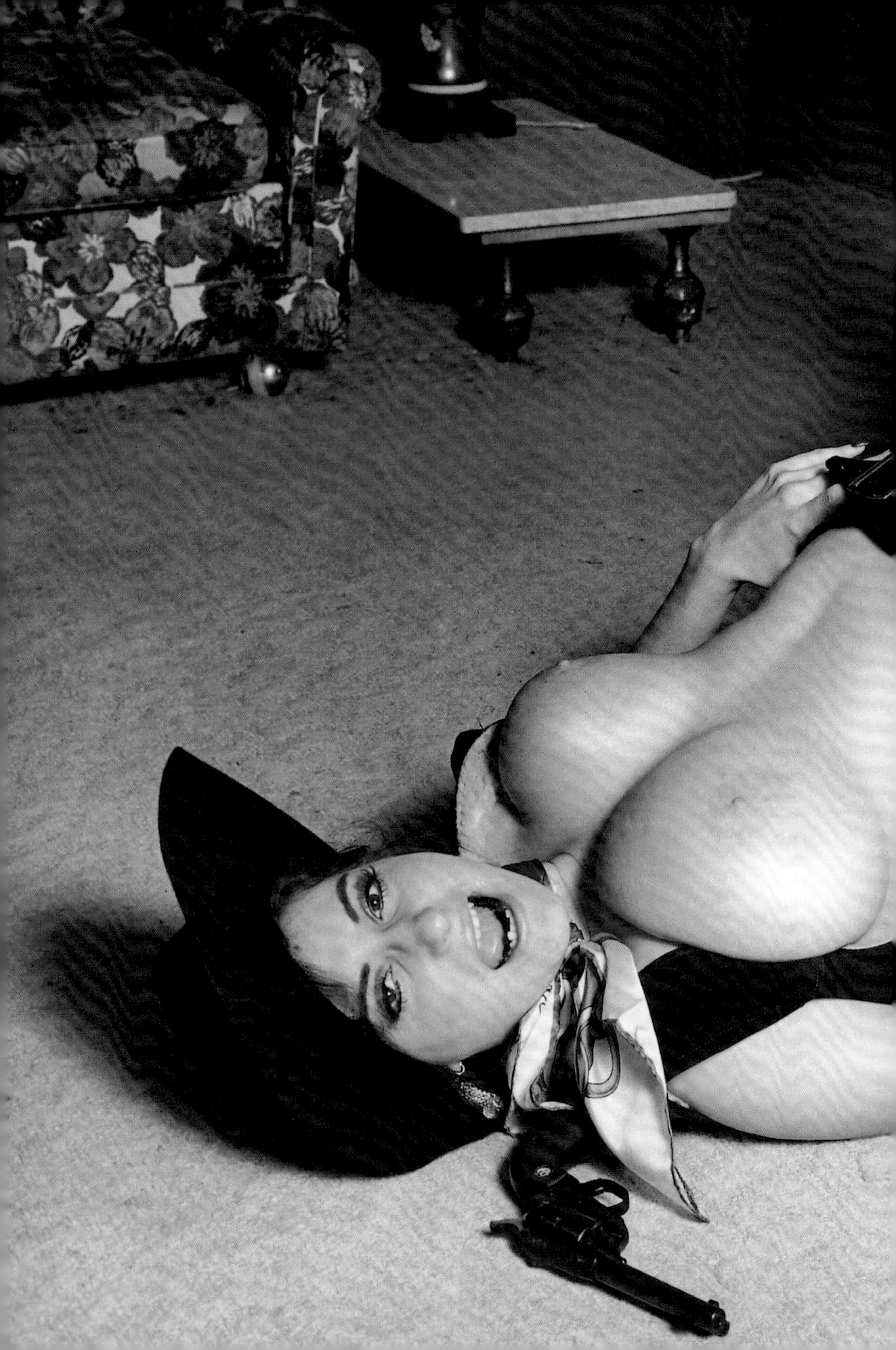

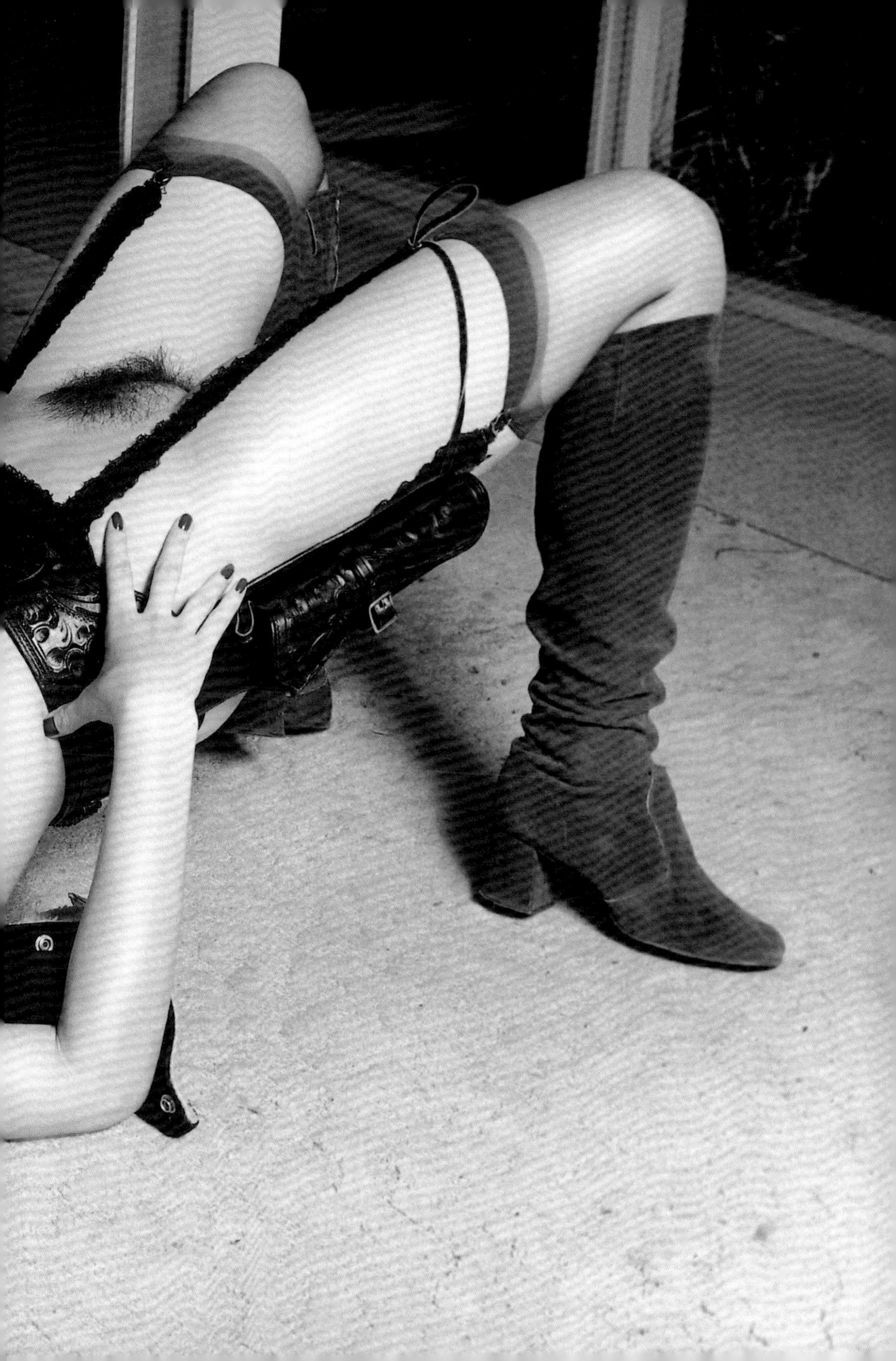

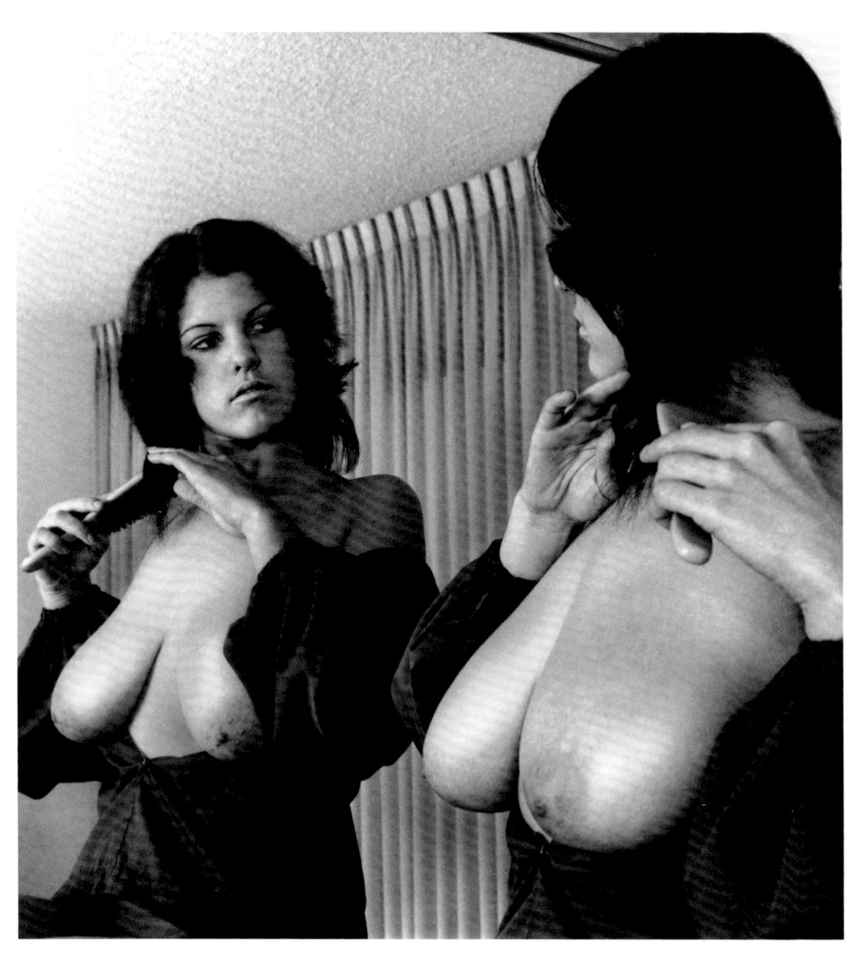

Brandy Hart

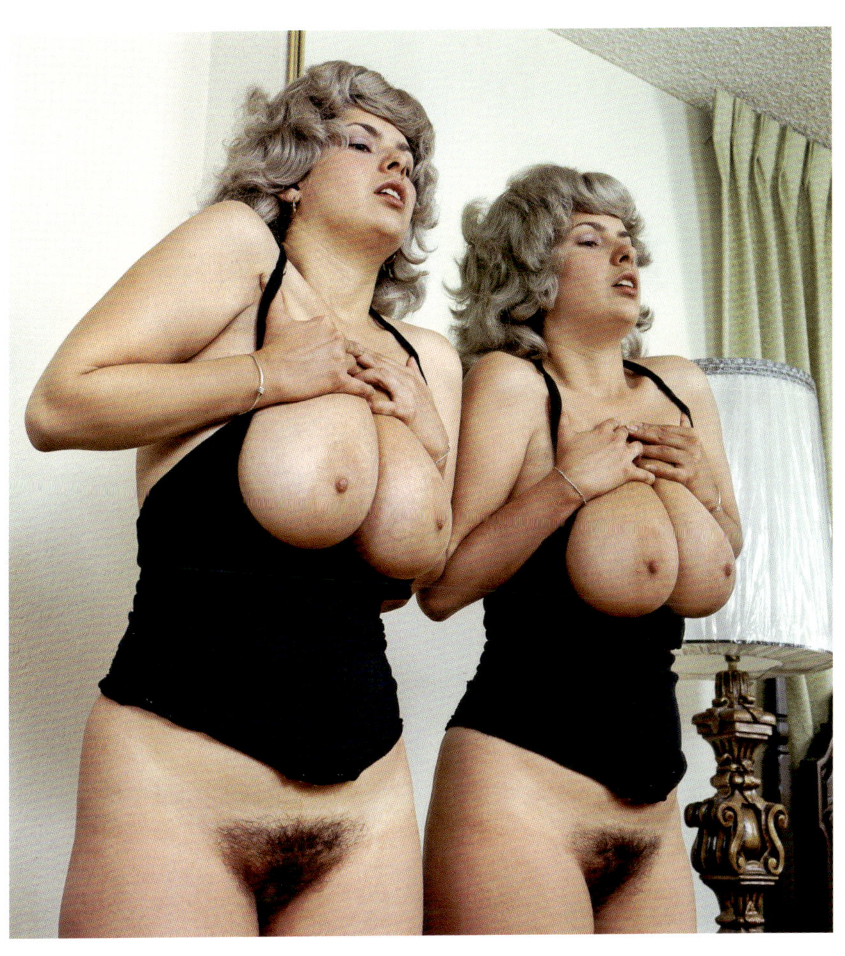

ABOVE Unknown PAGES 168-169 Lori Martin

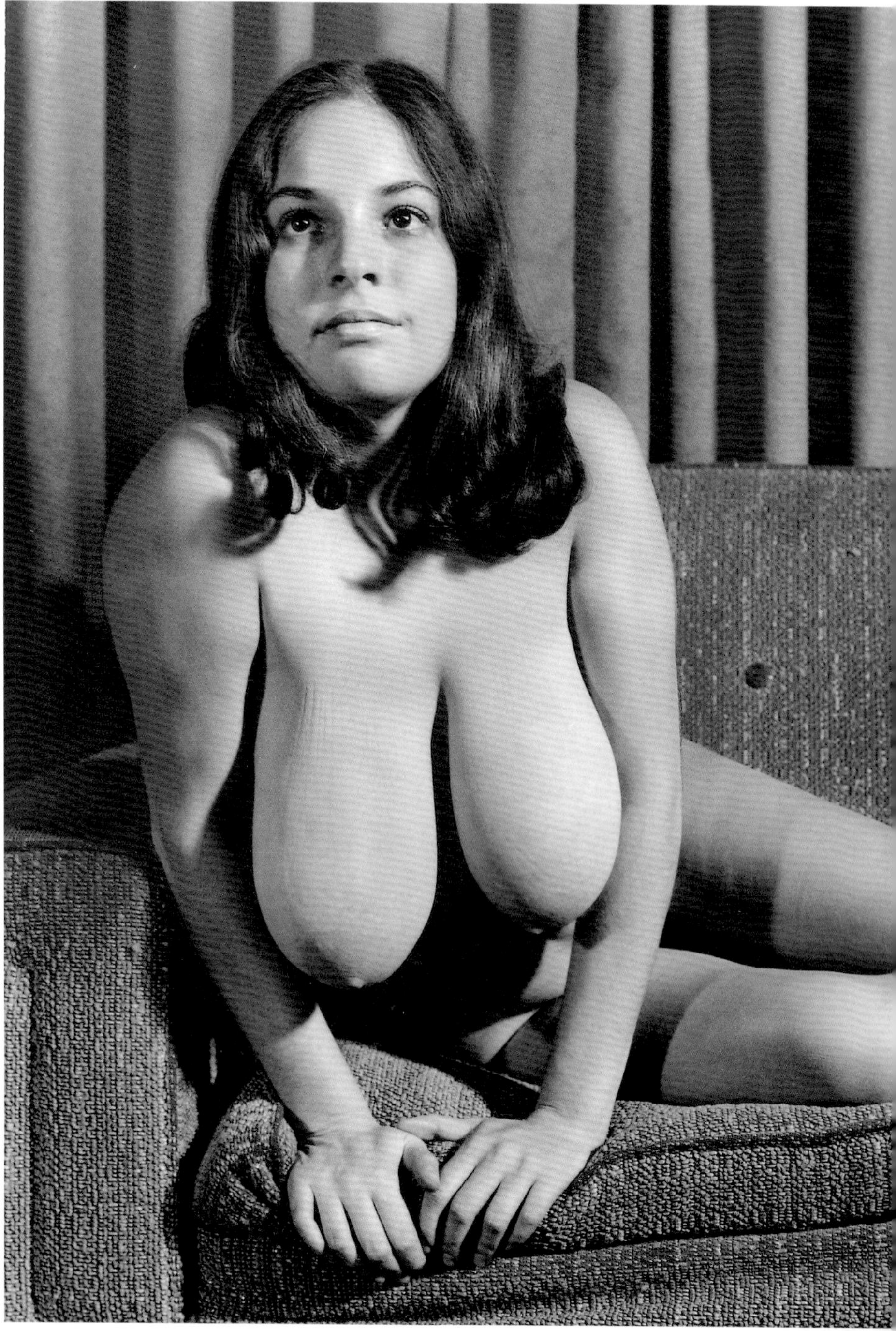

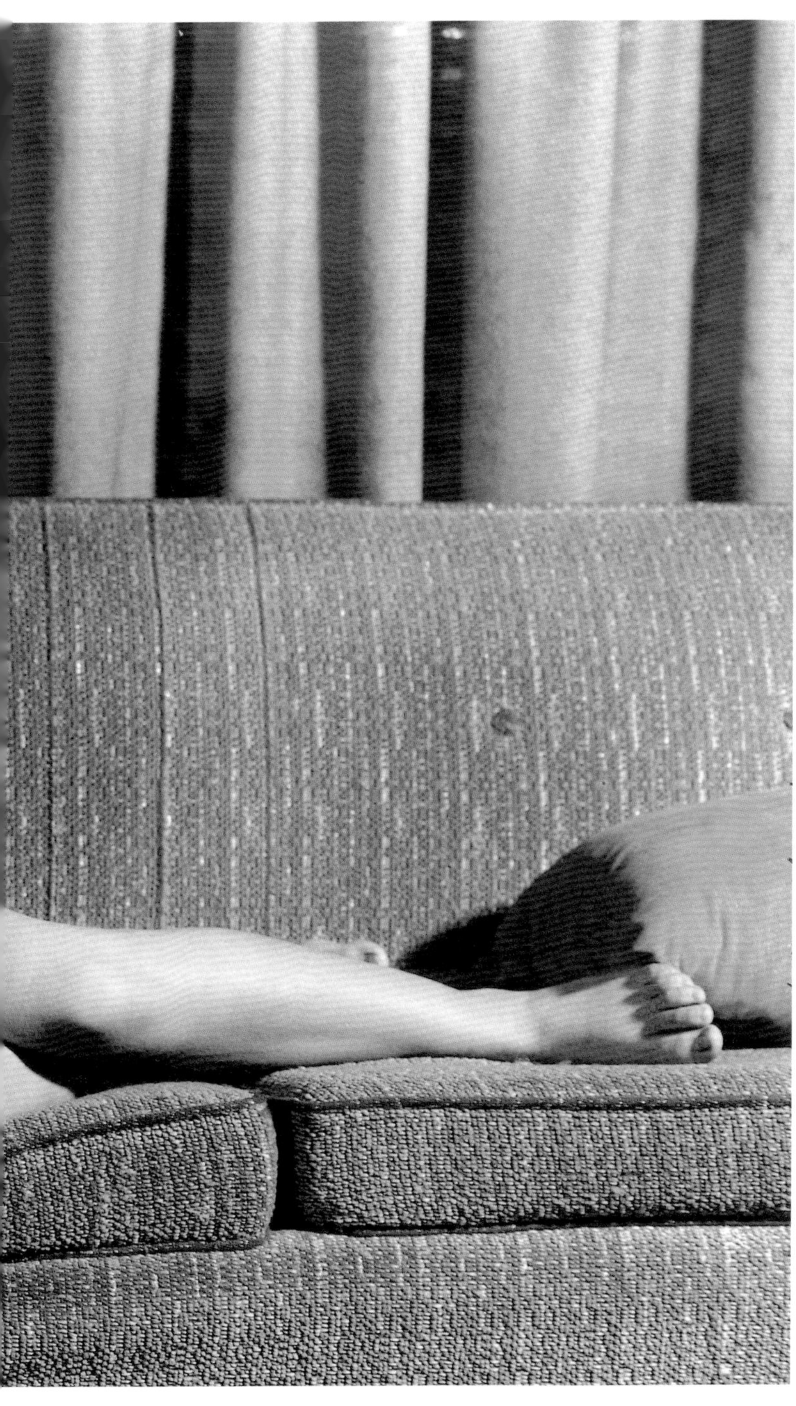

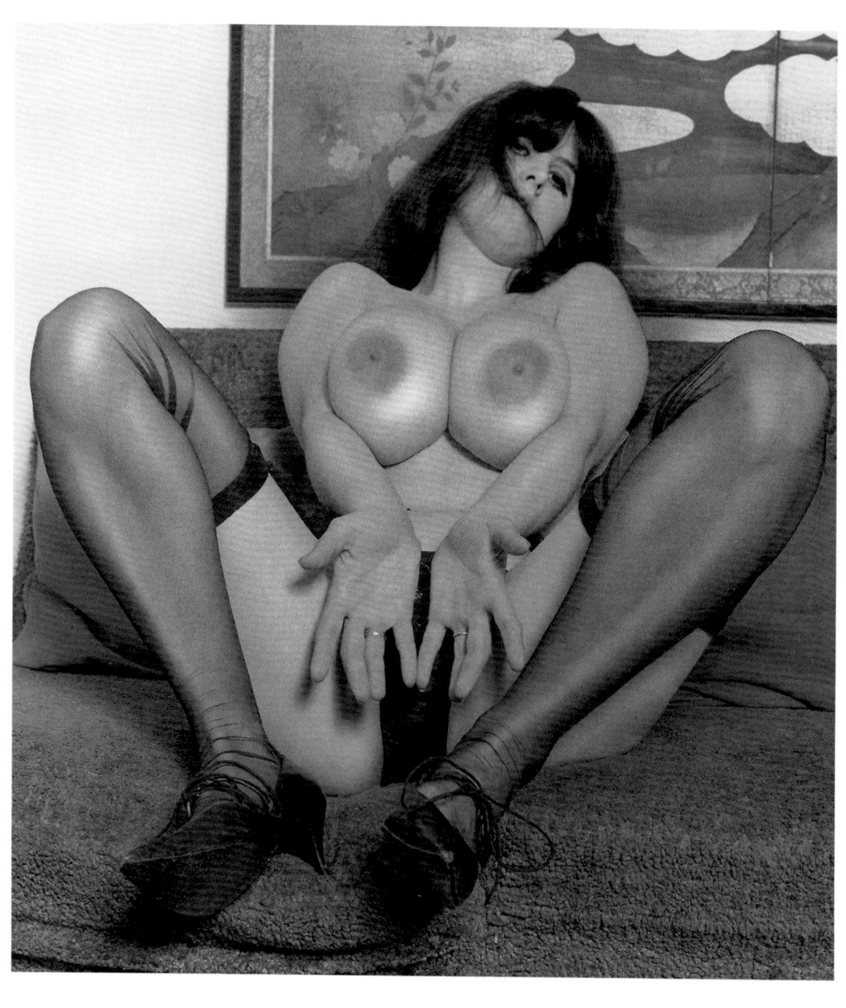

ABOVE Ann Day OPPOSITE Darlene English

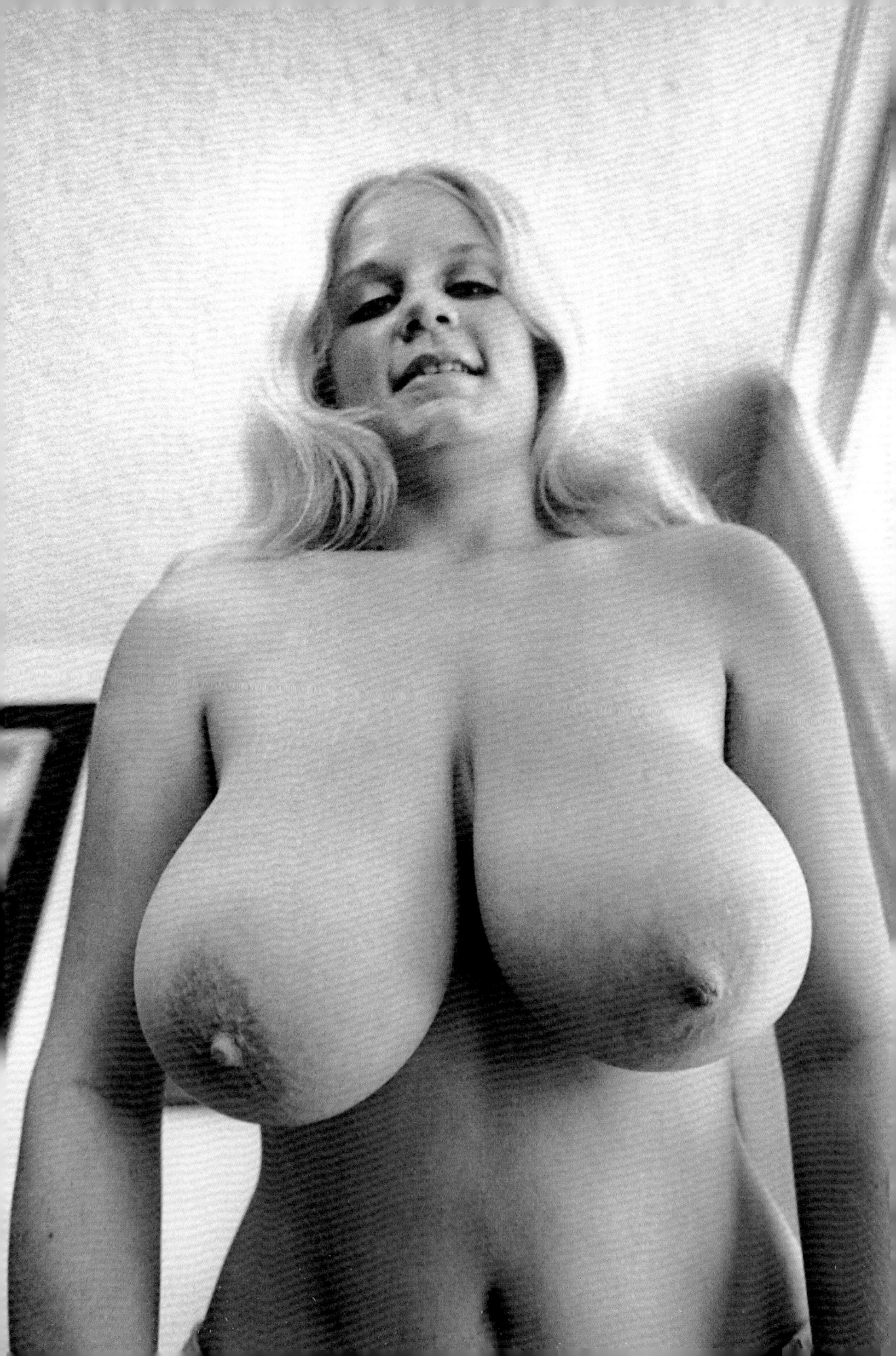

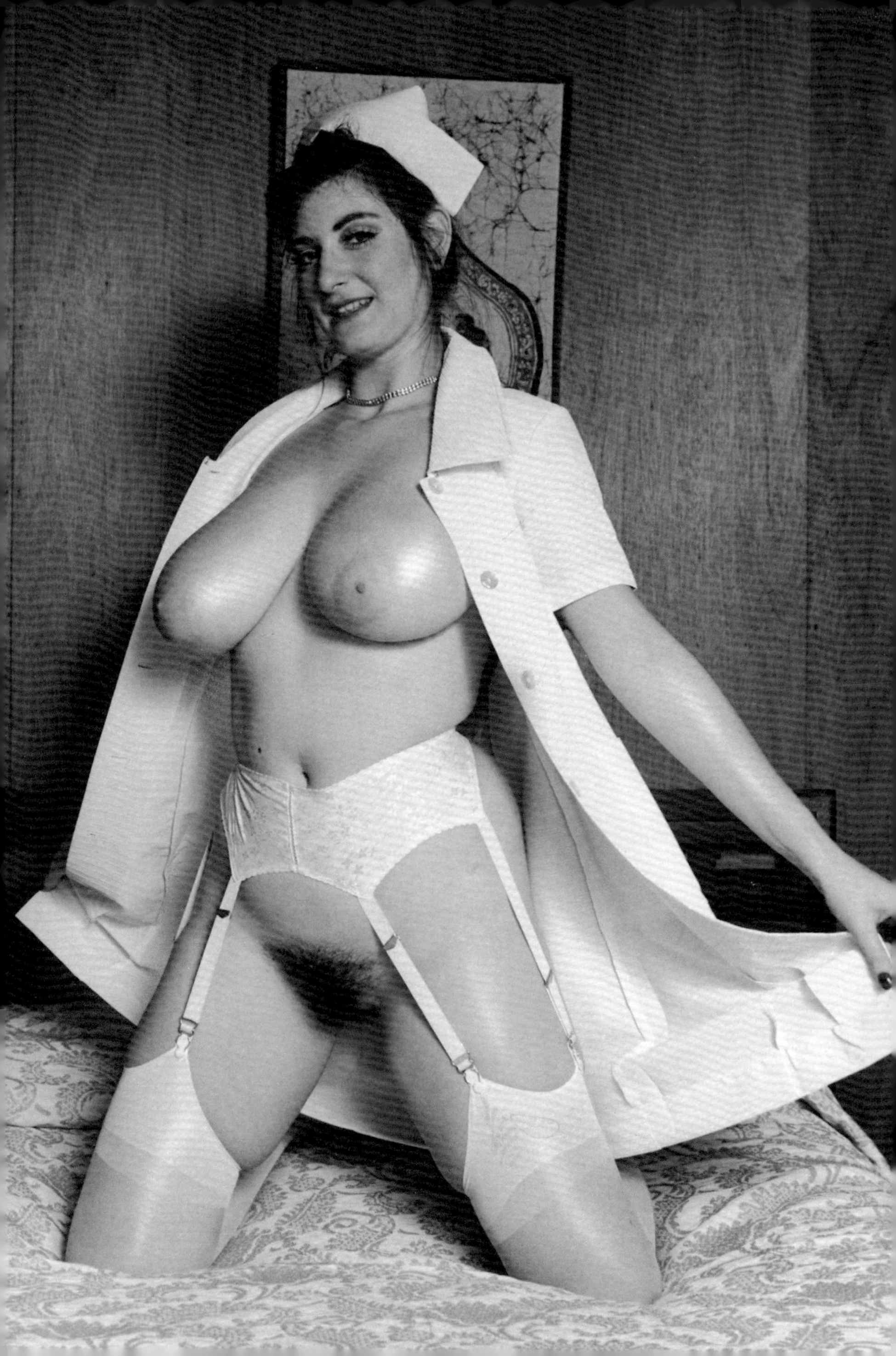

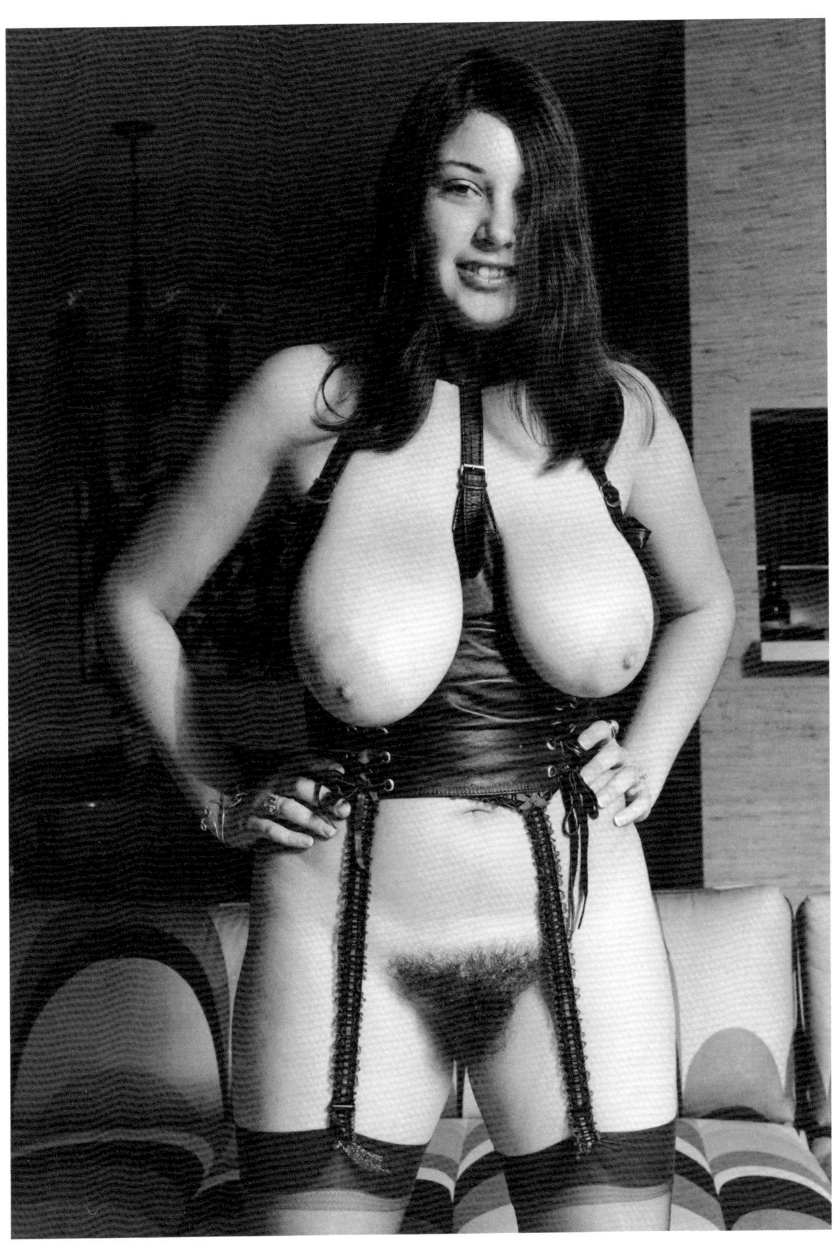

OPPOSITE Michelle Weiner   ABOVE Theresa Jackman

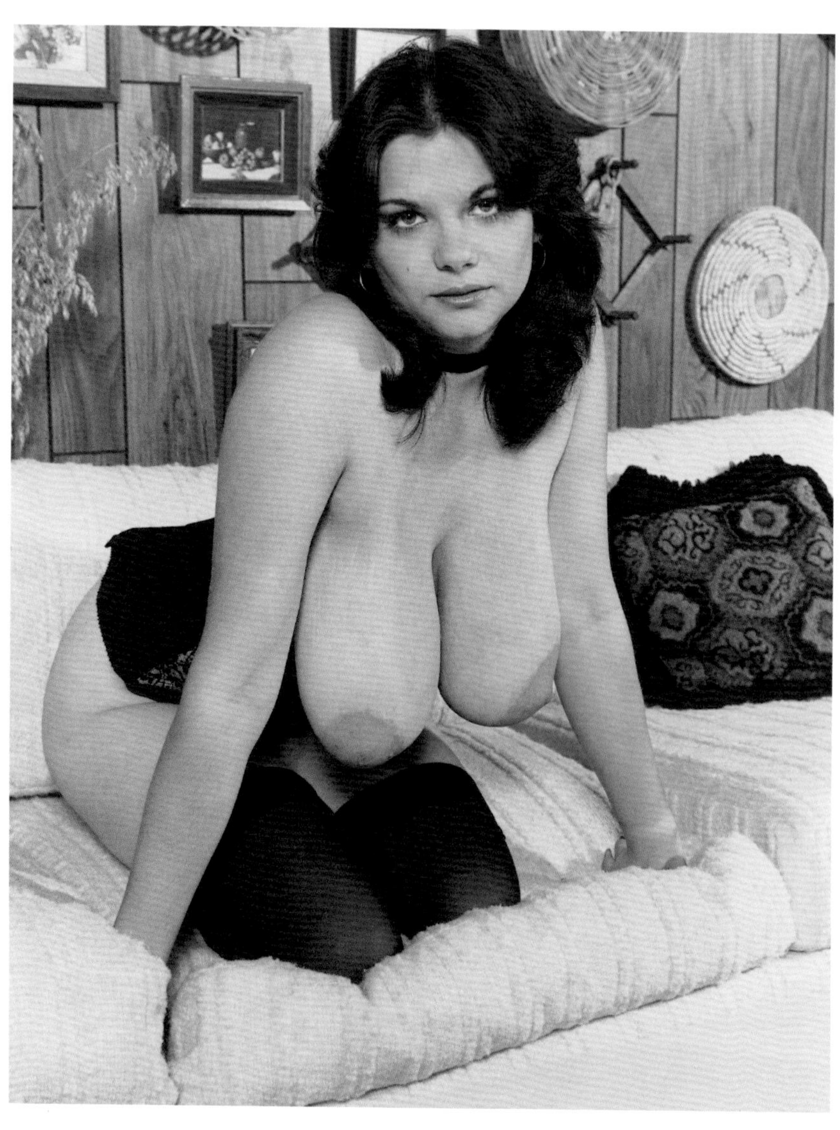

ABOVE Mary Waters OPPOSITE Lynn Townsley

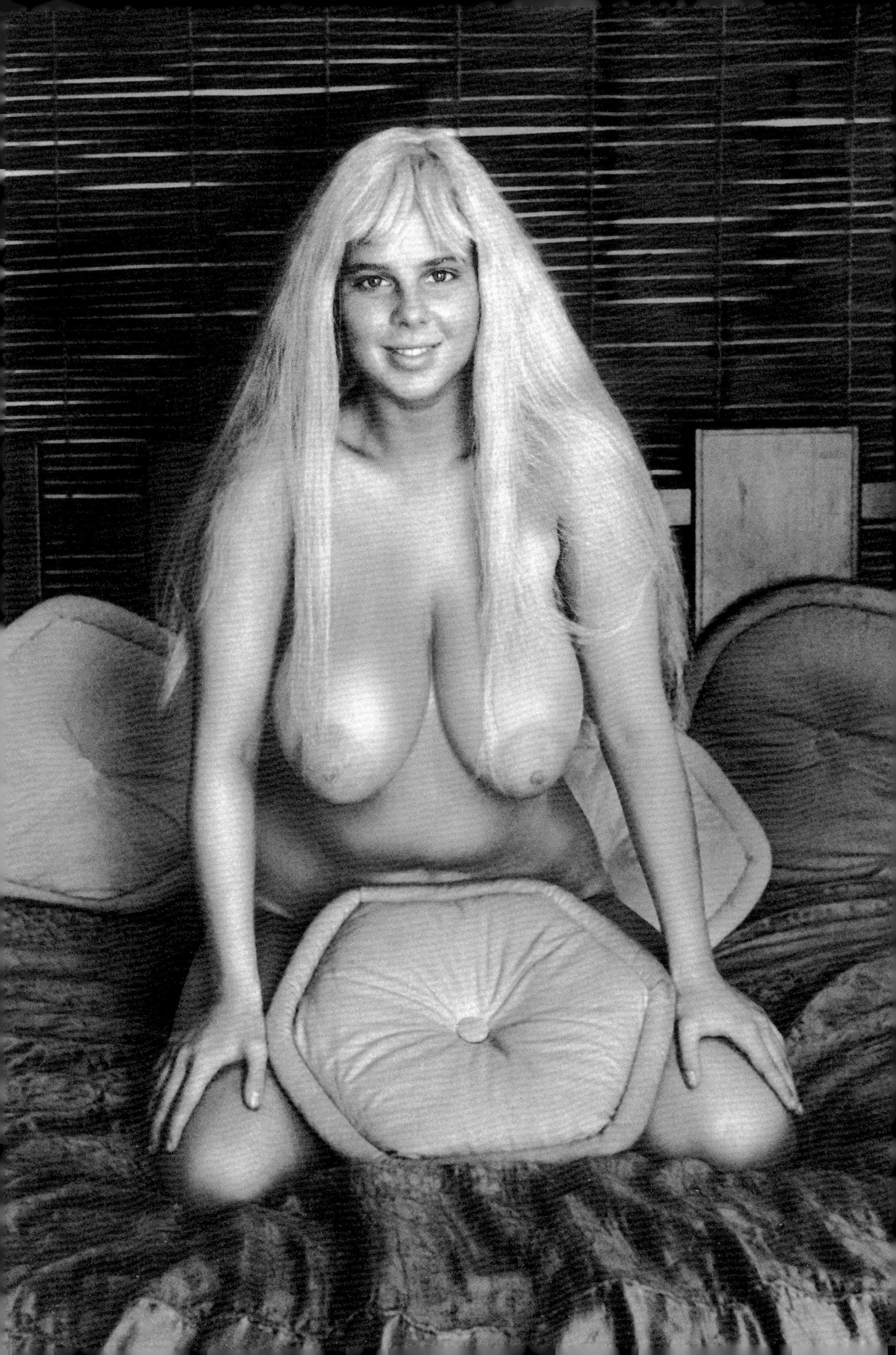

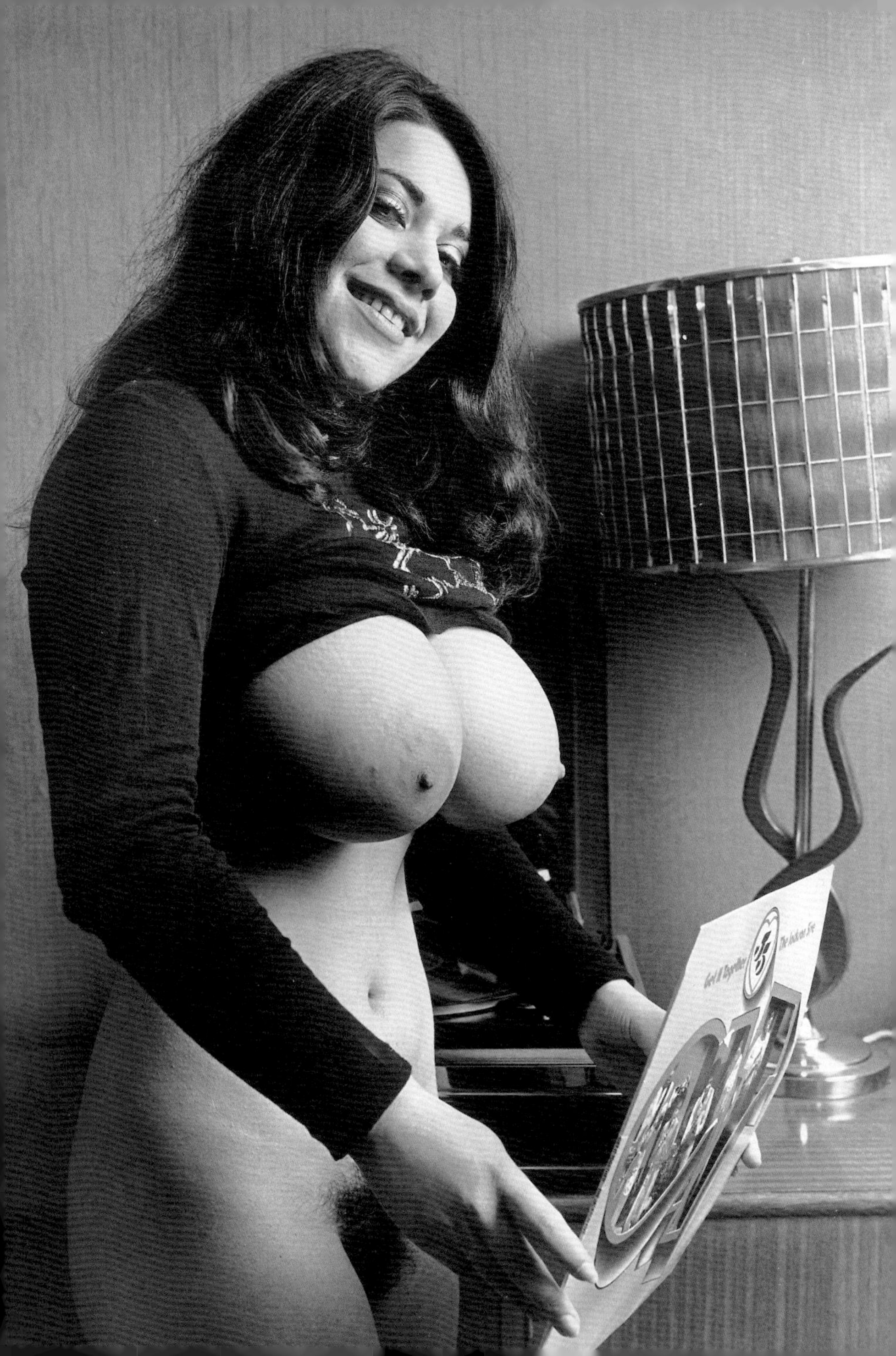

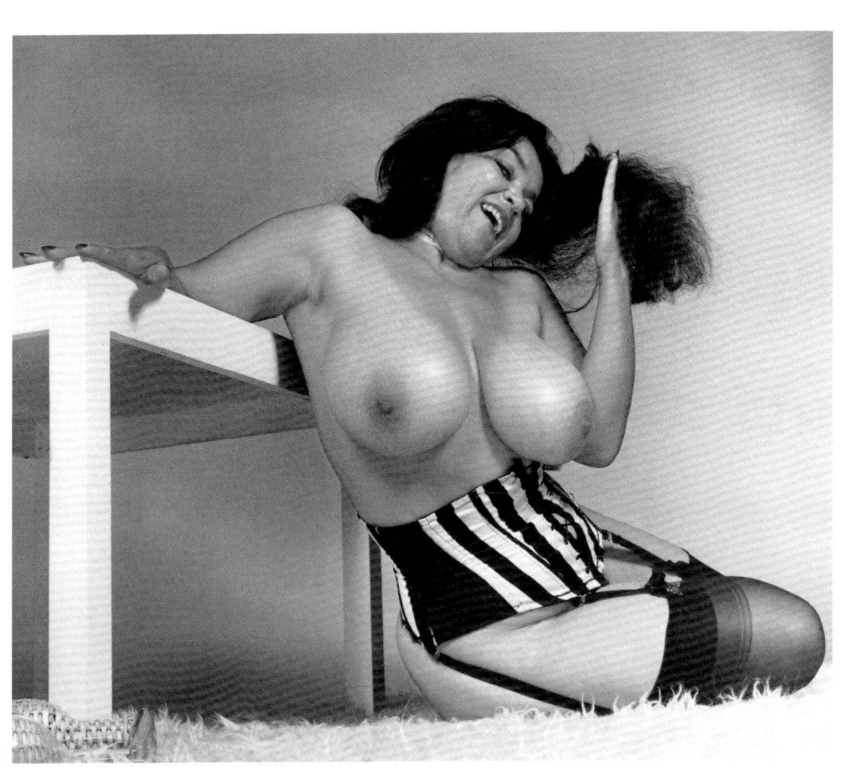

OPPOSITE Clyda ABOVE Maria Lopez PAGES 178-179 Joyce Spaeth

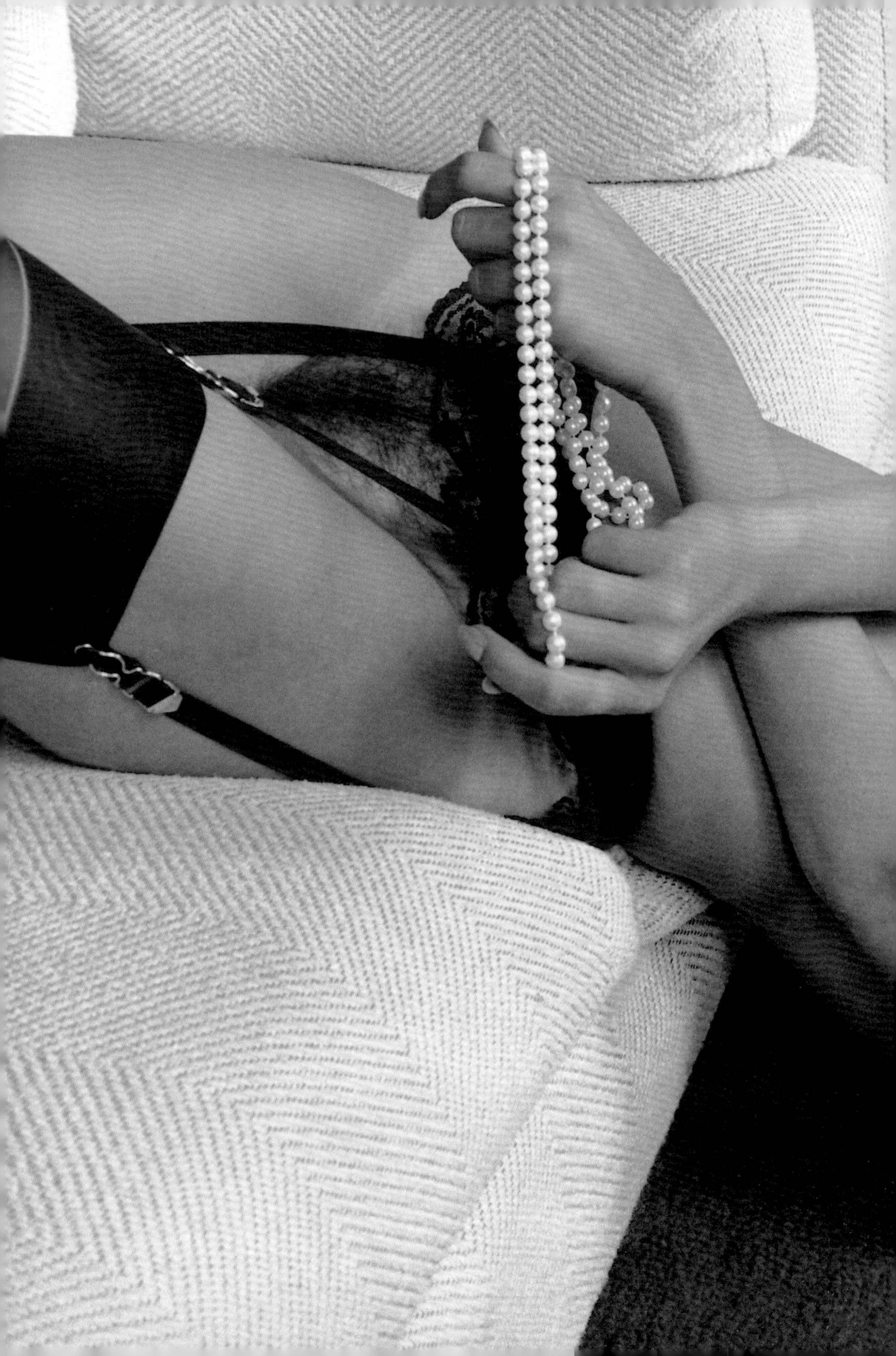

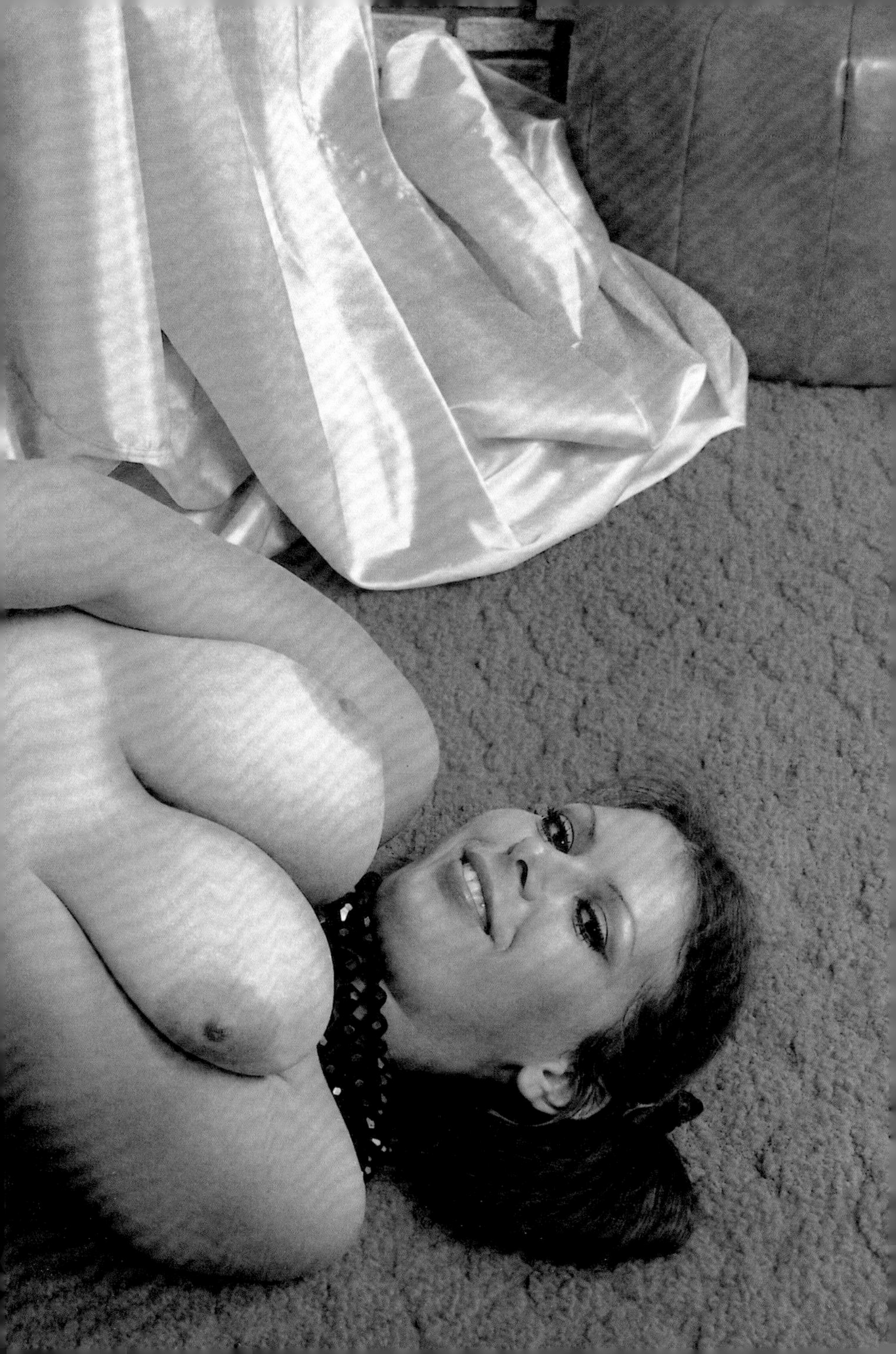

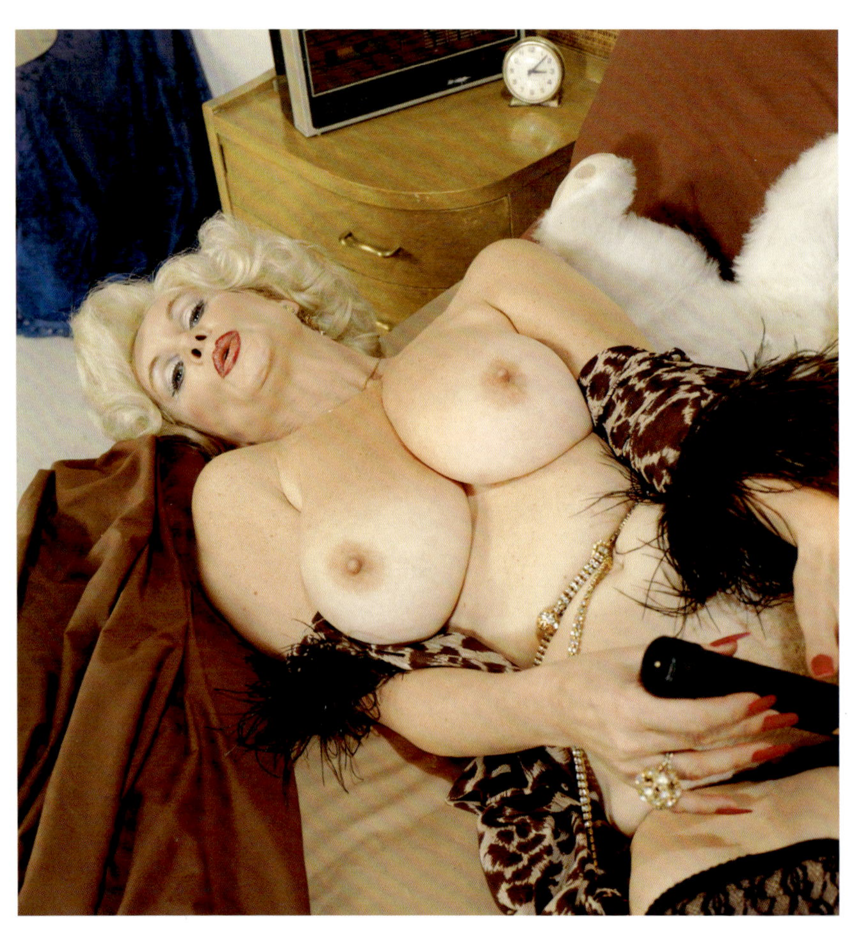

ABOVE Helga Sven OPPOSITE Elaine Collins

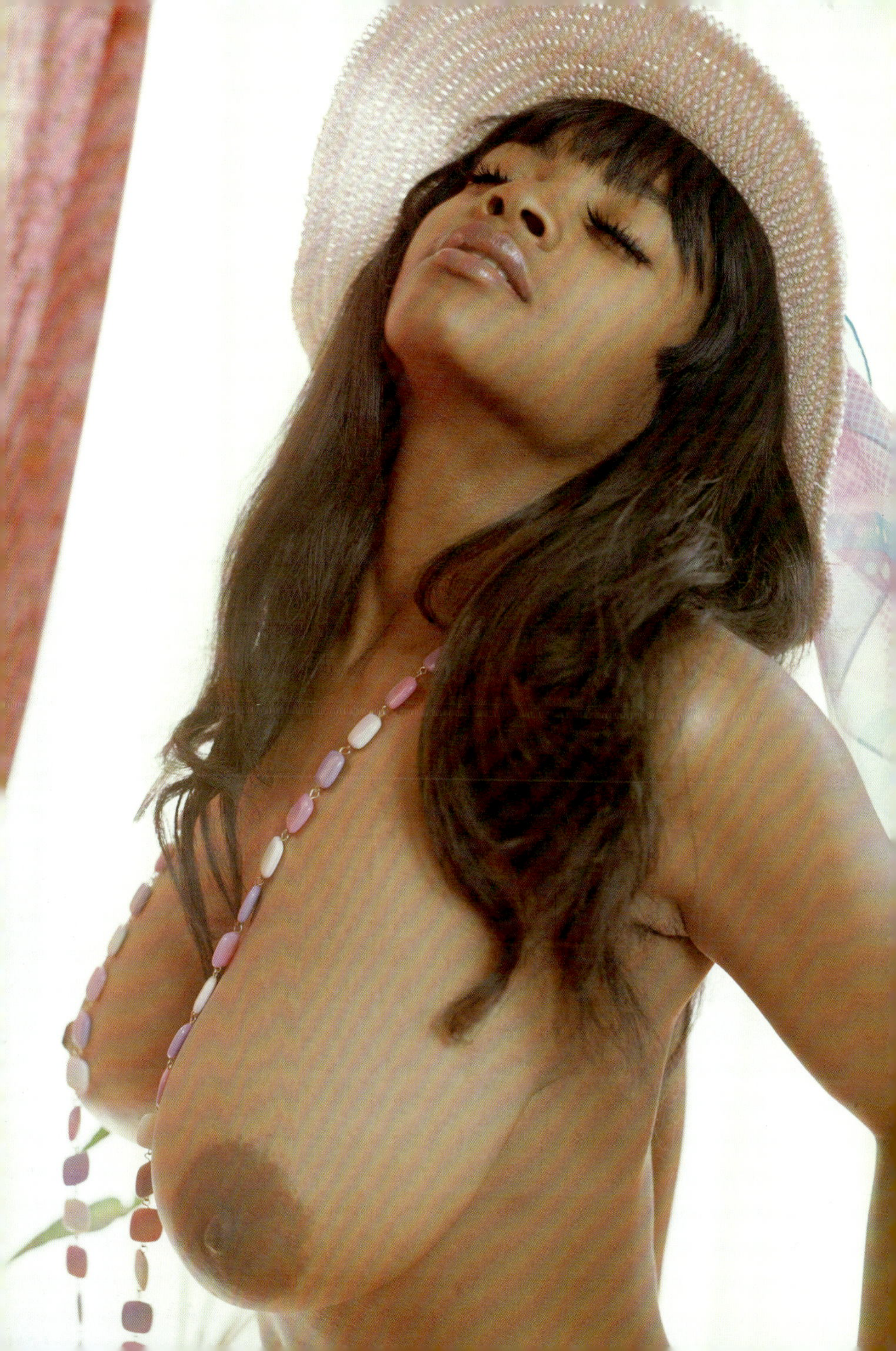

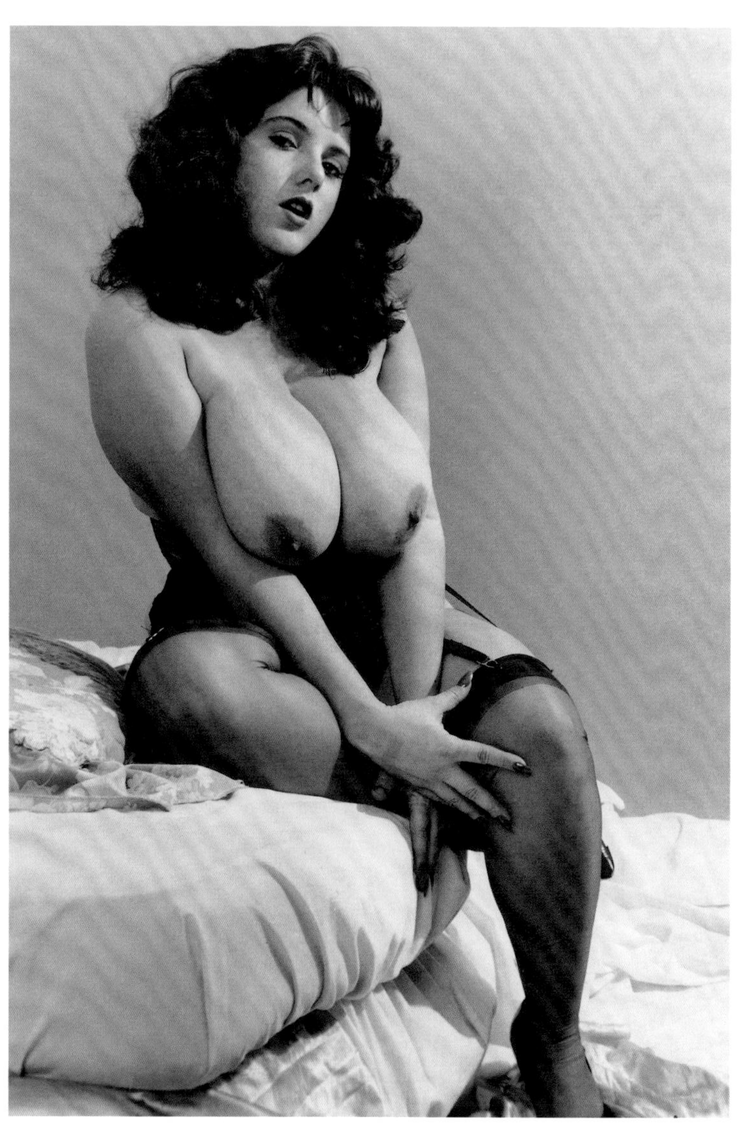

ABOVE Candye Kane OPPOSITE Anna West

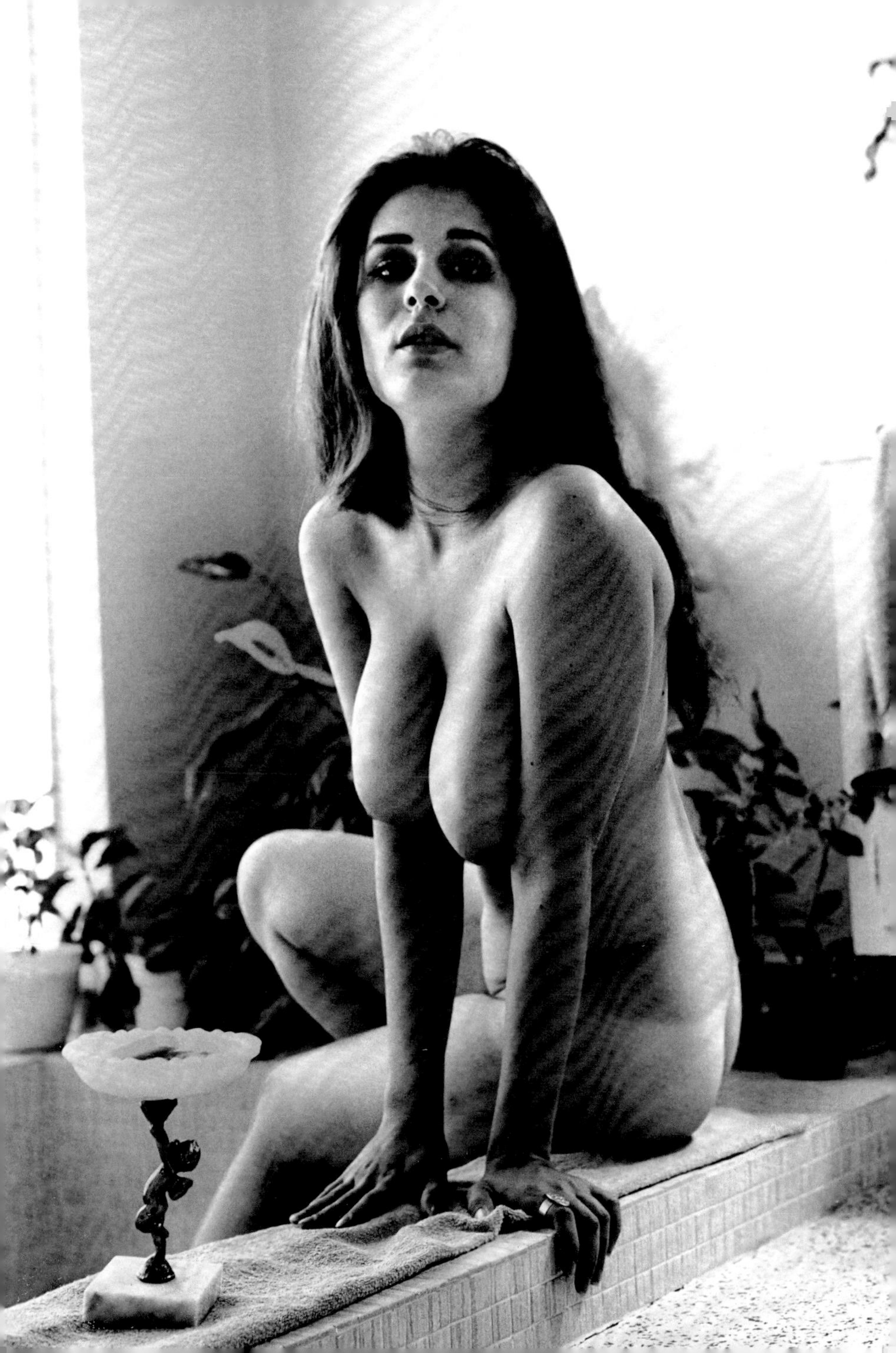

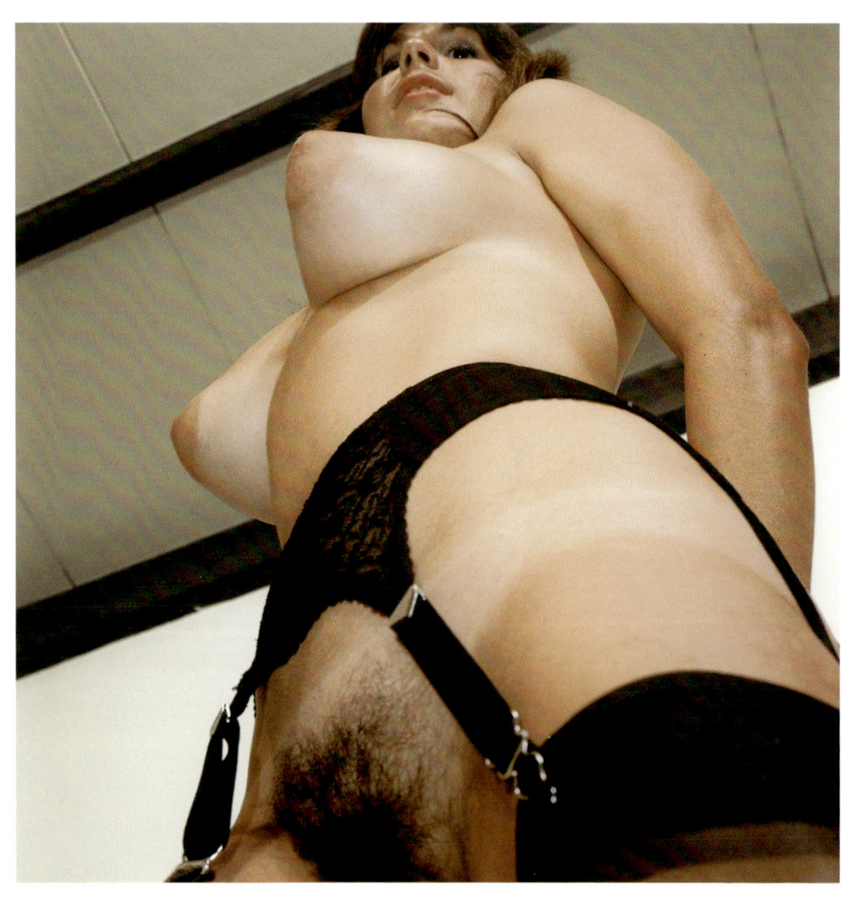

Unknown

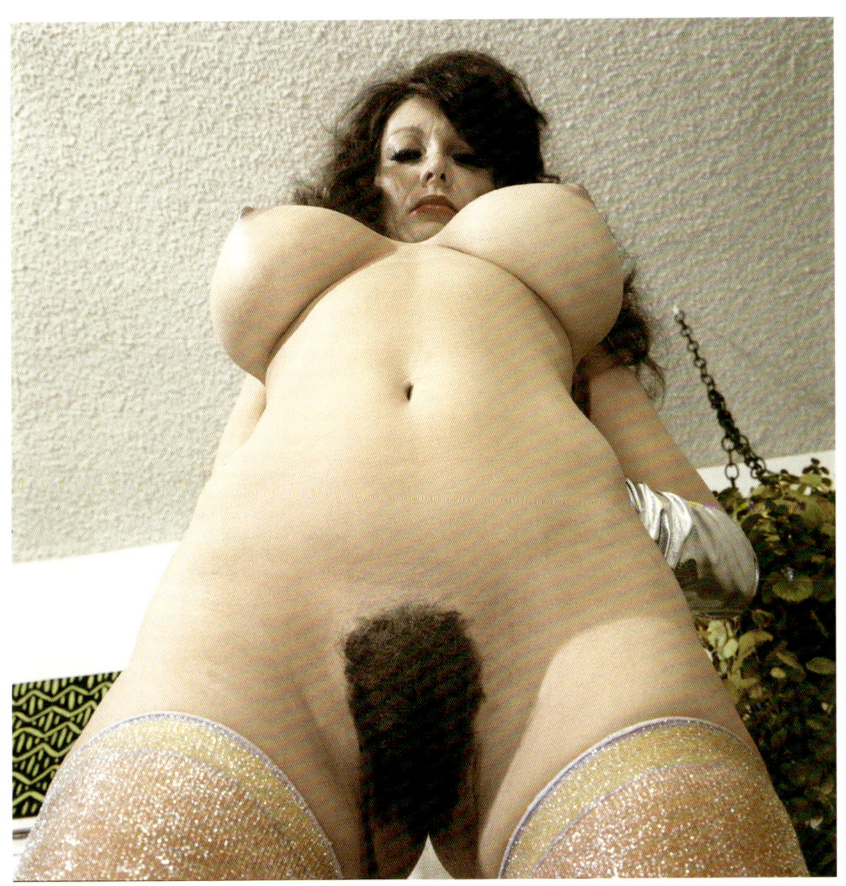

Unknown

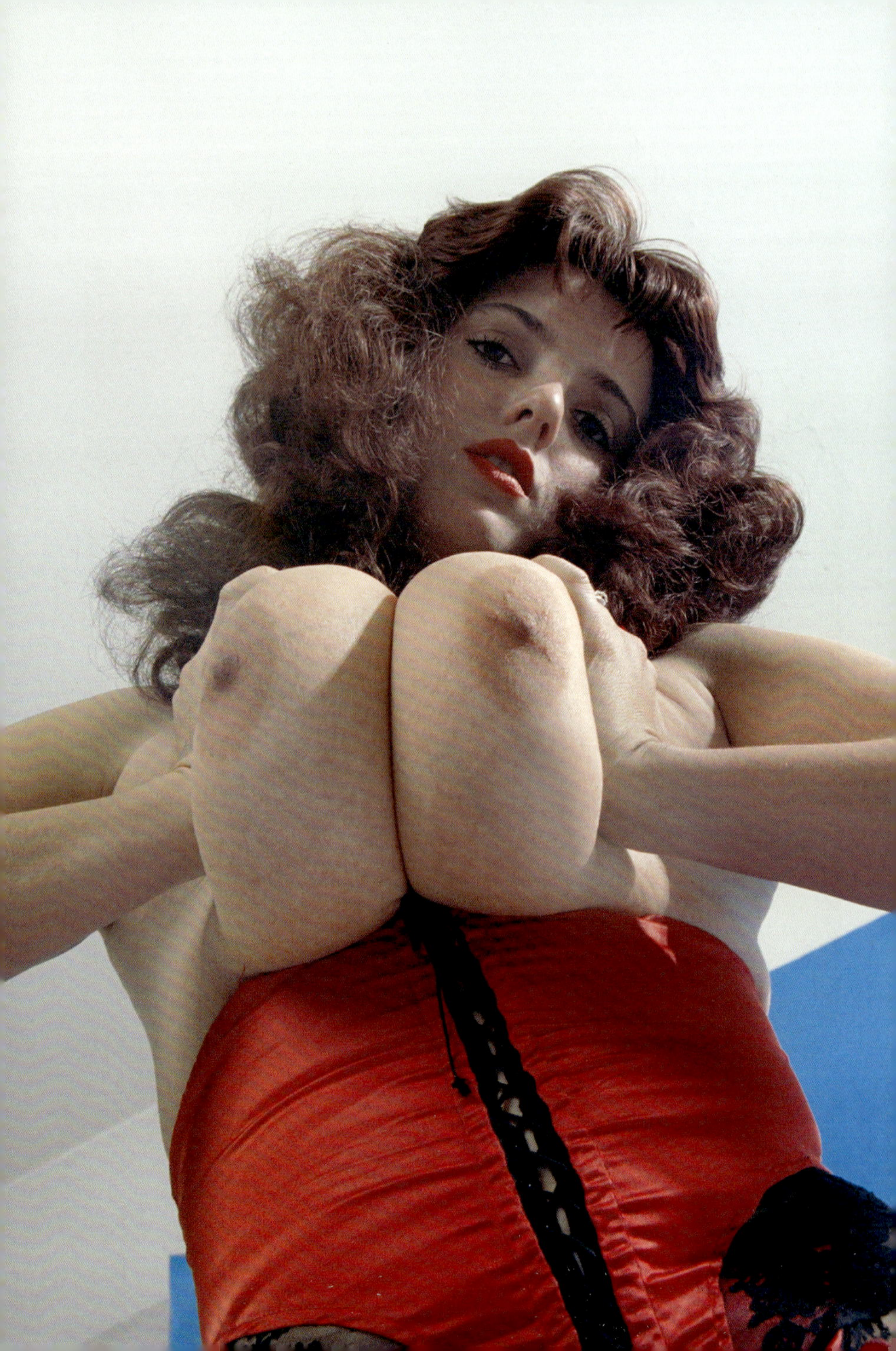

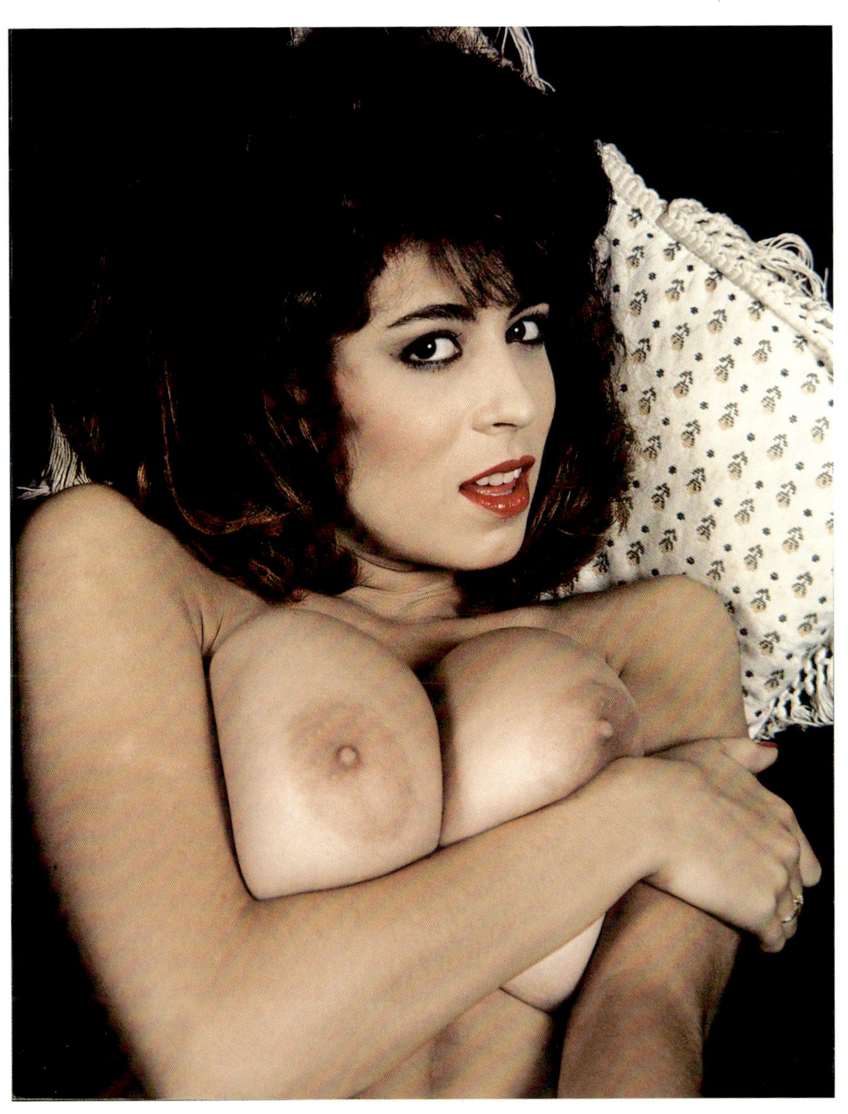

OPPOSITE Candye Kane ABOVE Christy Canyon

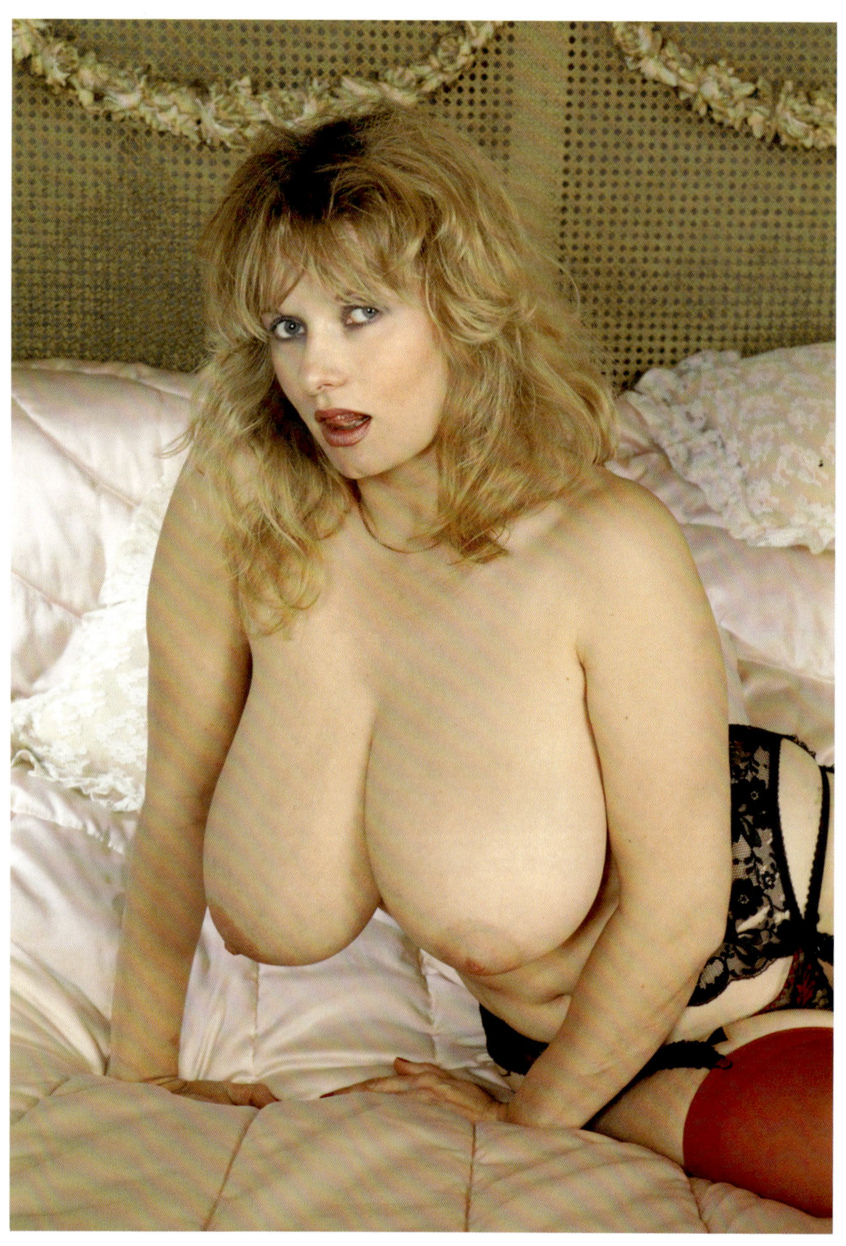

ABOVE Big Toni OPPOSITE Norma Stitz

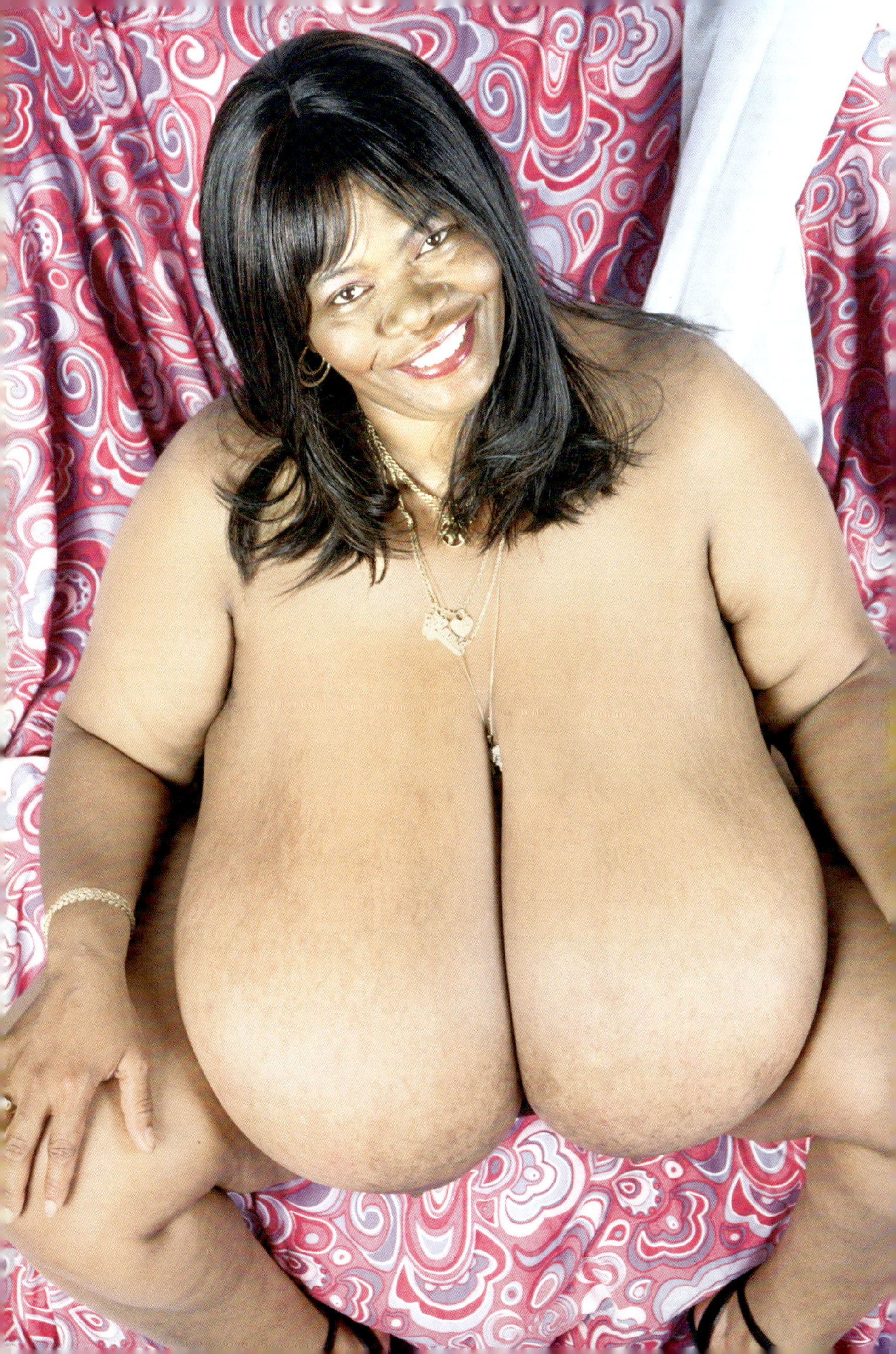

Acknowledgments

I would like to thank A.R.S. Inc., specialists in voluptuous vintage erotica, for providing most of the beautiful prints in the book. They can be reached through yesgirls@yesterdaygirls.com.

Additional photos were gratefully received from the following photographers, collectors and models: Michelle Angelo: page 70. Tyrone Cox: page 189. Robert Ellison: pages 24, 144/145, and 148. Dian Hanson: pages: 25, 29, 43, and 46. Lance Kincaid: page 16.

Special thanks to Ed Fox for his front and back cover photos of the astounding Kelly Madison; to John Cebollero, who created the statuette of Candy Samples on page 1; and to Josh Baker and Jessica Sappenfield for design.

Any credit omissions are unintentional, and appropriate credit will be given in future editions if such copyright holders contact the publisher.

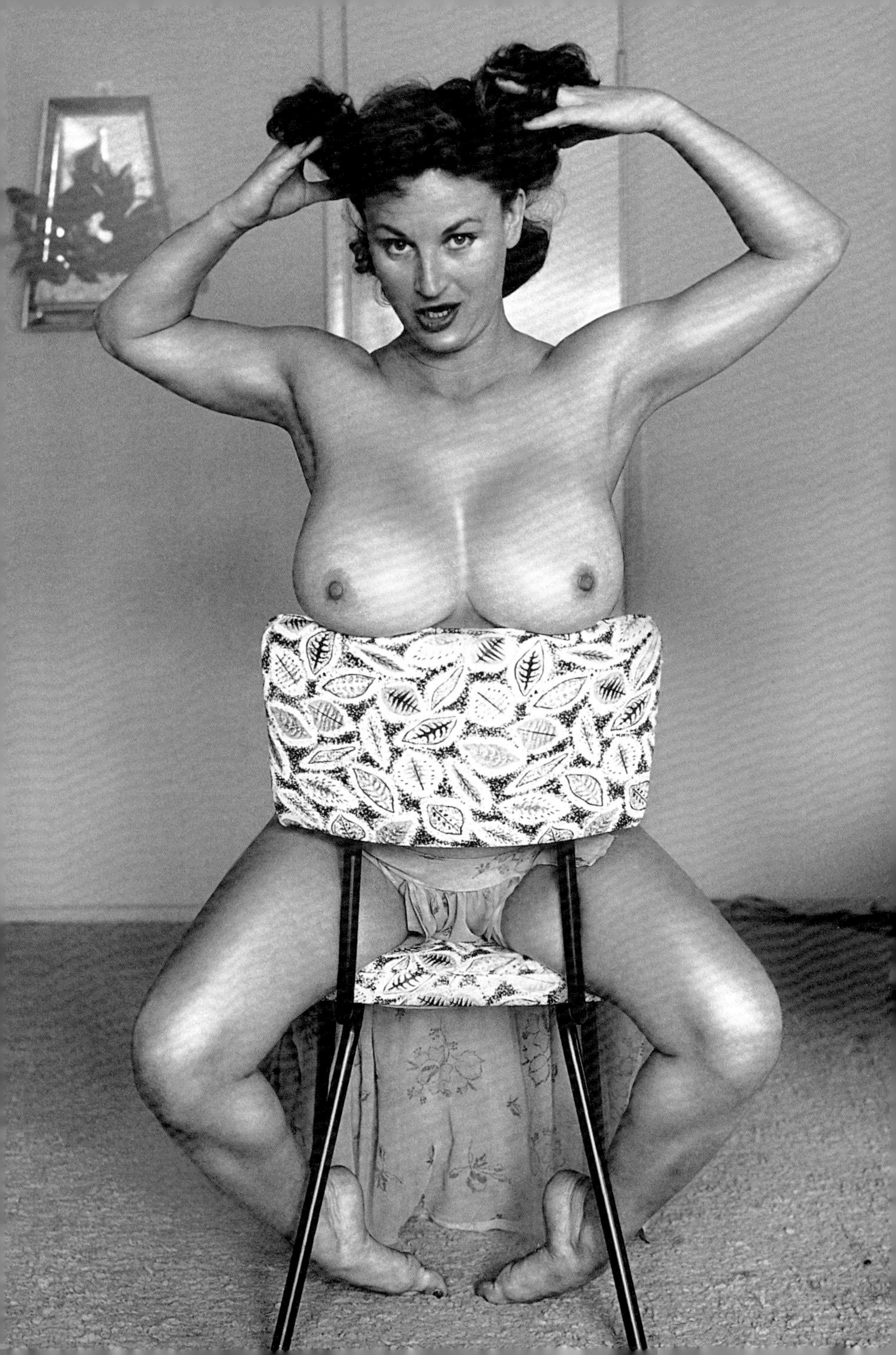

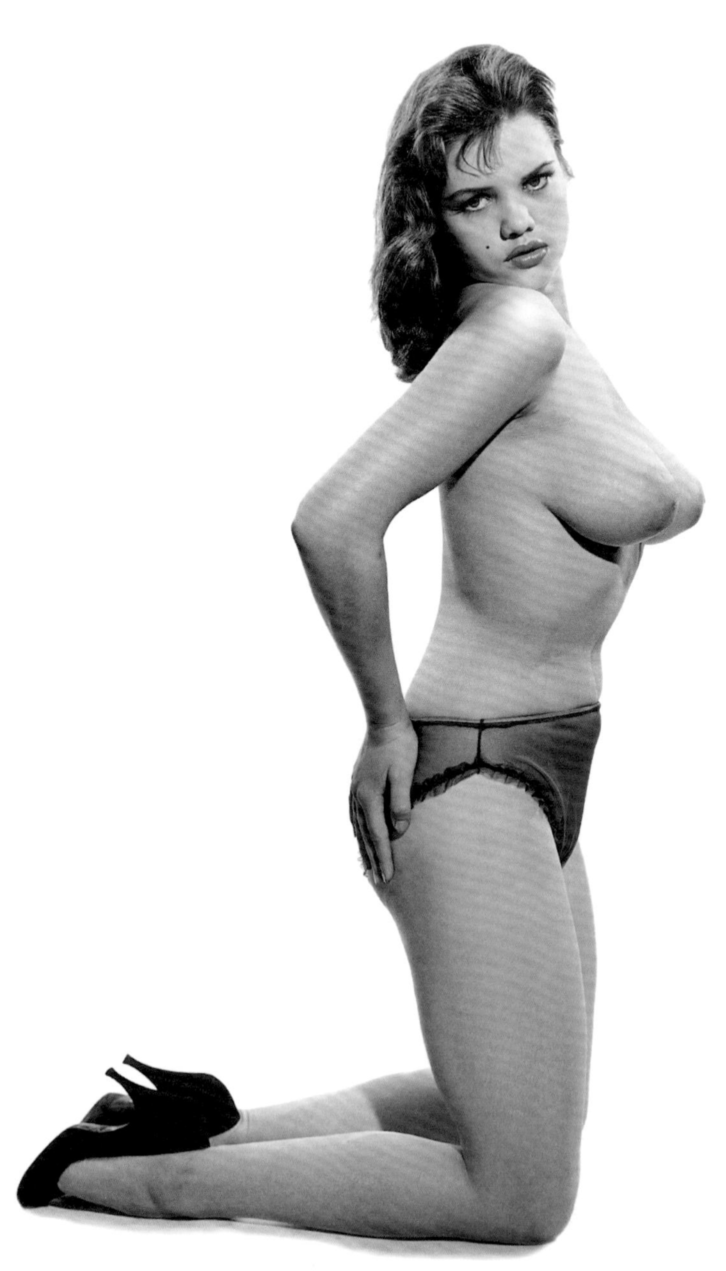

FRONT AND BACK COVERS Kelly Madison by Ed Fox
ENDPAPERS Gee Whiz, circa 1958
PAGE 1 Candy Samples statuette by John Cebollero
PAGE 2 Caren Castro, circa 1960
PAGE 191 Cherrie Knight, circa 1958
LEFT Rosina Revelle, circa 1958

All texts, interviews, and commentaries contained in this volume are those of the individual writers and interview subjects and do not necessarily represent the views and opinions of TASCHEN GmbH or any of its respective affiliates or employees.

All photographs are the sole possessions of the listed photographers and archivists. No photo from this book may be reproduced in any way without express written permission from the owner.

EACH AND EVERY TASCHEN BOOK PLANTS A SEED!
Each year, we offset our annual carbon emissions with carbon credits at the Instituto Terra, a reforestation program in Minas Gerais, Brazil, founded by Lélia and Sebastião Salgado. To find out more about this ecological partnership, please check: taschen.com/institutoterra
Inspiration: unlimited. Carbon footprint: (almost) zero.

Want to see more? Visit taschen.com to view our current publications, browse our latest magazine, and subscribe to our newsletter.

© 2025 TASCHEN GmbH
Hohenzollernring 53, D-50672 Köln
taschen.com

German translation by Egbert Baqué, Berlin
French translation by Alice Pétillot, Bayonne

Printed in Italy
ISBN 978-3-8365-7890-5

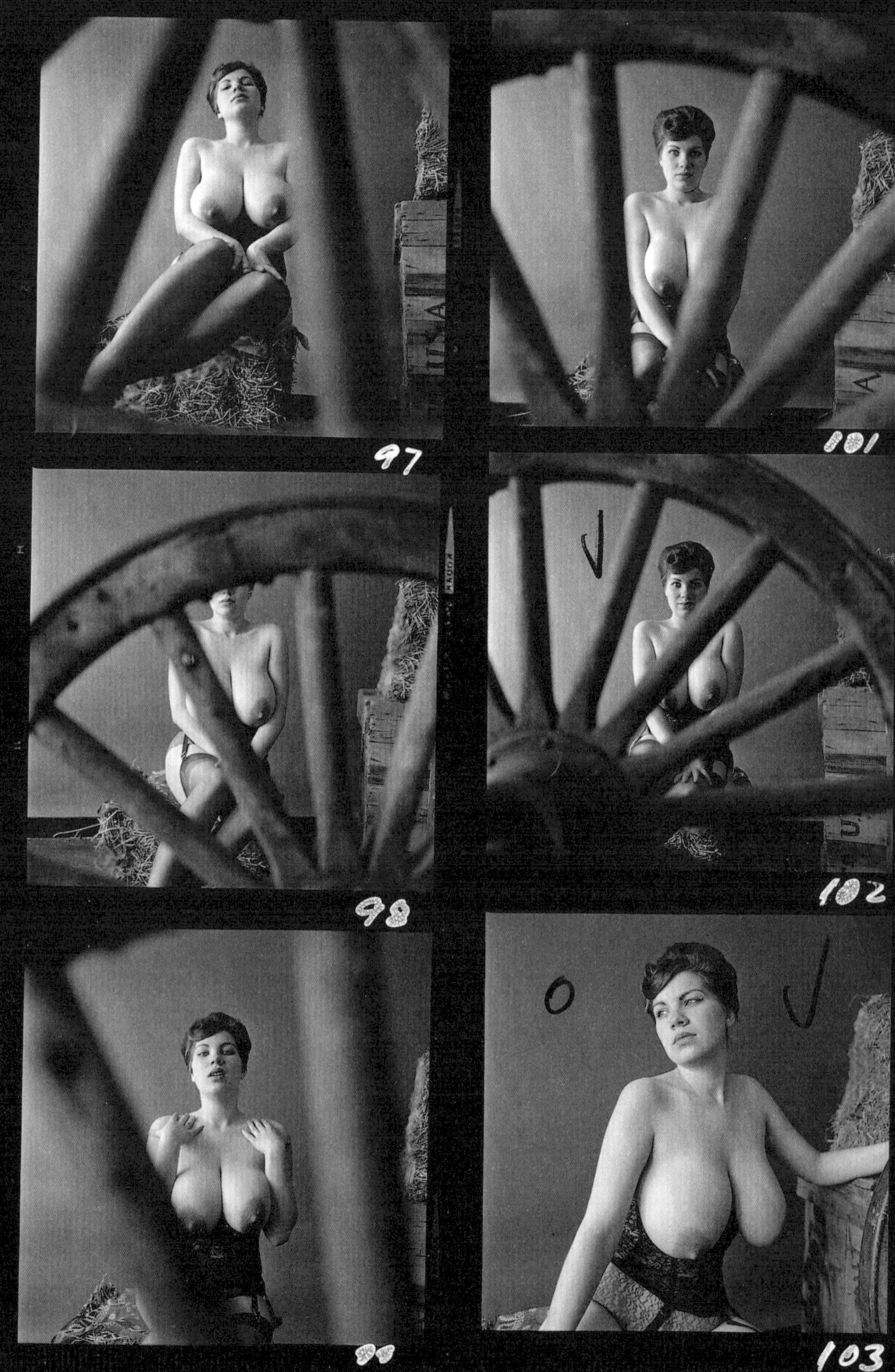
97
101
98
102
99
103